PATERNOSTER THEOLOGICAL MONOGRAPHS

The Will of Him Who Sent Me

An Exploration of Responsive Intra-Trinitarian Willing

PATERNOSTER THEOLOGICAL MONOGRAPHS

The Will of Him Who Sent Me

An Exploration of Responsive Intra-Trinitarian Willing

Andrew Moody

Copyright © Andrew Moody 2016

First Published 2016 by Paternoster

Paternoster is an imprint of Authentic Media
PO Box 6326, Bletchley, Milton Keynes MK1 9GG

authenticmedia.co.uk

The right of Andrew Moody to be identified as the author of this Work has been asserted
by him in accordance with the Copyright, Designs
and Patents Act 1988.

All rights reserved. No part of this publication man be reproduced, stored in a retrieval system, or transmitted, in any form or by any means, electronic, mechanical, photocopying, recording, or otherwise, without the prior permission of the publisher of a license permitting restricted copying. In the UK such licenses are issued by the Copyright Licensing Agency, Barnard's Inn, 86 Fetter Lane, London EC4A 1EN.

British Library Cataloguing in Publication Data
A catalogue record for this book is available from the British Library

ISBN 978-1-84227-846-8
978-1-78078-075-7 (e-book)

Printed and bound by Lightning Source

PATERNOSTER THEOLOGICAL MONOGRAPHS

Series Preface

In the west the churches may be declining, but theology—serious, academic (mostly doctoral level) and mainstream orthodox in evaluative commitment—shows no sign of withering on the vine. This series of *Paternoster Theological Monographs* extends the expertise of the Press especially to first-time authors whose work stands broadly with the parameters created by fidelity to Scripture and has satisfied the critical scrutiny of respected assessors in the academy. Such theology may come in several distinct intellectual disciplines—Historical, dogmatic, pastoral, apologetic, missional, aesthetic and no doubt others also. The series will be particularly hospitable to promising constructive theology within an evangelical frame, for it is of this that the church's need seems to be greatest. Quality writing will be published across the confessions—Anabaptist, Episcopalian, Reformed, Arminian, and Orthodox—across the ages—patristic, medieval, reformation, modern, and counter-modern—and across the continents. The aim of the series is theology written in the twofold conviction that the church needs theology and theology needs the church—which in reality means theology done for the glory of God.

Series Editors

Trevor A. Hart, Head of School and Principal of St Mary's College School of Divinity, University of St Andrews, Scotland, UK

Anthony N.S. Lane, Professor of Historical Theology and Director of Research, London School of Theology, UK

Anthony C. Thiselton, Emeritus Professor of Christian Theology, University of Nottingham, Research Professor in Christian Theology, University College Chester; and Canon Theologian of Leicester Cathedral and Southwell Minister, UK

Kevin J. Vanhoozer, Research Professor of Systematic Theology, Trinity Evangelical Divinity School, Deerfield, Illinois, USA

Abstract

Questions surrounding the operations of the divine will with regard to the Trinitarian life of God *ad extra* and *ad intra* feature in a range of contemporary discussions. This thesis presents the case for one possible model wherein divine willing is viewed as occurring according to the causal taxis of the divine persons, and where God's contingent action becomes the context for a real intra-trinitarian response from the Son to the Father. The Father, the Son and the Spirit have one will; but this will is 'the Father's will', which the Son receives and expresses as Son. This thesis focuses on the responsive intra-trinitarian willing of the Son.

In the first half of the thesis, this concept of responsive intra-trinitarian willing is defended as having a legitimate claim to orthodoxy. Its volitional and causal taxis is held to be consistent with pro-Nicene orthodoxy. Its depiction of the persons as distinct willing agents is tested against the dyothelitic theology of Maximus the Confessor. Its assumption of a special affinity between the Logos and creation (which gives rise to the incarnation) is shown to have precedent in the theology of key Western theologians such as Thomas Aquinas and Bonaventure.

In the second half, post-Reformation examples are supplied of a more strongly responsive intra-trinitarian willing which depicts the Son as accepting the free decisions of the Father, with (in some versions) the Father planning contingent reality for the glory of his Son. It is argued that this pattern can be seen to fit well with the themes of the Bible and is able to provide a rich and suggestive means of integrating anthropology, soteriology and trinitarian theology. Finally the proposed synthesis is used as a point of entry into three contemporary discussions on the Trinity: Hegelian, participationist and evangelical.

Table of Contents

Abstract	vii
Table of Contents	viii
Diagrams	x
Abbreviations & Conventions	xi
Acknowledgements	xiv
Introduction	1
Some Preliminary Statements	5
Limitations	8
1. Is the Priority of Paternal Will compatible with Pro-Nicene Orthodoxy?	10
Introduction	10
Father as Principium in Ancient and Modern Theology	11
Questioning the Modern Trend	20
The Question of Will	42
Divine Willing Beyond Athanasius	46
Conclusion	57
2. Does Dyothelitic Orthodoxy Permit Personal Agency?	59
Introduction	59
The Dilemma of Persons & Natures	60
Responsive Intra-Trinitarian Willing as Monothelite Heresy	63
Divine Will in the Theology of Maximus the Confessor	66
Conclusion	79
3. Is Intra-Trinitarian Willing Possible after Augustine?	80
Introduction	80
The Complaint Against the West	81
The Mixed Legacy of Augustine	85
Father, Son and Incarnation in the Medieval Synthesis	94
Divine Relations in Thomas Aquinas	100
Divine Willing in Medieval Theology	105
Conclusion	115
4. Can We Find Positive Examples of Intra-Trinitarian Willing?	116
Introduction	116
Christ the Centre?	116

Contents

Creation as Pro-Filius – John of the Cross	118
Triune Willing in the Covenant of Redemption	122
Jonathan Edwards	133
Some Final Observations Concerning the Pactum Salutis	146
5. Does Responsive Intra-Trinitarian Willing Fit with Scripture?	**153**
Introduction	153
Equal is as Equal Does	157
The Harmony of Function and Ontology	162
High Christology from Below	164
The Logos and the Mediator	171
Jesus Christ: The Logos Made Manifest	176
Assembling the Pieces	182
Some Potential Objections	183
6. Does Prioritising Divine Filiality Mean Neglecting the Holy Spirit?	**191**
Introduction	191
Some Observations Concerning the Filioque	193
Biblical Resonances	202
Conclusion	213
7. How does RITW Address Contemporary Theological Discussion?	**215**
Introduction	215
The Ghost of Hegel and the God who Becomes	216
Neoplatonism Redivivus: A Response to Modern Participationism	223
Observations Concerning the Current Evangelical Trinitarian Debates	231
Conclusion	**243**
Bibliography	**245**

Diagrams

Figure 1:   *A model for triune decision-making*   78

Figure 2:   *Alternate models for divine decision-making*   110

Abbreviations & Conventions

Abbreviations

Amb.	*Ambiguum/Ambigua*
ANF	A. Roberts, J. Donaldson & A. C. Coxe, *The Ante-Nicene Fathers: Translations of the Writings of the Fathers Down to A.D. 325* ed. Schaff, Philip (Grand Rapids: Eerdmans, 1989)
ASV	American Standard Version
CA	*Contra Arianos*
CD	K. Barth, *Church Dogmatics,* trans. G. W. Bromiley, ed. G. W. Bromiley & T. F. Torrance, 4 volumes (Edinburgh: T&T Clark, 1956-1969)
CE	*Contra Eunomium*
CGent.	*Summa Contra Gentiles*
CMax.	*Contra Maximinum*
CQLS	*Commentaria in Quatuor Libros Sententiarum*
DeFid.	*De Fide ad Gratianum*
DeRud.	*De Reductione Artium ad Theologiam*
DeTrin.	*De Trinitate*
DeInc.	*De Incarnatione*
DeSpir.	*De Spiritu Sancto*
DeSyn.	*De Synodis*
DisEnd.	*Dissertation Concerning the End*
FV	filial volition
IJST	*International Journal of Systematic Theology*
Institutes	J. Calvin, *Institutes of the Christian Religion,* trans. F. L. Battles, ed. J. T. McNeill, 2 volumes (Philadelphia: Westminster Press, 1960)
JETS	*Journal of the Evangelical Theological Society*
Misc.	*Miscellanies*
NCC	Niceno-Constantinopolitan Creed
NIGCT	The New International Greek Testament Commentary
NIV	New International Version

Abbreviations and Conventions

NPNF	P. Schaff (ed), *A Select Library of the Nicene and Post-Nicene Fathers of the Christian Church. two series,* 28 volumes (Edinburgh: T&T Clark, 1895)
NRSV	New Revised Standard Version
Or.	*Oratio*
Pan.	*Panarion*
PG	J. P. Migne, *Patrologiae Graeca,* 162 volumes (Paris: Migne, 1857-1866)
PL	J. P. Migne, *Patrologiae Latina,* 217 volumes (Paris: Migne, 1844-1855)
RITW	responsive intra-trinitarian willing
RO	Radical Orthodox
SJT	*Scottish Journal of Theology*
SQL	*Sententiarum Quatuor Libri*
ST	social trinitarianism
Summa	*Summa Theologiae* (nb. Latin quotations from *Corpus Thomisticum,* (Navarre: Fundación Tomás de Aquino Universitatis Studiorum Navarrensis, 2006) http://www.corpusthomisticum.org, (accessed September, 2009); English as cited)
WJE	Works of Jonathan Edwards

Abbreviations and Conventions

Miscellaneous Conventions

1. Unless otherwise noted all English Bible references are taken from the NRSV

2. Typically Greek words are not transliterated, though exceptions are made when the word is a technical term that is used frequently in modern theological discussion in transliterated form, for example: *arché, homoousios/homoiousios, hypostasis logoi/Logos, ousia, monarchy, perichoresis, tropos.* In general the rule here is that the terms are transliterated when discussed in abstraction but written in Greek when spoken of in the context of a particular Father's use of the term.

3. Transliterated Greek terms are generally italicised but not when they are adapted to English word forms: for example "*hypostasis*" is italicised but "hypostatic" is not.

4. Abbreviations for patristic works generally follow contemporary practice of removing words and indicating the break by a capital letter: thus *De Trinitate* becomes *DeTrin.*; *Contra Maximinum* is designated by *CMax.*.

5. All writers, dead or living, are spoken of in the present tense as regards their writing hence: Athanasius contends; Peter Lombard argues.

Acknowledgements

The thinking behind this project has been a work of decades: from a church Bible-study in the mid 1980s; to a series of essays, debates and online interactions during the first decade of the new millennium. Along the way many people have helped (and often forced!) me to think hard about the issues explored here: my former lecturer Dr Kevin Giles – whose energy and scholarship on this issue did much to compel me take up post-graduate study; conversation-partners Matthew Paulson and Mark Baddeley (currently at Berkeley and Oxford respectively) who greatly aided my attempts to explore the nature of orthodox trinitarianism in the early years of my research; long-time friends Andrew Prideaux and David Walter whose insights and encouragements provided catalysis and energy at crucial points along the way; Dr Jean Williams who provided invaluable feedback and proof reading in the final stages; and, of course, my ever-wise and patient supervisor, Dr Peter Adam of Ridley Melbourne – without whom I would never have reached this point. Thanks is especially due to my family. I remain thankful to my parents and siblings for their heritage of Christian thought and devotion to the Lord Jesus. I am grateful to my dear children, Emma and Jack, who offered many prayers for this project on my behalf and who were so generous in allowing me the time to study. Finally, beyond all telling, I am indebted to my beautiful Jenny; my strength, help and love. She has been God's greatest earthly gift to me through all this – and our marriage a sweet echo of the true wedding still to come.

Gloria Patri, et Filio, et Spiritui Sancto.
Sicut erat in principio, et nunc, et semper, et in saecula saeculorum.

I yearned to know just how our image merges
into that circle, and how it there finds place;

but mine were not the wings for such a flight.
Yet, as I wished, the truth I wished for came
cleaving my mind in a great flash of light.

Here my powers rest from their high fantasy,
but already I could feel my being turned –
instinct and intellect balanced equally

as in a wheel whose motion nothing jars –
by the Love that moves the sun and other stars.

Dante Alighieri, *Paradiso* 33.136-145[1]

---

[1] Dante Alighieri, *The Paradiso,* trans. J. Ciardi. *Signet Classics Series* (New York: Signet Classics, 2001).

Introduction

In the widely heralded rebirth of trinitarian theology since the second half of the twentieth century, the matter of how the divine persons relate in eternity has been a recurring issue. How does the Trinity, as it is revealed in the context of the human Jesus, connect with divine life outside creation? How "social" are the relationships within the Godhead? To what extent can the Trinity be used as a template for human social relationships?

These questions have generated important debates and seminal contributions in a number of different disciplines. In systematic studies, enquiries concerning the status of the immanent Trinity have generated a range of quite different theories of how God relates to the world.[2] In analytic philosophy the question of "social trinitarianism" has been related to the more fundamental problem of how the persons are one and three.[3] And, in Christian ethics and ecclesiology, the pattern of Christ's obedience – and how it correlates to the life of God *ad intra* – has figured prominently (and contentiously) as a model for human relationships, within marriage, church, and society.[4]

---

2   Some of these diverse viewpoints include the Hegelian idea that God's own trinitarian life is in some way determined by salvation history or that God's triunity is a correlate of his choosing to be God for us. Varieties of this approach occur in the works of Jürgen Moltmann, Wolfhart Pannenberg, Robert Jenson and (possibly) Karl Barth; see more on this in Chapter 7. Another broad trend in modern theology here is the return of Neoplatonism or exemplarism as espoused by Hans Urs von Balthasar – see, P. J. Casarella "The Expression and Form of the Word: Trinitarian Hermeneutics and the Sacramentality of Language in Hans Urs von Balthasar's Theology" in *Glory, Grace, and Culture: The Work of Hans Urs von Balthasar,* ed. E. Block (Mahwah: Paulist Press, 2005), 37-65 – or, more recently: D. B. Hart, *The Beauty of the Infinite: The Aesthetics of Christian Truth* (Grand Rapids: Eerdmans, 2003); K. Tanner, *Jesus, Humanity and the Trinity: A Brief Systematic Theology*. Scottish Journal of Theology, Current Issues in Theology (Edinburgh: T&T Clark, 2001).

3   Able representations of both sides of this debate can be found in C. Plantinga "Social Trinity and Tritheism" in *Trinity, Incarnation and Atonement: Philosophical and Theological Essays,* ed. R. J. Feenstra & C. Plantinga (Notre Dame: University of Notre Dame Press, 1989) and K. Kilby, "Perichoresis and Projection: Problems with Social Doctrines of the Trinity", *New Blackfriars* 81.957 (November 2000): 432-445.

4   Various applications of this approach occur across the major Christian traditions, with different trinitarian models being invoked to support hierarchy or egality in society, church or marriage. One important example in the context of ecclesiology is the disagreement between Miroslav Volf and Joseph Ratzinger; M. Volf, *After Our Likeness: The Church as the Image of the Trinity*, Sacra Doctrina (Grand

Introduction

The nature of divine will and willing has become an important sub-theme in each of these discussions. In systematic theology the problem is often posed in terms of whether God is free as regards the world.[5] In the philosophical realm, attention has been drawn to the threat to divine unity posed by the idea that the persons might be separate centres of volition (and conversely the spectre of modalism that might arise where volitional distinction is rejected).[6] And for those interested in the social implications of trinitarian theology, attention has focussed on whether the individual persons relate in a hierarchical fashion, and what such a taxis might say about the equality of those occupying the "subordinate" postion (ie. the Son and Spirit).[7]

Against the backdrop of these discussions there is, I believe, a need to subject the topic of trinitarian willing to greater scrutiny in historical, biblical and systematic perspectives. Certainly there have been isolated historical studies that attend to the question of divine will in various theologians.[8] And

---

Rapids: Eerdmans, 1998), 67-72. A parallel discussion occurs within evangelicalism where the analogy between the Trinity and gender relations. For initial overviews see R. Letham, *The Holy Trinity: In Scripture, History, Theology, and Worship* (Phillipsburg: P&R, 2004), 479-496; M. J. Erickson, *Who's Tampering with the Trinity?: An Assessment of the Subordination Debate* (Grand Rapids: Kregel, 2009) and F. Sanders, *The State of the Doctrine of the Trinity in Evangelical Theology*, trans. Nov. 18, 2004), 13-16.

5   For helpful surveys (for and against, respectively) see: T. Peters, *God as Trinity: Relationality and Temporality in Divine Life,* 1st edition (Louisville: Westminster, 1993), and P. Molnar, *Divine Freedom and the Doctrine of the Immanent Trinity: In Dialogue with Karl Barth and Contemporary Theology* (Edinburgh: T&T Clark, 2002).

6   Fairly pronounced examples of each tendency might be seen in Richard Swinburne's somewhat theogonist characterisation of the three persons as "Gods" – R. Swinburne, "Could There Be More Than One God?", *Faith and Philosophy* 5.3 (1988): 225-241, 232-233 – and Brian Leftow's insistence that the triune persons represent a single "trope"; B. Leftow "Anti Social Trinitarianism" in *The Trinity: An Interdisciplinary Symposium on the Trinity,* ed. S. T. Davis, D. Kendall & G. O'Collins (Oxford: Oxford University Press, 1999), 204.

7   The most notable prosecution of this case from an egalitarian perspective can be found in the work of Anglican clergyman, Kevin Giles. See his two major volumes on the topic: K. Giles, *The Trinity & Subordinationism: The Doctrine of God and the Contemporary Gender Debate* (InterVarsity Press, 2002-09) and K. Giles, *Jesus and the Father: Modern Evangelicals Reinvent the Doctrine of the Trinity* (Grand Rapids: Zondervan, 2006).

8   For example: E. P. Meijering "The Doctrine of the Will and of the Trinity in the Orations of Gregory of Nazianzus" in *God Being History: Studies in Patristic Philosophy*, (New York: American Elsevier Pub. Co, 1975); G. Pelland, "La "Subjectio" du Christ Chez Saint Hilaire", *Gregorianum Roma* 64.3 (1983): 423-452; I. A. McFarland, "'Willing is not Choosing': Some Anthropological Implications of Dyothelite Christology", *IJST* 9.1 (2007): 3-23; D. Bathrellos, *The*

indeed divine filiality (including filial "obedience" or responsiveness) has played a significant part in modern exemplarist/Neoplatonist theology.[9] Yet these are generally not brought into contact with the disputes listed above. Nor do they directly address the modern shibboleths of the contemporary theological scene which are likely to render them as beside the point.[10]

I will suggest too in this thesis that there are traditional resources in this debate that have not been properly brought to bear in modern discussion: first because they have not been properly understood by some modern theologians – I am thinking here of the basic structure of pro-Nicene trinitarianism; and, second, because the proposals or insights might be overlooked as obscure or overly speculative – thus, for example, the Medieval doctrine of *rationes*, or the Reformed covenant of redemption. There remains a need to correct the record in the case of the first, and to bring the second into the conversation.

This thesis represents an attempt to meet these needs. My overall strategy is to defend and flesh out a carefully circumscribed model for divine willing and inter-personal contingent action. But initially, my question is simply whether it is legitimate for orthodoxy to posit any kind of volitional distinction of taxis to the divine persons. To this end I will conduct some soundings in historical theology to clear away some modern misconceptions and more closely outline what might or might not be permissible for an orthodox theory of intra-trinitarian willing. The structure of my argument in the first half of the thesis is as follows:

Chapter 1. I will examine the matter of the Father's monarchy (ie. his causal priority as regards the Son and Spirit) and challenge contemporary attempts to

---

Byzantine Christ: Person, Nature, and Will in the Christology of St. Maximus the Confessor (New York: Oxford University Press, 2005).

9 Although I will explain these terms more fully in Chapters 2 & 3 the key idea is that the Son's natural derivation from the Father (as Image or Logos) becomes the template and or form of creation's contingent birth. The preeminent exponent of this ancient tradition in modern era is Hans Urs von Balthasar, though the general pattern finds diverse forms (see Chapter 6).

10 And in some cases such expositions of intra-trinitarian willing have themselves been subject to sharp criticism. The modern critique of the Reformed covenant of redemption (see Chapter 5) or the hostile reception of von Balthasar by the likes of Alyssa Lyra Pitstick – see A. L. Pitstick, *Light in Darkness: Hans Urs von Balthasar and the Catholic Doctrine of Christ's Descent into Hell* (Grand Rapids: Eerdmans, 2007), 299-308 and John Milbank – eg. J. Milbank, *The Suspended Middle: Henri de Lubac and the Debate Concerning the Supernatural* (London: SCM Press, 2005) 77.

Introduction

downplay it. I will argue that pro-Nicene[11] theology cannot be understood apart from a strong and literal sense of paternity[12] and, furthermore, that this structure was an important ground for the orthodox Fathers' understanding of how the Father and the Son could have "one will". Just as the Son is God by virtue of his filiality, so he has the Father's will by virtue of that same relationship: his will is *filial volition* (FV).

Chapter 2. Through an examination of the dyothelitic theology of Maximus the Confessor, I will attempt to forestall the idea that orthodoxy is inimical to any inter-personal willing between the divine persons who share the one will. I will press the point that the concept of "natural will" should not be taken to *exclude* personal responsiveness on the part of the Son and, furthermore, that the Maximian concept of *logoi* (eternal forms) implies a theory of divine decision which might be cast in terms of paternal initiative and filial response.

Chapter 3. Here I will trace out some of the themes emerging from Medieval European theology to qualify some misconceptions concerning the nature of "Western" trinitarianism. I will supply evidence of the enduring vitality of pro-Nicene patriarchy in the Western despite the unipersonalist heritage of Augustine. I will also show how one major theme in the scholastic milieu makes intra-trinitarian taxis *the* structuring principle for the creation and incarnation. I will also take a close look at how key doctors understand contingent willing as regards the divine persons.

Chapter 4. Next my attention will switch to more positive matters. Drawing on Post-Reformation sources (and one Counter-Reformation source), I will present a positive case for intra-trinitarian willing that is responsive as well as filial. The theory I will commend proposes that, in relation to contingent action, divine decisions might be seen to begin with the Father and be are embraced by the Son in line with the order of subsistence. I will contend that the kind of responsive intra-trinitarian willing (RITW) imagined by John of the Cross or Jonathan Edwards is an orthodox speculation that enables a rich and attractive vision of salvation history.

Chapter 5. Having thus laid out the completed form of my proposal and defended it as a possible expression of orthodox theology, I show how the model aligns with the themes of the Bible. I argue that the pro-Nicene taxis of

---

11   I will discuss the meaning of this term in the next chapter. For now, it is sufficient to say that it signifies the general orthodox consensus arising out of the trinitarian debates of the fourth century.

12   This reference to "literal" begetting should not be taken as anthropomorphic. As we shall see in the next chapter, the orthodox Fathers take the pattern in either an analogical (human fathering is a copy of divine) or univocal sense (there is a common essence to both divine and creaturely begetting) but hedge both around with negation and clarification.

divine persons accords well with the picture that emerges from the Fourth Gospel and the letters of Paul. Probing deeper, I will argue that the interlocking themes and typologies that inform New Testament anthropology and soteriology also fit with the patriarchal/filiocentric vision of salvation history outlined in Chapter 5. I will make the case that a carefully drawn theory of RITW can be powerfully integrative and can avoid the charges that might be brought against it.

Chapter 6. Against objections that the *filioque* and sending of the Spirit by the Son disrupt paternal priority and show alterations to intra-trinitarian relations, I conduct a brief survey of alternative pneumatological models. I suggest that there are good biblical and historical reasons to view the second and third persons as co-processional (at the *ad intra* level), and that this can help us understand how the Spirit and Christ operate during Christ's earthly sojourn. I will also demonstrate that a radicalised Spirit Christology can enrich our understanding of the church's standing.

Chapter 7. I conclude by showing how RITW can throw light on a number of contemporary discussions. I compare my own model of divine "history" with other modern Hegel-influenced models, and also make some general observations concerning the recent renewal of interest in the concept of Neoplatonist participation. I reflect on the state of the current Evangelical debate over filial obedience; and discuss the contemporary practice of using trinitarian relations as a template for human relationships.

Some Preliminary Statements

The daunting reality for anyone seeking to explore the question of how the eternal Son relates to the Father is that it very soon becomes apparent that this problem is inextricably linked to many others. What bearing does the Son's filiality have on *this* matter – and what *is* that filiality anyway? How does it relate to Christ's human nature and relationship with God? My argument in this thesis is that filiality is the Son's way or "mode" of being divine,[13] and that both

---

[13] I do not mean by this that he is only a mode or mask of the one person "God" as *per* Sabellianism, simply that there are different ways the Father and Son have their common divinity (ie. "are God"). "mode of subsistence", which I will employ in this sense now and again, is a translation of τροπος ὑπαρξεος – that phrase associated with (but not much used by) the Cappadocians: cf. J. Farrelly, *The Trinity: Rediscovering the Central Christian Mystery* (Oxford: Rowman & Littlefield, 2005), 87 and R. P. C. Hanson, *The Search for the Christian Doctrine of God: The Arian Controversy 318-381* (Edinburgh: T&T Clark, 1988), 692. In later theology we find Jonathan Edwards and using "manner of subsisting" – J. An Edw aUr ndps u, b l i s h e d Essa http://www.ccel.org/ccel/edwards/trinity/files/trinity.html, (accessed March, 2008)

Introduction

the Bible and important voices in church history testify, not only to the *fact* of God's unity and plurality, but that this unity and plurality hold together in the patriarchy of God the Father. As Augustine writes in *De Doctrina Christiana* 1:

> In the Father there is unity (*unitas*), in the Son equality (*aequalitas*), and in the Holy Spirit, a harmony of unity and equality (*unitatis aequalitatisque concordia*). And the three are all one because of the Father, all equal because of the Son, and in harmony because of the Spirit.[14]

In the next chapter I will contend that the patriarchy, equality and unity implicit in this statement are the essence of the pro-Nicene consensus of the fourth century:[15] God is one, because the Father *is* God; three, because the Son and Spirit are exactly like him and have all he has; and undivided, because this equality is neither coordinate nor partitive but derivative, continuous and unbroken. And everything we might say about God is true in this way. The divine power is first *the Father's power,* which is also possessed personally (hypostatically) by the Son without this signifying two powers (two *ousias*). The divine wisdom is from the Father, occurring again in the Son in an unbroken unity of knowing. And the divine will is that set of desires which is first in the Father, and reiterated in the Son via his eternal "birth" (begetting) – possessed in perfect unity and harmony.[16]

It is this last point that is most significant for this thesis. If there is a modality wherein the Son possesses a will that is the Father's but also his own

---

(see below) – and Karl Rahner speaking similarly of "distinct manners of subsisting" (*distinkten Subsistenzweisen*); K. Rahner, *The Trinity,* trans. J. Donceel (London: William Clowes & Son, 1970), 109-117. Karl Barth similarly speaks of "*Weisen*" of being/existence for which Bromiley and Torrance render "mode"; CD 1/1:360.

14   Latin and English Translation from Augustine, *De Doctrina Christiana,* ed. R. P. H. Green. *Oxford Early Christian texts* (Oxford: Clarendon Press, 1995), 16-17.

15   Readers may legitimately protest that the synthetic role played by the Spirit in this (apparently proto-Hegelian) dialectic is an Augustinian (filioquist!) innovation and seems to serve the same purpose as the essence in pro-Nicene theology – see H. U. von Balthasar, *Theo-logic: The Spirit of Truth.* vol. 3 (San Francisco: Ignatius Press, 2005), 54. My intent here, however, is not to address pneumatological issues nor to explain exactly what the unifying element *is* (Essence or Spirit) but simply to provide a neat exemplification of what I see as the pro-Nicene tension: monarchy, equality, unity.

16   This raises questions about whether the "divine will" should not also be held to include the volitional centre – the existential experience of wanting. I have perhaps made it sound here like the Father and Son like two individuals who like the same thing by virtue of their common nature (like two humans having the same attitude to fresh air). Is this correct? We will examine the matter more closely in Chapter 2.

(I will call this *filial volition* – FV), then there is also some congruence between that modality and the conformity of will we see in the life of Jesus.[17] To establish this, I will refer to a persistent theological tradition that regards the Son's filiality as in some way archetypal of his incarnation (and creation in general). I will also indicate specific cases where the "obedience" of Jesus has been applied in an analogical sense to the relationship between the Father and the Son in eternity.[18]

I also intend to present a more difficult case here. I will argue that it is legitimate also to speak of the Son as not simply possessing the Father's will in reiterative unity but *actively receiving* it; both in his incarnate life, and in his life as Son. In other words, there is an ordered and *responsive intra-trinitarian willing* (RITW) that might also be seen as an expression of FV *and which itself* gives rise to the obedience of Christ on earth.[19] RITW means that the Son is not simply begotten with the Father's preferences in eternity, he also – in a limited way – takes them on himself as coming from another *hypostasis* as an adjunct to the unbroken unity of the *ousia*.

These brief statements encapsulate the objective of the first half of this thesis. The points I plan to defend are these:

1. That the divinity of the second person of the Trinity derives from his relation to the Father according to a pattern of filiality, equality and unity.

2. That this pattern also applies to, and defines, filial volition (FV).

3. That, in additional to this filial volition, there is also a responsive intra-trinitarian willing (RITW) that arises out of FV and becomes "obedience" in the context of the incarnation.

---

17 For example Anne Hunt summarises Paschal-oriented theologians such as Hans Urs von Balthasar, François Durwell and Ghislain Lafont thus:

> His obedience is grounded in his divine personhood ... [his] mission, which he fulfills by his obedience, is properly his own. It is not given to the Son accidentally but as a modality of his eternal personal being and as the extension into creation of his procession from the Father.

> A. Hunt "Trinity and Paschal Mystery: Divine Communion and Human Conversation" in *Theology and Conversation: Towards a Relational Theology*, ed. J. Haers & P. d. Mey. *Bibliotheca Ephemeridum Theologicarum Lovaniensium* (Leuven: Leuven University Press, 2003), 80.

18 To summarise the general point: the Son is to Christ as FV is to Christ's obedience.

19 So Smail: "If purposeful initiation is the *proprium*, the defining hypostatic characteristic of the Father, *willing responsiveness* is the *proprium* of the Son"; T. A. Smail, "In the Image of the Triune God", *IJST* 5.1 (2003): 22-32, 29.

Introduction

Limitations

To cope with the difficult material and ambitious scope of this thesis it has been necessary to omit a number of areas of discussion that might have been included. Most conspicuous by its absence is any thoroughgoing treatment of the Holy Spirit: apart from a brief discussion in Chapter 6, I have confined my investigations to relations between the first two persons of the Godhead. This is primarily because the Bible simply does not treat the intra-trinitarian relationships between the Spirit and the other persons as an object of revelation in the same way it does the Father/Son bond. But also because it is the Son – and not the Spirit – who consistently depicted as recipient and respondant with regard to the Father.

Other omissions have been made in the areas of historical research; there is little attention given to pre-Nicene trinitarianism or to the protracted Christological controversies of the fifth and sixth centuries. These too are regrettable but considered decisions. In the first case, the reasoning is that post-Nicene trinitarianism is generally held to be more consistently anti-subordinationist and more authoritative than earlier theology, so that a case for RITW gains little from claiming precedent before Nicaea but achieves much more if it can find support from the Nicene Fathers themselves. In the case of the Christological debates, my hope has been that the monothelite issue can function as a way of addressing those aspects of the Antiochene/Alexandrian dipole which have closest bearing on the matter at hand.

Finally, evangelical readers may be dismayed to be dragged through such deep thickets of historical and systematic discussion before reaching the chapter on biblical theology. In that case, I would plead their indulgence and assure them that this is does not mean that my biblical theology is a post-justifiction of ideas gleaned from other sources. Although I believe there are many helpful things to learn from our antecedents in this discussion, it is also true that the structure of this thesis is less reflective of the way in which I came to my conclusions, than the objections I anticipate to them. If the biblical theology I advance is to avoid a *prima facie* condemnation as heterodox it will be necessary to first demonstrate what trinitarian orthodoxy actually *is;* and what it might or might not allow.

A Broad Synthesis

Against the trend in much contemporary doctoral research, this thesis presents an argument that is synthetic rather than narrowly analytic. In line with the traditional conception of systematic theology, the aim is to explore and test a theological model in a number of different contexts – historical, biblical and rational[20] – rather than achieve total mastery in one precise area. This generalism is, of course both a weakness and a strength. If the reader is under the impression that what follows is anything like the last word on patristic or scholastic models for divine fathering; covenant theology; biblical anthropology, Neoplatonism or Hegelian trinitarianism then he or she will certainly be disappointed! But if it is recognised that this is a wide-angle work that seeks to show connections and commonalities between traditions and theological structures then the explanatory appeal of the overall system might be appreciable. The yardstick by which the thesis should be judged, is the degree to which it coheres and produces a credible *whole*; are the diverse studies that buttress the main argument convincing *enough* to constitute strong collective support?

I do not delude myself that my arguments at each point will persuade every reader. Nor, in many cases, would I contend that mine is the only legitimate way to understand God and the world – that would be to overstate my intent. What I am attempting here is, not to prove that RITW is "the one true version of orthodox theology", but to to set it forth as a possible scheme that is *at least* coherent, and demonstrably orthodox. If the overall model exercises a greater attraction to the mind of the reader then that is a welcome outcome, but not the standard by which the work should stand or fall.

---

20 In other words, the first three legs of the so-called Wesleyan quadrilateral. It is my hope that the last element, pertaining to existential experience should emerge in doxology as we observe the whole picture: its theocentrism, Christocentrism, and its rich anthropology.

Chapter 1

Is the Priority of Paternal Will compatible with Pro-Nicene Orthodoxy?

> It is no inconsistency, therefore, that the Father alone is the source and origin of the divine will, while nevertheless the Son himself personally wills the same. The Arians' proof for the Son's subordination, his obedient work, itself becomes now the mystery of oneness of will ... the Son in his entire filial existence absorbs the entire will of the Father.
>
> – Christoph von Schönborn[21]

Introduction

If the concept of divine filiality and filial volition on which I am basing my thesis is to be considered orthodox, it will have to be tested against the conclusions of the fourth century Fathers. They, more than any who went before or after them, were forced to face squarely the question of the Son's subordination. And it is they, through their labours and their production of the great creeds of Nicaea and Constantinople, who retain the right to be treated as expert witnesses.

Perhaps surprisingly, however, I also believe that fourth century theology is the most promising place to begin a defence of RITW. The orthodox Fathers moved toward a general consensus, finally formalised at Constantinople in 381 [a consensus I will call "pro-Nicene"[22]], which involved the idea that the Son

---

21 C. von Schönborn, *God's Human Face: the Christ-Icon* (San Francisco: Ignatius Press, 1994), 38.

22 I am using a term that has been recently been given a particular scope in the writings of Michel René Barnes and Lewis Ayres – see for example M. R. Barnes "The Fourth Century as Trinitarian Canon" in *Christian Origins: Theology, Rhetoric and Community,* ed. L. Ayres & G. Jones (London: Routledge, 1998), 47-67, and L. Ayres, *Nicaea and its Legacy: An Approach to Fourth-Century Trinitarian Theology* (Oxford: Oxford University Press, 2004) 236ff – to mean that shape of theology which crystallised out of the post-Nicaea skirmishes of the 360s-380s, rather than just that which informs Nicaea itself. I think this is a generally helpful way of approaching the fourth century disputes (see below) though I also believe there is a common thread (namely the connection of the *homouosion* to

receives the divine nature from his Father. In this chapter I will show that this causal or derivational relationship was also seen by the Fathers to include the divine will; the result being that the Son can truly be said to "do the Father's will" in every action he performs. This by itself is not full-blown RITW – the "R" (responsiveness) in the acronym implies something more active on the part of the Son – but it is certainly FV and might prepare the way for RITW.

Father as Principium in Ancient and Modern Theology

But already this is moving too quickly. To suggest that pro-Nicene theology was in some way *built* on the concept of the Father as source or cause is far too strong a statement for many modern theologians. In both popular writing and systematic theology it is commonplace to read that Nicene theology eliminated "all forms of subordination";[23] or that Nicaea and Constantinople *almost* succeeded in establishing the equality of the persons but that a root of subordinationism remained in the orthodox tradition in the doctrine of divine begetting;[24] or that Athanasius succeeded in promulgating a genuine equality between the persons in contrast to the Cappadocian Fathers who undermined the principle with their insistence on the Father's monarchy;[25] or that the Cappadocians succeeded where Athanasius fell short.[26] The fact that these

---

fatherhood) that runs through all the orthodox theology from Alexander to Constantinople.

23 So D. S. Cunningham, *These Three are One: The Practice of Trinitarian theology. Challenges in Contemporary Theology* (Oxford: Blackwell Publishers, 1998), 112; D. G. Bloesch, *God the Almighty: Power, Wisdom, Holiness, Love. Christian Foundations* (Downers Grove: InterVarsity Press, 1995), 174 (Bloesch also suggests that subordinationism persists in Athanasius and that there is an orthodox form); Barth CD 1/1.382.

24 For example P. Helm, *John Calvin's Ideas* (Oxford: Oxford University Press, 2004), 51-52; M. J. Erickson, *God in Three Persons: A Contemporary Interpretation of the Trinity* (Grand Rapids: Baker Academic, 2003), 299, 309; E. A. Johnson, *She Who Is: The Mystery of God in Feminist Theological Discourse* (New York: Crossroad, 1992), 194-197; L. Hodgson, *The Doctrine of the Trinity. The Croall Lectures 1942-1943* (London: Nisbet, 1944), 102.

25 T. F. Torrance, *The Christian Doctrine of God, One Being Three Persons* (Edinburgh: T&T Clark, 1996), 182-183; W. J. La Due, *The Trinity Guide to the Trinity* (Harrisburg: Trinity Press International, 2003), 90; W. Pannenberg, *Systematic Theology*, trans. G. W. Bromiley, 3 volumes (Grand Rapids: Eerdmans, 1988), 1.279-280.

26 For example R. E. Olson, *The Story of Christian Theology: Twenty Centuries of Tradition & Reform* (Downers Grove: IVP, 1999), 172-173. Olson writes; "Athanasius held on to a relic of subordinationism by affirming the 'monarchy of the Father' ... he laid the foundation and others – namely the Cappadocian Fathers

claims tend to refute one another merely serves to highlight the fact that the modern temper is very much against *any* prioritising of the Father over the Son and Spirit and that many contemporary theologians are convinced that any such causal or derivational order should be thought of as mere historical detritus.

As one might expect, things are a little more complicated with regard to academic literature which focuses more closely on the fourth century. Yet here, too, there is a tendency to minimise the idea that the equality of the Son is founded on his derivation from the Father. Preferred readings of fourth century orthodoxy depict a view in which the divine essence *itself* gives rise to the Son; or in which the begetting of the Son by the Father takes place *within* the logically prior essence such that the begetting itself is not the basis of the consubstantiality.[27]

Dividing the Persons in Modern Patristics

A key instigator of this line of interpretation is E. Meijering. In research published in the late 1960s and '70s analysing the theology of Athanasius (c.295-373) and Gregory Nazianzen (329-390), Meijering seeks to demonstrate the points of contact and divergence between the theology of these Fathers and Platonic philosophy. In an early monograph,[28] he observes that Athanasius uses Platonic forms of language and arguments to show the connections between the created order and the divine Image and Logos/Reason from whom that creation is derived.[29] Yet, he adds, Athanasius also completely overturns Greek philosophy by making the divine Sonship an immutable aspect of God's

---

– built on it". See also A. Coppedge, *The God Who Is Triune: Revisioning the Christian Doctrine of God* (Downers Grove: IVP Academic, 2007), 98-101.

27 An alternative form occurs in N. G. Awad, "Between Subordination and Koinonia: Toward a New Reading of the Cappadocian Theology", *Modern Theology* 23.2 (April 2007): 181-204, 190, 193. Awad argues that the persons constitute the Godhead/essence by their *koinonia*. This construal of relationship-as-being has strong affinities with the views of John Zizioulas (see for example J. Zizioulas, *Being as Communion: Studies in Personhood and The Church* (Crestwood: St. Vladimir's Seminary Press, 1985) 39-41), although Awad is at pains to disprove Zizioulas' version of Cappadocian theology in which the Father is the source of divine equality in the Son and Spirit. We will return to Awad below.

28 E. P. Meijering, *Orthodoxy and Platonism in Athanasius. Synthesis or Antithesis*, corrected reprint edition (Leiden: E. J. Brill, 1974). This is a corrected version of the same work released in 1968.

29 Ibid., 118-119.

essence³⁰ – thereby negating the inherent hierarchical subordinationism found in the teaching of both Platonism and Origen.³¹

In a later essay Meijering returns to similar territory,³² wondering about the apparent inconsistency in Athanasius' Origenistic (so Meijering argues³³) depiction of the Father as the ἀρχή (*arché*) and αἰτία of the Son and his occasional *rejection* of the same terminology.³⁴ Having pointed out that Athanasius' varied attitude to ἀρχή can be explained by the fact that the word can mean both "eternal origin" (which Athanasius accepts) and "temporal beginning" (which he rejects); Meijering then puzzles over the apparent variation in the use of αἰτία and the logical problem its occasional affirmation seems to present. He writes:

> How can it then be explained that Athanasius, knowing that causality implies superiority and inferiority, calls the Father the cause of the Son and nevertheless rejects any inferiority of the Son to the Father?³⁵

Meijering's suggested answer is that Athanasius uses causation and origination between the Father and Son to provide a means of ontologically unifying the persons.³⁶ Because "the Son is the offspring of the Father's οὐσία ... there is only one divine οὐσία and one divine ἀρχή is the origin of the son". The

---

30 Ibid., 124-126.

31 Ibid., 129-131.

32 E. P. Meijering "Athanasius on the Father as Origin of the Son" in *God Being History: Studies in Patristic Philosophy*, (New York: American Elsevier Pub. Co, 1975), 89-102.

33 Examination of the context of those passages where Meijering sees the rejection of αἰτία (*CA* 2.53, 54, 62) indicates that he has missed the sense of Athanasius' argument. In both cases the issue is not the causal relationship between Father and Son but the "reason" (as Newman correctly translates it in NPNF), for the Son being called "Son" or "Word" or "Radiance". In contrast to the words of Hebrews 2 or Proverbs 8, which speak of those titles as being *achieved* in salvation history (τὴν εἰς ἡμᾶς αὐτοῦ κατ' εὐρεγεσιαν γενομένην ἀνανέωσιν) – *CA* 2.53.1, 1 in Athanasius, *Athanasius: Werke*, ed. H. G. Opitz & M. Tetz (de Gruyter, 2001) – these other terms (ἀπαύγασμα – *CA* 2.53, 20ff; Λόγος – *CA* 2.54, 10; μονογενὴσ Υἱός – *CA* 2.62, 23) are spoken μένης αἰτίας, ἀλλὰ ἀπολελυμενος (*CA* 2.62, 23). In other words, there is no additional αἰτία required for him to be so called because these are simply what he *is*.

34 Meijering, *Father as Origin*, 95-100.

35 Ibid., 95.

36 Ibid., 99.

Trinity is the ἀρχή and simultaneously "within this ἀρχή" the Father is the ἀρχή of the Son,[37] thus excluding "any divine hierarchy".[38]

To Meijering this drawing together of intra-trinitarian causality and equality is an unexpected Hegelian synthesis of irreconcilables.[39] And he contrasts this with what he regards as a less impressive achievement from Gregory Nazianzen.[40] Emphasising the differences between Athanasius and Gregory's views on the relationship between the Father's will and the Son's begetting,[41] and picking up those passages where Gregory writes that the Father is "greater" on account of being the cause of the Son,[42] Meijering concludes that Gregory is here influenced by Platonism and has been forced into a "logically untenable" position by "maintaining that the Father is the cause ... and in this respect 'greater' than the Son while at the same time stressing that the Son is not only co-eternal but also ὁμοούσιος with the Father".[43] Gregory's repeated pronouncements that the Son is *naturally* equal with the Father who begets him do not secure him the same respect that Meijering accords Athanasius, but merely compound the contradiction.[44]

Meijering's belief that the Fathers might be sorted according to sound and unsound theories of paternal causation persists amongst subsequent scholars, albeit with rather different conclusions. T.F. Torrance, for example, sees Gregory in the same terms as Athanasius, judging his theology to be a decided advance on that of Basil of Caesarea (330-379).[45] While Basil (and Gregory of

---

37 Ibid., 96.

38 Ibid., 99.

39 Ibid., 100.

40 Meijering, *Doctrine of the Will*, 229ff.

41 Ibid., 227-228, 232.

42 Ibid., 229-230.

43 Ibid., 232-233.

44 It is worth noting that Meijering regards Hilary of Poitiers in a similar light, though his treatment is much less hostile. In his later work E. P. Meijering & J. C. M. van Winden, *Hilary of Poitiers on the Trinity: De Trinitate 1, 1-19, 2, 3.* vol. 6. *Philosophia Patrum* (Leiden: Brill, 1982), 184, Meijering writes of the "striking similarity" between Hilary's Tertullian-influenced subordinationism and the Cappadocian mixing of "Athanasian orthodoxy with the subordinationist views of Origen".

45 See T. F. Torrance, *Theology in Reconciliation: Essays Towards Evangelical and Catholic Unity in East and West,* American edition (Grand Rapids: Eerdmans, 1976), 32-40; Torrance, *Doctrine of God,* 178ff. For a more recent presentation of arguments similar to Torrance's see Awad, "Subordination and *Koinonia*", 190, 193. Awad suggests that, in contradistinction to Basil, Gregory might be seen to be

Nyssa – c.335-394)[46] imply an unacceptable hierarchy of deity by making the Father's *hypostasis* the ἀρχή and αἰτία of the *ousia*, Son and Spirit, Gregory follows Athanasius, who regarded such views as bolstering the "Arian deviation".[47] Instead of the *monarchy* of the Father,[48] Torrance claims to find in both Gregory and Athanasius a nascent *perichoretic* conception of the *ousia* as "being in its internal relations";[49] the persons "mutually containing and interpenetrating one another ... [to] constitute a perfectly homogenous communion".[50] Thus he writes that:

> ... the inner trinitarian order [of Father, Son, Spirit] does not apply to the Deity or the Being of the divine persons which individually and all together have absolutely in common, but only to the mysterious economy which they have among themselves as persons within the unity of the Godhead. ... [Gregory Nazianzen] did not share the view of St Basil or his brother Gregory [of Nyssa] that the unity of God is ensured by tracing it back to the Father as the one underived Person, but insisted that the whole Trinity ... is the Principle (Ἀρχή) of the Oneness of the Godhead.[51]

---

offering a *koinonial* model wherein the three persons together "constitute" the *ousia*.

46   Torrance seems to regard Gregory of Nyssa in a more positive light in earlier writing – eg. T. F. Torrance, *The Trinitarian Faith: The Evangelical Theology of the Ancient Catholic Church* (Edinburgh: T&T Clark, 1988), 240 – but later brackets him with his brother as promoting a "causal series" model of the Trinity; Torrance, *Doctrine of God*, 178.

47   Ibid., 181.

48   I will use this expression to signify the idea that the Father is the sole source (ἀρχή or *principium*) of divine life, not to signify that he is "king" of the Godhead.

49   Ibid., 182.

50   Torrance, *Reconciliation*, 33.

51   T. F. Torrance, *Trinitarian Perspectives: Toward Doctrinal Agreement* (Edinburgh: T&T Clark, 1994), 136-138. Interestingly, Torrance here seems to have supplied us with *two different grounds* for divine unity: a monistically conceived "Deity" or "Being" which is "absolutely in common" beneath or behind the persons; and an economic *perichoresis* which arises out of their interactions. But as Colin Gunton asks, what are we to make of these formulations? If Torrance does not intend modalism – and Gunton is sure he doesn't – why deploy this distinction between "unified being" and the persons which suggests it? See C. E. Gunton, *Father, Son and Holy Spirit: Essays Toward a Fully Trinitarian Theology* (London: T&T Clark, 2003), 48.

For a more recent contributor to this tradition of Torrance see J. R. Meyer, "God's Trinitarian Substance in Athanasian Theology", *Scottish Journal of Theology* 59.1 (2006): 81-97.

Whether this is an accurate characterization of either Athanasius or Gregory is a question to which must return below.

Beyond Torrance, two of the most influential patristic scholars of the last decade, Michel René Barnes and Lewis Ayres also divide the Nicene Fathers according to their theories of causation, though their divisions do not correspond with those of Meijering or Torrance.

For Barnes and Ayres the traditional description of the Arian controversy is over-simplistic and too reliant on the partisan accounts of Athanasius.[52] Rejecting the notion that Arianism was an "alien theology" which appeared, conspired, was briefly triumphant and then dispatched, Barnes and Ayres attempt to contextualise the controversy as a collision between theological trajectories that had been present within both the Eastern and Western halves of the empire for centuries.[53] Thus, instead of a clash between *heresy* and *orthodoxy,* they prefer to contrast those who emphasise the unity of God with those who stress the diversity,[54] or those who want to talk more about the difference between the Logos and God with those who emphasise their similarity.[55]

From within this modern historiographical framework Barnes and Ayres analyse the Nicene debates in terms of new developments and broad movements rather than a *return* to orthodoxy championed by individual theologians. Athanasius is thus regarded as less significant than those who come after him, and pro-Nicene theology is viewed as something that emerges after Nicaea.

But here too, questions of intra-trinitarian causality remain central. Barnes writes that Cappadocian theology – in particular that of Gregory of Nyssa – differs from that of Athanasius by not using

> ... 'generation' to ground a doctrine of 'common nature' or 'one essence' in the Trinity. Whereas Athanasius and his contemporaries use the doctrine of divine generation to prove that the Father and Son have the

---

52 Barnes, *Trinitarian Canon,* 53.

53 Ibid., 47. See a more detailed delineation of these strands in Ayres, *Nicaea,* 41ff, 78ff.

54 Barnes, *Trinitarian Canon,* 50-51.

55 Ayres, *Nicaea,* 41-42. This is not, of course, to deny that there are differences between Ayres and Barnes – though they are certainly very similar in their approach. For a comparison of their differences see M. R. Barnes, *The Power of God: Dunamis in Gregory of Nyssa's Trinitarian Theology* (Washington: Catholic University of America Press, 2001), 239-240, cf. ibid., 169-172.

same nature or essence, Gregory uses generation as the basis for distinguishing the persons.[56]

Thus whilst those who supported Nicaea in the late 350s "argued that the language of Father and Son referred to a relationship in which the offspring has the same nature as the source", Gregory retains the concept of causation, but simply as a way of guaranteeing that there is some difference between the hypostases.[57]

Ayres makes similar judgments both about Athanasius, Gregory of Nyssa and the drift of fourth century theology; arguing against those who would see the conflicts of the fourth century resolved by a restatement of "original Nicene" (principally Athanasian) theology.[58] Ayres produces three central tenets by which pro-Nicene theology might be characterised: (1) "the principle that whatever is predicated of the divine nature is predicated of the three persons equally and understood to be one"; (2) "clear expression that the eternal generation of the Son occurs within the unitary and incomprehensible divine being"; (3) "clear expression of the doctrine that the persons work inseparably".[59] Following Barnes, Ayres insists that in "fully pro-Nicene usage

---

56 M. R. Barnes, "Divine Unity and the Divided Self: Gregory of Nyssa's Trinitarian Theology in its Psychological Context", *Modern Theology* 18.4 (2004): 475-496, 483. Of course one might protest that *both* the paradigms mentioned here serve to distinguish the persons.

57 Ibid., 483-484. Oddly, Barnes argues that the grounding of essential continuity in the filial relationship is a post-Nicene development. Nicaea, he argues, makes the "essence language" itself carry the burden of continuity, and makes it seem as if "Father" and "Son" refer only to the incarnation. No doubt there were some, such as Marcellus of Ancyra, who might have been inclined to take it this way, just as there were others such as Eusebius of Caesarea who were happy to misconstrue γεννηθέντα ἐκ τοῦ πατροσ and ἐκ τῆς οὐσίας τοῦ πατρός as signifying only that God *himself* had created the Son. But it is rather difficult to believe that the majority of the 318 present could really have imagined that the essence language was *not* meant to be understood in terms of fatherhood and causation with words and phrases such as γεννηθέντα and μονογενῆ and θεὸν ἐκ θεοῦ, φῶς ἐκ φωτός featuring so prominently. This is not simply "essence language", it is a *conception* of continuity (or at least equality) based on a causal relationship. Yet Gwatkin may be correct in his suggestion that the ἐκ τῆς οὐσίας part of the creed was included to counter the Sabellian connotations of the ὁμοούσιον, and that this phrase was removed in 381 because it was no longer needed; see H. M. Gwatkin, *The Arian Controversy*, 2nd edition (Charleston: BiblioBazaar, 2008), 39.

58 Ayres, *Nicaea*, 236-237. Ayres makes his argument here in conscious rejection of the theses that the Cappadocians simply burnished and refined Athanaius' theology or that Cappadocian trinitarianism represents a decay of Nicene/Athanasian theology (as per Loofs, Harnack).

59 Ibid., 236.

... the Father/Son relationship is used only to show that the persons are distinct because now the eternal generation occurs *a priori* within the unitary and simple Godhead".[60]

Historical Eisegesis?

Now, in responding to these various readings of fourth century theology, it is worth observing initially that there is something suspicious in the way these scholars all agree on the undesirable character of the paternal *monarchy* (at least in connection with the divine essence) while being at odds on *which* fourth century theologians are responsible for its mitigation. Given this peculiarity, we might permit ourselves to wonder if there is a little eisegesis going on here; the modern theologian *knows in advance* what a consistent trinitarian theology looks like and sets out to find it.

Our suspicions might be aroused still further when we observe that what is presented as *fully developed* or *consistent* trinitarianism turns out to look very much like the theology of Augustine[61] – or at least theology that might be labelled "Western".[62] It is interesting that this characterisation of pro-Nicene

---

60   Ibid., 236.

61   It is surely no coincidence that Ayres makes Augustine the quintessential pro-Nicene theologian; ibid., 365.

62   This is not an attempt to defend the claim (typically associated with Théodore de Régnon) that the East begins with the persons (in some kind of social trinitarian scheme) while the West begins with the essence. As has been made clear in recent research, both the paradigm *and* its connection to de Régnon is problematic – see D. B. Hart "The Mirror of the Infinite: Gregory of Nyssa on the Vestigia Trinitatis" in *Rethinking Gregory of Nyssa,* ed. S. Coakley (Oxford: Blackwell, 2003) and K. Hennesey, "An Answer to de Regnon's Accusers: Why we should not speak of "his" paradigm", *Harvard Theological Review* 100.2 (2007): 179-197. Yet, as we shall see in Chapter 3, there surely remains a strong kernel of truth in the observation that from Augustine on, there really is a tendency in the West to make the triune being the "God" to whom we pray and who might be called a "he" in some metapersonal sense.

Moreover the irony here is that those who have been most prominent in their criticism of the "de Régnon" thesis – Barnes and Ayres – are championing the very same division in different contexts. For them "East" becomes the earlier theology of Athanasius and Nicaea; "West" is true pro-Nicene theology as it is said to appear in Gregory of Nyssa and Augustine. A logical question to ask at this point is whether we might not expect these differences between Athanasius and Augustine to be reflected in the Greek and Latin traditions that cherish them? Unless we imagine that the East is ready to give Augustine the last word on Nicene theology *over* Athanasius (or happy to set Athanasius *against* Gregory of Nyssa) then it would be remarkable if the division observed by Barnes and Ayres did *not* give rise to an East/West division. In short, if they are right about pro-Nicene theology, we should expect them to be wrong about de Régnon.

theology involving the persons as subsisting "within" or "from" a single being has been promoted almost exclusively by modern (often postliberal)[63] Westerners and has received a much less enthusiastic reception amongst the Orthodox.[64] We might ask, with John Behr, whether what we are seeing here "constitutes an appropriation of what [the Fathers] were doing by an Augustinian tradition of theology mediated through the categories of modern systematics".[65]

Ironically, the diversity we have seen above means that the case in favour of a strong and (near) universal fourth century endorsement of the Father's monarchy as the means of the Son's equality with the Father is already half made. I agree with Barnes and Ayres that Athanasius and the Nicene creed both rely on the concept; *and* with Meijering that Athanasius also manages to deploy it without compromising the Son's ontological equality. I also agree with Meijering that a similar commitment to the monarchy of the Father also appears in Gregory Nazianzen; *and* I agree with Torrance that Basil and Gregory of Nyssa are united in the same commitment.

---

63 See Hankey's critical comments on postmodern Augustinianism (a bracket which he extends around Ayres); W. J. Hankey, *Re-Christianizing Augustine Postmodern Style: Readings by Jacques Derrida, Robert Dodaro, Jean-Luc Marion, Rowan Williams, Lewis Ayres and John Milbank*, http://www.mun.ca/animus/1997vol2/hankey1.htm#N_81_, (accessed February, 2010).

64 This is a generalization, of course, and is immediately challenged by Orthodox theologians such as David Bentley Hart and Nonna Verna Harrison who come close to this position. Yet here we might give heed to Alan Brown's lament that sectors of (especially anglophone) Orthodox theology have been colonised by postliberal Anglicans who purport to find their own brand of Augustinian Thomism in the Fathers; A. Brown "On the Criticism of Being as Communion in Anglophone Orthodox Theology" in *The Theology of John Zizioulas: Personhood and the Church*, ed. D. H. Knight (Aldershot: Ashgate, 2007). John Behr, despite himself being critical of the East/West cliché -J. Behr, *The Nicene Faith*. vol. 2. *Formation of Christian theology* (Crestwood: St. Vladimir's Seminary Press, 2004), 414n27 – protests that in Ayres' hands "the de Régnon paradigm has been removed, not in order to allow these diverse writers to appear in their distinctiveness ... but rather to subsume their distinct voices within a particular (and particularly totalizing) discourse;" J. Behr, "Response to Ayres: The Legacies of Nicaea, East and West", *Harvard Theological Review* 100.2 (2007): 145-152. See also Morwenna Ludlow here on the influence that ecumenical impulses might have on correct understandings of the Cappadocians; M. Ludlow, *Gregory of Nyssa: Ancient and (Post)modern* (Oxford: Oxford University Press, 2007), 270.

65 See Behr, "Response", 145-146. In the same article he challenges Ayres' nomenclature for the "triune God", and restates the Eastern objection that such language sounds "distinctly modalist"; ibid., 148.

Questioning the Modern Trend

Before I develop my case further, however, I need to state as clearly as I can that what I am *not* trying to do is to put forward (or return to) a neat unified terminology or conceptual rendition of the fourth century orthodoxy. Pro-Nicene theology *necessarily* holds in tension a number of different perspectives and modes of speech – some of which sound quite like those held up by Torrance or Barnes as "final". As I averred briefly in my introduction, pro-Nicene theology is a tension of (paternal) monarchy, equality and unity. Whenever we express the *unity* aspect of this trialectic it will sound something like the kind of trinitarianism imagined (and seen as pro-Nicene) by the scholars just listed; the Father and Son occuring as relations within, or expressions of, the one undivided *being*.

And yet there are nonetheless problems with this form of expression. The idea that the Father Son and Spirit are relations *within a conceptually prior essence* and that the essence itself is not implicated in the processions suggests a framework that is rather alien to the pro-Nicene Fathers (at least before Augustine).[66] Rather we tend to find the reverse – that there is one essence/nature/godhead *in three persons.*[67]

Equality in the Father

More typically, however, it is the Father who perichoretically serves this enclosing function in Athanasius and the Cappadocians. The Son is *in* the Father and is thus never severed from the Father's nature; yet the Son is not simply *one* with the Father but *equal,* and in this sense has the Father('s nature) "in him". As Athanasius writes at length in *Contra Arianos* 3.1-6:

> [The statement "I in the Father and the Father in Me"] is proper and suitable to a Son only, who is Word and Wisdom and Image of the Father's Essence (εἰκόνι τῆς τοῦ Πατρὸσ οὐσίασ) ... For the Father is in the Son, since the Son is what is from the Father and proper to him, as in the radiance the sun, and in the word the thought, and in the stream the fountain ... Accordingly when the Father is called the only God, and we read that there is one God, and "I am", and "beside me there is no God", and "I the first and I the last", this has a fit meaning. For God is

---

66 Gregory Nazianzen comes closest to this unitary mode of speech (*Or.* 38.16; *Or.* 31.9, 15) under the terms of "godhead" (θεότης) or "nature" (φύσις), but not to the exclusion of paternal monarchy – as we will see below.

67 Athanasius (*CA* 1.18, 3.15); Gregory Nazianzen (*Or.* 28.31; *Or.* 33.16; *Or.* 34.9). As Harnack – A. von Harnack, *History of Dogma,* trans. N. Buchanan (London: Williams & Norgate, 1905), 4.118 – puts in relation to the Cappadocians; "We are to believe in one God, because we are to believe in one divine substance or essence ... in three distinct subjects or persons".

One and Only and first; but this is not said to the denial of the Son, perish the thought; for he is in that one, and first and only, as being of that one and only and first the only Word and Wisdom and Radiance. And he too is the first, as the fullness of the Godhead of the first and only (τοῦ πρώτου καὶ μόνου θεότητος), being whole and full God.[68]

What should be immediately apparent from this is that Athanasius' version of trinitarian *perichoresis* does not mitigate the Father's monarchy but confirms it.[69] In contrast to modern egalitarian renditions of *perichoresis*,[70] here there is a *direction* and an *asymmetry* informed by the principle that the Father is the source of all that the Son is, as well as an insistence on unity and equality because of the Father being fully *in* the Son.

Athanasius is not alone here. Basil writes to his brother of how the Son, existing in the Father eternally (ἀεὶ ἐν τῷ πατρὶ ὤν), can never be severed

---

68 Excerpts from 3.2, 3, 6 (NPNF 2.4.394-397; PG 26.325A-333C). Torrance strangely takes 3.3 as a denial that the "Son's Deity is originated by the Father" (Torrance, *Perspectives*, 63). Of course this is obviously right if we are talking about "two deities", but it is completely contrary to the meaning of the passage to turn this into the idea that "Father and Son together must be thought of as *principium*" with regard to the divine equality of the Son. Torrance indeed does have a point when he suggests that Gregory Nazianzen shows a greater willingness to reify and personify the triune being (see below). But to take this as a *denial* that the Son derives his essential equality from the Father is to read Calvin's idiosyncratic doctrine of *autotheos* back over Gregory (see Torrance, *Trinitarian Faith*, 28-29 and, on Calvin, Letham, *Holy Trinity*, 252-268).

69 It is worth noting in passing that the same orderliness is intrinsic to the later theology of John of Damascus (676-749) who presents a *locus classicus* of perichoretic doctrine:

> For we recognise one God: but only in the attributes of Fatherhood, Sonship, and Procession, both in respect of cause and effect and perfection of subsistence, that is, manner of existence, do we perceive difference ... the Son and Spirit being referred to one cause (εἰς ἓν αἴτιον), and not compounded or coalesced according to the synaeresis of Sabellius. For, as we said, they are made one not so as to commingle, but so as to cleave to each other, and they have their being in each other (καὶ τὴν ἐν ἀλλήλαις περιχώρησιν) without any coalescence or commingling.

De Fide Orthodoxa 1.8; NPNF 2.9.11.

70 See for example L. Boff & P. Burns, *Trinity and Society. Theology and Liberation Series* (Maryknoll: Orbis Books, 1988), 137; C. M. LaCugna, *God for Us: The Trinity and Christian Life*, 1st edition (San Francisco: Harper, 1991), 270-271. Interestingly the modern version of *perichoresis* sounds very much like an idea that Athanasius condemns as irreligious: the idea that the persons are "discharged into Each Other, filling the One the Other, as in the case of empty vessels, so that the Son fills the emptiness of the Father and the Father that of the Son"; cf. *CA* 3.1.

from the Father, adding that the Father is in the Son as a perfect form (μορφή) is beheld in a polished mirror.[71] Gregory in turn also agrees that the Father and Son are in the other in different senses (κατ' ἄλλην...ἔνοιαν). The Son is in the Father as the beauty of an image (εἰκόνος) partakes of its archetype (τῇ ἀρχετύπῳ μορφῇ); the Father is in the Son as the original beauty itself (πρωτότυπον κάλλος).[72] Later in the same work he argues that the very order (τάξις) of the Johannine (perichoretic) phraseology provides the interpretive key to orthodox dogma (εὐσεβὲς ἑρμηνεύει τοῦ δόγματος).[73] "I am in the Father" occurs first because the Father is not of the Son but the Son is of the Father; "the Father is in me" is added to show the true and exclusive connection between the two.[74]

Hilary of Poitiers (c.310-368) returns to the language of John 17 more than any other of the Fathers, connecting it to the priority of the Father and the perfect equality (and "indistinguishable unity")[75] of the Son in his sonship.[76] The "Father is in the Son" because the Son has nothing in himself (*nihil in se*) unlike the Father"; but the Son is in the Father because the Son is not from any other (*non est aliunde*): they "are" one but not "is" one through their similar and indifferentiable nature (*unum sunt ... per indissimilis naturae indifferentum ... ne unus sit*).[77] Elsewhere he develops the same theme in terms which Meijering would associate with subordinationism,[78] stressing the greatness of the Father *as Father* and the equality of the Son *as Son*:

> The one is from the other, and the two are a unity; not two made one, yet one in the other, for that which is in both is the same ... not to dispute the Father's powers or to depreciate the Son, but to reverence the mystery and majesty of his birth; to set the unbegotten Father above all rivalry (*nihil comparare*), and count the only-begotten Son as his equal in

---

71 *Epistolae* 38.4, 8 (PG 32.328C, 340C).

72 *CE* 1 (PG 45.445D, 447A).

73 *CE* 9 (PG 45.821A cf. NPNF 2.5.218).

74 Ibid.

75 *Naturae indifferentis*; *DeTrin.* 7.22 (PL 10.218C).

76 *DeTrin.* 2.8, 10; 3.4; 7.24, 26-27.

77 *De Syn* 64, PL 10.524A. The Father is greater (*majorem esse*) because he is father, but the Son is not less because he is son. Although there is no superiority as to *genere substantiae*, nevertheless the Son is subject (*subjectum*), being born of the other's nature (*nativitate naturae*). See also *DeTrin.* 7.31.

78 Meijering & van Winden, *Hilary,* 184. Meijering sees connections between Hilary and Tertullian here and notes similarities to the Cappadocians who "combine Athanasian orthodoxy with the subordinationist views of Origen".

eternity and might, confessing concerning God the Son that he is from God.[79]

Of course Hilary does *not* mean to say here that the Father's incomparable supremacy excludes the Son. Rather, the first person *is* the greatness and supremacy which the Son *also possesses as son*. Hilary is thus using the same conceptual framework as Athanasius who, as we saw above, calls the Father the "one God" but immediately adds that this is not said to the "denial of the Son".[80]

This way of prioritising the Father yet including the Son *in* the Father should warn us to be careful about the way we read the patristic comments on the monarchy. Statements that make the whole Godhead one monarchy should not be set against the idea that the Father is also the *arché*. The logic of indwelling would imply that both can be true: the paternal monarchy – begetting and procession – gives rise to a united monarchy *vis á vis* creation. As Torrance correctly states, "the monarchy of the Father within the Trinity is not exclusive of the monarchy of the whole undivided Trinity in relation to the whole of creation".[81] Or, in the words of Basil:

---

79 *DeTrin.* 3.4 (NPNF 2.9.63; PL 10.78A). Torrance manages to miss these parts of Hilary's text which explicate the verse he does cite (3.1): "One permanently envelopes, and is permanently enveloped by, the Other whom he yet envelopes"; Torrance, *Perspectives,* 120. Hilary's meaning certainly does not connote the kind of symmetry and mutuality that Torrance imagines.

80 And, of course, this is exactly how the creed of Nicaea is also structured. "We believe in one God, *the Father*" is followed immediately by the inclusion of the Son, the Lord, θεὸν ἐκ θεοῦ, ὁμοούσιαν τῷ πατρί, "through whom" the world was created.

81 Ibid., 120. The difficult question here is what exactly Torrance means by "Father". It is clear elsewhere that Torrance (like other Westerners) applies the designation "Father" to two different things; first the person who "considered relatively to the Son" and second to the "personal Being" of the one (triune) God "in himself" (see Torrance, *Doctrine of God,* 131). Torrance seems to think that it is only in the *second* sense that the Father can be called ᾽Αρχή or Μοναρχία. Although the person of the Father is considered "Father of the Son", this designation does not mean "that the Son is to be thought of as proceeding from the *person* of the Father" (see ibid., 140-141). This is a little bizarre. Torrance's framework also means that it is just as true to say that the Son is his own ᾽Αρχη; or that the Spirit is the ᾽Αρχη of the Son; or the Son is the ᾽Αρχη of the Father. Since each of the persons can be considered "absolutely" as the one essence he can thus be designated "Father" (as the term refers to the divine being, cf. ibid., 145) and can be referred to as the cause of any personal subsistence. It was to avoid just such absurdities as these that Medieval scholasticism prohibited the use of undifferentiated *essentia* language to speak of the processions: see Peter Lombard, *SQL* 1.5.1; Thomas Aquinas *Summa*

> Worshipping as we do God of God, we both confess the distinction of the persons (ὑποστάσεων), and at the same time [stand fast] by the monarchy (μένομεν ἐπὶ τῆς μοναρχίας). We do not fritter away the theology (θεολογίαν – here connoting the *res ad intra*) in a divided plurality, because one form (μορφήν), so to say, united in the invariableness of the Godhead, is beheld in God the Father, and in God the only begotten. *For the Son is in the Father and the Father in the Son; since such as is the latter, such is the former, and such as is the former, such is the latter; and herein is the unity.* So that according to the distinction of persons (προσώπων), both are one and one, and according to the community of nature (κοιόν τῆς φύσεως), one. How, then, if one and one, are there not two Gods? Because we speak of a king, and of the king's image, and not of two kings. The majesty is not cloven in two, nor the glory divided. The sovereignty and authority over us is one, and so the doxology ascribed by us is not plural but one; because the honour paid to the image passes on to the prototype.[82]

Exactly the same reasoning can be found in Athanasius' *CA* 4.1:

> For the Word, being Son of the one God, is referred back to him of whom also he is (εἰς αὐτόν, οὗ καὶ ἔστιν, ἀναφέρεται)[83]; so that Father and Son are two, yet the monad of the Godhead is indivisible and inseparable. And thus too we preserve one Beginning of Godhead and not two beginnings, whence there is strictly a monarchy. [84]

Beyond the Paternal Monarchy? The Case of Gregory Nazianzen.

To challenge this we should thus need not only to find the *words* μοναρχία or ἀρχή applied inclusively to the Son and Spirit (which is easy enough for the reasons just given), but to adduce patristic texts which indicate something other than the Father (eg. the essence or Trinity) acting as source or cause as regards the *hypostases* themselves, or to find explicit denials that the Father is the *arché*.

As to denials of the Father as *arché* there are, as far as I can tell, simply none in fourth century pro-Nicene theology. There are certainly statements that the Son is ἀνάρχου in terms of not having *a beginning in time* or a "new"

    1a.39.5; Duns Scotus *Lectura* 1.5.2. (commentary on *SQL*) – thanks to Oxford research student J. T. Paasch for pointing this out in private correspondence.

82   *De Spiritu Sanctu* 45 (NPNF 2.8.28; PG 32.149B). Emphasis added.

83   The last word here would seem to signify more than NPNF's "referred", having the connotation of being supported

84   NPNF *2.4.433* (altered), *cf.* PG *26.468B*. We will see the same idea emerging in Gregory Nazianzen's *Or.* 29.2 below.

The Will of Him Who Sent Me

essence different from the Father's, thus rejecting the possibility that he might be a contingent addition to the Father.[85] But this is not a denial that the Father has always been the source of the eternal Son.[86]

However, with regard to an alternative *arché* for the persons, there *is* one passage, often cited,[87] that might indicate this in Gregory Nazianzen. In his fifth

---

85 Two recently cited examples should be noted here. In *CA* 2.57 Athanasius argues that the Son has no beginning (οὐχ ἔχων αρχήν τοῦ εἶναι) but exists without beginning (ἀναρχως ὑπάρχη) in the Father – as the Father himself exists without ἀρχη (PG 26.269A, B). Kevin Giles – Giles, *Jesus,* 138 – argues that this denial that the "Son has an *arche*" arises out of Athanasius' rejection of hierarchy within the Godhead. On this reading, however, Athanasius is simply incoherent for, as Giles notes, this same text also states that the Son has no other ἀρχη than the Father. The reconciliation is provided in the next verse (2.58) which states that the Son exists as γέννημα Υἱὸν, οὐχ τινος ἀρχῆς ἀρξάμενον, ἀλλ' ἀΐδιον (my emphasis); he is caused with regard to the Father but ἀναρχη in with regard to time. See Meijering on the distinction between these two uses ἀρχή in Athanasius; Meijering, *Father as Origin,* 96.

Another challenge is provided by John Meyer (Meyer, "Substance", 91) who cites Gregory Nazianzen's concern that using the word την ἀρχήν might make him source of those who receive less (ἐλαττόνων) (*Or.* 40.43; PG 36.420B). Yet here again the context solves the problem. Gregory's intention is certainly not to deny causal relations between the persons. He names the Father as the one from whom the equality of being derives (ἐξ οὗ ἴσοις εἶναι) and insists that this is universally accepted (πάντων δοθήσεται). Yet he is concerned that an opportunistic hearer will seize on this word (see also *Or.* 39.12) to divide the nature (διχοτομήσης τὴν φύσιν). Consequently he stresses that greatness (μεῖζον) applies not to the nature (φύσιν), as if there were more than one, but only to cause (τὴν αἰτίαν), which is the Father. It is ironic that Meyer in his essay follows the very logic that Gregory is trying to guard against: assuming that if the Father is cause then there must be two essences resulting in either ontological subordination or tritheism (cf. ibid., 89, 92, 96).

See the fuller discussion of this text and some similar verses in J. P. Egan "αἴτιος/'Author', αἰτιία/'Cause' and ἀρχή/'Origin': Synonymns in Selected Texts of Gregory Nazianzen" in *Studia Patristica, vol. XXXII, Papers Presented at the Twelfth International Conference on Patristic Studies held in Oxford 1995,* ed. E. A. Livingstone (Louvain: Peeters, 1997).

86 See for example *De Se Ipso* PG 37.1248.40 where the Father's status as root and source (ῥίζα καὶ πηγή) is followed by reference to the Son as eternal seal (σφράγισμα ἀναρχου).

87 For surveys of recent writing on the passage see C. Beeley, "Divine Causality and the Monarchy of the Father in Gregory of Nazianzus", *Harvard Theological Review* 100.2 (2007): 199-214 and J. P. Egan "Primal Cause and Trinitarian Perichoresis in Gregory Nazianzen's Oration 31.14" in *Studia Patristica, vol. XXVII, Papers Presented at the Eleventh International Conference on Patristic Studies held in Oxford 1991,* ed. E. A. Livingstone (Louvain: Peeters, 1993).

theological oration (*Oratio* 31) Gregory parries the charge of tritheism by protesting that:

> To us there is one God, for there is one Godhead (θεότης), and all that is from him (τά ἐξ αὐτοῦ) has one ground (ἕν...ἀναφορὰν ἔχει), though we believe in three. For one is not more and another less God; nor is one first and another after; nor are they divided in will or parted in power; nor can you find here any of the qualities of divisible things; but the Godhead is, to speak concisely, undivided in separation (ἀμέριστος ἐν μεμερισμένοις); and there is one mingling of Light, as it were of three suns joined to each other. When then we look at the Godhead, or the first cause (πρώτην αἰτίαν), and the monarchy, that which we picture in our minds (φανταζόμενον) is one; but when we look at those in whom the Godhead dwells, and at the ones who timelessly have their being from the first cause (τά ἐκ τῆς πρώτης αἰτίας ἀχπόνως ἐκεῖθεν ὄντα) with equal glory – there are three whom we worship.[88]

In this passage we apparently *do* see something much closer to the position held up by the likes of Ayres, Barnes and Torrance. In the first line, Gregory appears to begin by describing the Godhead itself as "God" – designated with a masculine singular pronoun.[89] In the last sentence it seems that *all three* derive their subsistence from this πρώτης αἰτίας – signifying a coordinate, rather than derived, equality for the Son and Spirit. In the same oration (31.9) he elsewhere speaks of three persons in one nature (τριῶν ὑποστάσεων ἐν τῇ μιᾷ φύσει)[90] – apparently signifying the model championed by modern patrology (that the persons occur within the essence).

But it is not *quite* the same. In verses 9-11 of the same work Gregory deals with the argument that either the Spirit is *another son* or he must be a second God – the implicit premise being that sonship is the only non-divisive type of consubstantiality. Gregory denies this premise, pointing out that even in the created world there is more than one mode of generation. He enumerates

---

88 *Or.* 31.14; PG 36.147D, 149A. The translation is partly mine and partly from NPNF 2.7.322.

89 Beeley argues that consistency suggests that the τά ἐξ αὐτου in the first line refers not to the essence but to God the Father; *he* is the "God" referred to in the first instance and the Godhead that begins with him but includes the other two: Beeley, "Divine Causality", 210-211. This is certainly a possible reading of *Or.* 31.14 but it is less likely in the light of subsequent verses (28, 33) where Gregory does seem to personify the Godhead (not the essence) itself as an entity of worship. In the very final line he speaks of his desire to call others to worship "Father, Son and Holy Ghost, the one Godhead and Power. To him belongs all glory (αὐτῳ πᾶσα δοξα) and honour and might for ever and ever (31.33; NPNF 2.7.328, cf. PG 36.172B).

90 PG 36.144A.

heterogenesis (where like begets unlike), metamorphosis (where a creature changes nature) and autogenesis (as seen in the phoenix), and then speaks of another case,[91] of which part is generated and part not, without any loss of consubstantiality (οὐ γέννημα, τὸ δὲ γέννημα, πλὴν ὁμοούσια). This example, he notes, is most fitting (προσέοικεν) for the issue at hand. To take this to a final step, Gregory next (31.11) introduces the contrasting examples of Eve and Seth, who are shown to be consubstantial with Adam by different means. Eve shares in Adam as a piece (τμῆμα) of him, and Seth shares by begetting; yet they are certainly all ὁμοούσια with each other and with the creature (πλάσμα) that is Adam. They are the same thing together (ἀμφότεροι ταυτὸν ἀλλήλοις) for they are all humans (ἄνθρωποι γάρ).[92]

Almost every one of these examples – and especially those Gregory emphasises as most useful – associates the idea of sharing of essence with origination. Seth and Eve share in the same nature as Adam because they are *from him*; in a similar way the Son and Spirit share in the Father's nature because they issue from him, one by begetting and the other by procession.[93] While causation does *not* apply to essence as if there were different essences generated by filiation and spiration, yet the essence *is* associated with these causal relationships, for the commonality of essence is what arises from the begetting and proceeding.[94]

---

91 31.10; PG 36.144C The object implied by τοῦ αὐτοῦ presumably means another "species" rather than individual substance as per autogenesis or metamorphosis.

92 A similar point is made by Ambrose who deconstructs the Arian use of 1 Cor 11.3 to argue that if the Son and Father are related as man and woman (though he himself makes the statement apply only to Christ's humanity) then they must be consubstantial; *DeFid*. 4.3.28.

93 We should note that Gregory uses a similar argument in the contemporaneous *Or*. 30.10 (380AD, see Gallay's dating in J. A. McGuckin, *St. Gregory of Nazianzus: An Intellectual Biography* (Crestwood: St. Vladimir's Seminary Press, 2001) x). Here the Son is called "Son" because he is identical according to essence (ταυτόν...κατ' οὐσίαν) and because he is from that essence (κἀκεῖθεν). Lest we think this corresponds to the theory that the Father's person is thus uninvolved, this is followed up by arguments concerning what it means for the Son to be the Father's Word and impress and offspring. Gregory writes that he is of the Father and the Father not of him (τοῦτο ἐκεῖθεν, ἀλλ' οὐκ ἐκ τοῦτο Πατήρ) and that the Son and Father correspond to type and archetype (living reproduction and Living One – ζῶτος καὶ ζῶσα) and this in a way more precise or indistinguishable (ἀπαράλλακτον) than applies between Adam and Seth or any son to father (NPNF 2.7.316-317; PG 36.127A-129B).

94 Beeley traces the theme through a swathe of Gregory's *Orationes* (including 41.9; 29.3; 30.16; 31.14, 30; 38.15; 42.15), justifying his claims that "Gregory's doctrine of divine causality is ... clear and consistent" and that the Father's monarchy is the

Is the Priority of Paternal Will compatible with Pro-Nicene Orthodoxy?

Given all this, it is just too neat to flag *Oratio* 31.14 as Gregory's departure from the views of Athanasius and the other Cappadocians. While Gregory does certainly evince a tendency to speak of the triune Godhead *itself* as an object of worship,[95] and may sometimes indicate that the divine Nature is even in some sense ontologically foundational to the persons,[96] he does not see this as incompatible with the causal priority of the Father in the way that many modern theologians do. Rather his thinking hovers between a generic view of the persons *and* a realist view of the essence.[97] If the first is in focus then the persons are equal – like three suns together; Adam and Seth – with the Father as source of the other two: "[T]he Son is a concise demonstration of the Father's nature (τοῦ Πατρὸς φύσεως) ... a complete resemblance rather than like (ταυτόν μᾶλλον, ἤ ἀφομοια)".[98] If the second is in view then the divine nature itself is the common and simple element, manifesting itself first as

---

"foundational principle of trinitarian logic" for Gregory (see Beeley, "Divine Causality", 204, 207-209).

95   "The one is praiseworthy (τὸ ἕν ἐπαινετὸν) if rightly understood; and the Three when rightly divided, when the division is of persons, not of Godhead (προσωπων...μὴ θεότητος)". (*Or.* 37.22; NPNF 2.7.344; PG 36.308B). See also *Or.* 31.33.

96   Hence Gregory's willingness to oppose the "one" (nature) with the "three" (persons) rather than simply the "one" (Father) and the other "two" derived from him (though he certainly speaks in the latter terms too). For Gregory the Father too is a subsistence as well as a source of the Son and Spirit's subsistences. In light of this I prefer Richard Cross' reading of *Or.* 31.14 which exemplifies a Neoplatonic depiction of universals as cause of particulars over against the view of Beeley who takes "the ones who timelessly have their being from the first cause" as refering only to the Son and Spirit (with the Father himself as the "first cause"); R. Cross, "Divine Monarchy in Gregory of Nazianzus", *Journal of Early Christian Studies* 14.1 (2006): 105-116, 105-116.

97   So he writes famously:

>   Each [is] God because consubstantial; One God because of the Monarchia (ἐκεῖνο διὰ τὴν ὁμοουσιότητα, τοῦτο διὰ τὴν μοναρχιαν). No sooner do I conceive of the One than I am illumined by the Splendour of the Three; no sooner do I distinguish them than I am carried back to the One. When I think of any one of the three I think of him as the Whole (τοῦτο νομίζω τό πᾶν), and my eyes are filled, and the greater part of what I am thinking of escapes me.

>   *Or.* 40.41; NPNF 2.7; PG 36.417B, C. See too *Or.* 39.12; 40.41.

T.A. Noble's discussion of paradox in Cappadocian theology (derived in part from F. Dinsen) is pertinent here. See T. A. Noble "Paradox in Gregory Nazianzen's Doctrine of the Trinity" in *Studia Patristica, vol. XXVII, Papers Presented at the Eleventh International Conference on Patristic Studies held in Oxford 1991*, ed. E. A. Livingstone (Louvain: Peeters, 1993), 97.

98   *Or.* 30.20 (NPNF 2.7.317-318; PG 36.129A, B).

Father then (through generation) as Son and Spirit without any discontinuity or division.⁹⁹ Finally, when the two ideas come together the Father is both the first instantiation of the common essence and the one from whom the other two instantiations derive their equality (ἐξ οὗ ἴσοις εἶναι – cf. *Oratio* 40.43) without schism.¹⁰⁰ As he writes in *Oratio* 42.15:

> "That which is without beginning [later identified as the Father], and is the beginning [the Son], and is with the beginning [the Spirit], is one God. ... For the one's nature does not consist in the beginning (οὐ ... φύσις αὐτῷ ἡ ἀρχή), just as the other's does not consist in his being without cause (ἄναρχον). For these are the circumstances of the nature (περί ... τὴν φύσιν), not the nature itself. ... And the unifier (ἕνωσις) is the Father from whom and to whom is found the story of those who are ordered (ὃν ἀνάγεται τὰ ἐξῆς)."¹⁰¹

Or again, in terminology that is familiar to us now:

> ... monarchy is that which we hold in honour. It is, however, a monarchy that is not limited to one person, for it is possible for unity if at variance with itself to come into a condition of plurality; but one which is made of an equal nobility of nature (φύσεως ὁμοτιμία) and a concurrence of mind (γνώμης συμπνοία), and an identity of motion, and a convergence of its elements to unity – a thing which is impossible to the created nature – so that though numerically distinct there is no severance of essence (τῇ γε οὐσίᾳ μὴ τέμνεσθαι). *Therefore this one* (μονάς) *having from all eternity arrived by motion at Duality, stood ultimately at Trinity. This is what we mean by Father and Son and Holy Ghost. The Father is the Begetter and the Emitter* (γεννήτωρ καὶ προβολεύς); *without passion of course, and without reference to time, and not in a*

---

99 Gregory here seems happy to work with a model similar to that of Gregory of Nyssa who maintains that a generic view of, say, humans does not necessarily connote separation: for strictly speaking there is only *one* humanity (or "gold" or "type of tree") which occurs according to diverse "ways of existing" (ὅπως...αὐτὸν ει:ναι); see *On Not Three Gods* (*Ad Ablabius*) cf. PG 45.133D.

100 We should note here that we are not talking about a simply generic view of divine unity. As McGuckin notes, the divine being *is the Father's own being* McGuckin, *Gregory*, 294n.352. But McGuckin perhaps misses the implication that, at least sometimes, Gregory seems to regard the Father as the first instance of his own nature.

101 This translation is partly from NPNF 2.7.390, cf. PG 36.476A, B. It is difficult to see how the Father's monarchy as it is set out in this late *Oratio* (381AD cf. ibid., x) can be reconciled with Torrance's claim that Gregory experienced a late change of heart after formerly following the same line as Basil and Gregory of Nyssa (Torrance, *Perspectives*, 29-30), Torrance, *Trinitarian Faith*, 322.

corporeal manner. The Son is the Begotten, and the Holy Ghost the Emission.[102]

Real Fatherhood as the Core of Pro-Nicene Theology.[103]

Gregory's recourse to the analogy of Adam and Seth in understanding the Trinity takes us to what is perhaps the most serious deficiency in the modern attempt to sideline the Father's monarchy – that is, its tendency to downplay the concept of fatherhood itself. My contention here is that this is a central and defining principle of pro-Nicene theology. Whereas Arianism or Eusebianism see divine fatherhood in merely functional terms so that the Logos is a son in the same sense that the angels or the king of Israel might be described as "sons of God", and Marcellinist theology might regard "Son of God" as applicable only after the incarnation,[104] the orthodox distinctive *is* the proposition that the Father is the *true* or *literal* father of the Son.[105]

Is this too bald? For some it would certainly seem so. T.F. Torrance associates the attempt to "speak of divine Fatherhood and Sonship on the analogy of human fatherhood and sonship" with Arianism: whatever legitimate "figurative or metaphorical element" might be in the human terms, they "point utterly beyond" human reality when applied to God. Torrance argues that we must "set aside all analogies drawn from the visible world ... [not] think of the Father as begetting the Son or of the Son as begotten after the analogy of

---

102 *Or.* 29.2; NPNF 2.7.301 (emphasis added; altered – I am grateful for Dr Ray Laird's help with the translation here); PG 36.76B. It is important to note how Gregory highlights the paradox of oneness and threeness here. The equal value of nature (φύσεως ὁμοτιμία) or agreement of mind (γνώμης συμπνοία) would seem to indicates plurality, yet the genitive nouns are singular – one nature equal with itself; one mind in agreement with itself. Or, as he writes, numerically three without severance of essence. We will return to what this means for the concept of "obedience" between the Father and Son below.

103 I would like to acknowledge my debt here to my long-time friend David Walter who helped crystallize my understanding of the significance of divine fatherhood with some well-chosen analogies and observations.

104 See J. N. D. Kelly, *Early Christian Creeds* (London: Continuum International Publishing Group, 2006), 276.; S. Parvis, *Marcellus of Ancyra and the Lost Years of the Arian Controversy 325-345. Oxford Early Christian Studies* (New York: Oxford University Press, 2006), 130-131.

105 James Dunn asserts that in the fourth and fifth centuries it was "the understanding of Christ as Son of God which provided *the absolutely crucial category in defining the nature of Christ's pre-existent deity*"; J. D. G. Dunn, *Christology in the Making: A New Testament Inquiry into the Origins of the Doctrine of the Incarnation,* 2nd edition (London: SCM Press, 1989), 12 (my emphasis).

generation of giving birth with which we are familiar among creaturely beings".[106]

Hanson makes a similar (though subtly different) observation on the question of analogy in regard to the orthodox and Arians. In his eyes

> What the Arians were insisting was that the Bible does not speak analogously nor symbolically about God, but directly. When it described God as the Father and Christ as his Son, it could only mean that, like all [human fathering] ... Christ at one point must have been non-existent before he was begotten by his Father. The pro-Nicene theologians gradually realised that this could not be true, that if it was true it made nonsense of the biblical doctrine of God, and that the Bible speaks of God in language which is analogous, symbolical, but nevertheless true.[107]

Again, there is a basic truth here. It is certainly correct, and easily demonstrated, that Athanasius and the Cappadocian Fathers were at pains to distinguish human modes of existence and begetting from God. The Nicenes certainly did not imagine that God was a "like humans" or believe that one could "read off" a simple correspondence between divine and creaturely filiation. Qualifications abound: divine begetting carries no association of contingency or temporality; nor does it imply passion or abscission or corporeality or intercourse or maternity or mutability; nor does the perfect likeness between Father and Son (another distinction) imply that the Son must also be a father.[108] And it is also true that the orthodox criticize their

---

106 Torrance, *Doctrine of God,* 157-158. Torrance does allow some qualified analogical connection between human and divine fatherhood provided that the order of revelation is conceived of in the right direction (cf. ibid., 100-105). Rightly conceived, the concepts "do not build some kind of image of God with a point to point correspondance", but constitute a "divinely forged lens through which we may discern God's personal self-revelation as it shines into our minds; ibid., 105. This "theomorphist" (ibid., 106) version of the *analogia entis* seems absolutely correct to my mind, but the way he puts it is falsely antithetical (and suspiciously Barthian). No orthodox ancient or modern theologian would ever argue for a "point for point" correspondance. As always, the points of connection and disconnection must be read through in the light of the scriptural *analogia fidei*.

107 R. P. C. Hanson "Biblical Exegesis in the Early Church" in *The Cambridge History of the Bible*, ed. P. R. Ackroyd, C. F. Evans, G. W. H. Lampe & S. L. Greenslade, 1st paperback edition (New York: Cambridge University Press, 1963), 447.

108 For distinction between human and divine fatherhood and sonship see: Athanasius – *De Decretis* 20-26; *CA* 1.26-28, 2.35, *DeSyn*. 41-42, 51; Basil – *De Spiritu Sancto* 14; Gregory of Nyssa – *CE* 1.39, 2.7, 9, 3.3, 4.1, 9, 8.4; *On Not Three Gods* (*Ad Ablabius*); Hilary of Poitiers – *DeSyn*. 33; *DeTrin*. 3.2-3, 4.2, 6.9, 35, 7.28.

subordinationist opponents for imputing such creaturely aspects of fatherhood to God.

True vs. Adoptive Fatherhood in Nicene Dispute

But the deficiency of this way of reading the controversy is that from another – and I would suggest more significant – perspective, precisely the opposite is *also* true.[109] As Athanasius observes in *De Decretis* 6-10, the Arian contention is that the Logos is *not* a "true son" or literal offspring (he uses the example of Abraham and Isaac) – that he is only a creature who receives this title by grace and contingency as *per* angels or the kings of Israel or we ourselves. Whatever superior honour the Arians claim for this "Son" is beside the point. The difference for them is simply one of honour not nature (τιμῆ καὶ μὴ φύσει; v.9)[110], and describes something other than a true Son of God (ἀληθινὸν τοῦ Θεοῦ Υἱόν; v.10)[111]. They have failed to distinguish the two distinct ideas (διπλῆν...διάνοιαν; v.6)[112] connoted in Scripture by the word "son".[113]

For his own part, however, Athanasius is very clear what the word means in the case of the divine Son. "Let it be repeated", he writes, "a work is external to the nature, but a son is a the proper offspring of the essence".[114] "[W]ho hears of a son but conceives of that which is proper to the Father's essence"?[115] "For a son, which is by nature, is one with him who begat him".[116] Athanasius is convinced that the reason *why* the Son is coessential with the Father is *because* he is the Father's son just as human offspring necessarily share in their parents' natures.

---

109 For a helpful and nuanced treatment of this question see Catherine Osborne's rhetorical analysis of the Arian controversy in C. Osborne "Literal or Metaphorical? Some Issues of Language in the Arian Controversy" in *Christian faith and Greek philosophy in Late Antiquity: Essays in Tribute to George Christopher Stead. In Celebration of his Eightieth Birthday, 9th April 1993*, ed. L. R. H. Wickham, C. P. Bammel, E. C. D. Hunter & C. Stead. *Supplements to Vigiliae Christianae* (Leiden: Brill, 1993).

110 PG 25.429D.

111 PG 25.433A.

112 PG 25.433A.

113 See Simonetti's discussion of Athanasius' concept of (and emphasis on) natural fatherhood in M. Simonetti, *La Crisi Ariana Nel IV Secolo.* vol. 11. *Studia Ephemeridis Augustinianum* (Rome: Institutum Patristicum Augustinianum, 1975), 271.

114 *CA* 1.29; NPNF 2.4.323.

115 *CA* 2.34; NPNF 2.4.366.

116 *CA* 4.5; NPNF 2.4.435.

But what is that which is proper to and identical with the essence of God and an offspring from it by nature, if not by this very fact coessential with him that begat it? For this is the distinctive relation of a Son to a Father, and he who denies this, does not hold that the Word is Son in nature and in truth.[117]

If there are differences between human and divine paternity (and there are) it is not because God is not a true father and the Son not a true son but rather because *we aren't* true fathers and sons:[118]

> ... it belongs to the Godhead alone, that the Father is properly father (κυρίως πατήρ) and the Son properly son (κυρίως υἱός), for in them, and them only, does it ever hold that the Father is ever the father and the Son is ever son.[119] ... For God does not make man his pattern; but rather we men — for that God is properly and truly, Father of his own Son (πατέρες...τῶν ἰδίων τέκνων) — are also called fathers of our own children; for of him is "every fatherhood in heaven and earth named".[120]

Once again, these ideas are not unique to Athanasius. The identification of true or literal sonship as a major difference between the orthodox and Arian parties goes back to the earliest days of the Arian crisis (if not further)[121]. As Arius

---

117 *Ad Afros Epistola Synodica* 8; NPNF 2.4.493. I am not convinced by Kannengiesser's argument that this letter is pseudonymous — C. Kannengiesser "(Ps. -) Athanasius, Ad Afros Examined" in *Logos: Festschrift für Luise Abramowski zum 8. Juli 1993*, ed. L. Abramowski, H. C. Brennecke, E. L. Grasmück & C. Markschies. *Beihefte zur Zeitschrift für die neutestamentliche Wissenschaft und die Kunde der älteren Kirche* (Berlin: Walter de Gruyter, 1993) — given that a central platform of his argument rests on the notion that true Athanasian works (which he allows include *CA* 1-2) do not deliberate on *how* the Father and Son are coessential. As we have just observed above, the connection between natural sonship and essence is quite plain in *CA* 1-2 too.

See also references to the Son as genuine son in *DeSyn*. 41, 47, 54.

118 Though we must note that Athanasius *does* seem to see some overlap in the dependence of the Son *qua son* and the Son as incarnate man. See Simonetti on Athanasius' reading of Proverbs 8; Simonetti, *Crisi*, 278.

119 *CA* 1.21; NPNF 2.4.318; PG 26.57A.

120 *CA* 1.23; NPNF 2.4.320; PG 26.59C. Athanasius' use of Ephesians 3 serves as a check on Catherine Osborne's suggestion that his reasoning has a "plainly Platonic origin" (see Osborne, *Literal*, 159).

121 Widdicombe attributes both Alexander's and Athanasius' understanding of sonship to their Alexandrian forebear Origen. See P. Widdicombe, *The Fatherhood of God from Origen to Athanasius. Oxford Theological Monographs*, revised edition (Oxford: Clarendon Press, 2000), 136.

makes clear in his joint confession statement to Alexander (c.318-321),[122] though he might declare the Son *uniquely* begotten (γέννημα, αλλ' ουχ ως εν των γεγεννωμένων) he will not allow the Logos to be a Son in any literal sense:[123] he is the *immutable perfect* creation (αναλλοίωτον κτίσμα...τέλειον) but *creation* he remains nonetheless.[124] Similarly, Eusebius of Nicomedia protests against any natural conception of begetting which would signify, so he argues, "two unbegotten beings" or a "change of a corporeal nature" being attributed to God. He rejects explicitly the possibility that the Son could be "from him [God] or of him, as a portion of him, or by an emanation of his substance" and opines that he is no more a participant in the substance of the Father than other "begotten" creatures such as the Israelites (cf. Isa 1:2) or the dew (cf. Job 38:28).[125]

In stark contrast, Arius' bishop (and Athanasius' mentor) Alexander of Alexandria (d. 328) writes to his namesake in Constantinople of a *real* sonship. While Alexander does not use the *homoousios* terminology that would ultimately become the test of pro-Nicene theology, he nonetheless elucidates something similar using the language of natural filiality. Divine filiality, in Alexander's reckoning, has nothing at all in common with the adoptive sonship

---

122 Unless stated otherwise the date ranges here draw on the proposed timelines taken from Athanasius, *Urkunden zur Geschichte des Arianischen Streites, 318-328*, ed. H. G. Opitz. vol. 3. *Athanasius Werke* (Berlin: Berlin Academy, 1934); R. Williams, *Arius: Heresy and Tradition*, 2nd edition (Grand Rapids: Eerdmans, 2002) and Athanasius, *Athanasius Werke: Band III/Teil 1: Urkunden zur Geschichte des Arianischen Streites 318-328: Lieferung 3: Bis zur Ekthesis Makrostichos (Lieferung)*, ed. H. C. Brennecke, U. Heil, A. Von Stockhausen & A. Wintjes (Berlin: Walter de Gruyter, 2007). See comparative chart in A. West, *Documents of the Early Arian Controversy (Fourth Century Christianity)*, http://www.fourthcentury.com/index.php/ urkunde-chart-opitz, (accessed Oct, 2008).

123 See Athanasius, *DeSyn*. 16. Kelly calls Arius' conception of begetting as "purely figurative"; see J. N. D. Kelly, *Early Christian Doctrines*, 5th edition (London: Continuum International Publishing Group, 2000), 227-228. Osborne, pursuing greater precision, speaks of Arius using the terminology of sonship in a "much reduced sense". Osborne, *Literal*, 157.

124 *DeSyn*. 16; PG 26.709A. This sticking point remains for Arius' ideological descendent Eunomius. See his comments in *Liber Apologeticus* 16-18 – Eunomius, *Eunomius: The Extant Works*, ed. R. P. Vaggione. *Oxford Early Christian Texts* ed. H. Chadwick (New York: Clarendon Press, 1987), 53-59.

125 See his letter to Paulinus of Tyre, preserved in Theodoret's *Historia Ecclesiastica* 1.6 (NPNF 2.3.42). Similar protests can be found in the more famous Eusebius of Caesarea who also associates a nativity of "nature from nature" with passibility and schism; cf. A. Grillmeier, *Christ in Christian Tradition: From the Apostolic Age to Chalcedon (451)*, trans. J. S. Bowden. vol. 1. *Christ in Christian Tradition*, 2nd edition (London: Mowbray, 1975), 174.

of men but represents a "true, peculiar, natural and special sonship (γνησίαν ... ἰδιότροπον φυσικὴν ... κατερξαίτερον υἱότητα) ... of the paternal birth".[126]

On the basis of evidence such as this Christopher Stead regards the issue of sonship as a decisive determinant of the meaning of the *ousia* language of Nicaea. When read against the background of the disagreements just mentioned and in the context of μονογενες, the phrase ἐκ τῆς οὐσίας πατρός was included to show that the Son "derives from the father by a process comparable to natural generation as opposed to some process of 'making', like that of God's created works ... he is equal to, and one with, his Father as a true natural son, and not just a creature adopted or dignified with the name of Son".[127]

Thus the emphasis on literal sonship does not begin with Athanasius. Neither does it end with him. Both Eastern and Western parties produced official statements that explicitly insist on the idea. The Western-dominated council of Sardica c.344 issued a synodical statement which includes an affirmation that the Son is "truly the Son" explaining that this means a "being of one essence" – in contrast to those who are so called by merit or adoption. The Second (or "Lucianic") Confession produced at a similar time in Antioch also speaks of a Son who is the unchangeable image of the essence (ἀναλλοίωτον ...οὐσίας ...ἀπαράλλακτον εἰκόνα) – a true Son (ἀληθῶς Υἱοῦ) of a Father who is truly Father.[128] This proto-*homoiousian* creed served

---

126 *Historia Ecclesiastica* 1.4 (NPNF 2.3.38; PG 82.900B). Kelly also sees an implied sharing of nature (Alexander does not explicitly use the language of ὁμοούσιος or μία φύσις) in Alexander's use of Ps. 110:3; Kelly, *Doctrines,* 224-225.

127 C. Stead, *Divine Substance* (Oxford: Clarendon Press, 1977), 233. Stead's argument receives additional support from Ambrose who recounts an incident at Nicaea (possibly also mentioned by Theodoret; *Historia Ecclesiastica* 1.8, cf. Kelly, *Creeds,* 249-250) where a letter of Eusebius of Nicomedia is read out in which he protests that if we say "the Son is the true Son of God and uncreate, then we are in the way to confess him to be of one substance ὁμοούσιος with the Father". Ambrose produces this as proof that the real Arian agenda is denial of the fact that the Word is a true son of God (*verum Dei Filium*), and sees it as an occasioning factor for the Fathers to include the word ὁμοούσιος in the creed. See *DeFid.* 3.15; PL 16.614A, B.

128 Recorded in Athanasius *DeSyn.* 23; PG 26.721C, 724A. Despite Athanasius' ungenerous characterization, the creed contains little that would mark it as such and contains numerous statements that a true Arian would have found very difficult to accept; see ibid., 270-271. David M. Gwynn seems right to observe the inconsistency of Athanasius' toleration of the homoiousian party as basically orthodox while calling the creed on which they relied "Arian"; D. M. Gwynn, *The Eusebians: The Polemic of Athanasius of Alexandria and the Construction of the Arian Controversy* (Oxford: Oxford University Press, 2007), 225.

as a touchstone for moderate Eastern theology into the next decade,[129] being invoked both by the 358 synod of Ancyra (convened by Basil of Ancyra in response to the notorious Second Creed of Sirmium)[130] and by a *homoiousian* dominated conclave which met at Seleucia the following year.[131]

In this latter context, Basil and another leading *homoiousian*, George of Laodicea, both reveal their united commitment to a notion of *real essential* sonship. Basil, in the synodical statement just mentioned, prevaricates slightly on whether "son" is quite the correct word given its association with physicality.[132] But once these creaturely aspects are stripped away – leaving "the generation of another living being of like essence" (ὁμοίου καὶ κατ' οὐσίαν ζώου γενεσιουργία)[133] – then Basil is insistent:

> And if anyone ... does not take "begets me" literally (ἐπὶ τοῦ αὐτοῦ) and as a reference to essence but says that "He begets me" means the same as "he created me", ... confessing that he is a mere creature and not a son ... let him be anathema.[134]

George's letter, written around the same time,[135] operates on the same logic. Revealing standard Eastern sensitivities he complains first against Marcellus, who denies that the Son is a υἱὸν ἀληθῶς with self-existence (καθ' ἑαυτὸν ... ὑπάρχοντοσ)[136] and thus reduces him to a *mere* word. Next, and at greater length, he decries the *Anomoians*: the "current faction [who declare] that the Son is like the Father in will and activity but unlike the Father in being". He argues that both deny the Son is begotten, for to them he is merely a creation (μὴ εἶναι ἐκ τὸ Θεοῦ γεγεννημένον ... ἀλλὰ μόνον κτίσμα εἶναι).[137] For George the matter is clear; the Son's is a *true* begetting (γνησίως γεγεννημένος) and he is perfectly like his Father as a son from a father (ὡς

---

129 See Hanson's assessment of the significance of the creed for understanding the broad character of the East at this time (and its contrast with the more radically Arian First Creed) in Hanson, *Search,* 290-291.

130 The text is preserved in Epiphanius *Pan.* 73.2-11; cf. Epiphanius, *The Panarion of Epiphanius of Salamis,* trans. F. Williams. vol. 35-36. *Nag Hammadi studies Nag Hammadi and Manichaean studies* ed. J. R. Robinson & H. J. Klimkeit (Leiden: E. J. Brill, 1987).

131 See Socrates *Historia Ecclesiastica* 2.39.

132 Epiphanius *Pan.* 73.3.

133 *Pan.* 73.4; PG 42.409A. "For every father (πᾶσ πατήρ) is understood to beget an essence like his"; Ibid.

134 *Pan.* 73.11; ibid. p.445; PG 42.421D.

135 Ayres, *Nicaea,* 158n.78.

136 *Pan.* 73.12; PG 42.428A, B.

137 *Pan.* 73.13; PG 42.429A.

υἱὸς πατρί).¹³⁸ In that this relationship is held to be eternal,¹³⁹ essential¹⁴⁰ and mutually defining,¹⁴¹ George's argument is very close to that of Athanasius.¹⁴²

Similar arguments can also be found among the Cappadocians, as we have already seen in the case of Gregory Nazianzen. Basil defends those who hesitate over the *homoousion* by clarifying that the word is not to be understood in the sense that the Father and Son *both* derive coordinately as brothers from a common essence – an idea he regards as Sabellian.¹⁴³ Rather, a thing is *homoousios* with *another thing* (ἑτέρῳ)¹⁴⁴ – in this case the Son with the Father (ἐκ τῆς οὐσίας πατρός) from whom he is ineffably begotten.¹⁴⁵ We must retain the idea of divine generation (θείαν γέννησιν) without slipping into simply corporeal notions.¹⁴⁶

Gregory of Nyssa returns to the idea of fatherhood repeatedly – far more in fact than either his brother or Gregory Nazianzen. Like Athanasius, he distinguishes between the two senses of sonship, insisting that the relation of the eternal Son to the Father must be seen as true or natural.¹⁴⁷ Like Gregory Nazianzen, he draws specific connections between the example of Seth and the Son, indicating the continuity of essence in both cases.¹⁴⁸ And there is a particular emphasis here. While other pro-Nicenes might observe an apophatic

---

138   *Pan.* 73.18; PG 42.436D, 437B. The word γνησίως also has connotations of proper familial or genetic connection.

139   *Pan.* 73.14.

140   *Pan.* 73.22.

141   *Pan.* 73.19.

142   This is not to suggest that Athanasius is the source of this conception of filiality – see Barnes' warning along these lines in his response to Widdicombe; M. R. Barnes, review of *The Fatherhood of God from Origen to Athanasius* by P. Widdicombe, *Theological Studies* 56.3, (1995): 574 – simply that this is a widespread and basic element in pro-Nicene theology.

143   *Epistolae* 52; NPNF 2.8.155-156, cf. PG 32.393D, 396A.

144   Ibid.; PG 32.393C.

145   Of course this idea is also implicit in Athanasius; see Stead, *Substance,* 260.

146   See *Epistolae* 52.2-3; PG 32.393D, 396A. See Behr's brief discussion of the relation of this passage to Basil's conception of monarchy in J. Behr, *The Trinitarian Theology of St. Basil of Caesarea,* (1999) http://www.allsaints-stl.org/Trinitarian%20Theology%20of%20St.%20Basil%20of%20Caesarea%20-%20Web%20Version%202008.pdf, (accessed November, 2008), 4.

147   *CE* 1 (cf. NPNF 2.5.83-84), 2, 3, 4, 6. In *CE* 1 (NPNF 2.5.58) he accuses Eunomius of turning the Son into a "bastard" who "creeps ... into relationship with the Father, and is to be honoured in name only as a Son".

148   *CE* 2 (cf. NPNF 2.5.123).

distinction between divine begetting and the "separateness" associated with human fatherhood, Gregory argues that there is no real abscission in human fathering either: "a man in begetting a man from himself does not divide his nature" or mutilate himself, nor is the nature "split off and transferred ... to the other", but it remains entirely in the progenitor as well as "discoverable in its entirety in the latter".[149]

Divine Fathering and the Pro-Nicene Rapprochement

Finally, it is crucial to observe the prominence given to the concept of natural fatherhood in the writings of both Hilary and Athanasius *as they seek rapprochement* with elements of the *homoiousion* party. Both theologians seem to believe that where there is a real commitment to this creation-mediated paradigm there can also be agreement *despite* diffences in terminology; as if the heart of pro-Nicene theology *itself* were to be found in the idea of literal divine paternity. As Athanasius writes in a passage that names Basil of Ancyra specifically, those who disagree about the homoousion but still see the Son as a genuine and natural offspring (γνήσιον καὶ φύσει γέννημα) are not Arian lunatics (Ἀρειομανίτας) but rather brothers with whom there can be brotherly discussion.[150]

Hilary also dwells on the logic of natural fathering in his own discussion of the Faith of the Easterns, both because the creeds he is discussing use this language, and because his own understanding of the concept of essence

---

149 *CE* 2 (cf. NPNF 2.5.109). The same idea is also found – albeit with less emphasis on fatherhood *per se* – in Gregory's letter to Ablabius where he adds that a basic response to the question of whether the Trinity is divided like three humans is to insist that humans are not really divided either, for there is only one humanity. See *On Not Three Gods* (*Ad Ablabius*) (cf. NPNF 2.5.332ff). Stead (rightly, I believe) argues that this *kind* of argument influences Kelly and Prestige in their assessment that the Cappadocians had a "concrete" view of the essence. See C. Stead "Why Not Three Gods? The Logic of Gregory of Nyssa's Trinitarian Doctrine" in *Studien zu Gregor von Nyssa und Der Christlichen Spätantike,* ed. H. R. Drobner & C. Klock. *Supplements to Vigiliae Christianae* (Leiden: Brill, 1990), 157-158. For Stead, however, this observation comes in the context of a wider and general complaint that Gregory is simply illogical in his argumentation, confusing the Platonic form of humanity with humanity itself. But Gregory never mentions Plato as the basis of these arguments but rather seems more interested in the analogy of Adam and Seth. It is possible therefore that the concrete universal "humanity" Gregory has in mind is the same as that which sees humans included in Adam (eg. Rom 5:12-19).

150 *DeSyn.* 41; PG 26.764D, 765A. Reference to true sonship (Υἱός τε ὢν ἀληθῶς...) also occurs – admittedly somewhat passingly – in *Tomus ad Antiochenos* 7 (cf. PG 26.804C).

demands it.[151] Having transcribed the odious Second Creed of Sirmium, Hilary then cites and explains the 358 Ancyran response mentioned above. In his commentary on the first declaration of the true sonship (*vere filium* in his translation), Hilary explains that the Son is an image who shares in his progenitor's "species" (*speciem*).[152] To the third anathema, which again mentions true sonship, Hilary argues that there can be no difference between Father and Son as regards nature and genus (*generis indifferentis*) "since the Son is the image of the Father in species, and ... a son begotten of the substance of his father does not admit of any diversity of substance".[153] There can be no inferiority either in kind or amount (*qualis et ... quanta*) for "this is the essence of true sonship (*hoc vere est esse filium*)".[154]

Recourse to the logic of true sonship and fatherhood occurs so frequently in Hilary as to appear to be a *central element* of his theological system.[155] And it is to this commonality of understanding that Ayres looks to explain the theological alliance that develops between Hilary and his Eastern friends. In that the "character of a perfect birth" is the key to understanding the divine unity and diversity,

> ... common cause could emerge between Hilary and his Eastern counterparts ... [in whom] we find a similar focus on the significance of the Son's generation from the perfect Father.[156]

Ayres acknowledges that, while we cannot know how much contact Hilary had with Athanasius, their attitude to rapprochement is similar.[157]

---

151 See Gerald O'Collins' observations concerning the centrality of God's (he means the first person's) fatherhood for Hilary in G. O'Collins "The Holy Trinity: The State of the Questions" in *The Trinity: An Interdisciplinary Symposium on the Trinity*, ed. S. T. Davis, D. Kendall & G. O'Collins (Oxford: Oxford University Press, 1999), 15. Ayres ascribes this emphasis to Hilary's indebtedness to "earlier Latin theology", specifically Tertullian and Novation; Ayres, *Nicaea*, 179-181. This may be correct and, if so, simply further reminds us of the ubiquity of the concept.

152 *DeSyn.* 12-13; PL 10.490B.

153 *DeSyn.* 15; NPNF 2.9.7 (altered) cf. PL 10.492A.

154 Ibid.

155 See for example, *DeTrin.* 1.27; 2.5, 8; 3.11; 6.5-52; 7.2, 5, 7-8, 10-15, 17, 21, 23, 26-27, 29-31, 36, 41, 60-61; 12.2, 12-17, But many of the verses between those just cited could also be included. In the light of this it is very puzzling to read Carl Beckwith's observation that Hilary uses father/son imagery "only sparingly", in contrast to Basil of Ancyra's "strained analogies"; see C. Beckwith, *Hilary of Poitiers on the Trinity: From De Fide to De Trinitate. Oxford Early Christian Studies* (Oxford University Press, USA, 2009), 101.

156 Ayres, *Nicaea*, 184.

Is the Priority of Paternal Will compatible with Pro-Nicene Orthodoxy?

To note the strength of this thematic connection is not to suggest that a reference to "true son" – without explicit reference to essence or general "natural" fathering – can infallibly indicate a common pro-Nicene theology,[158] nor is it to deny that there are important *differences* between the homoousian and homoiousian conception of divine sonship (we will come to these shortly).[159] But the recurrence of this concept of natural or essential fatherhood across the various theological strands – its significance in the final rapprochement between the *homoousian* and *homoiousian*, and its persistence – must cast a shadow of doubt over theories which see fourth century theology as moving away from intra-trinitarian causality models. If fatherhood is a central idea, then the commonality of essence would seem to be *all about* one individual coming from another and *thereby* being essentially the same.

The modern attitude to causation or origination in fourth century theology risks being both historically mistaken and logically problematic. The idea that the monarchy of the Father connotes his ontological superiority would have been strongly contested by those Fathers who are often enlisted as witnesses. In their understanding, the causality of true fatherhood means that the Son must be *equally* divine because *all sons* fully share in their father's natures.[160] As Hilary

---

157 Ibid. Ayres could have made his case even stronger by adding that Hilary and Athanasius both see the same *grounds* for agreement too.

158 Fathering language is also used by Eusebius of Caesarea (see Athanasius *Epistola Eusebii* 3) in his letter to his flock, by Asterius the Sophist in *fragment 20* (see ibid., 119) and also by the complex *homoian* Germinius of Sirmium – see D. H. Williams, "Another Exception to Later Fourth-Century 'Arian' Typologies: The Case of Germinius of Sirmium", *Journal of Early Christian Studies* 4.3 335-357, 346. Yet in none of these cases do we find a sonship that involves any sharing in the Father's essence. See Gwynn's discussion of Eusebius (Gwynn, *The Eusebians*, p.214) and, on Asterius, K. Anatolios, *Athanasius: The Coherence of his Thought*. Routledge Early Church Monographs (London: Routledge, 1998), 18-19 and W. Kinzig, *In Search of Asterius: Studies on the Homilies on the Psalms*. vol. 47. *Forschungen zur Kirchen- und Dogmengeschichte* (Göttingen: Vandenhoeck & Ruprecht, 1990), 127-132.

159 As Hilary (*DeSyn.* 89) and Epiphanius (*Pan.* 73.36) rightly observe, there is a dangerous ambiguity with *homoiousion*. If pushed to its logical conclusion then it could easily (as George realizes; see his discussion of subsistent persons – προσώπον ὑφεστώτων – in *Pan.* 73.16) lead to a genuine genericism that would render the Son as *another God*. At worst, its ambiguity could also provided comfort and cover to *real* Arian/Eunomian subordinationism where the Son is also seen as a new and *created* being. As long as the concept of *ousia* was doing the work of showing *both* the connection and distinction between the persons, homoiousionism could only ever be the last stop before a real division between Arians and pro-Nicene theology.

160 The same response applies to those modern theologians such as: B. B. Warfield – B. The B. BibliWarfield, Doc

puts it, "every son, by virtue of his natural birth is the equal of his Father, in that he has a natural likeness to him".[161]

The Question of Will

Hopefully these demonstrations of the importance of paternal causality in the Trinity have removed the objection that the idea of filial volition (wherein the Son's will *derives* from the Father's) should be regarded as sub-orthodox *simply because of its regard for paternal (causal) priority*. Paternal monarchy is the unifying principal in virtually every pro-Nicene affirmation of trinitarian equality and unity. But this scarcely gets us beyond general principles. We must now attempt to identify (if there was one) the pro-Nicene conception of the relationship between will and essence and determine whether the pro-Nicene Fathers would permit *any* sense in which the Father and Son have their own wills.

Will and Willing in Athanasius

For those on the Arian wing who reject the notion of a genuine sonship the question of will is plain enough: no *ontological* unity between Father and Son means that their relationship can *only* be one of will, for the Son is brought forth by the Father's will and *knows* the Father's will by (*post-facto*) participation and communication.[162] This was obviously unacceptable to the pro-Nicene party. As Athanasius is at great pains to point out in *Contra Arianos* 3.59-67, if the Son comes about as an act of the Father's will then he is son in the same sense as all other created "sons" – external to the maker (ἔξωθεν ... τοῦ ποιοῦντος).[163] In response to the Arian dilemma that the Son must be either begotten by will or necessity, Athanasius answers that begetting is neither by will (βουλήσει) nor by necessity (ἀνάγκῃ) but by nature (κατὰ φύσιν), which transcends will: the Father is father in the same way that he is good.[164] Moreover the Logos cannot be a product of will because, as

---

http://www.apuritansmind.com/ChristianWalk/ WarfieldBBTrinity.htm, (accessed May, 2008); or Leonard Hodgson – eg. Hodgson, *Trinity,* 222; or Millard Erickson – Erickson, *God in Three Persons,* 309. By refusing to recognise the difference between paternity and divinity, and by seeking to eliminate all subordinationism associated with the Father's status as *principium,* such authors make common cause with historic Arianism (consciously, in the case Hodgson and Erickson).

161 *DeSyn.* 73; NPNF 2.9.23. The argument comes in the familiar context of an Adam/Seth exemplar.

162 See Hanson, *Search,* 14-15, 565.

163 *CA* 3.62; PG 26.453B.

164 *CA* 3.66.

Is the Priority of Paternal Will compatible with Pro-Nicene Orthodoxy?

Athanasius argues from Proverbs 8:14 and 1 Corinthians 1:24, he is the Father's own *living will* (βουλὴ ζῶσα)[165] just as he is the Father's wisdom, strength and power.

Here some clarification is immediately in order. That the Son is the Father's will sounds like a partitive or psychological model[166] – as if the Son were the Father's *faculty* for volition or wisdom.[167] But as he makes clear elsewhere,[168] this is not what Athanasius means, nor do either of the words he uses here (βουλὴ and θέλημα) have such a connotation.[169] Rather, the Son is cast here as the fundamental object of the Father's will – that which he *wants* (and has) by nature, or, as Athanasius explains in *Contra Arianos* 3.65, "This is the Son by nature; 'in him is stored those things seeming desirous (βούλησις) to me".[170]

Now another model presents itself. To say that the Father *qua* Father loves and desires the Son sounds like a Trinity of distinct volitional agency – and to a real degree this seems to be what Athanasius has in mind. Despite wanting to disassociate the begetting of the Son from a free contingent act of willing, he still maintains that this natural and defining act is *accompanied* by willing. The Father wants to beget the Son and the Son wants the Father who begets him,

---

165 *CA* 3.63; PG 26.457A. The expression also occurs (with words reversed) in *CA* 2.2.

166 Not, I hasten to add, the "psychological model" associated with Augustine. Indeed Augustine protests against the idea that the "absurdity" Son should be so defined that the Father has "not in his own substance either counsel or will" or that "the Son makes the Father wise or willing". Rather, a better expression would be that the Son is will of will (*voluntas se voluntate*); *DeTrin.* 20.38, cf. PL 42.1087.

167 Again, Marcellus of Ancyra seems to be the chief exemplar of such a theory. Sara Parvis observes that "Marcellus hated this theology of two wills of the father and Son in perfect harmony: he would have said the Logos is the Father's will just as he is the Father's wisdom and the Father's δύναμις, and that it is Christ who has a second will, qua human being"; Parvis, *Marcellus,* 170. See also Ayres, *Nicaea,* 62ff and 106. Also Grillmeier's astute comparison between the monotheistic strategies of Eusebius of Caesaea (subordinationism) and Marcellus (partitive impersonalism); Grillmeier, *Christ (vol. 1),* 180-181.

168 See *CA* 1.28 and 4.2.

169 Prestige observes here that θέλημα is used rather than θέλησις – the former having less connotation of faculty and more to do with *acts* of will; G. L. Prestige, *God in Patristic Thought.* vol. 7. *SPCK large paperbacks* (London: SPCK, 1977), 256-257.

For the range of meanings expected from the Βουλ... group of words in general use and in Athanasius see Christopher Stead in C. Stead "The Freedom of the Will and the Arian Controversy" in *Substance and illusion in the Christian Fathers,* ed. C. Stead. *Collected studies* (London: Variorum Reprints, 1985), 255-256.

170 PG 26.461B.

just as the Father desires his own subsistence (ἰδίας ὑποστάσεώς ἐστι θελητής).[171] "The Son is also wanted by the Father (καὶ θελόμενός ἐστιν ὁ Υἱὸς παρὰ τοῦ Πατρός)", he writes at the start of *CA* 3.66,[172] before immediately adding a reference to John 5:20 that the Father loves the Son and shows him all he does.

This distinct volitional agency does not simply accompany the begetting, it also seems to *follow* the same pattern. In the same verse just cited Athanasius writes that "by the will with which the Son is willed (τῇ θελέσει ᾗ θέλεται), he also loves, wills and honours (ἀγαπᾷ...θέλει...τιμᾷ) the Father". Here θελέσις *does* occur – apparently indicating that the volitional faculty is common to the Father and Son. But is this commonality generic or concrete? That is to say, is Athanasius suggesting that the Son has the same *type* of will as the Father in the sense that Seth has the same nature as Adam, or that the same volitional centre is simultaneously deployed by both of them? This is not an easy question to answer, but Athanasius' comments a few sentences further on seem to suggest that somehow both are true.[173] Explaining what it means for the Father and Son to desire (θέλει) one another, he writes that this is not to be understood as a shaping of nature by will, but rather:

> ... a true/legitimate (γνησιότητα) nature and an individual similar expression of essence (οὐσίας ἰδιότητα...ὁμοίωσιν). For as with radiance and light one might say, that there is no foregoing will (βούλησιν) in the light, but it is its natural offspring, being willed (θελόμενον) of the light which begat it; not by considered planning (ἐν σκέψει βουλήσεως), but in nature and truth. So regarding Father and the Son, one might rightly say, that Father loves (ἀγαπᾷ) and desires (θέλει) the Son, and the Son loves (ἀγαπᾷ) and desires (θέλει) the Father.[174]

As we might expect, this is impossible for us to hold in our minds. Yet the themes are familiar enough for us to see that Athanasius' concept of will is following his concept of essence.[175] The Father and Son belong together and mutually define each other as a single "system"; yet, at the same time, the Son

---

171   PG 26.561C.

172   PG 26.461C.

173   If so it would mean that Athanasius is operating with the same realist/generic dialectic that we saw in the case of Gregory Nazianzen above. Here it is will (rather than divinity) that seems to flow unbroken between the persons, though each of them is simultaneously a true willer.

174   PG 26.464B, C.

175   See Prestige, *Patristic Thought*, 256.

is *another* like the Father.[176] In will, as in essence, they are unified *and* equal; *homoousious and homoiousios*; one *ousia* and two *hypostases*. At least for Athanasius my opening suggestion concerning filial volition is vindicated. The Son expresses and does the Father's will simply because the only will he *has* is that which is that which comes perfectly, and naturally and eternally from the Father.

A Parting Question on Contingent Decisions

Before we leave Athanasius there is a final question to ask about the difference between the natural willing associated with the generation of the Son and the contingent willing associated with creation. Athanasius has made clear that there are no "might have beens" or prevenient choices as regards the Son, but this would not appear to be the case with regard to creation.[177] In *De incarnatione* 3.1 Athanasius makes it clear that the world was not created spontaneously (αὐτομάτως) because there was forethought involved (μὴ ἀπρονόητα).[178] In *CA* 2.77 he supplies the image of a wise architect, proposing (προθέμενος), deliberating (βουλεύεται) and preparing his plans (βουλὴ ... ἡτοιμάσθη).[179]

---

176 We can find Basil speaking in very similar terms in *De Spir* 16.38 where he balances the individual equality of the three persons against a dynamic picture of the Father as the willer who wills solely through his Son; "the Father who creates all by will alone doesn't need the Son but at the same time wills through the Son" (Οὕτω γὰρ ἂν οὔτε Πατὴρ προσδεηθείη Υἱοῦ, μόνῳ τῷ θέλειν δημιουργῶν) the participle he uses here for the Father's action is cognate of the word he uses for the Son's agency in the previous sentence – ἀλλ' ὅμως θέλει διὰ Υἱοῦ); PG 32.136C. The result is that a diverse unity: "the Lord [here, the Father] who commands (προστάσσοντα Κύριον); the Word who effects (δημιουργοῦντα Λόγον); the Spirit who makes it all firm"; ibid.

177 John Zizioulas puts it well:

> The one divine will shared equally by all three persons and lying behind the creation of the world, in accordance with Athanasius and Nicaea, does not emerge automatically and spontaneously as it were out of itself, but is initiated by a person, namely the Father as "the willing one".

> J. D. Zizioulas, *Communion and Otherness: Further Studies in Personhood and the Church,* ed. P. McPartlan (London: T&T Clark, 2006), 121.

178 PG 25.101A.

179 PG 26.309C. See Stead's comments here; Stead, *Freedom,* 256-257. Stead seems inexplicably critical of Athanasius, regarding his distinction between accompanying desire and contingent willing (as regards the Son) as "bizarre", and finding his views on God's free-will as simply inconsistent. I cannot see the logical problem in either case, though Stead's highlighting of these two aspects of divine will in Athanasius is nonetheless fruitful.

But if God's will for the world is not "natural" (as it is in the case of the Son) – that is, if it is *free* -how are the contingent determinations present in both the Father and the Son? The *original* natural connection will surely not suffice; that will simply provide the parameters of the things that God *might* do. Here again it is difficult to get a completely clear answer, but one section of *Contra Arianos* takes us tantalizingly close. In *CA* 2.31, Athanasius contrasts God's relationship to his under-workers (ἀνθρώπων ὑπουργάς – angels, prophets etc.) to that which he has with his Word. In the case of the former, he writes, there is a transmission of information – a hearing, questioning and answering that follows the deliberation of God – for created agents are dependent on the mediating Word himself. But the Word himself is subject to no such mediation or intervening communication, "for that which he ["he" appears to mean "Father"] imagined (δόξαν) and determined (βουληθὲν), the Word immediately (εὐθὺς) brought into being and finished off (ἀπηρτίζετο)".[180] A few lines on, Athanasius once again draws the comparison between the agency of creatures and that of the Word, observing that:

> ... when the Word himself works and creates, then there is no questioning and separation (ἀπόκρισις), for the Father is in him and the Word in the Father; but it suffices (ἀρκεῖ) to make a decision (τὸ βούλεσθαι),[181] and the work is done; so that the word 'he said' is a token of the intention (βουλήματος) for our sake, and 'It was so,' denotes the work which is done through the Word and the wisdom, in which wisdom also is the Father's act of willing (βούλησις).[182]

Once again, this is extremely difficult to penetrate and draws together the same dynamic tension we have observed in the case of the Word's own status as will. In the first place there seems to be a sense in which the Father decides something, *immediately communicates it to the Word,*[183] who, in turn, immediately effects it; yet in the second case there is the more difficult idea that the Word/Wisdom/Willing seems to somehow *be* the Father's act of "going

---

180 PG 26.213A.

181 Stead points out that this form has "marked tendency to represent a process in which one or more alternatives are considered"; ibid., 256.

182 *CA* 2.31; NPNF 2.4.365 (altered) cf. PG 26.213B.

183 The idea that the Father's will is "in" the Son comes out implicitly in *CA* 3.31 and explicitly in *CA* 3.76. Meanwhile Mark Baddeley points out a stronger example of the interpersonal motif in *Contra Gentes* 46 where Athanasius repeatedly uses the language of command (προτάσσω) to describe the "let us" statements of Genesis 1 – God speaking to his Word; M. Baddeley, *Complementarianism and Egalitarianism (part 3): The Coming Divide (iii),* (The Sola Panel) http://solapanel.org/article/complementarianism_and_egalitarianism_part_31/ #5772, (accessed November, 2011).

out" from himself in contingent decision making – much as the Son is already in his *nature* the *radiance* of the Father.[184]

Both these images belong together; the first preserves the Son's genuine agency and ensures that his inherited divinity is really *his*; the second guards against ditheism or subordinationism – as if the Son were exterior to the Father's inner life after all. And both also have bearing on our discussion of RITW. The second, dynamic model shows us that the Son's going-forth from the Father is not simply an eternally complete historical fact but that it is also retranscribed in every free act of God toward all that is *not God*. Meanwhile the first by itself simply *is* RITW; the Father wills and the Son simultaneously does the Father's will.

Divine Willing Beyond Athanasius

The themes that emerge from this brief study of Athanasius can also be detected to varying degrees in other key pro-Nicenes of the later fourth century.[185] The highlighting and rejection of subordinationist attempts to reduce divine relations to a matter of will is commonplace.[186] So too, however, is the acknowledgement amongst the orthodox that the begetting of the Son is *also* willed as well as eternal.[187] Beyond this, three general observations might be made: (1) the pattern of causal relationships between the persons of the Trinity is commonly held to include will and gives rise to a community of will; (2) this causality extends to the *opera ad extra* and may sometimes be seen to align

---

184 Richard Hanson notes Origen's preference for "will proceeding from the mind and of light proceeding from the sun as the best model for the production of the Son"; Hanson, *Search*, 65-66. The same dynamism is present here; although Athanasius is at pains to say that the begetting also transcends any act of will, he also sees the Son *in* every act of contingent willing.

185 This is not to deny that there are also some subtle differences too. For example, as Meijering observes (Meijering, *Doctrine of the Will*, 227-230), Athanasius and Gregory connect will and begetting in different ways. While Athanasius stresses the fact that begetting is natural and willed, Gregory makes the begetting itself an *eternal act of will*. Here Gregory, influenced it would seem by the sensitivities of his homoiousian background, places a greater emphasis on the individuality and equality of the persons, while Athanasius in turn wants to retain a stronger stress on dynamic continuity.

186 So for example: Gregory of Nyssa – *CE* 1.34 (cf. NPNF 2.5.81), 4.6 (NPNF 2.5.165) 12 (*pars altera*) (NPNF 2.5.255); Ambrose – *DeFid.* 4.103-105; Epiphanius – *Pan.* 26.5-6; Hilary – *DeTrin.* 1.28, 8.3, 8.5, 8.17, 9.1, 9.70; Socrates – *Ecclesiastica Historia* 2.40.

187 Examples include: Gregory of Nyssa – *CE* 8.2 (cf. NPNF 2.5.202); Hilary – *DeSyn.* 59; Epiphanius – *Pan.* 26.6; Gregory Nazianzen – *Or.* 29.6-8.

with the humanity of Christ; (3) there is a degree of flexibility in the language and emphasis as regards the order of willing from Father to Son.

1. The pattern of causal relationships between the persons of the Trinity is commonly held to include will.

Once again of course, this is the FV option – the Son expresses and does the Father's will because *as Son* he receives everything that is the Father's including his will. The priority of the Father here guards against polytheism. At the same time, the fact that the Father *is father* – that he has a Son perfectly like him – means that there are two distinct *willers* (volitional centres) who necessarily want the same thing because they have the same *will* (or naturally determined set of desires or inclination – see next quote). As Gregory of Nyssa (from whom I have taken the expression "community of will")[188] writes in his response to Eunomius, there is:

> ... no divergence of will (διαφορὰ ... ἐν θελήματι) between the Father and the Son, but the image of goodness is after the archetype of all goodness and beauty, and as, if a man should look at himself in a glass ... the copy will in all respects be conformed to the original, the shape of the man who is reflected being the cause of the shape on the glass, and the reflection making no spontaneous movement (κινεῖσθαι) or inclination (ἐπικλίνεσθαι) unless that movement and inclination is begun (ἄρξαντος) by the original, but, if it move, moving along with it – in like manner we maintain that our Lord, the image of the invisible God, is immediately and inseparably (ἀμέσως) one with the Father in every movement of his will. If the Father will anything, the Son who is in the Father knows the Father's will, or rather he is himself the Father's will. For, if he has in himself all that is the Father's will ... he needs not, therefore, to know the Father's will by word, being himself the Word of the Father, in the highest acceptation of the term.[189]

Gregory parallels much of what we have already seen from Athanasius here: the explicit connecting of the Father's *arché* with will; the rejection of any intervening "word" between the Father and Son and the insistence on the immediacy of the "communication" between them;[190] the balance of individual equality – "the Son ... knows the Father's will" – with dynamic continuity – "the Son ... is the Father's [will/Word]". But there also seems to be a particular stress on the *ongoing* joint willing of the Father and Son. The Son('s will) is from the Father as Son (both naturally and contingently), not simply in some

---

188 "κοινωνία τοῦ θελήματος" cf. *CE* 1.34 (NPNF 2.5.81), 2.15 (NPNF 2.5.132).

189 *CE* 12 (*pars altera*) (cf. NPNF 2.5.272 altered cf. PG 45.981D-984A).

190 See also on this *DeSpir.* (NPNF 2.5.320).

frozen eternity, but in "every movement" (πᾶσαν θελήματος κίνησιν) of the Father's activity.

More of this is to be found in the other Cappadocians and beyond. Basil distinguishes the "transmission of will" from a process like verbal command, comparing it rather to "the reflection of an object in a mirror, passing without note of time from Father to Son".[191] He insists that the will is "concurrent with the essence" such that the Image of the Father is "like and equal, or rather the same" in this matter too.[192] Gregory Nazianzen, emphasising the simplicity of the divine nature and the priority of the Father, includes will in the list of qualities which "tell forth" (ὃν ἀνάγεται) the ordered persons (τὰ ἑξῆς) from the Father.[193]

2. This causality extends to the *opera ad extra* and may sometimes be seen to align with the humanity of Christ.

In modern trinitarian discussions it is commonplace to find invocations of the doctrine that all works of the Godhead are undivided (*omnia opera Trinitatis ad extra indivisa sunt*). The maxim is sometimes ascribed to Augustine, but the principle itself precedes him. Those of the pro-Nicene generation that went before him were very clear that the persons of the Trinity worked as one, but they were equally clear that the way the divine persons work together is determined by the taxonomy of their subsistence. As Gregory of Nyssa writes in *On Not Three Gods* (*Ad Ablabius*), responding to the challenge that his theology represents tritheism;

> ... in the case of the divine nature we do not similarly learn that the Father does anything by himself in which the Son does not work conjointly, or again that the Son has any special operation apart from the Holy Spirit; ... there exists one motion and disposition of the good will (μια τις γίνεται τοῦ ἀγαθοῦ θελήματος κίνησις τε καὶ διακόσμησις) which is communicated from the Father through the Son to the Spirit. ... [For example] when we learn concerning the God of the universe, from the words of Scripture, that he judges all the earth, we say that he is the judge of all things through the Son: and again, when we hear that the Father judgeth no man, we do not think that the Scripture is at variance with itself – for he who judges all the earth does this by his Son to whom he has committed all judgment; and everything which is done by the only-begotten has its reference to the Father, so that he himself is at once the judge of all things and judges no man, by reason of his having, as we said, committed all judgment to the Son,

---

191 *DeSpir.* 20 (NPNF 2.8.14).

192 *DeSpir.* 21 (NPNF 2.8.13). Note the unity/equality tension.

193 *Or.* 42.15, PG 36.476B.

while all the judgment of the Son is conformable to the will of the Father; and one could not properly say either that they are two judges, or that one of them is excluded from the authority and power implied in judgment. ... We find that the power which we conceive as preceding this motion, which is the only-begotten God, is the maker of all things; without him no existent thing attains to the beginning of its being: and, again, this same source of good has its beginning from the will of the Father (ἐκ τοῦ πατρικου Βουλήματος ἀφορμᾶται).[194]

For Gregory here the Father's monarchy operates through the *opera ad extra* exactly as in the immanent Trinity; not to exclude the Son and Spirit from equal honour, but to ensure that each of the three persons is seen to be fully involved in the works of the Godhead without multiplying sources of divine power or action. As Athanasius balances the dynamic model of the Son as the Father's "going out" in contingent willing against the interpersonal model of the Son receiving and executing the Father's will (such that the Father is retained as the author and Son is *also* seen as a real agent worthy of praise), so Gregory rings the same dynamic tension into his own conception of salvation history. The result, as the Nyssen writes elsewhere, is that for:

> ... those who with simplicity of heart receive the preaching of the cross and the resurrection, the same grace should be a cause of the same thankfulness (Ἴσης εὐχαριστίας) to the Son and to the Father, and now that the Son has accomplished the Father's will (τὸ πατρικὸν θέλημα τοῦ Υἱοῦ τελειώσαντος) ... inasmuch as our salvation would not have been wrought, had not the good will of the Father proceeded to actual operation for us through his own power. And we have learnt from the Scripture that the Son is the power of the Father.[195]

This pattern is also seen through the lens of the incarnation. We have seen that there is a fundamental difference for pro-Nicenes between the Father's unity of will with his Son and that which exists in the case of *created* agents; yet this does not mean that the relationship that Jesus *the man* enjoys with the Father is to be thought of as completely alien to (or obscuring) of his divine filiality. In *De Spiritu Sancto* 19, Basil elides the agency of the Son in creation and incarnation – treating the words of Jesus as fair exegesis of the Logos.

> He shepherds; he enlightens; he nourishes; he heals; he guides; he raises up; he calls into being things that were not; he upholds what has been created. Thus the good things that come from God reach us "through the Son", who works in each case with greater speed than speech can utter. ...On the other hand, and lest we should ever be drawn away by the

---

194 NPNF 2.5.334-335 cf PG 45.126-129.

195 *CE* 12.3 (NPNF 2.5.245, cf. PG 45.900-901).

greatness of the works wrought to imagine that the Lord is without beginning, what saith the Self-Existent (αὐτοζωή)? "I live through the Father, "and the power of God? "The Son has power to do nothing of himself". And the self-complete (αὐτοτελὴς) wisdom? "I received a commandment what I should say and what I should speak.[196]

There is more to come. In the next verse (20) – citing a catena of verses from the Farewell Discourse (John 12:49, 50, 14:24) which might point to a subordinate status or deficiency in that the Son must obey the Father and speak his words – Basil chooses not to write these off as expressions of Jesus' humanity, but again interprets them as manifestations of the divine life itself:

> [I]t is not because he lacks the ability to choose (οὐκ ἀπροαίρετος) or that he is mindless (ἀνόητος),[197] nor yet because he has to wait for a signal (συνθημάτων), that he employs language of this kind. His object is to make it plain that his own mind (οἰκείαν γνώμην) has a continuous (ἀδιαστάτως) unity (ἡνωμένως) with the Father. Do not then let us understand by what is called a "commandment" a peremptory mandate (λόγον προστακτικὸν) made known by organs of speech, and giving orders to the Son, laying down the law (νομοθετοῦντα) concerning what he ought to do as if he were an obedient subordinate (ὡς ὑπακόῳ). Let us rather, in a sense befitting the Godhead, perceive a transmission of will (θελήματος διάδοσιν). ... Thus on all sides is demonstrated the true doctrine that the fact that the Father creates through the Son neither constitutes the creation of the Father imperfect nor exhibits the active energy of the Son as feeble, but indicates the unity of the will; so the expression "through whom" contains a confession of an antecedent cause, and is not adopted in objection to the efficient cause.[198]

Gregory Nazianzen also derives truth about the Logos from the words of Jesus – albeit with a much stronger inclination to *distinguish* those passages referring to the divine nature from those that bespeak his humanity. In his fourth theological oration (*Oratio* 30) he deals with the subjections of the incarnate Christ, presenting the case that his sufferings and ongoing obedience are part of his function as our representative (vv. 4-6). Gregory clarifies that the learning of obedience and tears belong to the Christ; *not the Word*, who cannot die, nor be described as obedient:

> ... in his character of the Word he was neither obedient nor disobedient [as] such expressions belong to servants, and inferiors, and the one

---

196 *DeSpir.* 19; NPNF 2.8.12 – altered cf. PG 32.101C.

197 Migne has ἀνόμητος.

198 NPNF 2.8.13 – altered cf. PG 32.103B, C.

applies to the better sort of them, while the other belongs to those who deserve punishment. But, in the character of the form of a servant, he condescends to his fellow servants, nay, to his servants, and takes upon him a strange form, bearing all me and mine in himself, that in himself he may exhaust the bad.[199]

But, like Basil, Gregory interprets other scriptural verses concerning Jesus as pointing to his (divine) filiality. As we have already touched on above, Gregory interprets John 14:28 to refer to the Father's priority *as cause* (*Or.* 30.7). Two verses later he makes a similar assessment of the Son's receiving inheritance, judgment, power or glory etc: such things certainly belong to the humanity but also to God (τῷ Θεῷ) in the sense that these things are with him (συνυπάρχοντα) from the source (ἀπ' ἀρχῆς) and by reason of nature (λόγῳ φύσεως).[200] In verse 11, John 6:57 is exegeted in the same way: "For their being itself is common and equal, even though the Son receive it from the Father. It is in respect of this that it is said I live by the Father".[201] In the *opera ad extra* (as demanded by the John 5 context) this means that the Father and Son work in perfect unity: "the Father impresses (ἐνσημαίνεται)[202] the form of these actions (αὐτῶν πραγμάτων τοὺς τύπους) and the Word brings them to completion (ἐπιτελεῖ) – working not as a slave nor as unlearned but as knowledgeable (ἐπιστημονικῶς) and as a master (δεσποτικῶς) – that is to say, like the Father (πατρικῶς)".[203] Gregory says that this pattern explains the way the Godhead works to found and preserve the world in John 5:17, Psalm 104:4-5 and Amos 4:13: the Father and Son thus have a "sameness of authority and honour" (τῆς ἐξουσίας ὁμοιτίμιαν).

3. There is room for a variety of expression concerning the way the Father and Son work together.

What should be apparent from the above excerpts and discussion is that much orthodox fourth-century trinitarianism is built on a series of dialectical tensions. The Father must be seen as the ultimate source of the Son's actions *yet* the Son must also be seen as a sufficient source of his own actions. The Father communicates his will to the Son *yet* that communication must be purged of any verbal or temporal connotations. The Son receives and does the Father's will *yet* the receipt of that will is *eternally complete* such that it is also his own.

---

199 NPNF 2.7.311.

200 PG 36.113C.

201 NPNF 2.7.313.

202 In *Or.* 33.33 the word is contrasted with a merely outward re-colouring, signifying the total conformity expected of those baptized.

203 PG 36.117A, B.

Is the Priority of Paternal Will compatible with Pro-Nicene Orthodoxy?

The Son is inextricably connected to the Father as his radiance and will-in-action *yet* the Son *qua* son is also a reiteration of the Father.

And it should be also clear here that there is room for some variation here within these polarities. A theologian who emphasizes the eternally-complete aspect of the Father/Son relationship will produce a differently hued trinitarianism from another who is more inclined to portray the filial bond as dynamic and ongoing: the first might sound more tritheist, the second more "subordinationist". A theology that emphasizes the *differences* between the Father-to-Son communication and creaturely forms will sound different from one that wants to stress that what transpires between the divine persons *is* some type of communication: in modern terminology, the second will sound more "social".[204]

Useful examples can be seen if we compare and contrast the writings of Hilary of Poitiers and his fellow Westerner Ambrose of Milan (c.340-397). For Hilary, it is important to stress that the unity of will that comes from true natural birth connotes a free agency for the Son (in his own right) *and* that his will is one with the Father. As he writes in book 9 of *De Trinitate* in a lengthy treatment that traces the knots of the paradox:

> Their nature is such, that the several action of each implies the conjoint action of both, and their joint activity a several activity of each. Conceive the Son acting, and the Father acting through him. He acts not of himself, for we have to explain how the Father abides in him. ... But he would not be in the unity of the divine nature, if the deeds which he does, and wherein he pleases, were not his own, and he were merely prompted to action by the Father abiding in him. The Father then in abiding in him, teaches him, and the Son in acting, acts not of himself; while, on the other hand, the Son, though not acting of himself, acts himself, for what he does is pleasing. Thus is the unity of their nature retained in their action, for the one, though he acts himself, does not act of himself, while the other, who has abstained from action, is yet active.[205]

In the next verse Hilary deploys this same dialectical machinery against the opportunism of those who would wield John 6:37 against the Son. "Perhaps you say, the Son has no freedom of will (*voluntatis libirate*)." [206] But Hilary will not allow this. The Son is free to do what *he* will but the character of what he wants comes from the Father "under the aspect of one indistinguishable

---

204   See the definition at the start of the next chapter.

205   *DeTrin.* 9.48; NPNF 2.9.172.

206   PL 10.320A.

nature". As he puts it in verse 50, "the Son plainly wills all that the Father wills, for wills of the same nature cannot dissent from one another".[207]

Significantly, although Hilary here casts the oneness of will in terms of nature, he derives the *evidence* for it (or expression of it) from the words of the human Jesus,[208] and the result of this is that the bishop's theology begins to sound like a sort of social trinitarianism. On the one hand, he maintains that "obedience to death" has nothing to do with the "form of God" (*Dei forma*) (v.14, cf. vv.38-38), and that the conformity of will of the Son is *different* from obedience.

> His conformity to the Father's will is ... more than to obey a will: the latter would imply external necessity, while to do another's will requires unity with him, being an act of volition. In doing the will of the Father the Son teaches that through the identity of their nature his will is the same in nature with the Father's, since all that he does is the Father's will.[209]

Yet, on the other hand, Hilary tends to hold together the priority of the Father in relation to the Son with the contingency of the human servant. In verse 53, for example, he exegetes John 14.28 as relating the "mystery of [the Word] taking the servant's form", yet immediately switches to speaking of *divine filiality*: asking whether "it is an indignity to the only-begotten God, that the unbegotten God is his Father ... [and] gives him the only-begotten nature"? He insists that it is not, for the Son is neither self-generated nor born from nothing but comes as a living nature from living nature (*Non enim suae originis est Filius, neque nativitatem sibi non exstans ipse conquisivit ex nullo: sed ex*

---

207 At the end of verse 52 this is expressed in language reminiscent of the *homoiousion/homoousion* dichotomy – the Son has a nature *like* the Father's that we "might know that in Father and Son there is no distinction of nature". (NPNF 2.9.173).

208 The relationship between the two natures of Christ is a major sub-theme in book 9 (see 5.3ff). Hilary distinguishes three phases of the scriptural testimony concerning the Word: before, after and during his earthly sojourn (v.6). Yet although he stresses that in the case of the earthly Jesus we must distinguish between those expressions which testify to his humanity and those which indicate his divinity (cf. vv.5-6, 14), Hilary is also concerned to press the unity of the person of Christ ("he took a new form but remained what he was. 5.14) and the coincidence of the human and divine in the deification achieved by the incarnation:

> [T]he whole Son, that is, His manhood as well as his divinity, was permitted by the Father's gracious favour to continue in the unity of the Father's nature, and retained not only the powers of the divine nature, but also that nature's self. For the object to be gained was that man might become God (v.38; NPNF 2.9.167).

209 Verse 50; NPNF 2.9.172.

Is the Priority of Paternal Will compatible with Pro-Nicene Orthodoxy?

vivente natura vivens natura exstans).²¹⁰ At this point Hilary seems suddenly to run together the obedience of the Son's incarnate humility with the relationship arising from his birth, speaking of the Son testifying in honour to the grace of his birth (*honorem testetur, et gratiam sumptae nativitatis in honore*) and rendering a debt to the Father who sent him (*quidem Patri debitum reddens, ut obedientiam suam mittentis deputet voluntati*).²¹¹ As in vv. 21 and 74 it thus seems that the Father's "sending" – and perhaps even the Son's obedience – is connected to the Father's paternal priority. By the end of book 9 the it is clear that Hilary's vision of the Son that looks to an "overlap" (as well as a difference) between the second person's relationship with the Father as Son and as man:

> What the Father knows, the Son does not learn by question and answer; what the Father wills, the Son does not will by command. Since all that the Father has, is his, it is the property of his nature to will and know, exactly as the Father wills and knows. But to prove his birth he often expounds the doctrine of his person, as when he says, I came not to do mine own will, but, the will of him that sent me. ... His will is, therefore, the same in nature as the Father's will, though to make plain the fact of the birth it is distinguished from the Father's.²¹²

Things are slightly different with Ambrose of Milan (c.340-397). In *De Fide Ad Gratianum* (written c.378-380)²¹³ and *De Spiritu Sanctu* (381) Ambrose reveals a trinitarian scheme that strives to play down parallels between the human subordination of Jesus Christ and the filial dependency of the eternal Son. While Ambrose certainly insists on the same paradigm of real sonship to explain how Father and Son share the same essence²¹⁴ (and sometimes deploys the same dynamic image of light and radiance so commonly found amongst his Eastern brethren²¹⁵) begetting, to him, is for all intents and purposes purely

---

210 *DeTrin.* 9.53; PL 10.324A.

211 Ibid.

212 *DeTrin.* 9.74 (NPNF 2.9.181).

213 Dating from B. Ramsey, *Ambrose. Early Church Fathers* (London: Routledge, 1997) 61-62.

214 "[I]f we seek to know his natural rank and dignity, he is so truly the very Son of God, that he is indeed God's own Son (*usque Filius Dei verus ... et proprius*). ... To deny that the Son of God is begotten [of God] is to deny that he is God's own Son, and to deny Christ to be God's own Son is to class him with the rest of mankind, as no more a Son than any of the rest"; *DeFid.* 1.17.108, 110 (NPNF 2.10.219, cf. PL 16.553C). See extended discussion of the differences between human and divine generation in *DeFid.* 1.11-12. See prosecution of Arians on the reality of the Son's begetting in *DeFid.* 3.15.124ff.

215 *DeFid.* 1.13.79; "[The Son is] the brightness of eternal light, for brightness takes effect in the instant of its coming into existence ... Think not, then, that there was

historical.[216] Ambrose has very little interest in the *relational* dynamism that Hilary explores and, rather, draws strict lines of demarcation between the human and the eternal Son. It is only as man that the Son suffers,[217] it is only as man that he submits his will to the Father's, or calls the Father "greater"[218] or "God",[219] or is sent,[220] or has the Father as head,[221] or prays,[222] or speaks God's words.[223] In direct contrast to Gregory Nazianzen or Hilary, who make apparently subordinationist passages such as John 5:26 or 14:28 or 1 Corinthians 8:6 etc. refer to both the contingence of the man Jesus *and* the dependence of the eternal Son on the Father,[224] Ambrose generally interprets them all as referring to the human nature. Although Ambrose acknowledges that "many learned men (*pleri ... doctores*)[225] allow that the Son hears, and that the Father speaks to the Son through the unity of their Nature",[226] this is more apparent than real: the Son only *seems* to have heard (*videtur audisse*)[227], and what is really described is the inseparable cooperation (*indissociabile*

---

ever a moment of time when God was without wisdom, any more than that there was ever a time when light was without radiance", (NPNF 2.10.214).

216 *DeFid.* 1.11.72; 4.9.111. Not that it ever happened in time, of course.

217 *DeFid.* 2.7.52-53.

218 *DeFid.* 2.8.61; 4.12.169. There is a tantalizing hint, however, that Ambrose is prepared to allow more than he will admit (for tactical reasons). In 2.8.66 he asks whether his opponents think of the Father as greater because he is Father. His answer, without absolutely denying the assertion, is that the word "Father" cannot mean a difference in age, nor does duty (*pietas* – the word frequently has connotations of familial obligation) detract from natural equality (*non ... naturae detrimentum*) (PL 16.573C). There are other glancing connections between divine filiality and humanity in *DeFid.* 2.11.99 and 4.10.122. Daniel Williams may be correct here that Ambrose's interests here are captive to his polemical strategy, the "sole task [of defending and substantiating] the absolute essential unity of the Father and Son"; (D. H. Williams, *Ambrose of Milan and the End of the Nicene-Arian Conflicts. Oxford Early Christian Studies* (Oxford: Clarendon Press, 1995), 145).

219 *DeFid.* 1.15.91-92.

220 *DeFid.* 2.9.74-79.

221 *DeFid.* 4.3.41ff.

222 *DeFid.* 4.5.56-57.

223 *DeFid.* 2.9.79-80. "[T]hat which he speaks cannot be solely from him, for in him all that is, is naturally derived from the Father"; (NPNF 2.10.234).

224 For Hilary's treatment of such verses, see for example: *DeTrin.* 2.10-11; 11.12; *DeSyn.* 75.

225 PL 16.675C.

226 *DeFid.* 5.11.132; NPNF 2.10.301.

227 PL 16.675D.

cooperationis)²²⁸ – that is, the "unity of will and of power (*voluntatis atque virtutis*)²²⁹ which exists both in the Father and in the Son ... for there is one opinion and one operation in the Trinity (*una sententia et operatio Trinitatis*)".²³⁰

Ambrose's (by-and-large) segregation of causal order[231] from the *opera ad extra* raises questions of how the works of the three can be unified.[232] How are the Son and Father one God if their unity is a *finished* historical act (of begetting) in eternity[233]? He needs to supply an alternative balancing element to keep the equality of the persons signifying a coordinate divinity (or tritheism), and this he does by referring to the substance (*substantia*) of God itself. The *substantia* itself is one and undivided; its power and will is undivided; and therefore (as he never tires of reiterating) the works of the Trinity are undivided.[234] In *De Spiritu Sancti* (2.9.100) he disagrees with those who would use 1 Corinthians 8:6 to justify a "from the Father" and "through the Son" pattern of ontology and operation:

---

228 Ibid.

229 Ibid. See Williams' comments on Ambrose's peculiar use of this term in connection the Trinity; Williams, *Ambrose of Milan*, 144.

230 *DeFid.* 5.11.133 (NPNF 2.10.301 – altered cf. PL 675D-676A). We can see a similar pattern of argument in Ambrose's treatment of dependency passages such as John 6.58 (*DeFid.* 4.10.118ff). For the largest part such passages are taken to apply to the contingency of the incarnation, yet there is also a passing concession (4.10.133) that the "the Son lives by the Father, because he is the Son begotten of the Father ... because he came forth from the Father, because he is begotten of the bowels of the Father, because the Father is the Fountain and Root of the Son's being"; (NPNF 2.10.279).

231 In several places he stresses Scripture's occasional variation from the traditional order of Father-Son-Spirit; eg. *De Spiritu Sancti* 3.16.117 or 4.11.136 or 5.9.115-117; the last reading: "the order of the words is often changed; and therefore thou oughtest not to question about order or degree, in the case of God the Father and his Son, for there is no severance of unity in the Godhead"; (NPNF 2.10.299).

232 This was indeed the major Arian accusation of Ambrose according to Williams; ibid., 144.

233 This is less of a problem in schemes which imagine the processions as both complete and ongoing (eg. solar radiance, or fluvial effluence). For a very helpful discussion of the different conceptions of eternal generation and their significance see J. S. Rhee, *A History of the Doctrine of Eternal Generation of the Son and its S i g n ï Ṯṛïnïtaṟiaṉïsm̃, c e* http://www.jsrhee.com/QA/thesis1.htm, (accessed January, 2010).

234 And often unordered; *Non ergo alicui prior vel secundus est actus, sed idem unius operationis effectus; De Spiritu Sancti* 2.12.136 (PL 16.772A).

> ... these expressions suit either the Father or the Son or the Holy Spirit, ... no distinction of the divine power can arise from particles of this kind, there is no doubt but that all things are of him through whom all things are; and that all things are through him through whom all are; and that we must understand that all things are through him or of him in Whom all are. For every creature exists both of the will, and through the operation and in the power of the Trinity, as it is written: "Let us make man after our image and likeness."[235]

Ambrose here represents the beginning of what might now be described as the Western or "Latin" paradigm – beginning with the one being instead of the one Father. Yet, complicating this, it is important to see that there is still much here that could be stereotypically described as "Eastern". As already noted, Ambrose strongly retains the view that the causal relationship between the Father and Son is the *way* both can be seen as consubstantial: his reification of the *substantia* or Trinity itself exists alongside (I would suggest somewhat uncomfortably) the pro-Nicene ordered model.

Conclusion

We are now in a position to itemise some general observations about what light the fourth century trinitarian debates might cast on our contemporary discussion concerning the ordered relatationship between the Son and the Father. Here is a brief summary of where the argument stands:

1. The pro-Nicene position retains the concept of real sonship as an important correlate of the *homoousios* doctrine. This perfect and eternal derivation of the Son from the Father differentiates heretical subordinationism from the orthodox position and undergirds the language of essence or nature.

2. The notion that the Son *qua* Son is perfectly *like* the Father – or alternately, wholly *shares* in what the Father is – extends to every aspect of the divine nature including power, knowledge and will.

3. This means that the Son inevitably wants what his Father wants, for his begetting means that he shares the same natural will and is thereby in perfect agreement with the Father. The statement "he does his Father's will" is therefore just as true as "he does his own will". The first acknowledges the derivational relationship that exists between Father and Son; the second emphasizes the state of affairs that results from that begetting.

---

235 NPNF 2.10.127. See the similar argument in *DeFid*. 4.11.139-157.

4. The fact that the Son's will is from the Father might be imagined as either a purely past-complete historical reality, or both complete and dynamically continuous. The second conception sounds more relational and may be seen to fit with the active conformity of the human Jesus. The first model is inclined to treat any such historicising as a threat to the Son's full eternal equality.

5. With regard to the will of God, the pro-Nicene position excludes:

    – Arian subordinationism, with the implication that the eternal Son needs to be told the Father's wishes as if he did not already possess the Father's character (and thus will) by begetting.

    – Modalist or Marcellanist conceptions of the Son which either reduce him to a faculty, part or impersonal projection of the Father.

    – Tritheistic depictions of the Father and Son as two distinct aseities without an accompanying declaration of unity.

6. The pro-Nicene position less clearly addresses these questions:

    – Is the triune God to be envisaged as a thing or entity in its own right, such that "he" is the basis on which Father and Son are one as well as three?

    – How does the human nature of Christ relate to the filiality of the Son in terms of his relationship to the Father?

    – How do Father and Son make contingent decisions about issues where their natural will allows them more than one option?

These three questions will direct our enquiries from this point on.

Chapter 2

Does Dyothelitic Orthodoxy Permit Personal Agency?

> In Christ alone can His Human will submit itself to the divine will, because He alone has two wills. Conversely, if there is only one identical divine power of will there can be no obedience in the Trinity. Seen in this light, the Son can obey the Father only with respect to the submission of His human will to the divine will of the Father, which latter is identically the same as the divine will of the Son.
>
> – Alyssa Lyra Pitstick[236]

Introduction

In the previous chapter, I demonstrated how the pattern of paternity and subsistence which informs pro-Nicene orthodoxy, *also* informs the fourth century Fathers' view on divine willing: the Son wills what the Father wills by virtue of being begotten by the Father. But this does still not quite give us two willing agents. The precise nature of "will" here is still too vague and might (as we saw with Athanasius, Hilary and Ambrose) be understood in a slightly different ways, ranging from: the idea that the Son *is* the Father's act of willing; to something more analogous to two human persons wanting the same thing.

In this chapter, I will attempt to shine a little more light on this question by examining a moment in church history when the relationships between will, person and nature came to the fore in theological discussion. My argument will be that the orthodox commitment to the singularity of natural will was not meant to exclude all sense of existential individuality (agency) on the part of the persons – and nor should it be taken that way today. Father and Son share a single will, but they are not a single willing *agent*. Moreover, it is the very structure of their difference that – at least according to one major strand of Christian tradition – gives rise to redemptive history.

---

[236] Pitstick, *Light in Darkness*, 299.

The Dilemma of Persons & Natures

The theory of responsive intra-trinitarian willing, as I have been describing it, is a sub-species of social trinitarianism; that is, it is a theology which posits that the persons of the Trinity relate to each other as distinguishable psychological entities, each with their own consciousness and will.[237]

To make a complementary observation using more ancient terminology, RITW has affinities with Alexandrian theology. While Antiochene theories more sharply distinguish the natures of Christ and tend to see them as separately operant, RITW regards the subjective unity of the Son's person to be the moving principle in both his humanity and divinity. Jesus *is the Logos* living through his human nature.

Both these descriptors signal fearsome historical and theological issues. The Alexandrian idea that the Son and Christ are "one person and one subsistence" aligns well with the orthodox formula of Chalcedon, but makes it harder to grasp the relationship between hypostasis and nature.[238] On the other hand, ST

---

237 T w l œ a r i fai i œ tr i h dre: e s r
   (1) The form of ST that I am advocating is not *purely* social – that it is, it does not take the position that the *only* thing connecting the persons is an accordance of will. For a reasonably careful presentation of ST that displays a greater-than-average awareness of pro-Nicene trinitarianism, see Plantinga, *Social Trinity*.

   (2) To be opposed to RITW does not necessarily mean being anti-ST. Although some critics of RITW certainly do reject ST on the basis of something that sounds like unipersonalism (see, for example, the quote from Alyssa Lyra Pitstick at the head of this chapter), others do not – see Erickson, *Tampering*; G. A. Cole, *He Who Gives Life: The Doctrine of the Holy Spirit* (Illinois: Crossway, 2007), 65-67, cf. 172-173.

238 This matter is fundamentally complicated by the fact that pro-Nicene theology used *hypostasis* as particularistion of an essence – leading to a puzzle over whether Christ signifies two *hypostases* (one divine, one human). History saw two basic attempts to escape this conundrum involving: (1) the creation of a new category of person (πρόσωπον) separate from *hypostasis* (the Nestorian solution); or (2) viewing Christ's human *hypostasis* as a kind of *expression* of his divine *hypostasis* (a scheme later termed *enhypostasia*). It is the second option that informs this thesis, yet, if it is possible to maintain the subjective unity of the person *through* the hypostatic dichotomy of Antioch (Nestorius would have insisted that it is – see McGuckin, below) then there is no final reason why RITW should not also be assimilable to that tradition too. Whether this is possible is beyond us here, though interested readers may pursue the question through discussion in: J. Pelikan, *The Spirit of Eastern Christendom (600-1700)*. vol. 2, *The Christian Tradition: A History of the Development of Doctrine*, 5 volumes (Chicago: University of Chicago Press, 1971), 39-48; A. von Harnack, *History of Dogma*, trans. N. Buchanan, 7 volumes (London: Williams & Norgate, 1905), 4.226-252; and, most especially, J. A. McGuckin, *St. Cyril of Alexandria: The Christological*

is a relative novelty. Despite occasional claims to the contrary,[239] neither Cappadocian theology nor classical theology generally can properly be described as having a "social" conception of the Godhead. The primary preoccupations in each case are categories such as derivation and nature – not psychological individuality.[240] Certainly it might be accurate to speak of a general consensus that each person is equal in their individual possession of the divine essence and its attributes. However, while this seems to suggest real subjective diversity (there are *three* who know and will etc.),[241] the unifying motifs that accompany this equality motif curtail ST speculation fairly abruptly. ST, if it can be said to exist in classical orthodoxy, looks like three individuals thinking exactly the same thing in timeless succession (first the Father, then the Son and Spirit)[242]: which is a somewhat difficult start if we want to think of them as having plans and attitudes toward each other.[243]

Further complications arise from the issue of whether the psychological life displayed in Jesus is a product of his person or his human nature. For Descartes-influenced moderns, to be a person *just is* to be a psychological entity; thus it is hard for us to imagine how the Logos and Jesus could be the "same person" without this signifying a continuity or translation of

---

Controversy: Its History, Theology, and Texts (Crestwood: St. Vladimir's Seminary Press, 2004), 159ff.

239 For example Zizioulas, *Being as Communion,* 36-41; S. J. Grenz, *The Social God and the Relational Self: A Trinitarian Theology of the Imago Dei* (Louisville: Westminster John Knox Press, 2001), 31.

240 See the helpful discussions in S. Coakley, *Powers and Submissions: Spirituality, Philosophy and Gender. Challenges in Contemporary Theology* (Oxford: Blackwell, 2002), 109-129, and L. Turcescu, "'Personal' versus 'Individual', and Other Misreadings of Gregory of Nyssa", *Modern Theology* 18 (2002): 527-539. I think it is possible that the reaction against ST is a little overstated here – see Morwenna Ludlow's carefully stated protest – Ludlow, *Gregory of Nyssa,* 265-270 – and further balanced treatment in R. E. Olson & C. A. Hall, *The Trinity. Guides to Theology* (Grand Rapids: Eerdmans, 2002), 36-41.

241 We will see this spelled out in greater detail by Maximus the Confessor. But the point here is that, insofar as the persons are held to be hypostasisations of a single real *ousia,* there is not a great deal of difference between the opinions of the Cappadocians and Boethius when the latter says that a person is *"naturae rationabilis individua substantia"* (*Contra Eutychen et Nestorium* 3). Aquinas uses the same logic with *suppositum*: *"persona nihil aliud sit quam suppositum rationalis naturae"*; *De Unione Verbi* 1.

242 See for example, Basil of Caesarea: Epistolae 38.4, 8; *DeSpir.* 20.

243 Karl Rahner makes the point thus: "there is properly no mutual love between Father and Son, for this would presuppose two acts. But there is loving self-acceptance of the Father (and of the Son, because of the taxis of knowledge and love), and this self-acceptance gives rise to distinction"; Rahner, *Trinity,* 106.

consciousness from heaven to Bethlehem. Yet this too raises difficulties. If it is the continuity of subjectivity and consciousness that makes Jesus the Logos, then it seems we must say either that he ceased to have the mind of God while he was in the cradle,[244] or that the omniscient Logos remained lurking behind the child-mind of the baby in the manger.

ST and Alexandrian Christology here exhibit the dangers associated with theology that emphasises persons (ie. personalism): ST – at least in its strongest forms – threatens to divide the Godhead into three volitional and noetic aseities, just as Alexandrian Christology risks turning Jesus into an Apollinarian shell or a Eutychian hybrid. But of course equal dangers lurk on the other side. The polar opposite of ST is simply modalism.[245] The end-point of Antiochene theology is Nestorianism (or adoptionism).[246]

Where between these extremities do we find orthodoxy? Does it favour personalism or a natures-theology? And where do these quandries leave RITW's claim to orthodoxy? Can a theory that imputes personal volition to the Logos, and identifies that volition with the obedience of Christ, avoid dividing the Godhead or confounding the Son's human and divine natures? In this chapter I will attempt to answer these questions by examining an aspect of the Monophysite controversy that has particular bearing on RITW – the dispute over Monothelitism in the seventh century.

---

244 "What was happening to the rest of the universe during the period of our Lord's earthly life ... was [the world] let loose from the control of the Creative Word"? W. Temple, *Christus Veritas: An Essay* (London: Macmillan, 1925), 142-143.

245 A rather striking example of this can be found in Brian Leftow's rejection of ST: "For the Son to be in the forefront of an act is just for God to be more prominent in one role (or state, etc.) than he is in others. So thanking the Son is thanking the same individual God who is Father and Spirit". Leftow, *Anti Social*, 238.

246 Thus Jesus turns out to be a quite separate individual from the Son, with a different relationship to the Father. As Tozer puts it:

> The dialogue involving the Father and the Son recorded in the scriptures is always to be understood as being between the eternal Father and the man Christ Jesus. The instant, immediate communion between the persons of the Godhead ... knows not sound nor effort nor motion.

A. W. Tozer, *The Knowledge of the Holy*, reprint (original 1961) edition (Carlisle: Authentic, 2008), 29.

The same approach can be found in Baillie's contention that a serious theologian can "...hardly maintain that it was the second person of the Trinity praying to the first" – D. M. Baillie, *God was in Christ: An Essay on Incarnation and Atonement. Faber paper covered editions* (London: Faber and Faber, 1961), 88-89.

Responsive Intra-Trinitarian Willing as Monothelite Heresy

At first blush it might seem counter-intuitive to associate RITW with a position called *Mono*thelitism; after all it is the RITW contention that there is *more* than one centre of volition in the Godhead. Yet Monothelitism, with its assertion that the incarnate Son possesses a single unified faculty of willing (or volitional centre), contains a significant overlap with RITW position in that both tend to envisage will as a property of *person* rather than of nature. Monothelitism, as espoused by its original advocates, certainly declared that there was only one divine-human will present in the person who became Jesus. But it also thereby implied (as its critics were quick to point out) that there are three volitional centres within the Godhead. The resonance with the RITW thesis should be clear.[247]

Orthodox Dyothelitism – Divine Unipersonalism?

In response to Monothelitism the *Dyo*thelitic orthodox settlement hammered out at the Sixth Ecumenical Council (Constantinople III) in 680-681 insisted that Christ possessed *both* a human *and* a divine will. If Jesus were both man and God, as Chalcedon had stipulated, then he must have two wills since will is a function of nature. As the council wrote in its *Prosphoneticon to the Emperor*:

---

247 A fact which RITW critics have not been slow to label as heresy. Kevin Giles says: "orthodoxy absolutely rejects the possibility that the divine three each have their own will"; Giles, *Jesus*, 203, cf. 310. Phillip Cary makes a similar observation in his review of the Giles book:

> [RITW advocates] insist that there is a distinctive kind of role differentiation in the Trinity, a subordination in role though not in being, so that the Father has the role of giving commands and the Son has the role of obeying them. The problem is that this is only conceivable if the Son's will is at least conceivably different from the Father's. But Nicene orthodoxy says it is not. There is only one will in God.

> P. Cary, "The New Evangelical Subordinationism: Reading Inequality into the Trinity", *Priscilla Papers* 20.4 (2006): 42-45.

A similar point is made by Alyssa Lyra Pitstick who states the problem with regard to Hans Urs von Balthasar's version of (divine) filial obedience;

> if Jesus is to have a mission it means he must be sent, but to be sent necessarily implies a sender [yet] the existence of a sender raises the spectre of the heteronomy. ... [For Maximian orthodoxy] faculties flow from natures, Jesus obeys with his Human will the single divine will of the Father, Son and holy Spirit. In contrast, Balthasar wants to say that Jesus humanly obeys the Father, but in doing so, he obeys *as Son*.

> Pitstick, *Light in Darkness*, 144-145.

> And as we recognize two natures, so also we recognize two natural wills and two natural operations. For we dare not say that either of the natures which are in Christ in his incarnation is without a will and operation: lest in taking away the proprieties of those natures, we likewise take away the natures of which they are the proprieties. ... For should we say that the human nature of our Lord is without will and operation, how could we affirm in safety the perfect humanity? For nothing else constitutes the integrity of human nature except the essential will, through which the strength of free-will is marked in us; and this is also the case with the substantial operation. For how shall we call him perfect in humanity if he in no wise suffered and acted as a man?[248]

As this statement makes clear, if will then is a product or aspect of *nature*, it is immediately apparent that there can be only one common will within the Godhead, just as there must be two wills in the Christ. Any thought that the persons might possess their own individual wills must lead us to conclude that there is a tritheistic schism within the nature itself. Thus the council's letter to Pope Agatho explicitly denounces those who speak of a "personal will":

> For if anybody should mean a personal will, when in the holy Trinity there are said to be three persons, it would be necessary that there should be asserted three personal wills, and three personal operations (which is absurd and truly profane). Since, as the truth of the Christian faith holds, the will is natural, where the one nature of the holy and inseparable Trinity is spoken of, it must be consistently understood that there is one natural will, and ... natural operation.[249]

This pronouncement by an ecumenical council appears to present a serious problem for the RITW position. If the concept of "personal will" is heretical then any theory which depends on it (as RITW surely does) must also be excluded from orthodoxy. If there is no personal distinction in the "natural will" of the Godhead then there is no possibility of the Father *as Father* wanting anything for the Son or the Son *as Son* wanting anything for the Father. Love as we normally conceive it as is completely excluded.[250]

---

248 NPNF 2.14.129.

249 NPNF 2.14.123.

250 Though we should note, on the other hand, that the *Dyothelitic* formula also surprisingly elevates a kind of RITW to the status of orthodoxy. For although it might well mitigate against us conceiving of the eternal Son as "obedient" before the incarnation it also insists that he is eternally and presently submissive in his human nature. As long as the Son is human as well as God he must also be thought of as having a subordinate will (as well as his divine will) since, as we saw above; "nothing else constitutes the integrity of human nature except the essential will,

But if the orthodox formula is taken at face value, this also raises disturbing questions. If the human will of Jesus Christ is free, does that mean it has a separate volitional aseity apart from that of the Son? It would seem that it must if the Son (*qua* Son) has no will of his own. What Dyothelitism *simpliciter* seems to present us with is an undifferentiated divine will influencing a free human will, with the Son as simply some kind of nodal point or divine conduit through which the monad and the human intersect. Or if we take it another way, then the Son's incarnation is the only thing which *facilitates* his having his own will. Before the incarnation he has no volitional capacity save that which he shares with the Father and Spirit: apart from the singular volition of Father-Son-Spirit the Son *qua* Son has no desire or aspiration at all. Only when he becomes man does the *person* who is the Son become capable of choosing or wanting anything *as Son*, leaving us to wonder whether the incarnation generates his distinctiveness.[251]

An Alternative Approach

We have seen enough in our discussion of pro-Nicene theology to warn us against such a monadic conception of divine willing, for unity of will no more connotes a single "willing subject" in God than it does in humans. The will of a nature is expressed discretely according to the *tropoi hyparxeos* who exemplify

---

through which the strength of free-will is marked in us". And the incarnation, as the council insists, is an "inseparable union".

The eternal submission of (the humanity of) Jesus Christ has historically played a crucially positive role in the conception of Christ as our priest who enables and (vicariously) mediates our service and praise to the Father. As T.F. Torrance writes concerning this theme as it is found in Cyril of Alexandria;

> Christ is himself the true worshiper of God, who in his vicarious mediation (μεσιτεία) is himself our redemption (ἱλασμοσ) and worship (προσκύνησισ, λατρεία), himself the altar (θυσιαστήριον), and as such the pattern (ὑπόδειγμα) of all our service in prayer, adoration and worship, which we offer in and through and with him to the Father.
>
> This worship which characterized the whole life and obedience of the Incarnate Christ in the form of a servant, and [is] fulfilled in a heavenly mode in which Christ continues to exercise his priesthood as man.

Torrance, *Reconciliation*, 178-179.

See similar constructive observations along these lines in R. Doyle, "The One True Worshiper", *The Briefing* 236 (1999): 6-9; also Fred Sanders – F. Sanders, *The Deep Things of God: How the Trinity Changes Everything* (Illinois: Crossway, 2010), 221-223 – who draws on Andrew Murray to highlight the continuity between Christ's sonship, humanity and eternal priesthood.

251 This approaches the radical views of modern theologians like Cathering Mowry LaCugna and Ted Peters who want to suggest that God depends on salvation history to become who he is. I will discuss this issue at greater length in Chapter 7.

it. The real question is whether the distinction between the *tropoi* is sufficient to allow anything like a real relationship. Is there any way to see the subsistent hypostases as anything more than mirrors or straight reiterations of the natural will (of the Father) such that they can act and respond to each other as persons? I believe that if we take a closer look at one of the arch defenders of Dyothelitic orthodoxy we will see that there is.

Divine Will in the Theology of Maximus the Confessor

Maximus the Confessor (581-662), the one-time favoured court secretary of Emperor Heraclius, came into sustained contact with the Monothelite dispute: first in Africa where he served under the anti-Monothelite Sophronius; and later through a respectful debate conducted in 645 with Pyrrhus, Patriarch of Constantinople. Maximus wrote a number of important works which were important both to this debate and a host of other issues. He has received particular attention in the modern era, with the renewal of interest in Byzantine theology amongst its inheritors – particularly Gregory Palamas and, (in modern times) Vladimir Lossky.[252] Maximus was ultimately tortured and martyred for his resistance to the Imperial will on Monothelitic doctrine.[253]

In Maximus' writings, particularly in the minutes of his public *Disputation with Pyrrhus*, we quickly see the key points of difference between the Monothelite and Dyothelite doctrines. Pyrrhus insists that two wills must signify two persons, for "it is impossible not to imply some 'willer' along with the will itself",[254] Maximus argues that in *that* case the Trinity must either be

---

252 See; D. J. Geanakoplos, "Some Aspects of the Influence of the Byzantine Maximos the Confessor on the Theology of East and West", *Church History* 38.2 (1969): 150-163; V. Lossky, *The Mystical Theology of the Eastern Church* (London: James Clarke & Co, 1957).

253 J. Chapman, *Catholic Encyclopaedia; St Maximus of Constantinople,* (New York: New Advent, 1911) http://www.newadvent.org/cathen/10078b.htm, (accessed March, 2007).

254 Maximus the Confessor, *The Disputation with Pyrrhus of Our Father Among the Saints Maximus the Confessor,* trans. J. P. Farrell (South Canaan: Saint Tikhon's Seminary Press, 1992), 5. He also argues that "It is impossible for two wills to exist in one person without opposition"; ibid., 7.

Hans Urs von Balthasar acutely observes that Monothelitism is a "precursor of the personalistic nominalism of the late Middle Ages and modern culture"; H. U. von Balthasar, *Cosmic Liturgy: The Universe According to Maximus the Confessor,* trans. B. E. Daley (San Francisco: Ignatius Press, 2003). Also remarkable is the Monothelite opposition between nature and volition such that "natural will" might be seen as a contradiction in terms; I. A. McFarland, "Naturally and by Grace': Maximus the Confessor on the Operation of the Will", *Scottish Journal of*

one person, or have three different wills, which is manifestly absurd.[255] Pyrrhus' response to this is that, if willing is natural, disagreements between humans must indicate a multitudinous divergence of human will also.[256]

Maximus' answer to this challenge here and elsewhere[257] is to elucidate the distinction, already discussed above, between the natural faculty of willing (*logos* expressed as θέλημα φυσικον or θέλησισ) which is identical in everyone, and the mode of willing (*tropos* expressed as θέλημα γνώμικον or γνώμη – *gnomie*) by which individuals express that will.

> The will and the mode of willing (πῶς θέλειν) are not the same just as the power of sight and the mode of perception are not the same. All things which have an identical nature have identical abilities (τοῖς ὁμοφυέσι καί ὁμογενέσι προσόν). But the mode of willing, like the mode of perception ... is only a mode (τρόπος ...τοῦ θέλειν) of the use of that power, of the employment of will and of perception. And the same distinction may be applied to other things as well ... the will to eat or not to eat, to walk or not to walk. But these negatives [ie. not to eat or walk] are not applicable to the will as such, but only to the particular mode of willing. In other words, things come to pass by choices [of those who will – τῶν θελητῶν].[258]

Thus to Maximus all human persons are endowed with the capacity for choice and with the same natural "wants" through their common natural will, which is given by God and is inviolable.[259] Yet how people respond to this good will is varied. On an *individual basis* humans deliberate and choose as they exercise their common human will.

Theology 58.4 (2005): 410-433, 423. This anticipates the dilemma posed in modern times by existentialism and, later, poststructuralism.

255 Maximus the Confessor, *Disputation*, 5.

256 Ibid., 9.

257 McFarland, "Willing", 8.

258 Maximus the Confessor, *Disputation*, 10; PG 91.292D-293A.

259   PYRRHUS: Virtues, then are natural things?

   MAXIMUS: Yes, natural things.

   PYRRHUS: If they be natural things, why do they not exist in all men equally, since all men have an identical nature?

   MAXIMUS: But they do exist equally in all men because of the identical nature ...[though] we do not all practice what is natural to an equal degree.

   Ibid., 32-33

Clearly, then Maximus is not offering us a monadic view of natural will which obliterates the distinction between individuals.[260] As expressions of our humanity, we live out the will which we possess. Yet how does this apply to Christ? More especially, what relation is there between the *logos/tropos* distinction in Christ's humanity and divinity? Is the Son a mode of divine will, and does the he make *choices* out of his divine will in the same way individual humans do?

To give an answer to these very complicated questions, it is important first to recognize a certain ambivalence in Maximus about the way human choosing works.[261] While individual willing might be fundamental to human existence,[262] the current outworking of human willing is, for Maximus, almost entirely negative. Humans were made with a good natural will but an undeveloped *gnomic* will. The original intent was that Adam should learn to align his choices with the will embedded in him so that ultimately, by habit, the two should be fused together[263] – yet the fall led to a corruption in the human *gnomic will*. Hereafter, individuals are plagued by an inability to "think straight", or realize in their choices, the good that still resides in their natural will.[264] Good ends are now pursued by illegitimate means,[265] and the whole of human moral experience becomes characterized by deliberation and decision.

---

260 Whether Maximus is followed by the Sixth Ecumenical Council on this point is a more complex question. Both Alloys Grillmeier and Demetrios Barthrellos observe in the 449 *Tome of Leo* a latent Nestorian tendency to hypostasise the natures as willing subjects; Bathrellos, *Byzantine Christ*, 176-188; Grillmeier, *Christ (vol. 1)*, 536.

261 Maximus is not entirely consistent on whether this deliberating is an aspect of human nature or fallenness. For a helpful survey of his various positions, see McFarland, "Naturally", (esp. 415 n. 23).

262 See J. P. Farrell, *Free Choice in Saint Maximus the Confessor* (South Canaan: Saint Tikhon's Seminary Press, 1989), 114 and McFarland, "Willing", 18.

263 This schema informs but is not explicit in the *Disputation* (though see his comments on asceticism and virtue; on page 33). For a fuller examination of this, including Maximus' distinction between *image* and *likeness* (human constitution as formed by freely exercised discipline), see P. Christou, "Maximus Confessor on the Infinity of Man", in *Maximus Confessor; Acts du Symposium sur Maxime le Confessor, Fribourg, 2-5 September 1980* (Fribourg, Suisse: Éditions Universitaires, 1982) http://www.verujem.org/maksim_ispovednik/panayiotis_christou.htm, (accessed June, 2007) and A. G. Cooper, *The Body in St Maximus: Holy Flesh, Wholly Deified* (Oxford: Oxford University Press, 2005), 97-102.

264 "What happens through the fall is that a perversion of man's capacity for self-determination takes place – not an annihilation – which predisposes man for constant misuse ... That is to say, it forms in man a sinful disposition of will [*gnomie*]"; Lars Thunberg, cited in McFarland, "Naturally", 416n26;

Against this backdrop, Maximus is at pains to stress that the divine person who is enhypostasized[266] has *gnomie* neither in his divine nor human willing. If *gnomie* signifies a hypostatic *divergence* from nature[267] then it is pernicious both to his righteous humanity and his deity.

[I]f free choice is a characteristic of the *hypostasis* of Christ, then by virtue of this will, they cut him off from the Father and Holy Spirit,

---

Andrew Louth helpfully summarises the situation in A. Louth, *Maximus the Confessor. Early Church Fathers* (NewYork: Routledge, 1996), 61:

> [W]ith fallen creatures, their own nature has become opaque to them, they no longer know what they want, and experience coercion in trying to love what cannot give fulfillment. For, in their fallen state, rational creatures are no longer aware of their true good, which is God. Various apparent goods attract them: they are confused, they need to deliberate and consider and their way of willing [at a personal level] shares in all this.

Maximus himself, in his *Letter 2: On love* (ibid., 87) writes that

> [the Devil] has separated us in our inclinations from God and from one another .... He has divided nature at the level of mode of existence, fragmenting it into a multitude of opinions and imaginations.

265 Following Daniel Jones we might find a helpful example in the case of a thief who believes his thieving will be *good* for him. The fact that he looks for the good indicates that his nature is still intact, yet everything after that aspiration to the good is awry. The choices he makes to secure good things – in other words, the mode in which the desire for good is deployed – lead to disaster. D. Jones, *Synergy in Christ According to Saint Maximus the Confessor,* (2005) http://energeticprocession.files.wordpress.com/2007/02/synergy-in-christ-according-to-saint-maximus-the-confessor.doc, (accessed March, 2007), 9.

266 By *"enhypostasis"* I mean the neo-Chalcedonian doctrine (common to Byzantine theologians such as Maximus and the two Leontii of Jerusalem and Byzantium) that the person of the Logos becomes the personhood of the (otherwise anhypostasic) man Jesus Christ. See Bathrellos, *Byzantine Christ,* 94.

267 "[I]t was only this difference of gnomic wills that introduced into our lives sin and our separation from God. For evil consists in nothing else than this difference of our gnomic will from the divine will" – *Opuscule 3* 56B in Louth, *Maximus,* 197 – or;

> It is important to note here that while Maximus tends to reserve the terminology of gnomic will for fallen humanity, other Medieval theologians do not have the same qualms about simply identifying it with the personal occurrence of natural will in a hypostasis. Demetrios Bathrellos traces this usage in Pseudo-Cyril and John of Damascus, concluding that "the rejection of Monothelitism does not mean that a carefully qualified Monothelite *terminology* could not be used in order to express the unity of the two wills and energies of Christ.

Bathrellos, *Byzantine Christ,* 202-207.

making him different [from them] in will and thought. For that which is ascribed to the Son hypostatically, [that is] in a distinctive way, is certainly not shared by the Father and Spirit.[268]

Similar logic applies to the way Maximus understands the obedience of Christ. Echoing Gregory Nazianzen, Maximus insists that the words of Philippians 2 – that Christ "became obedient to death ... of the cross" – must apply

> not in his deity but in his humanity for neither obedience nor disobedience are proper to the deity, according to the Fathers. For these things are appropriate to those in an inferior position, and under subjection.[269]

And again;

> He thus delights to do the will of the Father, not according to his deity, but according to his humanity, for the Father's will is also his will, since he is also God by essence.[270]

Maximus' line of argumentation here is clear. Since the divine will is a function of the Son's nature, he possesses it not, as it were, through inter-personal *communication* with the Father but naturally. He cannot in this sense be called "obedient".

Once again, however, this does not mean that there is no *taxis* in the possession and employment of this will. While Maximus repudiates the idea of an errant *gnomic* will amongst the persons he nonetheless affirms a modality in the divine will. There *are* three "willing persons" sharing the same natural wants. Thus, Louth argues, Maxmimus warns against the "collapse of theology [into]Arian polytheism, Sabellian atheism, and a pagan kind of Godhead that fights against itself".[271]

But (in the same *Opuscule*) Maximus also writes that

> if there is one will of the triad beyond being, there will be a Godhead with three names and a single person (μονοπρόσθπος ἔσται Θεότης τριώνυμος).[272]

Maximus' way of understanding the hypostatic modalities of the divine will is completely consistent with the Cappadocian scheme (albeit more developed).

---

268 *Theologia et Polemica* PG 91.29B-C cf. translation in Farrell, *Free Choice,* 118.
269 Maximus the Confessor, *Disputation,* 45.
270 Ibid., 45.
271 Louth, *Maximus,* 196; PG 91.53B.
272 *Opuscule 3* in ibid., 195; PG 91.52B.

The Father is orginator or designer of the economy; the Son and Spirit are its effectors. As he writes in *The Chapters On Knowledge*:

> Just as the human word which proceeds naturally from the mind is messenger of the secret movements of the mind, so does the Word of God, who knows the father by essence as Word knows the Mind which has begotten it (since no created being can approach the Father without him), reveal the Father whom he knows. As the Word of God by nature, he is spoken of as the "messenger of the great plan of God".
>
> The great plan of God the Father is the secret and unknown mystery of the dispensation which the only begotten Son revealed by fulfilling in the incarnation, thus becoming a messenger of the great plan of God the eternal Father. The one who knows the meaning of the mystery and who is so incessantly lifted up both in work and in word through all things until he acquires what is sent down to him is likewise a messenger of the great plan of God.[273]

In these stanzas we see more of the outlines of Maximus' thinking. On the one hand, the Word knows "by essence"; on the other hand, as communicator he is "messenger". The first signals that the Son's knowledge of the Father is natural since he possesses it, not *subsequent* to his being, but *along with it* as he receives the essence. Yet at the same time, in the incarnation, this "begotten" knowledge gives rise to the mission in a way that can be cast in interpersonal terms, as signified by the word "messenger". Maximus shows us what we have seen with other Fathers – that there is a congruence or "fit" between the way the eternal *hypostases* exist according to their *tropoi* and what takes place in the economy.[274]

But Maximus also takes us a step further. The final sentence in the quote above, where he writes of humans being "likewise" messengers of God's plan, is indicative of a special affinity between the Word of God and humanity. The Son as *Logos* is held to be the eternal source of the *logoi* of humans (and every

---

[273] Translation from G. C. Berthold, *Maximus Confessor: Selected Writings. Classics of Western Spirituality* (New York: Paulist Press, 1985), 152.

Maximus the Confessor, *Disputation*, 41; translation from ibid., 152.

A similar statement occurs in the *Disputation with Pyrrhus* he argues that " ... the incarnation was the work of the divine will alone, of the good pleasure of the Father, the Son accomplishing it in himself, and the Holy Spirit cooperating"; Maximus the Confessor, *Disputation,* 41

[274] Maximus describes the incarnate Logos as a composite or synthetic *hypostasis* (ὑπόστασις σύνθετος) in that the one person is fully possessed of two distinct natures; PG 91.204, 491, 517, 529, 555. Schönborn paraphrases the event which gives rise to this as that in which the "mode of his being God becomes the mode of his being man"; von Schönborn, *God's Human Face,* 114.

other nature): the Logos *contains* the logoi as blueprints[275] or ideas of creation,[276] so that in this sense our eschatological conformity to *our* logos will be a confirmation of Christ's centrality.

> The *logoi* of all the separated and partial things are contained ... by the *logoi* of the universal and generic; the *logoi* of the most generic and most universal things are held together by wisdom, and those of partial things, variously held fast in those generic ones are contained by sagacity ... [But] the Wisdom and Sagacity of God the Father is the Lord Jesus Christ who both holds together the universals of beings by the power of wisdom, and contains their fulfilling parts by the sagacity of thought.[277]

Under this framework, both humans and the Son draw their action or grounding from the Father. The grand plan of God is for there to be a single principle and a single movement in operation throughout all reality. Both created beings *and* the *hypostases* of the Son and Spirit can in this sense be seen in the same light. As Maximus writes in *Ad Thalassium 2*:

> [God] is bringing about the assimilation of particulars to universals until he might unite creatures' own voluntary inclination to the more universal natural principle of rational being through the movement of these particular creatures toward well being, and make them harmonious and self-moving in relation to each other and to the whole universe. In this way there shall be no divergence between universals and particulars. Rather one and the same principle shall be observable throughout the universe, admitting no differentiation by the individual modes according to which created beings are predicated, and displaying the grace of God effective to deify the universe. It is on the basis of this grace that the

---

275 Thanks to Daniel Jones for this helpful image: see Jones, "Synergy in Christ", 12.

276 In *Amb. 7* the *logoi* are described variously as potentialities (1081A), predeterminations or products of the divine will (1085A). See Blowers & Wilken, *Cosmic Mystery*, 57, 61.

277 Louth, *Maximus,* 161. Or similarly:

> [The believer] will also know that the many *logoi* are the one Logos to whom all things are related and who exists in himself without confusion, the essentially and individually distinctive God, the Logos of God the Father. He is the beginning and cause of all things in whom all things were created, in heaven and on earth, visible and invisible ... Because he held together in himself the *logoi* before they came to be, by his gracious will he created all things visible and invisible out of non-being.
>
> *Amb.* 7 (PG 1080A); P. M. Blowers & R. L. Wilken, *On the Cosmic Mystery of Jesus Christ: Selected Writings from St. Maximus the Confessor: Popular Patristics Series* (Crestwood: St. Vladimir's Seminary Press, 2004), 54-55.

divine Logos, when he became man, said, "My Father is working even now, and I am working" (Jn. 5:17). The Father approves this work, the Son properly carries it out (ὁ μὲν, εὐδοκιαν ὁ δε, αὐτουργῶν), and the Holy Spirit essentially completes both the Father's approval of it all and the Son's execution of it, in order that the God in Trinity might be "through all and in all things" [Eph. 4:6], contemplated as the whole reality proportionately in each individual creature as it is deemed worthy by grace, and in the universe altogether, just as the soul naturally indwells both the whole of the body and each individual part without diminishing itself.[278]

Thus, just as the *logoi* of particulars and universals are encompassed in the Logos, so now it is that same Logos who moves all *logoi* toward their goal (which is him) – while he himself finds *his principle* in the Father. Both humans and the Logos himself are grounded in the same ultimate principle.[279]

Maximus is, we should note, scarcely the first to draw strong connections between the eternal and necessary participation of the Son and the contingent *ad extra* participation of created beings in God. Earlier thinkers such as Clement and Irenaeus or, (later) Origen and Marius Victorinus, also see humanity's imaging of God as related specifically to the Logos who is the true and eternal image.[280] Indeed, the doctrine of participation is crucial even to Athanasius,[281] who speaks of God creating humans according to the Logos and

---

278 Translation in Blowers & Wilken, *Cosmic Mystery,* 99-100; PG 90.272 B-C.

279 We might also reiterate that in the incarnation, both the human willing and divine willing are hypostatically united in the same *person:* "To profess about Christ that his natures are not without their proper existence ... does not mean creating several *hypostases* or acting subjects; rather it means, in line with the orthodox faith, affirming their existences and their essential and proper activities"; PG 91, 205BC, translation from von Schönborn, *God's Human Face,* 116.

280 Irenaeus describes humanity as created after the Image of God (the Logos) such that the coming of the Son is both a self-revelation and a restoration/fulfillment of humanity; see *Adversus Haereses* 3.18.1, 3.22.3 5.16.1. For the other Fathers mentioned see A. Nichols, *Light from the East: Authors and Themes in Orthodox Theology* (London: Sheed & Ward, 1999), 172ff.; Anatolios, *Athanasius: The Coherence of his Thought,* 56-57; and A. Louth & M. Conti, *Genesis 1-11.* vol. 1. *Ancient Christian Commentary on Scripture* ed. Thomas C. Oden (Downers Grove: IVP, 2001), 27.

281 Of course Athanasius generally contrasts the Son's connection to the Father with creaturely "participation" (eg. "He is the Father's Power and Wisdom and Word, not being so by participation" *Contra Gentes* 46.8; NPNF 2.4.29); cf. T. G. Weinandy, *Athanasius: A Theological Introduction. Great Theologians Series* (Aldershot: Ashgate, 2007), 23-24. But this only because the terminology of μετοχή has been deployed by the Arians to designate a contingent partial and

then remaking them into the form of the same true Image through the incarnation and atonement:

> For by men's means it was impossible, since they are but made after an image; nor by angels either, for not even they are (God's) images. Therefore the Word of God came in his own person, that, as he was the Image of the Father, he might be able to create afresh the man after the image. ... he took, in natural fitness, a mortal body, so that while death might in it be once for all done away, men made after his image might once more be renewed. None other then was sufficient for this need, save the Image of the Father.[282]

This special relationship between the Logos and humanity – whether described under the terms Exemplarist,[283] Participationist,[284] Stoic,[285] Platonic, Middle-Platonic,[286] Neoplatonic,[287] Irenaean,[288] Franciscan[289] or simply Biblical[290] – will come to be seen as more important as we progress.[291]

---

    external relationship. In *CA* 1.5.16 he speaks at length in these terms, stating that "to be participated (εἶναι μετέχεσθαι) is the same as to beget" (PG 26.45A).

282 *DeInc*. 13.7-9; NPNF 2.4.42.

283 T. Tollefsen, *The Christocentric Cosmology of St Maximus the Confessor. Oxford Early Christian Studies* (Oxford: Oxford University Press, 2008), 21-27.

284 Ibid., 190-193; W. Jenkins, *Ecologies of Grace: Environmental Ethics and Christian Theology* (Oxford: Oxford University Press, 2008), 191-192.

285 Anatolios, *Athanasius: The Coherence of his Thought*, 4.

286 Ibid. 4.

287 C. Elsee, *Neoplatonism in Relation to Christianity; An Essay* (Cambridge: Cambridge University Press, 1908), 104-106, or F. C. Copleston, *A History of Philosophy*, 9 volumes (Tunbridge Wells: Burns & Oates, 1999), 27-28.

288 K. Anatolios "The Influence of Irenaeus on Athanasius" in *Studia Patristica Vol. XXXVI - Critica et Philologica, Nachleben, First Two Centuries, Tertulian to Arnobius, Egypt before Nicaea, Athanasius and his Opponents (Paperback)*, ed. E. A. Livingstone (Leuven: Peeters, 2000) or Z. Hayes, *The Gift of Being: A Theology of Creation. New theology Studies* (Collegeville: Liturgical Press, 2001), 102-103. However Hayes detects the theme as early as the *Shepherd of Hermas;* Anatolios, *Influence*, 101.

289 I. Delio, "Revisiting the Franciscan doctrine of Christ", *Theological Studies* 64.11 (March 1, 2003): 3-23.

290 Meijering, *Platonism*, 43.

291 My convention from this point will be to prefer the terms *exemplarism* and *participationism*: the first because it emphasises the person or filiality of the Son as that from which creation is derived; the second because it refers to the same scheme from the aspect of those derived from (thereby participating in) him.

Meanwhile, however, we should caution that Maximus is not saying that the Son is contingent or derivative in the same way as created things. The language of the Father *approving* and the Son *performing* may sound in this context, like one person telling the other what to do; but we have also seen the same language used to describe the modality of the persons. The Son does not (1) exist and then (2) receive instruction from the Father. Any truly heteronomous hearing and *choosing* the Father's will would sever the Son from the Father's nature,[292] or signify a movement or development in God that would be equally anathema.[293] The Son always has the same will as the Father in that he has the same nature.

A Question Concerning Divine Decision Making

How then, we might ask, does God make decisions? Already we have seen that, for Maximus, "natural will" can only be *actualised* as "willing" or "choosing" by hypostases:

> The ability to will and the [mode of] willing (πεφύκνει θέλει, καί θέλειν) are not the same, and the ability to speak and speaking are not the same either. For the ability to speak exists always [in man] by nature, but [man] does not always speak, for the former belongs to essence and is held by the *logos* of nature, whereas the latter belongs to deliberative desire (Βουλή), and is modeled by the [*gnomie*] of him who speaks; therefore the ever-existing ability to speak belongs to nature, but

---

Where I refer to the same general scheme under the heading "Neoplatonist", I will distinguish it from the "classical" form which makes creation a natural outgrowth (as opposed to a free production) of God. See A. Hunt, *The Trinity: Insights from the Mystics* (Collegeville: Liturgical Press, 2010), 55.

292   That is, it would signify a before and after in the Son's possession of the divine will in an Arian sense. If will is natural then "there was once when he willed not" is the same as "there was once when he was not". See again his stipulation that allocating free choice to the hypostasis severs him from the Father and Spirit;

Theologia et Polemica 29B-C.

In contrast, humans do exercise free will in their surrender to God;

> Do not be disturbed ... I have no intention of denying free will. Rather I am speaking of a firm and steadfast disposition, a willing surrender, so that from the one whom we have received being we long to receive being moved as well.

Amb. 7 (PG 91.1076B) Blowers & Wilken, *Cosmic Mystery*, 52.

293   "For it belongs to God alone to be the end and completion and the impassible. God is unmoved and complete and impassible"; *Amb. 7* (PG 91.1073B) ibid., 50. c.f. (1069B) Note the contrast with the previous quote from PG 1076B.

the mode of speaking belongs to the *hypostasis,* and the same goes for the ability to will (πεφυκέναι θέλειν) and the [mode of] willing (θέλειν) ... the former belongs to the essence, whereas the latter to the deliberative desire of the willer.[294]

Thus natural will forms the "wants" and the *ability* to choose; but it is only persons who *experience* wanting and *exercise* choice. Does this not mean that if God is to make free choices then these choices must be made at a hypostatic level? It will not do to invent a *super-mode,* as if God were able to choose as "The Trinity" – Maximus has already described this above as a God with one person and three names.[295] Nor will it suffice to argue that the single nature can only ever suggest one course of action, such that the three persons would always agree. Maximus has clearly indicated that God is *free* in his willing[296] – that he is able to choose between equal goods. Thus, the *logoi* are described as predeterminations (προορισμοί) or divine "wills" (θεῖα θελήματα).[297] God's dealings with the world are by grace; he is under no moral obligation to make the world, nor constrained to make it in any particular way.

> God would not be a creator were he deprived of a natural will and activity; if it is true that he made heaven and earth willingly and not drawn by any necessity, if David speaks the truth in the Spirit, "The Lord made all things he wanted in heaven and on earth, in the seas and in all the depths" (Ps 135:6).[298]

---

294 *Opuscule 3*; Bathrellos, *Byzantine Christ,* 162, cf. PG 91.48A-B.

To anticipate the discussion of our next chapter, the same contention is made by Thomas Aquinas who cites Aristotle to the effect that actions cannot be attributed to natures but only persons/*supposita*; *Summa* 3.20.1.

295 *Opuscule 3* 52B in Louth & Conti, *Genesis,* 195.

296 See Balthasar's discussion of Maximus' opposition to all forms of pantheism; von Balthasar, *Cosmic Liturgy,* 124-125. On the contrast between Maximus and Origen's theory of eternal/necessary creation see Jones, "Synergy in Christ".

297 *Amb. 7* (PG 91.1085A) c.f. Cooper, *Body in Maximus,* 92-93. Paul Jungwirth, in an excellent online essay, notes the distinction here between the singular will of God and the plurality of God's "wills", concluding that the *logoi* must be seen as "decisions" of the will; P. Jungwirth, *Maximus Study Guide,* http://9stmaryrd.com/shared/st_maximus_intro.pdf, (accessed April, 2007), 3.

298 Berthold, *Maximus,* 20. See too, Thunberg & Allchin, *Microcosm,* 81. There is admittedly some difficulty here, given the range of meanings given to *"logoi"* by Maximus. In the *Chapters on Knowledge,* Maximus distinguishes between those works which he began to create and those he did not:

> The works of God which did not happen to begin in time are [those] in which participated beings share according to grace, for example, goodness and all that the term goodness implies ... For all virtue is without beginning,

This question of how God makes these decisions is never explicitly addressed by Maximus; yet his theological framework suggests a solution nonetheless. If each of the persons equally partakes of the one divine will, and that same natural will can accommodate a plurality of divine courses of action, then it might be that the person of the Father "chooses" and the person of the Son "obeys" or executes a particular course of action (see *Figure 1*). This possibility retains the distinction between human obedience and filial; for whilst human obedience moves the created person from without, in accordance with divine intentionality, Filial obedience sees the Son moved to do what *already lies within him* (ie. by the natural will he shares with the Father). Thus, the Son who has the Father's will by virtue of begetting, might also receive instruction on *which* natural good to pursue from the Father's *hypostasis*. We can see an hints of this in the later Palamite concept of divine energies which designate the free *determination* of the Trinity as regards the eternal ideas.[299] .

Such a hypostatic willing may appear to open the door to tritheism or a schism in the Trinity – what if the Father should wish to pursue one option and the Son another? Yet, here again, Maximus presents us with a solution in his conception of human will in the eschaton. In the final state of Christians in the *eschaton*, our *gnomic willing* will be so aligned with God that our

---

>   not having any time previous to itself. Such things have God alone as the eternal begetter of their being.
>
>   Berthold, *Maximus*, 136-137
>
>   Here, it would seem, there is a necessity about the *logoi* in that they participate in God himself – although the fact that Maximus speaks of them in terms of "grace" seems to imply that even here there is divine freedom. At the other extreme, *logoi* inhere in accidentals such as colour and shape, which God clearly does not have and which would seem therefore to be freely assigned. Cf. M. Törönen, *Union and Distinction in the Thought of St. Maximus the Confessor. Oxford Early Christian Studies* (Oxford: Oxford University Press, 2007), 43.

299 See the helpful explorations of the Byzantine (and earlier!) distinction between divine essence and willing in , 237-239 and J. Meyendorff, *Byzantine Theology: Historical Trends and Doctrinal Themes,* 1st edition (New York: Fordham University Press, 1974), 131-132.

>   Much more could be written about this topic and the debate over whether Maximus' *logoi* theory corresponds to Gregory Palamas' concept of energies. Since some *logoi* are derived from God's eternal goods (recapitulated in the Logos), they are in a real sense "divine" – which seems to fit well with the Palamite theory of eternal energies which are God yet not his essence (see, for example, Lossky, *Mystical Theology,* 67ff). However, as van Rossum helpfully observes, "Palamas' theology is in fact a *doctrine of God* while Maximus' doctrine of the λόγοι deals with the *world* which is anchored and rooted in God"; J. van Rossum "The Logoi of Creation and the Divine 'Energies' in Maximus the Confessor and Gregory Palamas" in *Papers Presented at the Eleventh International Conference on Patristic Studies, 1991,* ed. E. A. Livingstone (Leuven: Peeters, 1993), 216.

free will ... will surrender voluntarily to God and will have been taught to refrain from willing anything other than what God wills. ... [As] a seal conforms to the stamp against which it is pressed, and has neither desire nor capability to receive an impression from something else, or to put it forthrightly, it does not want to.[300]

Similarly

[O]ur manifold and natural diversities converge into one ... no being will continue to possess motion that is aimless and deprived of his presence. It is with respect to this presence and by our reference to the goal of the divine plan that we are called "gods" (John 10:35) and "children" (John 1:12) and "body" (Eph. 1:23).[301]

Figure 1. A model for triune decision-making

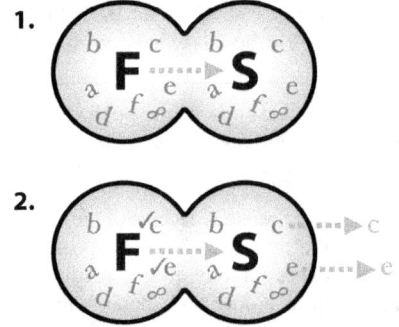

1. The Son's birth from the Father in eternity includes the full array of logoi *(later* rationes *or* ideas*) associated with the essential will (a-∞).-*

2. The Father freely decides which logoi *to deploy contingently, giving rise and shape to salvation history. The Son receives and enacts the Father's decision.*

- In some schemes the logoi might be shown around the Son only, on the theory that they are "in the Logos" and the Father possesses them solely in him. This might raise questions about the Father's personal sufficiency but would not trouble this scheme.

Maximus is here speaking of how human hypostases will be characterized. Why could the same not also be said of the *hypostasis* of the Son: that for all

---

300 *Amb. 7*; Blowers & Wilken, *Cosmic Mystery,* 52; cf. PG 91.1092C.

301 *Amb. ad Iohannem* quoted in Cooper, *Body in Maximus,* 109.

eternity he not only possesses the Father's will naturally, but delights to conform to the Father's choices from within that will? Such an extrapolation from Maximus' scheme seems immune to the objections he otherwise raises against *gnomic* willing in the Godhead, and aligns with Maximus' own way of understanding volition.

Conclusion

From this brief examination of Dyothelitic theology, it should now be clear that it is far too simple to assert that the unity of divine will signifies an outright repudiation of ST. The natural will, as Maximus explains it, is expressed *through* the diversity of the *tropoi*, and the *tropos* that *is* the Logos is expressed through the human willing of Christ. There is no need for us to reject the distinct subjectivity of the second person of the Godhead, nor to divide his subjectivity from that of Jesus. Applying the pronouncements of Constantinople III to John 6:38 ("I have come down from heaven, not do do my own will, but the will of him who sent me"), Joseph Ratzinger observes:

> Here it is the divine Logos who is speaking, and he speaks of the human will of the man Jesus as his will, the will of the Logos. ... There are not two "I"s in him, but only one. The Logos speaks in the I-form of the human will and mind of Jesus; it has become his I, has been adopted into his I, because the human will is completely one with the will of the Logos. United with the latter, it has become a pure Yes to the Father's will. [302]

Finally, as we have just seen, it may be that Maximus' theory of eternal *logoi* might actually necessitate - a *stronger* view of the divine persons. If we take his passing comments about decision – making seriously then God's freedom as regard creation implies a person or persons choosing to create.

---

302 J. C. Ratzinger, *Behold the Pierced One,* trans. G. H. Ignatius (San Francisco: Ignatius Press, 1986), 39. Ratzinger argues that the natural/tropical model represents a "central distinction which is fundamental to the Council" and to the thought of Maximus, and allows the admission of "much that had been regarded as Monophysite"; ibid., 39-40, n. 18.

Chapter 3

Is Intra-Trinitarian Willing Possible after Augustine?

> Augustine introduces a tendency to draw apart the being of God – what he is eternally – and his act – what he does in time ... the drive is to treat God unipersonally, with his personhood located in his oneness not his threeness. ... [T]he way God meets us in time as Father, Son and Spirit is at best secondary to the way we are to understand that he really is, in himself.
>
> – Colin Gunton[303]

Introduction

Thus far I have shown that a commitment to the primacy of the Father is a central and persistent feature of early orthodoxy. I have repeatedly illustrated the contention that Fathers see a correspondence between the Son's eternal mode of subsistence and his life and obedience as a man. Yet for many modern scholars, such demonstrations merely confirm the difference and diversity between East and West. The argument goes that Eastern trinitarianism *typically* begins with the plurality of the Godhead (possibly even signifying something like ST) while the West's emphasis is on the oneness of God – leading to the conclusion that, whatever I might be able to prove as regards Maximus or, say, the Cappadocians, has little bearing on matters west of the Danube.

In this chapter, I will test this theory and indicate both its strengths and weaknesses. I will provide evidence that, despite genuine developments wrought in the West, the basic pattern of pro-Nicene theology remains. I will show that Augustine's heirs remain very interested in the diversity of the divine persons (and their modes of willing), and that they retain the belief that redemptive history exemplifies the life of God *ad intra*. Finally, I will briefly examine a couple of important scholastic opinions concerning divine *contingent* action, and suggest how a more genuinely social model of the triune willing (RITW) might serve their aims.

---

303 C. E. Gunton, *The Promise of Trinitarian theology,* 2nd edition (Edinburgh: T&T Clark, 2003), 4.

The Complaint Against the West

To ask questions concerning the relationship between the obedience of Christ and divine filiality is to join a much wider modern discussion concerning the right and wrong ways to begin thinking about the triune God. Since the 1967 publication of Karl Rahner's seminal monograph *The Trinity* – with its *Grundaxiom* that "the economic Trinity is the immanent"[304] – there has been a steady, indeed growing, swathe of articles and books on this topic.

Many of these, along with Rahner himself, connect the issue of economic/immanent commensurability to the viability of trinitarian doctrine itself.[305] They argue that the Augustinian and Thomist-influenced tradition of Western Christendom squandered its pro-Nicene heritage by beginning with the unity of God (*De Deo Uno*) instead of the diversity of the persons.[306] With

---

304 Rahner, *Trinity*, 22-23; (1967 is the date of the German edition).

> I should clarify at this point that I am taking Rahner as *expressivist* rather than Hegelian. That is, I believe that he is arguing for a congruence between the economic and immanent Trinity, not that the immanent Trinity arises from history.

305 > [T]he Augustinian-Western conception of the Trinity, as contrasted with the Greek conception ... begins with the one God, the one divine essence as a whole, and only afterwards does it see God as three in persons ... if one starts from the basic Augustinian-Western conception, an a-trinitarian treatise "on the one God" comes as a matter of course before the treatise on the Trinity".

> Ibid., 17.

> See K. Rahner, *Theological Investigations*, trans. C. Ernst. vol. 1, 23 volumes (London: Longman & Todd, 1961), 146-148. It should also be noted, as Timothy Lee Smith reminds us, that Karl Barth made the same observation on the connection between the immanent and economic Trinity thirty years before Rahner in CD 1.1.382; T. L. Smith, *Thomas Aquinas' Trinitarian Theology: A Study in Theological Method* (Washington: Catholic University of America Press, 2003), 6. n.17. Fergus Kerr observes the same critique directed at Aquinas in a 1951 work from Hans Urs von Balthasar; F. Kerr, *After Aquinas: Versions of Thomism* (Oxford: Blackwell, 2002), 183.

306 So Colin Gunton (see above); Gunton, *Promise*, 4. Similar comments occur in LaCugna:

> Trinitarian doctrine after Augustine concerned itself with the relations internal to the Godhead, largely disjoined from what we know of God through Christ in the Spirit. Medieval Latin theology, following Augustine and reaching its high point in Thomas Aquinas, solidified the whole trend toward separating the theology of God from the economy of salvation by treating *De Deo Uno* and *De Deo Trino* as discrete treatises.

> LaCugna, *God for Us*, 10.

essentialism elevated over *personalism*,[307] and with simple monotheism displacing the God revealed through Jesus Christ[308] – the Trinity was ultimately reduced to a postscript so that it could be safely excised without making any significant difference at all.[309]

Yet this often-repeated rendition of trinitarian theology (dubbed *Rahnerian* henceforth in this work, though it extends beyond him) is not without its problems. Leaving aside for now the difficulties raised by Rahner's identification of economy with immanence, the historical generalisations which form the foundation of his thesis, look less sure than they once did. In recent years, Rahner and those who follow his lead have come in for some severe criticism,[310] with the paradigm of "East vs. West" regarded as too easy – too facile with regard to complexity and diversity,[311] and too unaware of historical

---

For a critical, but admirably careful, response to both Rahner and LaCugna on this point see H. Rikhof "Aquinas' Authority in the Contemporary Theology of the Trinity" in *Aquinas as Authority: A Collection of Studies Presented at the Second Conference of the Thomas Instituut te Utrecht, December 14-16, 2000*, ed. P. v. Geest, H. J. M. J. Goris & C. Leget. *Publications of the Thomas Instituut te Utrecht* (Leuven: Peeters, 2002).

307 By "personalism", I mean the idea that the persons themselves are the primary object of thought as regards God (an idea often wistfully associated with Cappadocian theology), while "essentialism" conversely looks first to the triune essence. For a fairly strident depiction of the East/West division along these lines see S. N. Bulgakov, *The Comforter*, trans. B. Jakim (Grand Rapids: Eerdmans, 2004), 59-60.

308 See Catherine Mowry LaCugna especially on this point; LaCugna, *God for Us*, 81ff.

309 "Despite their orthodox confession Christians are, in their practical life, almost mere 'monotheists'" Rahner, *Trinity*, 10. See a survey of similar comments in O'Collins, *Holy Trinity*, 1-2.

310 Andrew Louth observes that there is "a growing consensus in patristic scholarship that this characterization of the differences between Latin West and Greek East is little more than a caricature"; A. Louth, review of *Persons in Communion: Trinitarian Description and Human Participation* by A. Torrance, *Heythrop Journal* 42.4, (2001): 529-530. In the case of Augustine, Lewis Ayers vindicates Louth's claim by stringing a list of like minds including: F. Bourassa, J. Arnold, B. Studer, M. Löhrer, R. Williams, T. J. Van Bavel and J. Milbank; L. Ayres "The Fundamental Grammar of Augustine's Trinitarian Theology" in *Augustine and his Critics: Essays in Honour of Gerald Bonner*, ed. R. Dodaro & G. Lawless (London: Routledge, 2000), 71 n. 3. The list would be much longer still if it were to be compiled today.

311 For an excellent survey of the East/West issue through the eyes of contemporary scholarship see A. G. Roeber, "Western, Eastern, or Global Orthodoxy? Some Reflections on St. Augustine of Hippo in Recent Literature", *Pro Ecclesia* 16 (2008): 210-223.

developments in both East and West. Counter arguments press that Augustine's opponents have mis-read him (or not read him)[312] – indeed that the West's critics have generally *wilfully abused* their sources;[313] that the East is equally implicated in the retreat from trinitarianism;[314] that it is neo-scholasticism and not Augustine or Thomas themselves who should be blamed for the West's putative modalism;[315] and so on.

The issues associated with the Rahnerian critique are not entirely new to us by this stage. In Chapter 1 I observed, tested – and found somewhat wanting – the fashion amongst patristic scholars that would characterise the development of orthodoxy as a progress away from the causal priority of the Father, toward the idea that God is that *within which* the persons subsist. In Rahnerian terms, this view of the Trinity that I challenged is the typically "Western model", and we saw that it *is* actually different from pro-Nicene orthodoxy. Thus far, then, with Rahner and against his critics.[316]

But now there is another question to ask. If that which has been labeled Western is different from pro-Nicene theology, whom *does it represent* beyond modern (largely Western) scholars? Is it really *Western* at all? Already we have seen in Ambrose that there is something like it in his reluctance to connect divine filiality to the incarnation; but we also observed that he remains ardently committed to the idea of paternal causality in the *opera ad intra*. How does this position compare with Ambrose's more famous disciple, Augustine? Is the great fountainhead of Western Christianity guilty, as charged by his critics?[317]

---

312 M. R. Barnes, "Augustine in Contemporary Trinitarian Theology", *Theological Studies* 56.2 (1995): 237-250. Barnes observes the diminished set of texts used in modern studies of Augustine – in particular the absence of reference to the saint's polemical works such as *CMax*. (to which I will refer below).

313 Roeber, "Western Eastern", 218 (relying on Barnes).

314 LaCugna, *God for Us,* 181-205.

315 Barnes notes the influence of modern anti-Nicene French Augustinians such Henri Paissac and André Malet; Barnes, "Augustine". Ayres indicates a still earlier "rise of anti-trinitarian thought in the seventeenth and eighteenth cent"; Ayres, *Nicaea,* 407 n. 46. LaCugna observes that the Rahner critique is "truer of neo-Thomism and manual theologies than of Thomas himself"; (LaCugna, *God for Us,* 168) – (Herwi Rikhof expresses frustration that LaCugna appears not to remember this when conducting her research more generally; Rikhof, *Aquinas' Authority*, 230).

316 And it is interesting to note that a number of those who champion the "Western" version of pro-Nicene theology (see for example Lewis Ayres and Michel René Barnes) are also those who critique the East West division as presented by Rahner.

317 Besides those already cited, other critics include Paul M. Collins (P. M. Collins, *Trinitarian Theology, West and East: Karl Barth, the Cappadocian Fathers and John Zizioulas* (Oxford: Oxford University Press, 2001)), J.P. Mackey, David Brown and John O'Donnell – cf. Barnes, "Augustine".

And what of the Medieval scholastics who followed in Augustine's train? Was their much-condemned systematising and speculation a further blow to a truly personalist trinitarianism?

Obviously a full response to these arguments is beyond the scope of this thesis. But we should undertake *some* examination of the matter. If the Rahnerian theory is thoroughly debunked, then RITW – which is invested in a particular aspect of the economic/immanent debate – might well be a collateral casualty.[318] On the other hand, if the reality of the matter is more complicated than Rahner *et al.* suggest, then it is important that we try to gain some perspective on that complexity so that we can see how it might align with (or forestall) RITW. These questions are, after all, the very same areas of enquiry we slated as needing further attention at the end of Chapter 1:

Is the triune God to be envisaged as a thing or entity in its own right such that "he" is the basis on which the Father and Son are one? (*Or, in Rahnerian terms: how legitimate and mainstream is essentialism?*)

How does the human nature of Christ relate to the filiality of the Son in terms of its relationship to the Father? (*Is the economic Trinity the immanent Trinity?*)

And, although it fits less easily into the standard Rahnerian debate, we will also find some more interesting leads on our third question: how do the Father and Son make contingent decisions in questions where their natural will allows them more than one option?

---

318   This is especially the case given that Rahner himself makes a passing reference to something that sounds like RITW as he warns against using the concept of the two natures to eliminate obedience from divine filiality:

> May we really say without more ado that from the concept of the Son of the synoptic Jesus we must eliminate his obedience to the Father, his adoration, his submission to the Father's unfathomable will? For we eliminate them when we explain this kind of behaviour in him only through the hypostatic union as such.

Rahner, *Trinity*, 62

See Mark Baddeley on this point too; M. Baddeley, "The Trinity and Subordinationism: A Response to Kevin Giles", *Reformed Theological Review* 63 (2004): 29-42, 37-38.

The Mixed Legacy of Augustine

Despite the formidable rejoinders to the Rahnerian thesis mentioned above[319] – and despite what I myself will say below – I think the critical take on Augustine does embody fundamental truths. Augustine really does sometimes make it sound as if the divine nature itself is a metapersonal subject – a single entity who *just is* the Father, Son and Spirit. His introduction of extrabiblical analogies, which liken the persons to the various internal aspects of an individual human being (memory, understanding and will, self-love and self-knowing, sight and perception and so on),[320] *do* make it more difficult to think of there being real inter-personal exchange between the subsistents. If C.S. Lewis is right to warn that when we change imagery we change religion,[321] then Augustine's introduction of extra-biblical tropes into the bloodstream could only ever lead to a change in the way Westerners imagined God.[322]

More formally, Augustine's rules for speaking about the triune substance ensure the same metapersonalism is injected into the major arteries of the Western tradition.[323] In a formula of speech that was to become enshrined in the

---

319   Eg. Ayres, *Grammar*. For a recent careful and measured response see J. Behr "Augustine and the Legacy of Nicaea" in *Orthodox Readings of Augustine,* ed. G. E. Demacopoulos & A. Papanikolaou (Crestwood: St. Vladimirs Seminary Press, 2008).

320   *DeTrin.* 9-11.

321   C. S. Lewis, *God in the Dock: Essays on Theology and Ethics* (Grand Rapids: Eerdmans, 1970), 237.

322   It is a mark of how ingrained this habit of thought is, that even a modern Westerner who proposes to criticize Augustine and point back to the Eastern model, ends up with the bizarre denial that

> within the Trinity there is no reciprocal "Thou". The Son is the Father's self-utterance which should not in turn be conceived as "uttering", and the Spirit is the "gift" which does not give in its turn. John 17, 21; Gal. 4, 6; Rom. 8, 15 presuppose a *creaturely* starting point for the "Thou" addressed to the Father.

Rahner, *Trinity,* 76 n. 30 (emphasis original)

Catherine Mowry LaCugna's observation that Rahner becomes more muted as he progresses are apposite; LaCugna, *God for Us,* 109.

323   It should be added that, as Thomas Aquinas observes in the prologue of *Contra Errores Graecorum*, the West has a problem with terminology over the polyvalent nature of the word "substance" which might mean *either* signify *hypostasis/suppositum* (hence Boethius', "*individua substantia*" in *Contra Eutychen et Nestorium* 3) or essence. Augustine himself indicates the depth of the problem in a very revealing manner in *De Doctrina Christiana* 1.9: "Each of these [persons] is a full substance and all together are one substance (*singulus quisque horum plena substantia, et simul omnes una substantia*)"; – Augustine, *Doctrina,* 16-17.

Quicunque Vult,³²⁴ and rehearsed *ad infinitum* throughout the Middle Ages, Augustine writes:

> ... whatsoever is said of that most eminent and divine loftiness in respect to itself, is said in respect to substance, but that which is said in relation to anything, is not said in respect to substance, but relatively; and that the effect of the same substance in Father and Son and Holy Spirit is, that whatsoever is said of each in respect to themselves, is to be taken of them, not in the plural in sum, but in the singular. For as the Father is God, and the Son is God, and the Holy Spirit is God, which no one doubts to be said in respect to substance, yet we do not say that the very Supreme Trinity itself is three Gods, but one God. So the Father is great, the Son great, and the Holy Spirit great; yet not three greats, but one great. ... And the Father is good, the Son good, and the Holy Spirit good; yet not three goods, but one good ... the Father is omnipotent, the Son omnipotent, and the Holy Spirit is omnipotent; yet not three omnipotents, but one omnipotent.³²⁵

In one sense of course there is nothing new here. None of Augustine's pro-Nicene predecessors would ever have wanted to say there that the Trinity involved a *plurality* of divinity or goodness or power. Yet this language of *unus magnus ... bonus ... Deus ... omnipotens* gives a quite different impression from that which might have been given by speaking of one *goodness* of *deity* or *omnipotence* shared by three persons.³²⁶ Augustine has reified the essence to the extent that it is both goodness *and* one who is good; omnipotence *and* one who is omnipotent (*Et haec Trinitas unus Deus, solus, bonus, magnus,*

---

324 On the *Quicunque*'s connection to Augustinian theology (rather than Athanasian!) see J. N. D. Kelly, *The Athanasian Creed* (Edinburgh: Adam and Charles Black, 1964), 80-82 and J. Pelikan, *A History of the Development of Doctrine.* vol. 5. *The Christian Tradition,* 5 volumes, paperback edition (Chicago: University of Chicago Press, 1971), 351. The connection however is made abundantly clear upon a reading of *DeTrin.* 5.8.9 and 7.3.4.

325 *DeTrin.* 5.8.9; NPNF 1.3.91, cf. PL 4.917.

326 As John Behr rightly describes it:

> [T]he word "God" *is* being used in a new manner by Augustine; the approach and framework *has* changed ... not that of the "de Régnon paradigm" which alternates between starting with the one substance or three persons. ... It is rather the difference between starting with the one God, who is Father, and beginning with the Father, Son and Spirit who are each, and together, the one God.

Behr, *Augustine Legacy,* 163. (emphasis original).

aeturnus, omnipotens: ipse sibi unitas, deitas, magnitudo, bonitas, aeternitas, omnipotentia.).[327]

As Catherine Mowry LaCugna demonstrates,[328] the Western church was changed by this in both its prayer and praise. This is the same concept of the Trinity-as-a-single-entity that would be attacked by Joachim of Fiore in the thirteenth century and would be defended (and now officially enshrined) in the ensuing Fourth Lateran Council of 1215 – where the Trinity would become a "certain incomprehensible entity" (*quaedam summa res*) which is simultaneously the Father, Son and Spirit individually and together (*veraciter est pater et filius et spiritus sanctus tres simul personae ac sigillatim quaelibet earundem*).[329] David Brown may be right in his warning that this is trinitarianism at its most incoherent;[330] certainly it is Western theology at its most idiosyncratic.

Another point at which I tend to agree with the critics of Augustine is the charge that his way of conceiving the *Imago Dei* inevitably leads to a distancing of the persons of the Godhead from the creation.[331] While, as we saw in the last chapter, earlier Christian thinkers from Irenaeus on see human

---

327 *DeTrin.* 5.11.12; PL 4.919.

328 See Catherine Mowry LaCugna's study revealing the emergence and growth of prayer to the Trinity; LaCugna, *God for Us,* 111ff. Of course LaCugna does not regard Augustine as the only source or influence for Western theology and specifically notes the impact of the struggle against Visigothic Arianism as a catalyst.

329 From G. Alberigo, J. A. Dossetti & P. P. Joannou, *Conciliorum Oecumenicorum Decreta,* (Bologna: Istituto per le Scienza Religiose, 1973) http://ldysinger.stjohnsem.edu/ @magist/1215_Lateran4_ec12/02_lat4_c01-22.htm, (accessed August, 2009). This is not to offer endorsement of Joachim's collectivist Trinitarianism, merely to agree with his diagnosis of the Lombardian *quaternitatem ... communem essentiam*; ibid.

Joachim's position here is prefigured in the nominalist Roscellinus of Compiègne (d. c.1125) whose insistence that the Trinity was *tres res,* occasioned Anselm's *De Incarnatione Verbi.* Roscellinus presents a classic anticipation of modern social trinitarianism, pressing that we are forced to choose between a Trinity of distinct individuals with an agreement of wills (tritheism to the Synod of Soissons, 1092) or to admit that the Father and Spirit were also incarnate with the Son; see J. Pelikan, *The Growth of Medieval Theology (600-1300).* vol. 3. *The Christian Tradition: A History of the Development of Doctrine,* 5 volumes (Chicago: University of Chicago Press, 1971), 264-266.

330 D. Brown, *The Divine Trinity* (London: Duckworth, 1985), 291.

331 See for example C. E. Gunton "The Doctrine of Creation" in *The Cambridge Companion to Christian Doctrine,* ed. C. E. Gunton. *Cambridge Companions to Religion* (Cambridge: Cambridge University Press, 1997). My criticism is slightly different from Gunton's much fuller treatment though there is a significant overlap.

imaging of God as both protologically and teleologically connected to the second person of the Trinity, Augustine (at least the mature Augustine)[332] prescinds from this tradition with his speculation that the *imago* relates to the way the individual is like (per *vestigia*) the Trinity.

Important implications would flow from this: firstly it would make it harder to see any particular relation between the Son *as Son* and the man Jesus Christ. Formerly there had been a generally uniform conviction that the Old Testament theophanies were the Logos sent by the Father, and (as we have seen) that there was a certain fitness to the Son becoming man. But Augustine erodes these connections. Humans are in the image of the *Trinity* – not in the image of the Son (as per Irenaeus). Nor can Augustine find place for *sonship* in the mediatorial office of the Logos; Christ is mediator solely as man[333] – or sometimes as man in conjunction with his divinity[334] – but not as Son. As to the theophanies, they might involve any of the persons – or even the whole Trinity.[335]

The corollary of this would be the loss of any *real* contact between humans and the persons of the Godhead. For example, in Medieval theology, as it retranscribes Augustine, the relations between the persons of the Godhead pertain *only* to themselves while all that God does in regard to creation is

---

332 It is fairly clear that a different situation exists with the younger Augustine. In his early *Unfinished Literal Commentary on Genesis* (c.394) Augustine agrees with the older interpretation of the *Imago Dei* as mentioned above; (Augustine, *On Genesis*, trans. E. Hill, ed. J. E. Rotelle. *The Works of Saint Augustine* (NY: New City Press, 2002), 148-150). Yet a 426 postscript added to the document just mentioned, observes that, while it is a "sufficient explanation ... insofar as the likeness of God to which man was made can be taken to be the very Word of God, that is to say, the only-begotten Son", nevertheless, "there is a preferable choice of meaning in these divine words ... that man was made to the image, not of the Father alone or of the Son alone or of the Holy Spirit alone, but of the Trinity itself". ibid., 148-151. The same exegesis is set forth without equivocation in his complete *Literal Meaning of Genesis* 19.29, cf. ibid., 233-234.

For a fuller treatment of Augustine's theories of the *Imago* – including similar passages from the *Soliloquies* and *De Vera Religione* see J. E. Sullivan, *The Image of God. The Doctrine of St. Augustine and its Influence* (Dubuque: The Priory Press, 1963), 192-195.

333 See for example, *Confessions* 43.68; *Tractate* 82.4, 105.7, 121.4. See discussion in S. Edmondson, *Calvin's Christology* (Cambridge: Cambridge University Press, 2004), 22-24.

334 Eg. *Tractate* 124.5; *Letter* 137.3, cf. NPNF 1.1.477.

335 *DeTrin.* 2.35. See Scott A Dunham's explanation of how Augustine's logic here seeks to undercut the functional subordination implied in a consistent Father-sends, Son-sent dynamic; S. A. Dunham, *The Trinity and Creation in Augustine* (New York: State University of New York Press, 2009), 32-33.

described as God *simpliciter*. The Logos, therefore, might be described as God's Son – and so might humans (by adoption) too – but this analogical connection is not to be taken to mean that we can participate in *his (the Son's)* relationship with the Father. *Our* Father is not *the* Father but the faceless Trinity itself.[336] We are kept on the outside, beyond the perimeter of divine life.

All these shifts in the tradition wrought by Augustine have significance for this thesis. The more the triune nature is reified, the less room there is for contemplation of the distinct subjectivity and relationships of the individual persons. The more the filial is separated from the human, the less we will be able to see the incarnation as a real episode in the life of the Son.[337]

Augustine as a Pro-Nicene

But Augustine's legacy is by no means monolithic. He may be the source of Western trinitarianism, but to brand him (or Western trinitarianism) as cryptomodalist – the binary opposite of the East – is far too simple. Augustine's psychological analogy of mind, self-knowledge and self-love, for example, *can* be construed as unipersonal. But if the Father is identified as the mind from which the knowledge and love originate (which is how Augustine sees it), then we have something that looks like a hybrid of the old-sun radiance analogy and the true sonship idea – the Logos is now a *mental* reiteration of the Father (echoing *sonship*), *within the one dynamic system* (as in radiance). In Anselm's *Monologion* we see this analogy shaped into birth language,[338] incidentally

---

336 For explanation of this principle in Aquinas see G. Emery, *The Trinitarian Theology of Saint Thomas Aquinas*, trans. F. Murphy (Oxford: Oxford University Press, 2007), 163-168, or for a more critical approach; see T. C. O'Brien's observations in Thomas Aquinas, *Father, Son and Holy Ghost (Ia. 33-43)*, trans. T. C. O'Brien. vol. 7. *Summa Theologiae*, 61 volumes, paperback edition (Cambridge: Cambridge University Press, 2006), 246ff.

337 More on this in chapters 5-6. Meanwhile a relevant example concerning the will of Christ can be found in Hugh of St Victor's short treatise on the "Four Wills of Christ" (*De Quatuor Voluntatibus in Christo*), PL 176.841-846. Despite the promising title, Hugh's analysis boils down to an Antiochene dichotomy of natures (three of the four "wills" are human). Strikingly, Hugh manages to conduct his entire analysis without a single reference to the mode of willing wherein the *person* of the Son possesses and expresses the divine will.

338 Hence, it may be clearly apprehended in the supreme Wisdom, which always thinks of itself, just as it remembers itself, that, of the eternal remembrance of it, its coeternal Word is born. Therefore, as the Word is properly conceived of as the child, the memory most appropriately takes the name of parent. ... The Son is, therefore, the memory of the Father, and the memory of memory, that is, the memory that remembers the Father, who is memory, just as he is the wisdom of the Father, and the wisdom of wisdom, that is, the wisdom wise regarding the wisdom of the Father; and the Son is indeed

giving rise to a vision of the Logos/creation connection that is strongly redolent of that found in Maximus.[339]

A wider examination of Augustine's corpus also reveals that he himself is certainly not wholly wedded to these famous (latterly infamous) analogies and emphases. Augustine's thinking seems to exhibit the same hybridisation as we see in Ambrose; there *is* a unipersonal theme, but then there is also the traditional depiction of Father as ontological *principiuim* the source of the Son. Indeed at points, Augustine stresses this *more* strongly than Ambrose and sounds more like Hilary. In De Trinitate 4.19.26-4.20.29 Augustine dwells at length on the theme that the *modus* of the *opera ad extra* relate to the eternal Son's derivation from the Father without impairing the Son's equality:

> He was not sent in respect to any inequality of power, or substance, or anything that in him was not equal to the Father; but in respect to this, that the Son is from the Father, not the Father from the Son; for the Son is the Word of the Father, which is also called his wisdom. ... he is sent (*movere*), not because he is unequal with the Father, but because he is "a pure emanation (*manatio ... claritatis*) issuing from the glory of the Almighty God". For there, that which issues, and that from which it issues, is of one and the same substance. For it does not issue as water issues from an aperture of earth or of stone, but as light issues from light. (*De Trinitate* 4.20.27)[340]

For Augustine in these verses, the sending of the Son is *not the same* as his begetting; yet it is directly related to the fact of his derivation. "For as to be

---

memory, born of memory, as he is wisdom, born of wisdom, while the Father is memory and wisdom born of none.

Monologion 48, cf. Anselm, *Proslogium; Monologium: An Appendix In Behalf Of The Fool By Gaunilo; And Cur Deus Homo,* trans. S. N. Deane (Chicago: The Open Court Publishing Company, 1903, reprinted 1926) in Anselm, *Medieval Sourcebook: Anselm (1033-1109): Monologium,* http://www.fordham.edu/halsall/basis/anselm-monologium.html, (accessed 2009, August).

339 Anselm explains that the self-utterance of the Word simultaneously gives rise to the creation because the Word contains all the Father's wisdom which is later used to create (*Monologion* 33-34). Wayne Hankey may be correct to see a Dionysius-mediated Neoplatonism here – though Augustine is explicitly claimed as the source in the preface; W. J. Hankey "Dionysius Becomes an Augustinian: Bonaventure's Itinerarium VI" in *Studia Patristica, vol. XXIX, Papers Presented at the Twelfth International Conference on Patristic Studies held in Oxford 1995,* ed. E. A. Livingstone (Louvain: Peeters, 1997), 256.

340 *DeTrin.* 4.20.27; NPNF 1.3.83, cf. PL 42.907.

born, in respect to the Son, means to be from the Father; so to be sent, in respect to the Son, means to be known to be from the Father".[341]

In the earlier *De Fide et Symbolo* (393) Augustine develops the same theme at greater length. Noting the many passages enlisted to deny the Son's equality and cosubstantiality by heretical self-styled teachers (*impias haereticorum mentes*), Augustine argues that such texts rather refer to the Son in his incarnate humility and also to his derivation from the Father:

> "For the Father is greater than I" and, "The head of the woman is the man, the head of the man is Christ, and the Head of Christ is God" and, "Then shall he himself be subject unto him that put all things under him" and, "I go to my Father and your Father, my God and your God", together with some others of like tenor. Now all these have had a place given them, not with the object of signifying an inequality of nature and substance; for to take them so would be to falsify a different class of statements, such as, "I and my Father are one" (*unum*); and, "He that hath seen me hath seen my Father also"; and, "The Word was God", for he was not made, inasmuch as "all things were made by him"; and, "He thought it not robbery to be equal with God", together with all the other passages of a similar order. But these statements have had a place given them, partly with a view to that administration of his assumption of human nature in accordance with which it is said that "He emptied himself": not that Wisdom was changed, since it is absolutely unchangeable; but that it was his will to make himself known in such humble fashion to men. Partly then, I repeat, it is with a view to this administration that those things have been thus written which the heretics make the ground of their false allegations; *and partly it was with a view to the consideration that the Son owes to the Father that which he is (Filius Patri debet quod), – thereby also certainly owing this in particular to the Father, to wit, that he is equal to the same Father, or that he is his peer (utique Patri quod eadem Patri aequalis aut par est), whereas the Father owes whatsoever he is to no one.*[342]

A somewhat similar discussion occurs in *De Diversis Quaestionibus Octoginta Tribus* 69 (also written around the early 390s). Considering whether the eschatological subjection of the Son to the Father expressed in 1 Cor 15:26-27 signifies the Son's person or humanity, Augustine answers "both"; it *is* clear that it is the resurrected Christ who is in view (69.2, 7). But it also applies to the Son. In speaking of the Father subjecting all things to the Son, writes Augustine, Paul "calls to our attention and announces ... not only with respect to the form of a slave, but also with respect to the source from whom he takes

---

341 *DeTrin.* 4.20.29; NPNF 1.3.84.

342 *De Fide et Symbolo* 9.18; NPNF 1.3.329, cf. PL 40.190 (emphasis added).

his existence, and on account of whom he is equal to him from whom he takes his existence".[343]

Lest we think that this is simply Augustine in a younger, Neoplatonic, frame, he makes a return to this theme in his interactions with the Arian bishop Maximinus in 427-428. In the transcribed debate, Maximinus pushes Augustine hard on the issue of the Son's earthly subjection to the Father, arguing that it signifies the ontological superiority of the Father over the Son. Augustine's resp0nse, both in the debate and in his two subsequent written refutations, maintains the same tension seen in his earlier work – albeit with a few variations. For a start, passages such as John 14:28; Philippians 2:6-9 and First Corinthians 15:28 and so on are said to apply solely to the humanity of Christ.[344] Augustine advises Maximinus that passages which show the Son to be less than the Father (*minor Patre Filius videatur ostendi*) should be read *ex forma servi*.[345] Yet it must be understood that this demarcation is not a simple one. Immediately following the injunction just mentioned, Augustine uses an illustration which shows how the eternal Son might *also* be depicted as obedient without threat to his equality. He writes:

> Let me use a human example for the sake of those who think in bodily terms. Take two human beings, a parent and a child. If the child is obedient to the parent and for some reason asks the parent for something and thanks the parent and finally, is sent somewhere by the parent where the child says that he has not come to do his own will, but that of the one who sent him, does this show that the child is not of the same substance as the parent? Why then do you rush into such a great sacrilege ... and say that the Son of God does not have one and the same substance with the Father?[346]

In a sense this is a very limited analogy; willed conformity of action does not orphan human offspring, so (*a fortiori*) why should it sever the Son *if* we were to think of him as obedient in his divinity? But later there is a more

---

343 Augustine, *Responses to Miscellaneous Questions: Miscellany of Eighty-Three Questions; Miscellany of Questions in Response to Simplician; and, Eight Questions of Dulcitius*, trans. R. Boniface, ed. R. F. Canning. *The Works of Saint Augustine, Part 1* (New York: New City Press, 2008), 125.

344 *CMax.* 1.5-6, 8, 19. In the last passage cited here, Augustine uses 1 Cor 15 to argue that the humanity of Christ remains in subjection to the Father for eternity – an idea that is also stressed by Cyril of Alexandria; see Torrance, *Reconciliation*, 178-179.

345 *CMax.* 2.14.8, cf. Augustine, *Arianism and other Heresies: Heresies, Memorandum to Augustine, To Orosius in Refutation of the Priscillianists and Origenists, Arian Sermon, Answer to an Arian Sermon, Debate with Maximinus, Answer to Maximinus, Answer to an Enemy of the Law and the Prophets*, trans. J. E. R. R. J. Teske (New York: New City Press, 1995), 286.

346 *CMax.* 2.14.8, cf. PL 42.775.

positive recurrence of the same theme. Following a restatement of the same argument – a human son is not prevented from being human through his compliance (*tamen obsequendo esse non desinet homo*)[347] – he argues that

> ... if true reasoning admits that the equal Son obeys his equal Father, we do not deny the obedience, but if you want to believe that he is inferior in nature by reason of this obedience, we forbid it. In no way would God the Father, in order to have the obedience of the only Son, want to deprive him of his nature.[348]

Here then is a thoroughly ambivalent attitude to the terminology of filial obedience. Augustine is not bothered much if the term is used to *signify* the Son's *sonship* as long as it is not *also* intended to derogate from his equality *as son*.

This slightly unclear tension between human contingence and filial derivation also reoccurs two chapters later: Mark 14:36 – "not my will but yours" – is ascribed to the human will. Yet John 6:38 – "I came down from heaven, not to do my will but the will of the one who sent me" might be spoken of the man Jesus but -

> ... can also be interpreted insofar as he is the only-begotten Word. Thus he said that it was not his will, but his Father's, because whatever the Son is comes from the Father, though whatever the Father is does not come from the Son. In this sense he also said, "my teaching is not mine, but comes from him who sent me" John 7:16, because he who is the Word of the Father is also the teaching of the Father and certainly does not come from himself.[349]

Augustine's legacy, then, is quite mixed with regard to the issues that bear on our discussion. Even without considering the influence of the pre-Augustinian Nicenes on the Western tradition, or the input of later Eastern theologians such as Pseudo-Dionysius, this main fountainhead of Western theology *already* supplies enough ambivalence to thoroughly complicate any pronouncements we might want to make regarding RITW and the West. In that Augustine both appears to retain the pro-Nicene taxonomy *and* to think of God as a single agent, we might expect to find our enquiries about the connections between divine filiality and humanity met with both a "yes" and a "no". "Yes", if the personal distinctions between the persons are to the fore; "no" if the absolute unity of the subjective being is in view.

---

347 *CMax*. 2.18.3, cf. PL 42.786.
348 *CMax*. 2.18.3, cf. ibid., 298.
349 *CMax*. 2.20.2-3, cf. ibid., 301.

Father, Son and Incarnation in the Medieval Synthesis

Perhaps it is unsurprising, given the situation with Augustine, that this same ambivalence should also be a hallmark of Western Medieval theology. One issue raised repeatedly in the Medieval period (and frequently cited in the debates initiated by Rahner) provides a useful exemplification: namely the question of whether any person of the Trinity might have become incarnate.

It is relatively well known that Thomas Aquinas and other major Medieval theologians held that any of the three persons might have equally assumed flesh: the issue has been critically revisited both by Rahnerians wishing to defend the correspondence between the *ad intra* and *ad extra*,[350] and also by their opponents.[351] What is too seldom realised, however, is that Medieval

---

[350] Amongst Catholics, Karl Rahner, denounces the idea in the most emphatic terms, pressing that the most ancient tradition before Augustine never countenanced such a theory and that, if followed, it would "create havoc" with theology by abolishing any connection between the missions and the processions; Rahner, *Trinity*, 11-14, 28-31. See too K. Rahner, *Foundations of Christian Faith: An Introduction to the Idea of Christianity,* trans. W. V. Dych (London: Darton Longman & Todd Ltd, 1978), 214ff. Hans Urs von Balthasar takes a similar line; see A. Hunt, *The Trinity and the Paschal Mystery: A Development in Recent Catholic Theology. New Theology Studies* (Collegeville: Liturgical Press, 1997), 66-67.

T. F. Torrance and John Thompson evince similar sentiments from the Barthian wing. John Thompson links the idea that any of the persons might have taken flesh to historical (and regrettable) divorce between Christology and trinitarian theology; J. Thompson, *Modern Trinitarian Perspectives* (New York: Oxford University Press, 1994), 21-22. T.F. Torrance suggests that it is "the *actuality* of God's exclusive revelation and communication of himself ... that decides the hypothetical question of whether the incarnation of another divine person was a possibility"; Torrance, *Doctrine of God,* 199-200. (Torrance goes on to quote Rahner, though it is difficult to imagine that he would be wanting to affirm Rahner's axiom for the same *reasons* that Rahner does given his ambivalence toward the Father's priority.)

Other expressions of the same approach can be found in Robert Jenson; R. W. Jenson, "God's Time, Our Time: An Interview with Robert W. Jenson", *The Christian Century* 123.9 (2007): 31-35; B. A. Ware, *Father, Son and Holy Spirit: Relationships, Roles, and Relevance* (Wheaton: Crossway, 2005), 81-83 and Letham, *Holy Trinity,* 390 ff.

[351] Bernard Lonergan gives a recitation of the (neo-)Thomist position in B. J. F. Lonergan & M. G. Shields, *The Ontological and Psychological Constitution of Christ* (London: Lonergan Research Institute, University of Toronto Press, 2002), 139. For a Protestant defence of the same notion see Millard Erickson's response to Bruce Ware in Erickson, *Tampering,* 205-208; also his comments on Aquinas in Erickson, *God in Three Persons,* 295. A more nuanced response occurs in Giles, *Jesus,* 270-271, though both Erickson and Giles make the same mistake of reading the preliminary question of *Summa* 3.3.8 as being Aquinas' own opinion that it would have been better if the Father had become human.

theology actually gives *just as much* comfort to those championing Rahner's *Grundaxiom* as it does to their "Western" opponents.[352] For example, in *Distinctio* 1, Book 3 of his massively influential *Sententiarum Quatuor Libri* Peter Lombard (d. 1160), does indeed allow that the Father or Spirit might have (or might still!) become human (*Sicut enim Filius homo factus est, ita Pater vel Spiritus Sanctus potuit et potest*).[353] Yet this short statement is preceded by a lengthy explanation of why it is fitting (*ordine congruo/congruentius/ convenienter*) that the Son take flesh.

First, it is fitting that the Word as Wisdom (*sapientia*) by which God established the world, should also come as a lamp for human infirmity (*humanae infirmitatis lumine*).[354] Second, it is appropriate that the Word be the messenger because he is from another (*ab alio*), while the Father *a nullo alio est*: Peter cites a catenary of verses from *De Trinitate* and *In Ioannis Evangelium* to demonstrate Augustine's position that the one sent should be the one given birth (*mittitur quod genitum est*).[355] Third, the Son is the one to become flesh because he alone is the Son of God and thus appropriately becomes the Son of Man (... *qui erat in divinitate Dei Filius, ipse fieret in homine hominis filius*). The alternative – that there might be a different "son" in heaven and on earth, or that the Father might be simultaneously (*pater et filius*)

---

[352] Anne Hunt, for example, contrasts Aquinas with Hans Urs Von Balthasar on the grounds that the first says that any of the persons might have become incarnate while Von Balthasar sees the mission of the Son as "most profoundly appropriate"; Hunt, *Paschal Mystery - Development,* 66. The problem here is that, as we will see, Aquinas would say that too. Perhaps the best recent treatment of this matter with regard to Rahner's claims is from Fred Sanders: F. Sanders, *The Image of the Immanent Trinity: Rahner's Rule and the Theological interpretation of Scripture.* vol. 12. *Issues in Systematic Theology* (New York: Peter Lang, 2005), 62-68, 85.

For an extremely helpful exception to this pattern see F. Neri, *Cur Verbum Capax Hominis: Le Ragioni dell'incarnazione della Seconda Persona della Trinitá fra Teologia Scolastica e Teologia Contemporanea* (Rome: Editrice Pontificia Università Gregoriana, 1999). Neri demonstrates the stability of Scholastic opinion on the suitability of the Word's incarnation until the advent of neo-scholasticism.

[353] *SQL* 3.1.2; Latin text in, *Bibliotheca Augustiana,* (Augsburg: Ulrich Harsch) http://www.hs-augsburg.de/~harsch/Chronologia/Lspost12/PetrusLombardus/pet_s000.html, (accessed September, 2009). Philipp Rosemann argues that Peter does not "wish to suggest that the scope of God's possible action is limited to what actually occurred in history"; P. W. Rosemann, *Peter Lombard. Great Medieval Thinkers* (Oxford: Oxford University Press, 2004), 122. This is an acute observation and will become relevant to us below in our discussion of the Medieval concept of God's *potentiae*.

[354] Here he uses the parable of the woman with the lost coin (Lk 15:8-10) as an allegory for (the woman) Wisdom.

[355] *DeTrin.* 4.28; quoted in *SQL* 3.1.1.

is dismissed with an extended quote from Gennadius' *Ecclesiasticis Dogmatibus* 2 (here ascribed to Augustine):

> Neither the Father nor the Holy Spirit assumed flesh, but only the Son, so that the one who was God the Son as to divinity might also be the Son of Man as to humanity; that the name of "son" might not pass to one who is not son by nature. Therefore God the Son was made Son of Man – a true birth from God as God the Son, and a true birth according to humanity as the son of man. ... So there aren't two Christs nor two sons but God and man are one Son.[356]

This same dichotomy just observed also emerges in Peter Lombard's major successors; Bonaventure (1221-1274) and Aquinas (1225-1274). Maintaining Peter's concern that an *inability* on the part of the Father and Spirit to assume flesh would reflect an inequality of *potestas* or *dignitas*, both insist that the other persons *certainly do* have the capability.[357] Indeed, in Aquinas' case there is even the alarming parsing of Augustinian unipersonalism into the contention that the divine nature *itself* might have become incarnate. He argues that even if we don't think about the three persons (*circumscriptis per intellectum personalitatibus trium personarum*) – there yet remains the single personality of God – as known by the Jews (*remanebit in intellectu una personalitas Dei, ut Iudaei intelligent*) which could perform the same function as the person of the Word.[358] Closely associated with this same metapersonalist perspective, Thomas also cites Augustine's argument that since the will and working of the persons are one, the missions of the Son and Spirit must also be from themselves[359] – ie. the Son and Spirit send themselves.[360]

---

356 Quoted in *SQL* 3.1.2; my translation.

357 See Bonaventure's Commentary on Lombard's Sentences – *CQLS* 3.1.1.4; Latin text from Bonaventure, *S. Bonaventurae Opera Omnia,* ed. A. C. Peltier (Paris: Ludovicus Vivès, 1864), 15. Also Aquinas' Commentary; *Scriptum Super Sententiis* 3.1.2.3.

Both theologians are at pains to stress in these passages that Anselm's strong statements concerning the connection between divine filiality and incarnation – see *Cur Deus Homo* 2; *De Incarnatione Verbi* 10, cf. Discussion in D. Deme, *The Christology of Anselm of Canterbury* (Aldershot: Ashgate, 2003), 138 – not be seen as a statement of necessity, merely of congruence; as are their own.

358 *Summa* 3.3.3. For observations of the same theory in other scholastic theologians, see R. Cross, *The Metaphysics of the Incarnation: Thomas Aquinas to Duns Scotus* (Oxford: Oxford University Press, 2002), 178 n. It is difficult to see how this can be reconciled with Thomas' later statement that it is only *supposita* or *personae* which can act and not *naturae;* cf. *Summa* 3.20.1.

359 Cf. *DeTrin*. 2.7ff.

Yet both Bonaventure and Aquinas *also* spill more ink over the appropriateness of the Son's incarnation. They reprise the arguments used by the Lombard already mentioned and add their own too. Aquinas accompanies his Augustinian-inspired assertions that the Son and Spirit send themselves, with other Augustinian-supported stipulations that it would never be fitting for the Father to be sent.[361] The missions, he argues, signify the internal *notions* of begetting and proceeding; they are the processions retranscribed in a *novum modum existendi* – or again, they are the eternal processions worked out *per gratiam* in time (*Missio ... est temporalis processio*).[362]

More significant still, is the way Aquinas develops the latent exemplarism in Lombard's *sapienta* argument just mentioned above. Aquinas says that it is most fitting (*convenientissimum*) that the Son become flesh because the Son and humanity are *similar* and thus suitably united (*Convenienter enim ea quae sunt similia, uniuntur*);[363] "the Word, God's eternal conception, is the examplar for all creation" (*verbum Dei, quod est aeternus conceptus eius, est similitudo exemplaris totius creaturae*).[364] Augustine's psychological analogy (Word as self-conception) is brought together with the *filiocentric* view of creation that we have already encountered in Athanasius and Maximus the Confessor.[365] We will return to this in relation to Aquinas' conception of the divine will momentarily.

---

360 *Summa* 1.43.8. He acknowledges that there is a *diversimode locuti* on this issue – that some insist that a person is only sent by the one whence he proceeds (with the sending of Christ by the Spirit to be ascribed only to the humanity). The reconciliation for Aquinas relies on the view that if the focus is on the relations between the persons (ie. *ad intra*) then a person is only sent by his *principium*, yet if the external (*ad extra*) effect of the mission is in view then the Trinity itself – and thus the person sent – is the sender and *principium*.

361 *Summa* 1.43.4.

362 *Summa* 1.43.1, 4. Thomas is unclear if there is only an aesthetic reason for this connection.

363 Thomas Aquinas, *The Incarnate Word (3a. 1-6)*, trans. R. J. Hennessey. vol. 48. Summa Theologiae, 61 volumes, paperback edition (Cambridge: Cambridge University Press, 2006), 110.

364 *Summa* 3.3.8. English translation in ibid., 111.

365 Gilles Emery says for Aquinas this emanationism wherein everything comes from God in the Word and returns to him through the Word undergirds everything; "*les relations de la créature au Créateur, le sujet de la théologie, les noms divins. la structure de son commentaire et, ultimement, la structure de toutes choses ... [t]out ce que nous disons de l'action de Dieu dans le monde*"; G. Emery, *La Trinité Créatrice: Trinité et Création dans les Commentaires aux Sentences de Thomas d'Aquin et de Ses Précurseurs Albert le Grand et Bonaventure. Bibliothèque Thomiste* (Paris: J. Vrin, 1995), 303.

For Bonaventure, meanwhile this same exemplarism constitutes the keystone of his whole theological system. He sees the Word as the perfect "internal" image of the Father and thus the template and perfector (*exitus* and *reditus*) of creaturely participation:[366] "that which comes after [ie. humanity] has to return to that which is the first of its kind [ie. The Word]" (*posterius per illud habet reduci, quod est prius in eodem genere*).[367] As he unpacks his theology of human artistry in *De Reductione Artium ad Theologiam*, the Logos is central to creation at every turn. The Logos is the first and true Similitude emanating from the Father (*a Summa mente ... aeternaliter emanavit similitudo, imago et proles*),[368] and thus the archetype of all cognition which relies on mental similtudes to operate.[369] The Logos is the interior exemplar (*exemplari interiori*) to which the Artificer (ie. the Father) turns in designing external work (*exterius opus*), ensuring that those created should be – not simply vestigially similar to the Most High, but in his image (*non solum ... vestigii, sed etiam imaginis*).[370] The Logos is one in whom coincides the initial forms (*rationes seminales*),[371] the final goals (*rationes ideales*) and the thinking rational end (*rationes intellectuales*) which actualises and mediates between them.[372]

---

366 *CQLS* 3.1.2.3. See I. Delio, *Simply Bonaventure: An Introduction to His Life, Thought and Writings* (New York: New City Press, 2001), 67-79, 84ff. Jacques-Guy Bougerol writes that, for Bonaventure, humanity is " ... the subject of a quasi-original relationship between God and himself"; J. G. Bougerol "Bonaventure" in *Encyclopedia of Christian Theology*, ed. J. Y. Lacoste (London: Routledge, 2005), 228. Capuchin scholar Bernardino Garcia de Armellada puts it similarly – for Bonaventure creation is an *ad extra* copy of the Son/Word: "*Porque el Verbo existe en Dios, puede darse la creación en cuanto palabra 'ad extra', en cuanto imagen del Hijo*". The Son stands as the origin and exemplar of the world: "*según el modo que a esta le es propio - es el origen ejemplar del mundo*". See B. G. de Armellada, *Cristo Crucifado, Dios-Hombre en San Buenaventura*, http://franciscanos.net/teolespir/bernardi4.htm, (accessed September, 2009), 4.1.4.

367 *CQLS* 3.1. a4. q2 (cf. Bougerol, *Bonaventure*, 227). The comment is immediately supported by an invocation of *DeTrin.* 4.27.

368 *DeRud.* 8. Latin text originally from Bonaventure, *Opera Omnia S. Bonaventuræ* (Quarrachi: Collegio San Bonaventurae, 1882-1902) and obtained online: <http://www.forumromanum.org/literature/bonaventura/reduct.html>. The English translation of the same work can be found in; Bonaventure, *De Reductione Artium ad Theologiam: A Commentary with an Introduction and Translation*, trans. E. T. Healy, 2d ed edition (New York: The Franciscan Institute, Saint Bonaventure University, 1955).

369 See Hunt, *Insights*, 59-63.

370 *DeRud.* 12.

371 These correspond to the *logoi* of Maximus the Confessor.

372 *DeRud.* 20.

For each of these reasons it is of central importance that the incarnation be a manifestation of the Word. If the Logos is the similitude of the Father, then the incarnation is consummation of all cognition and revelation.[373] If the Son is the primary source for the Father's creative action, then nothing can bring back a sinful creation which is wandering from its course, than the one from whom it takes its form.[374] And if the Logos is the Alpha of creation then it will only reach its Omega when he assumes a human rational nature and brings it to perfection. As humanity represents a microcosm of creation – possessing flesh, spirit and intellect[375] – so the incarnate Logos is the perfection of all nexus:

> [W]e come to the conclusion that the highest and noblest perfection can exist in this world only if a nature in which there are the seminal causes, and a nature in which there are the intellectual causes, and a nature in which there are the ideal causes are simultaneously combined in the unity of one person, as was done in the incarnation of the Son of God. ... he is the Alpha and the Omega, that is, he was begotten in the beginning and before all time but became Incarnate in the fullness of time.[376]

Or again in verse 23:

> There is ... need of an intermediary in the going forth and in the return of things (*Necesse ... medium in egressu et regressu rerum*): in the going forth, an intermediary which will be more on the part of the one producing; in the return, one which will be more on the part of the one

---

373   [F]rom the mind of the Most High, who is knowable by the interior senses of our mind, from all eternity there emanated a Similitude, an Image, and an Offspring; and afterwards, when "the fullness of time came", he was united to a mind and a body and assumed the form of man, which had never been before. Through him the minds of all of us which receive that Similitude of the Father through faith in our hearts, are brought back to God.

       DeRud. 8, cf.Bonaventure, *De Reductione,* 49-50.

374   And since by sin the rational creature had dimmed the eye of contemplation, it was most fitting that the Eternal and Invisible should become visible and take flesh that he might lead us back to the Father. Indeed, this is what is related in the fourteenth chapter of Saint John: "No one comes to the Father but through me", and in the eleventh chapter of Saint Matthew: "No one knows the Son except the Father; nor does anyone know the Father except the Son, and him to whom the Son chooses to reveal him". For that reason, then, it is said, "the Word was made flesh". 53.

       DeRud. 12, cf.ibid., 49-50.

375   Christopher Cullen notes that for this reason, Bonaventure sees humanity as the greatest thing in the material universe; C. M. Cullen, *Bonaventure. Great Medieval Thinkers* (New York: Oxford University Press, 2006), 59.

376   *DeRud.* 20, cf. Bonaventure, *De Reductione,* 61.

returning. Therefore, as creatures went forth from God by the Word of God, so for a perfect return, it was necessary that the Mediator between God and man be not only God but also man so that he might lead men back to God.[377]

At this point it should be fairly obvious that the Rahnerian allegations concerning the West and its erasure of differences between the persons represent a very partial account. In contrast to the theory that Western trinitarianism is a long retreat to arid monotheism, the exemplarism of Lombard's heirs is *less* "Western" than Augustine's.[378] Bonaventure's depiction of the Logos/Christ in relation to the *rationes*, corresponds precisely with Maximus' understanding of the *logoi*.[379] His declaration that it must be the Word who redeems those made according to his own pattern is essentially the same argument used by Athanasius in *De Incarnatione*.[380] And, in each case, the *taxis* of the Trinity is maintained; the Father is the source or origin with the Logos his perfect eternal image. In creation, the Father configures contingent reality to correspond to his own Son (Similitude), ensuring that the Logos who becomes Christ is the mediator of creation from first to last.

Divine Relations in Thomas Aquinas

In the end, despite all the modern debate, the significance of the Augustinian (metapersonalist) legacy seems much less than we might expect.

---

377 *DeRud.* 23, cf. ibid., 63.

378 Nevertheless Augustine's own form of exemplarism, labeled "Middle-Platonist" by Mary Clark – M. T. Clark, *Augustine. Outstanding Christian Thinkers* (London: Continuum, 2000), 113-114 – ironically *does* seem to match that expected by Rahnerian critique; the *rationes* are simply eternal ideas in (presumably the triune) "God" without any reference to the Logos. See *Diversis Quaestionibus Octoginta Tribus* 46.

379 Eric E. Puosi observes that it was Bonaventure's understanding of intra-trinitarian relations that enabled his brokerage of ecumenical agreement between the Eastern and Western delegates at the (sadly disregarded) Council of Lyons in 1274; E. Puosi, *I Am Love* (Longwood: Xulon Press, 2007), 130-131.

380 [I]t was in the power of none other to turn the corruptible to incorruption, except the Saviour himself, that had at the beginning also made all things out of nought and that none other could create anew the likeness of God's image for men, save the Image of the Father; and that none other could render the mortal immortal, save our Lord Jesus Christ, who is the very life; and that none other could teach men of the Father, and destroy the worship of idols, save the Word, that orders all things and is alone the true only-begotten Son of the Father.

DeInc. 20; cf. NPNF 2.4.47.

True to the temper of their age,[381] the scholastics seem quite capable of holding one truth as incontrovertible without annihilating it by other factors that we would see as contradictory.[382] Thus the singularity of God, which might collapse into modalism if pursued in every context, is reserved for predication of *our* relationship with God.[383] If the focus is on the persons themselves, or (more problematically) on the Christ, then the factors in play are the same as before: natures expressed through modes (or *supposita/substantia*) of subsistence. If the question is raised why the creature Jesus is not son of the Trinity, Thomas answers with regard to his person and sonship: "son" is a personal category (rather than *natural*) – "*filiatio non determinat naturam, sed personam ... nullo modo potest dici filius Trinitatis*".[384]

Thus when we examine Aquinas we find just the same equivocation between filiality and humanity as we did in Augustine. As he rebuts the Arian view of the Son and incarnation in *Contra Gentiles* 4.8, he moves almost arbitrarily between filiality and humanity in his accounting for aspects of Jesus' life. Passages which speak of the Father as greater (John 14:28), or the Son as subject (1Cor 15:23-28), or obedient (John 15:10, 24:31 etc.) are confined to the humanity of Christ. Yet other statements which speak of the Son's dependence (eg. "the Son can do nothing of himself"; John 5:19) or describe him as *receiving* power (Matt 18:18) or knowledge, are seen in terms of the Son's eternal birth whence he derives everything. In the case of Phil 2:9-11, Thomas avoids the more obvious interpretation that would limit the achievement to Christ's humanity,[385] arguing instead that the exaltation really

---

381 C. S. Lewis summarises the situation well, observing in the Medieval mind, "the tranquil, indefatigable, exultant energy of passionately systematic minds bringing huge masses of heterogenous material into unity ... This is the Medieval synthesis itself ... All the apparent contradictions must be harmonized"; C. S. Lewis, *The Discarded Image: An Introduction to Medieval and Renaissance Literature* (Cambridge: Cambridge University Press, 1994), 10-11.

382 See Anne Hunt's comments on the nuanced trinitarianism and the "bland ... undivided undifferentiated Trinity" that replaced it in later theology; A. Hunt, *Trinity: Nexus of the Mysteries of Christian Faith* (Maryknoll: Orbis Books, 2005), 99-100.

383 For an excellent insight into how this works, see Gilles Emery's explanation of how "Father" means different things for humans ("the whole Trinity") and for Christ ("the first person of the Godhead") in post-Augustian (and especially Thomist) Western theology; Emery, *Trinitarian Theology*, 163-165.

384 *Scriptum Super Sententiis* 3.4.2. See also comments in Summa 3.23.2.

385 So, for example: Athanasius, *CA* 1.44-45, Augustine, *In Ioannis Evangelium Tractate* 104.3.

only designates the new proclamation *of the fact* that "the Son has from eternity received all power".[386]

> But the name higher than all names which every creature venerates is none other than the name of divinity. By this giving, therefore, the generation itself is understood in which the Father gave the Son true divinity. The same thing is shown by his saying that "all things are delivered to me by My Father" (Mat. 11:27). But all things would not be given to him unless "all the fullness of the Godhead" (Col. 2:9) which is in the Father were in the Son. ... For it is usual of Scripture to say that some things are or are made when they begin to be known. Now, the fact that the Son has from eternity received all power and the divine name was made known to the world after the resurrection by the preaching of the disciples.[387]

The same applies also to the concept of obedience. In the midst of his discussion of how obedience applies to Christ's humanity alone, Aquinas suddenly seems to *also* allow that it might be transcribed under filiality. As he writes:

> Clearly, then, in none of these can it be shown that the Son is subject to the Father except in his human nature. For all that, one should recognize that the Son is said to be sent by the Father invisibly and as divine, without prejudice to his equality to the Father, as will he shown below when we deal with the sending of the Holy Spirit.[388]

Aquinas manages to capture Augustine's mood perfectly. At the last moment it is alright *after all* to have the Father telling the Son what to do, as long as the sending is not held to signify *inaequalitas*. The subsequent treatment of the Spirit's sending, which he flags here, confirms the pattern:

> One must, then, say that the Son has an authority in regard to the Holy Spirit (*filius habeat aliquam auctoritatem respectu spiritus sancti*): not, of course, that of being master or being greater (*dominii vel maioritatis*), but in accord with origin only. In this wise, then, the Holy Spirit is from the Son. Now, let one say that the Son is sent by the Holy Spirit as well, because we read in Luke (4:18-21) that our Lord said Isaiah's words (61:1) were fulfilled in him: "The Spirit of the Lord is upon me, he has

---

386 *Contra Gentiles* 4.8.5-7; Thomas Aquinas, *On the Truth of the Catholic Faith: Summa Contra Gentiles,* trans. C. O'Neil, ed. J. Kenny (New York: Hanover House, 1955), 66.

The implication of this is that Christ's exaltation really has nothing do to with the cross; a rather alarming flight in the face of the text itself.

387 Ibid.

388 *Contra Gentiles* 4.8.10; ibid., 69.

sent me to preach the gospel to the poor". But consideration must be given this: the Son is sent by the Holy Spirit in accord with the assumed nature.[389] But the Holy Spirit has not assumed a created nature, so that in accord with it he can be called sent by the Son, or so as to give the Son authority in his regard. Therefore, this remains: it is considered as an eternal person that the Son has authority over the Holy Spirit (*respectu personae aeternae filius super spiritum sanctum auctoritatem habeat*).[390]

The same ambivalence exhibited in *Contra Gentiles* also shows up in Aquinas' lecture on John 5, this time cutting even closer to our topic.[391] Here, as Aquinas works to sift the human from the filial in the *locus classicus* of RITW theology, he acknowledges (with Augustine) that the words of verse 30 – "I can do nothing on my own. As I hear, I judge; and my judgment is just, because I seek to do not my own will but the will of him who sent me" – might be seen to belong *either* to the Son of Man or the Son of God. If it is the first, then the verse is interpreted along classic Dyothelitic lines; Jesus has a human will which is proper to himself (*quae est sibi propria, sicut est proprium eius esse hominem*) in addition to the one divine will which he has in common with the Father (*una divina quam habet eamdem cum patre*).[392] The statement of dependency meanwhile ("I can do nothing on my own") is simply a testament to the frailty of his humanity, which is empowered by God (*secundum quod inspiratur a Deo in anima*). But it is also possible to see these statements as referring to his filial dependence. In this vein, Aquinas suggests that the text "I cannot do anything of myself" speaks of "Christ, as the Divine Word showing the origin of his power ... For his very doing and his power are his being (*esse*); but being in him is from another, that is, from his Father. And so, just as he is

---

389 I will return to the question of the incarnate Christ's apparent subjection to the Spirit in Chapter 7.

390 Contra Gentiles 4.24.3; ibid., 135, cf. "Corpus Thomisticum" <http://www.corpusthomisticum.org/scg4001.html>.

391 Gilles Emery observes that in his work on John, Thomas draws together trinitarian theology and Christology to a much greater extent than he does in the *Summa*. "By participitiation in the personal property of the Word who is the Son, ... the faithful are deified and made 'connoisseurs of truth' and 'sons of God' by participation"; G. Emery "Biblical Exegesis and the Speculative of the Doctrine of the Trinity in St. Thomas Aquinas's *Commentary on St. John*" in *Reading John with St. Thomas Aquinas: Theological Exegesis & Speculative Theology,* ed. M. Dauphinais & M. Levering (Washington: Catholic University of America Press, 2005), 37.

392 *Super Ioannem,* 5 Lectio 5; "Corpus Thomisticum" <http://www.corpusthomisticum.org/cih05.html>.

not of himself (*a se*), so of himself he cannot do anything".[393] And even the *will* statement might be interpreted in a similar way:

> But isn't the will of the Father and Son always the same (*Sed numquid non est eadem voluntas patris et filii*)? I answer that the Father and the Son do have the same will, but the Father does not have his will from another, whereas the Son does have his will from another, ie., from the Father (*sed tamen pater non habet voluntatem ab alio, filius vero habet ab alio, scilicet a patre*). Thus the Son accomplishes his own will as from another, ie., as having it from another; but the Father accomplishes his will as his own, ie., not having it from another. Thus he says: I am not seeking my own will, that is, such as would be mine if it originated from myself, but my will, as being from another, that is from the Father.[394]

Michael Waldstein observes that, although Thomas often cites passages which tend to confine "obedience" to the human nature of Christ, he also – frequently in the same breath – attributes it to the Son under the terms of *subiectio* and *pietas* on account of the begetting.[395] Indeed Thomas seems to see no problem in running together quotes that would point in quite different directions:

> [The words "the Father is greater than I"] are to be understood of Christ's human nature, wherein he is less than the Father, and subject to him; but in his divine nature he is equal to the Father. This is expressed by Athanasius, "Equal to the Father in his Godhead; less than the Father in humanity": and by Hilary (*DeTrin.* ix): "By the fact of giving, the Father is greater; but he is not less to Whom the same being is given"; and (*DeSyn.*): "The Son subjects himself by his inborn piety" – that is, by his recognition of paternal authority (*auctoritatis paternae*); whereas "creatures are subject by their created weakness".[396]

As long as Arianism is avoided, Thomas wants to see the procession-mission connection as the meeting point for the life *ad intra* and *ad extra*, thus

---

393 Thomas Aquinas, *Commentary on the Gospel of St. John*, trans. J. A. L. Weisheipl, Fabian R. vol. 4. *Aquinas Scripture Series* (Albany: Magi Books, 1980), 321.

Emery notes that Aquinas' treatment of John 5:19 is essentially a rehash of Hilary's Emery, *Trinitarian Theology*, 20-21.

394 Thomas Aquinas, *John*, 322 altered.

395 M. Waldstein "The Analogy of Mission and Obedience: A Central Point in the Relation between *Theologia* and *Oikonomia* in St Thomas Aquinas's Commentary on John" in *Reading John with St. Thomas Aquinas: Theological Exegesis and Speculative Theology*, ed. M. Dauphinais & M. Levering (Washington: Catholic University of America Press, 2005), 103-104.

396 Summa 1.42 in Ibid.

maintaining the same teetering between humanity and filiality seen in pro-Nicene and Augustinian theology generally. The *ad extra* authority relationships displayed in the life of Christ might be seen either as expression of the *ad intra* processions or the assumed nature.

Divine Willing in Medieval Theology

But Medieval theology also has some other things to say which take it into new territory in regard to issues of divine willing. In my earlier discussions of Athanasius and Maximus, I flagged that there were questions that might be asked about how *contingent decisions* concerning creation and redemption might be made by the triune God. In the case of Athanasius, I observed the balance between the Son as the Father's going-forth from himself, with the image of the Father instantly communicating his will to the Son; and I asked whether such a model might fit with a responsiveness on the part of the Son in the case of contingent action.[397] I also raised the possibility as to whether there is room for something similar to be discovered in Maximus' vision of creation as a contingent actualisation of the eternal *logoi* contained in the Logos. Given Maximus' stipulation that decisions must be made by *hypostases,* should the decision to create, then, be seen as a sovereign act of the Father communicated to the Son?

Neither Athanasius nor Maximus are particularly interested in drawing these conclusions, of course. Nor, should be it confessed, are the great scholastic theologians of the twelfth and thirteenth centuries. But the Medieval theologians *are* extremely interested in the issue of divine will – particularly the free or contingent will that gives rise to created order. Debates over whether God's decision to create was free, reoccur throughout the Medieval period, implicating all the major players. On the one hand, the *rationalists* (or *intellectualists*) such Peter Abelard offer a revitalised classical Neoplatonism (really panentheism) wherein God can't help creating;[398] his nature is naturally self-diffusive and he was bound to do all the good he might.[399] At the other

---

397 The same question is posed as a problem by Aquinas in *De Veritate* 1 where (after Boethius) God is the unmoved mover, yet will seems to indicate movement.

398 Norman Kretzmann notes the specific condemnation of Abelard on this issue at the Council of Sens (1141) and the more general rejection of the view at Vatican I (1870); N. Kretzmann "A General Problem of Creation: Why Would God Create Anything at All?" in *Being and Goodness: The Concept of the Good in Metaphysics and Philosophical Theology,* ed. S. C. MacDonald (London: Cornell University Press, 1991), 220 n. 37.

399 See G. van den Brink, *Almighty God: A Study of the Doctrine of Divine Omnipotence.* vol. 7. *Studies in Philosophical Theology* (Kampen: Kok Pharos, 1993), 71. Arthur Lovejoy quotes Abelard thus:

extreme, later thinkers such as Peter Damian (1007-1072) propose a thoroughgoing voluntarism wherein God simply *deems things* good or bad by his own fiat.[400] In the midst of these views we find some clarifications that will turn out to be important for this thesis.

Aquinas and the Father's *Rationes*

The first clarification comes with Aquinas' attempt to deal with the problem of whether God was bound to create the world. As Arthur Lovejoy and others have noted,[401] Aquinas seems to make contradictory statements when it comes to this question. While he asserts strongly that God's essence and perfection cannot be augmented, he nevertheless wills that it be "multiplied ... in its likeness, which is shared by many" (*Summa Contra Gentiles* 1.75). Can this mean anything other than that God's perfect desire for the good, binds him to multiply created entities which participate in his goodness? For Lovejoy this effectively consigns Aquinas to a strong form of classical Neoplatonism where God's freedom *vis à vis* creation is pre-empted by his diffusiveness (*bonum est diffusivum sui essem*).[402] But if this is the case, Aquinas has been forced into this position despite himself, for his explicit intention is to proclaim that God is free as regards creation. As he goes on to explain, God's will toward creation must be seen as an expression of his will and desire for his own essence, as just mentioned, but it is not *necessary*. There are, as he observes, "infinite ways" that the infinite and perfect nature of divine goodness might be participated so God is not bound to any particular contingency:

> Moreover, God, in willing his own goodness, wills things other than himself to be in so far as they participate in his goodness. But, since the divine goodness is infinite, it can be participated in infinite ways, and in ways other than it is participated in by the creatures that now exist. If, then, as a result of willing his own goodness, God necessarily willed the

---

> We must inquire whether it was possible for God to make more things or better things than he has in fact made ... Goodness, it is evident, can produce only what is good; but if there are things good which God fails to produce when he might have done so, or if he refrains from producing some things fit to be produced, who would not infer that he is jealous or unjust – especially since it cost him no labour to make anything? ... Hence is that most true argument of Plato's, whereby he proves that God could not in any wise have made a better world than he has made.
>
> A. O. Lovejoy, *The Great Chain of Being: A Study of the History of an Idea. William James Lectures* (Cambridge: Harvard University Press, 1964), 71.

400 Ibid., 70, 156.

401 Ibid., 73ff.; Kretzmann, *Creation*, and W. L. Rowe, *Can God be Free?* (Oxford: Clarendon Press, 2004), 36-53.

402 This phrase from Pseuodo-Dionysius occurs repeatedly in Thomas' work.

things that participate in it, it would follow that he would will the existence of an infinity of creatures participating in his goodness in an infinity of ways.[403]

Further to this, as John Wippel shows,[404] Aquinas sees that God does not need to create anything at all – he *already* infinitely and perfectly possesses his own goodness in willing and loving his essence. In that case, as Wippel says, divine goodness is not something that *results from* the production of those contingent realities, but rather is it that *by which* they are ordered.[405] To put it in trinitarian terms,[406] God's creating is a contingent adornment to his begetting:

> [T]he Father speaks himself and every creature by his begotten Word, inasmuch as the Word "begotten" adequately represents the Father and every creature; so he loves himself and every creature by the Holy Ghost, inasmuch as the Holy Ghost proceeds as the love of the primal goodness whereby the Father loves himself and every creature. Thus it is evident that relation to the creature is implied both in the Word and in the proceeding Love, as it were in a secondary way (*quasi secundario*), inasmuch as the divine truth and goodness are a principle of understanding and loving all creatures.[407]

---

403 *CGent.* 1.81; Thomas Aquinas, *Contra Gentiles,* 258.

404 J. F. Wippel, *Metaphysical Themes in Thomas Aquinas II. Studies in Philosophy and the History of Philosophy,* revised edition (Washington: Catholic University of America Press, 2007), 232-239.

405 Ibid., 232-233.

406 To what extent Aquinas really understands this in trinitarian terms, is an interesting question. *CGent.* (1258-1261) seems to speak of God's self-knowing without much reference to it at all, whereas the later *Summa* clearly does express it. For contrasting opinions compare Norman Kretzmann's unflattering comparison of Aquinas with Bonaventure (who, Kretzmann argues, *does* fully develop a convincing trinitarian Neoplatonism) – Kretzmann, *Creation,* 223-228 – with Gilles Emery's argument that there is a deepening participationist/exemplarist theme at work in Aquinas from the *Scriptum Super Sententiis* onward; Emery, *Trinitarian Theology,* 41-44, 345ff. I suspect both commentators have a point here; Aquinas does seem much less excited by participationism than Bonaventure, though the theme *is* certainly a significant part of his theology.

407 *Summa* 1.37. On this theme Michael Waldstein (Waldstein, *Analogy of Mission,* 109) quotes Gilles Emery at length:

> This rule of the unity of operation of the persons *ad extra* (a principle shared by East and West) does not constitute the sole aspect of Thomas's doctrine on this point. If he holds firmly the unity of divine action ... required by the consubstantiality of the Trinity, he maintains equally clearly another principle: "the procession of the divine persons is the cause and the reason of the procession of creatures". This thesis is found in all of Thomas' works.

If Aquinas' vision of divine freedom is held together with this exemplarist (or participationist) scheme that locates the ideas of creation in the eternal Word, then what we have is just the voluntarist form of Maximus' *logoi* theory that I was proposing at the end of Chapter 2. Just like Maximus, Aquinas speaks of things pre-existing in God according to concept or "*rationes*" (*Omnia autem quodammodo praeexistunt in ipso per proprias rationes*),[408] yet his insistence on God's free-will means that not all of these *rationes* need to be, or will be, actualised. Decisions must be made.

Yet *how* are these decisions to be related to the persons of the Godhead? We have already learned that Aquinas maintains the distinction of Father and Son on the grounds of their mode of possession of the natural will (*pater non habet voluntatem ab alio, filius vero habet ab alio, scilicet a patre*). Can we also say that, in contingent matters, the Father *decides* a thing and then the Son *accords* and enacts it? This is a more tricky matter. Returning to Michael Waldstein's study on the connection between obedience in the humanity and filiality in Christ, we find that a number of the passages he adduces, clearly indicate that the Father's impartation of the will to the Son, *also* includes the Father's decisions. For example this passage from Aquinas' Lecture on John 12:49:

> All the divine commandments (*omnia mandata divina*) are in the mind of the Father, since these commandments are nothing other than the patterns of things to be done. And so, just as the patterns (*rationes*) of all creatures produced by God are in the Father and are called ideas (*ideas*), so the patterns of all things to be done by us are in his mind. And just as the patterns of all things pass from the Father to the Son, who is the Wisdom of the Father, so also the patterns of all things to be done. Therefore the Son says, "The Father who sent me has himself given me, as God, the commandment, that is, by an eternal generation he has communicated to me what to say within and what to speak without.[409]

> The connection of the double rule (unity of operation *ad extra* and causality of the trinitarian processions) comes not from modern interpretation, but is explicitly posed by Thomas. Thus, the causality of the trinitarian going-forth (*processus*) in the order of efficiency and of exemplarity unites the divine activity *ad extra* to the eternal generation of the Son and to the procession of the Holy Spirit: it furnishes from fact "the motive" of the divine economy.
>
> (Quote originally from G. Emery, "Essentialism or Personalism in the Treatise on God in Saint Thomas Aquinas", *Thomist* 64 (2000): 521-563, 527-528).

408 *CGent.* 1.75.

409 Waldstein, *Analogy of Mission*, 102; *Super Ioannem*, 12 Lectio 8, cf. "Corpus Thomisticum" <http://www.corpusthomisticum.org/cih12.html>.

This is a startling, but also difficult paragraph. By speaking of the Father having a mental act which is logically prior to the Son's birth, Thomas anticipates the later distinction between essential and notional action, wherein the Father is seen to have a distinct mental act that is separate from his paternity.[410] This would seem to make for a model that is more like RITW. Aquinas' language of "commands" and the inclusion of creatures in this transmission *also* points in this direction; if the Father is passing his decisions about contingent affairs to the Son, then we are almost at the point of saying that there is a non-necessary aspect to the Father's relationship to the Son. It is precisely this lack of necessity – in other words contingency – that we need if the persons are going to be able to truly respond to each other.

---

410 That is, the Father's mental life does not *cause* the Son as it would if we were to take the Augustinian psychological model in a literal sense. See Richard Cross' very helpful explanation of the disagreement between Duns Scotus and Henry of Ghent on this point; R. Cross, *Duns Scotus on God. Ashgate Studies in the History of Philosophical Theology* (Aldershot: Ashgate, 2005), 223.

Figure 2. Alternate models for divine decision-making

RITW triune model (cf. Figure 1)

1. The Son's begetting by the Father in eternity includes the full array of rationes/ideas associated with the essential will (a-∞).

2. The Father freely decides which logoi to deploy contingently, giving rise and shape to salvation history. The Son receives and enacts the Father's decision.

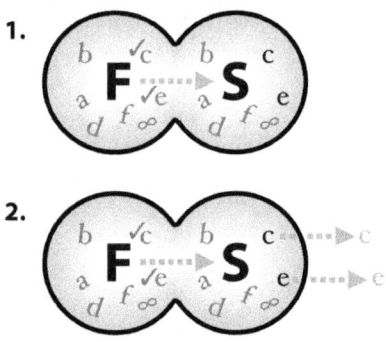

Aquinas' model

1. The Father decides which rationes (a-∞) to deploy contingently before *the Son's begetting. The Son is "born" with both the rationes and the contingent decisions concerning them already set.*

2. The Son enacts the Father's decision.

But we must not be too quick here. If the will spoken of includes contingent decisions then Thomas *also* believes that the Son is "born" with them already in his mind, which would seem to mitigate his free response. In that event we have a kind of hybrid of FV and RITW: the will that is passed includes contingent determinations (sounding like RITW), but it is a notional (or "natal") act (actually FV) *not* an interpersonal communication (see *Figure 2*).[411] Thomas, in line with his emphasis on divine simplicity, needs to insist on the (quite problematic) conception that the contingent acts of will constitute the divine essence just as the surely as the necessary acts of begetting and spiration.[412]

Exemplarism and Voluntarism in Bonaventure and Duns Scotus

Things are, once again, pushed a little further amongst the Franciscans. As with Thomas, Bonaventure and Duns Scotus (1266-1308) also maintain the priority of the Father in both the *opera ad intra* and the missions, yet the language is slightly stronger. Here the Father is first in terms of authority/authorship; his *innascibility* (aseity) makes him *summa auctoritas* (also *ultimum* or *reductio*) while the Son and Spirit, who fully and equally share in that authority, are dubbed *subauctoritas*.[413] In that the Son is both from the Father and thence equal sharer (*subauctoritas*) in the spiration of the third person (ie. the *filioque*),[414] he becomes the *medium*/centre between the Father

---

411 This is an early form of the so called "power differential" deployed by Medieval theologians to distinguish between the infinite potentiality of divine action (*potentia absoluta*) and *those specific acts* freely chosen by God (*potentia ordinata*). See L. Moonan, *Divine Power: The Medieval Power Distinction up to its Adoption by Albert, Bonaventure, and Aquinas* (Oxford: Clarendon Press, 1994).

412 "The divine will is God's own existence essentially"; *Summa* 1.19.2. See Bruce Marshall's summary of Aquinas' position; B. Marshall "Ex Occidente Lux: Aquinas and Eastern Orthodox Theology" in *Aquinas in Dialogue: Thomas for the Twenty-First Century*, ed. J. Fodor & F. C. Bauerschmidt. *Directions in Modern Theology* (Oxford: Blackwell, 2004), 42 n.29. The problems that arise in this case are: first, that inclusion of creation in the Son's necessary birth sounds suspiciously like nascent panentheism; and second, making contingent decisions God's essence sounds like a contradiction in terms.

413 Bonaventure, drawing on Hilary, relates the Father's self-causedness to the appropriateness of his being *auctor*: "*summa auctoritas est in Patre ratione innascibilitatis: ergo convenit hypostasi Patris ratione innascibilitatis generare*".; *CQLS* 1.27(part 1).2, cf. Bonaventure, *Bonaventurae Opera*, 1.436. See also *CQLS* 1.12.1-2.

414 See Duns Scotus; *Ordinatio* 1.12.2 – cf. useful, but hostile, summary in O. Bychkov, "What Does Beauty Have to Do with the Trinity", *Franciscan Studies* 66 (2008): 197-212, 205 – and Bonaventure; *CQLS* 1.12.1. For a helpful explanation in the case of Bonaventure see J. A. W. Hellmann & J. M. Hammond, *Divine and Created Order in Bonaventure's Theology* (New York: Franciscan Institute, 2001). Note that Bonaventure relies on the idea of eternal (but eternally complete) generation; cf. *CQLS* 1.9.4.

who is solely from himself, and the Spirit who is purely from the other persons.[415] The Son alone is both from another and a producer.

While insisting that this *subauctoritatis* does not connote the subjection of inferiority,[416] Bonaventure is nonetheless ready to describe it in hierarchical terms. In *Sermo* 21 of his *Collationes in Hexaemeron* he relates the hierarchies discovered in creation to the *coelestis monarchiae,* striving to demonstrate a harmony (or echo) between the Father, Son and Spirit and the hierarchy of the sun, radiance and heat, the psychological hierarchy of power, wisdom and will. Going further, he quotes Pseudo-Dionysius' definition of hierarchy as a deiform order of knowledge and action (*hierarchia* [*est*] *ordo divinis, scientia et actio ad deiformem*)[417] and strives to show how the same pattern that operates with the Godhead gives rise to contingent hierarchy amongst the angelic orders, within the church and amongst humans generally.[418]

And yet when it comes to the question of whether the persons of the Godhead participate in a common will as per creational hierarchies, then his answer seems that they do, but not through the same means of interpersonal commerce that characterises creatures. Father, Son and Spirit share the same will naturally, not by the *conformitas voluntatis* that comes from an extrinsic Spirit (as in our case),[419] but through their own Spirit. How this spiritual unity

---

415 See *Collationes in Hexaemeron* 1.11-14.

416 Here he contrasts divine relations from the *conditione separationis* of *inferioribus* where the difference in *esse* makes all the difference. Since the divine persons all share the same being and virtue there is "*aequalis nobilitatis in mittente et misso* [and] *subauctoritatis emanatio*"; CQLS 1.15.1.

417 *Collationes in Hexaemeron* 21.16-17; Bonaventure, *Bonaventurae Opera,* 9.135.

418 "*Cœlestis hierarchia est illustrativa militantis Ecclesiae. Oportet ergo quod Ecclesia militat habeat ordines correspondentes hierarchiae illustranti*". *Collationes in Hexaemeron* 22.2; ibid., 9.139. Bonaventure sees the church's hierarchy descending *proximately* from the threefold angelic hierarchy of Thrones, Seraphim and Cherubim.

419 Thus distinguishing the patterns of unity in divine and created reality, Bonaventure writes:

> [T]here is a twofold manner of unity among the Father and the Son, which is [also] among the members of Christ, namely [that] of nature and of will; but differently, because in us there is a unity of nature through a sharing in one common essence (*per participationem unius communis essentiae*), but we are not the essence itself. However the Father and the Son do not share the Essence as (something) diverse, nay they are the Essence itself. Similarly among us there is a conformity of will (*conformitas voluntatis*) through a gift of God, which unites us; but the Father and the Son are united not by having received a gift from another, but by Their own Spirit ...

might be worked out post-natally, or how *decisions* might actually be made, is left very vague.[420]

This is somewhat disappointing. The real significance of the Franciscan tradition, as has been observed by many commentators,[421] is a more highly developed theology of divine freedom. Heiko Oberman contrasts the approach of Thomas – who reconciles the natural and supernatural within the *Being* of God (as just witnessed above) – with the "Franciscan alternative" wherein the *personal decisions* of God mediate between all that he might do (*potentia absoluta*), and that which he actualises (*potentia ordinata*).[422] According to Oberman, this new (*via moderna*) emphasis on person and decision gave rise to a "metahistorical" (or "mythological") frame of reference with regard to creation and redemption.[423] Thomas had sought to flee any hint of divine mutability – even to the extent of collapsing God's free decisions into his essence – but Bonaventure and Duns Scotus envisage reality as controlled by the free interventions of God.

But this *freedom* is almost exclusively explored at the level of "God" – the Augustinian metaperson. When Scotus comes to the question of whether the Son has a distinct personal causality in relation to created reality, he brushes past the matter of how acts of will might work at the personal level, even as he

---

CQLS 1.10, *dubium* 5; Bonaventure, *Opera Omnia*, 1.207. Translation courtesy; A. Bugnolo, E. D. Buckner & J. C. Klok, *The Commentary Project*, (Boston: The Franciscan Archive) http://www.franciscan-archive.org/bonaventura/I-Sent.html, (accessed November, 2009).

420 The difficulty here is that the *filioque*, as explicated just above, demands that the Son be considered *before* the Spirit so how can the Spirit be the "natural" bond between the first and second persons?

421 For a comprehensive introduction to voluntarism in Bonaventure see Z. Hayes, "The Meaning of *Convenientia* in the Metaphysics of St. Bonaventure", *Franciscan Studies* 34 (1974): 74-100. For the more developed ideas of Scotus see W. L. Craig, "John Duns Scotus on God's Foreknowledge and Future Contingents", *Franciscan Studies* 46 (1987): 98-122 and R. Cross, *Duns Scotus. Great Medieval Thinkers* (Oxford: Oxford University Press, 1999), 52-57.

422 H. A. Oberman, *The Dawn of the Reformation: Essays in Late Medieval and Early Reformation Thought* (Grand Rapids: Eerdmans, 1992), 6. For an example of Bonaventure's attributing of the efficacy of the sacraments to the *pactione divina*, see *CQLS* 4.5.1. For extended discussion on this question in Franciscan theology see K. B. Osborne, *A Theology of the Church for the Third Millennium: A Franciscan Approach* (Boston: Brill, 2009), 187-189. Meanwhile the same general pattern is discernible in Calvin's suggestion that the incarnation was not a matter of absolute necessity but of decree; *Institutes* 2.12.1.

423 Oberman, *Dawn*, 6. See also N. Walker, *Sovereignty in Transition: Essays in European Law* (Portland: Hart Publishing, 2006), 250-251, for a discussion of the renewed emphasis on the will that arises out of the *potentia* distinction.

seems to set up a framework that demands it.[424] If, he writes to an interrogator, you want to discuss whether the Son might have a particular role in the voluntary determinations (*determinationem voluntatis*) of the divine will, then the answer is negative. It is not correct:

> ... to say that one person knows that another, and not himself, has made this sort of decision (*aliam ... disponere de operabili*) as regards this possible work, ... for our main conclusion of this article [is that], if there is but one will then what it decides is also one (*unius voluntatis una est dispositio*), and so if one person decides about a specific work (*disponat de hoc operabili*), in this particular way, it follows the other person who has the same will-act does so in the same way (*eandem voluntatem eodé modo imo eodem actu disponit*), and when he reflects in his mind upon this will-act (*actum voluntatis*) he will know that he is disposed to this particular work in the same way as the other persons are ... [425]

This is a rather complicated way to deny distinct personal volition as regards contingent decisions. Although Scotus stresses that there is one *actus,* his explanation of how this action is performed clearly implicates the persons: one person "makes the decision" and the others immediately feel the same way as if they had taken it themselves. But why should the free decision of one person so circumscribe the *disposition* of the others? Is this not simply a (meta-)temporalised form of Aquinas' theory concerning the Son being born with the Father's decrees already in place? Doesn't it also amount to the surrender of Duns' idea (maintained against Henry of Ghent) that each person possesses the same essential mental capacity *in se*? Wouldn't it be truer to *this* principle to see the "passive" persons *actively* embracing the decisions of the one who chooses: in other words *making* his decision their own? But we will come to that soon enough.

---

424 We should note again here the fact that was observed earlier concerning Scotus' insistence that each person individually possesses the *essential* capacities of God. This would, as Richard Cross recognizes, allow us to think of the persons as possessing really distinct roles *ad extra* without threatening tritheism; Cross, *Scotus,* 70-71.

425 *Quaestiones Quodlibetales* 8.24; translation from John Duns Scotus, *God and Creatures; The Quodlibetal Questions,* trans. F. Alluntis and A. B. Wolter (Princeton: Princeton University Press, 1975), 206-207; Latin text from Duns Scotus, J. B. Campanea, L. Durand & L. Wadding, *R.P.F. Ioannis Duns Scoti, Doctoris Subtilis, Ordinis Minorum, Opera omnia, quæ hucusque reperiri potuerunt* (Lugduni: Sumptibus Laurentii Durand, 1639), 12.209.

Conclusion

By this point it should be clear how deeply embedded paternal priority and causality are in orthodox trinitarianism. In spite of the rise of Western meta-personalism as a second tier in trinitarian theology, the pro-Nicene commitment to fatherhood continues as the means by which the Son is God. Moreover, we have seen that the mode of the Son's existence *as God the Son* remains crucial as a structuring principle in many scholastic explanations of salvation-history. The will of God *ad extra* has everything to do with the essential and rational procession of the Son and Logos from the Father.

Chapter 4

Can We Find Positive Examples of Intra-Trinitarian Willing?

[I]t was not anything in that human nature that moved him to predestinate it, or any thing else for it. Nor was the glory of that human nature made the end in the act of predestinating; but it was the glory of the second Person only, which God saw might be more fully manifested in this personal union than any other way: that was it that moved him, and that was made the end of all.

– Thomas Goodwin[426]

Introduction

To this point, I have been attempting to prepare the way for a more full-blooded theory of responsive intra-trinitarian, willing by calling attention to the shape and persistence of pro-Nicene trinitarianism. I have paid special attention to how causality and taxis apply to the willing of the divine persons in a number of key theologians. And, I have also suggested a way that taxis *might* work in the context of the contingent economy of God.

Nevertheless I have not yet supplied a clear example of any theologian who has pursued this last possibility, nor anyone who has sought to explore the pattern of filial volition as an inter-personal (or "social") relationship outside the context of Christ's humanity. There remains, in other words, a gap between filial volition and a true RITW. In this chapter, however, we will see that historical examples of a real RITW do exist, and that the vision they bring of reality is beautiful.

Christ the Centre?

What is history about? What is its focus? One standard answer to these questions, is that history is about Christ. Whether it is because Christ is the one in whom, and through whom, God achieves his purpose for created reality – an

---

426 T. Goodwin, *The Works of Thomas Goodwin, D.D., Sometime President of Magdalene College Oxford,* 8 volumes (Edinburgh: James Nichol, 1861), 1.102.

analogy of begetting; a full realisation of the eternal *rationes* and so on – or because he is the federal head and substitute for redeemed humanity, the focus on Christ himself is a recurring theme in every theological tradition.

But is Christocentrism the same as Filiocentrism? The Son of course is the hypostatic core of Christ – Jesus *is* the Son in our flesh (however we understand, or don't understand, that) but is this something that has significance for the Son himself, or is that which takes place in his humanity a completely external act – a "role" or office that he assumes for us?

The significance of the question is greater than might be immediately apparent. If it is Christ's *work* that is ultimate – if "being Christ" is only something the Son does *for us* without any personal stake or gain – then our salvation must terminate at a similar remove. In that case, being "in Christ" or "united with Christ" can only mean being joined to whatever restoration or mercy God has in mind for us. Similarly if, as we find in much exemplarism, it is Christ's *nature* rather than his person that is important to God, then our redemption might have meaning for God, but that meaning will not necessarily have a trinitarian dimension.[427]

On the other hand, if the Son himself is seen to be somehow personally invested in mission (ie. if he receives something that *he* values)[428] then our salvation moves into a different register. In that case, we potentially become the means by which the persons love and glorify each other.

---

427 Thus in his Parisian lectures Duns Scotus lays out what he sees as God's methodical willing (*ordinate volens*) in which :

> ... first, God treasures (*diligit*) Himself; second, he treasures himself in others (*diligit se aliis*) [the Son and Spirit], and this is a pure love; third, he wills that he be treasured by another, one who can love him with the highest love – in speaking about the love of someone extrinsic (*amore alicujus extrinseci*). And fourth, he foresees the union of that nature which owes him the highest regard (*summe diligere*), even apart from the fall.

> *Reportata Parisiensia* 3.7.9.4 J. Duns Scotus, *Ioannis Duns Scoti Opera Omnia Ordinis Minorum,* ed. J. B. a Campanea, L. Durand & L. Wadding (Paris: Vivès, 1891-1895), 23.303. See discussion in G. Florovsky, *Cur Deus Homo? The Motive of the Incarnation,* http://jbburnett.com/resources/florovsky/3/florovsky_3-6a-curdeushomo.pdf, (accessed November, 2009).

The catch here is that Christ is not considered as Son but only as a Mediator of creation.

428 The danger with talking like this is that God might be seen to be dependent on creation in a panentheist sense (see Chapter 6). This is not what I mean here, rather my argument assumes that there is such a thing as a contingent good which pleases God, and which does not threaten his perfection *in se*.

Creation as Pro-Filius –
John of the Cross

To find theology that is prepared to think in the terms just described, we must leap forward to the sixteenth century.[429] Here it first appears in the *Romance sobre el Evangelio "In principio erat Verbum" acerca de la Santísima Trinidad* (or *Romanzas*) of the Spanish Carmelite mystic, John of the Cross (1542-1591),[430] who reveals both a social conception of the triune voluntarism and a thoroughgoing Victorine sensibility with regards to the purposes of the persons *vis á vis* creation.[431]

Written by John in 1578 while he was in prison for his reformist enterprises, the cycle of nine ballads[432] traces the arc of creation and incarnation as a love story between the Father, Son and the latter's bride. John sets the scene with what initially appears to be a straightforward, albeit richly hued, depiction of trinitarian life: The Word (Son) lived in and with God at the beginning in a

---

429 This is not to deny glimpses of personalist *Filiocentrism* before this. See George Florovsky's detection of the theme in Rupert of Deutz who says that; "that both angels and men were made because of one man, Jesus Christ, so that, as he himself was begotten God from God, and was to be found a man, he would have a family prepared on both sides, becoming the centre of everything"; ibid. n. 3; cf. PL 169.72D-73A.

430 I remain indebted to Matthew Paulson who first helped me to see the significance of John of the Cross (and this particular work) in this connection.

431 Whether John is influenced by Richard directly is not certain – see B. Frost, *Saint John of the Cross, 1542-1591, Doctor of Divine Love: An Introduction to his Philosophy, Theology and Spirituality* (London: Hodder & Stoughton, 1937), 69, on this question – though his regard for the Victorine-influenced Bonaventure is certainly high. In an *Instruction for Novices* published in 1590 he singles out "the glorious doctor, Saint Bonaventure" as being worthy of special attention; see Anon. ("A Benedictine of Stanbrook Abbey"), *Mediaeval Mystical Tradition and Saint John of the Cross* (London: Burns & Oates, 1954), 56. With regard to John's overlap with voluntarism (as *nominalism*) see S. Payne, *John of the Cross and the Cognitive Value of Mysticism: An Analysis of the Sanjuanist Teaching and its Philosophical Implications for Contemporary Discussions of Mystical Experience* (Dordrecht: Kluwer, 1990), 5, 33. Payne outlines John's particular interest in questions of will and provides evidence from Crisógono concerning the influence of *nominalism* at the University of Salamanca where John trained.

432 ... or three, if the stanzas on the creation are considered as one. See, John of the Cross, *The Collected Works of John of the Cross: Romances*, (ICS Publications) http://www.carmelite.com /saints/john/works/p_10.htm, (accessed November, 2007). Unless otherwise noted the translation and numbering of the *Romanzas* is taken from G. Brenan, *St John of the Cross: His Life and Poetry,* trans. L. Nicholson (Cambridge: Cambridge University Press, 1975), 186-207; numbering is by ballad and verse.

state of perfect bliss; fully sharing in the Father's substance, glory and love. There are three lovers and yet they are one by virtue of the unity of their love, being and Spirit (cf. 1.1-9).

> This Being was each single one
> And they were tied by this alone
> In an inexpressible union
> For which no name is known.
>
> For it was infinite, the love
> Which wrought their unity.
> And this is called their essence,
> The single love possessed by three;
> And the more love grows to oneness
> The more it is increased. (1.10-11)

In stanzas two and three the mood becomes more speculative; the Father speaks to the Son of the delight he has in him, and declares that he will share himself with any who love the Son (2.7). The Father then proposes that he will give the Son a bride who will come to share in the life of the Trinity. She will:

> " ... eat her bread at our table. ...
> That she may know in such a Son
> The wealth of good I bear;
> And she will join with me in praising
> Your grace and glowing splendour". (3.2)

The Son responds in delighted accord, and in return declares that he will glorify his Father before the bride by showing her his own brightness which comes from the Father.

> "And I shall hold her in my arms,
> To burn there in your love,
> And she will glorify your goodness
> In eternal celebration". (3.5)

Thereupon the world is made and arrayed in earthly and heavenly beauty "that the bride may know the Bridegroom" (4.4). The movement of stanza four is toward the vision of erotic and ecstatic love between the Son and bride and the transport of the creaturely into the life of God:

> ... He would gather [her] up
> Tenderly into His arms,
> There give to her His love;
> And thus would bear her to the Father,
> United into one.

> Where she would joy with that same joy
> Possessed by God Himself;
> For as the Father and the Son
> And He who issues from them
>
> All live within each other,
> So also would the Bride. (4.14-17)

John's depiction of divine life and creation here is, of course, highly stylised, yet there is a serious theological foundation underpinning his poetry which is remarkable for several reasons. Firstly it provides a profound application of Richard of St Victor's theory that the perfection of trinitarian love consists in love, not simply for the other person, but in a generous desire that seeks to *share* the beloved with others so that the beloved will receive *additional* love.[433] While Richard (and Duns Scotus after him) uses the idea to show the necessity of a third within the Godhead, John cuts closer to the biblical source by making this love the *raison d'être* of creation. The Father wants to give *the Son* a bride who will adore and know him. The Son in return draws the bride into his love and adoration of the Father. In knowing the Son, she will also come to know and love the one from whom the Son comes. In every part of this network of relationships there is a sharing of love for the third: the Father drawing the bride into his love for the Son; the Son sharing his love of the Father with his bride; Father and Son bringing the bride to eat at their table and join their family. The scheme communicates a dazzling vision of openness and welcome between God and humanity.

John's way of imagining the relationship between God and human history is thus theocentric, trinitarian, filiocentric, patrocentric and personalist. It reminds us that it is *God* who is at the centre – salvation history is not *primarily* about us, or for us, but about the persons of the Trinity who find occasion to *further* love one another by means of us. Creation is instigated by the Father *for the Son* so that the Son might be known and loved by other persons. Simultaneously this filiocentrism becomes theocentric (or patrocentric) because the Son himself is the perfect expression of the Father and *personally devoted* to the Father such that both passively and actively he points his bride to her Father-in-law.[434] John imagines the Son answering the Father's proposal thus:

---

433 See "Book 3 of The Trinity", chapter IX in Richard of St Victor, *Richard of St Victor: The Twelve Patriarchs; The Mystical Ark; Book Three of The Trinity,* trans. G. Zinn. *Classics of Western Spirituality,* paperback edition (New York: Paulist Press, 1979), 392.

434 As Rowan Williams puts it in his profound essay on the *Romanzas:* "human relation with God lives in a tension between the nuptial and the filial"; R. Williams "The Deflections of Desire: Negative Theology in Trinitarian Disclosure" in *Silence and the Word: Negative Theology and Incarnation,* ed. O. Davies & D. Turner (Cambridge: Cambridge University Press, 2002), 119.

The Will of Him Who Sent Me

"And to the bride you give me
I will add my clarity.

That with its light my Father's worth
By her may be perceived,
And how this nature I possess
Was from His own received". (3.3-4)

We should note here that John is not suggesting that the Son increases in *intrinsic* glory or that he overcomes any *lack* through salvation history. Certainly the Son *himself* (and not merely the humanity he represents) receives something from the hand of the Father; but what he receives is the gift of a new context in which he is known – becoming known and loved by the bride offered to him by the Father.

Another notable aspect of John's depiction of the life of the Godhead is the way he daringly presents the social dynamic at work between the persons without compromising their unity of will. The Father proposes the idea of the bride; the Son accepts joyfully. Later the Father proposes that the Son assume flesh to increase the bride's delight (7.6) and the Son again agrees. Declaring his unity of will with the Father and adding his *own reasons* for doing the Father's will:

"My will is yours and yours alone,
The Son to him replied,
(*y la gloria que yo tengo es tu voluntad ser mía*),
So I accord with you, my Father,
[with you, Highness – *tu Alteza*][435] in everything you say". (7.7-8)

John's *Romanzas* offer a rich and evocative imagining of trinitarian life in a social framework and bring together a number of the issues that we have been tracing up to this point. There is a regard for the Son's person in the *opera ad extra*. There is an exploration of how contingent decision-making might work in the life of the Godhead. There is the depiction of a trinitarian order which neither connotes ontological subordination nor diverges from orthodox conceptions of equality but rather leads to the second person being exalted by the first, and accompanies begetting with active conformity.

Yet, before we leave John, it is worth observing that his vision also exhibits some curious deficiencies. Surprisingly, John seems confused about who exactly the bride *is* – whether she is the whole creation or righteous (*los justos*)

---

435 Nicholson's translation – in Brenan, *St John*, 202-203 – entirely eliminates the reference to the Father as *Alteza*. For a better (but more generally wooden) translation at this point see John of the Cross, *The Poems of Saint John of the Cross*, trans. W. Barnstone (New York: New Directions, 1972), 118.

humanity.[436] More perplexingly, John seems to almost completely miss the key moment in the romance between the Son and the bride. For while the apostle Paul marks the cross – whereby Christ gives himself up for his bride (Eph 5:25-27) – as the *archetype* of love between a man and woman, John is far more interested in the incarnation as the means by which the Son woos his wife.[437] John first suggests that the incarnation enables the bride to get to know her groom,[438] then follows it up with a discomforting melding of natal and nuptial imagery as the groom comes forth from the womb as his bridal chamber to embrace Mary.[439]

Triune Willing in the Covenant of Redemption

The downplaying of redemptive themes in the theology of John of the Cross seems strange to Protestant eyes. Yet at the same time this iconic figure of the Counter-Reformation is in a Spanish prison imagining conversations between the Father and Son, something similar is beginning to emerge in Reformation Europe. And here, as we might expect, the emphasis *is* very squarely on salvation from sin.

Beginning with Caspar Olevianus (1536-1587),[440] student of Calvin and Bullinger and co-author of the *Heidelberg Catechism,* the movement known as

---

436 Thus in 4.6 we read: "And though beings and places [ie. heavenly and earthly] were divided in this way, all are part of one body which is called the bride". Yet John also recognizes the particular connection between humanity and the Son wrought by the incarnation (7.6). In 4.14 John writes that "all the members of the just would be joined in him; they form the body of the bride".

437 A glancing reference to the atonement does occurs in stanza 7: "I shall look for my bride and take upon myself her weariness and labours from which she suffers so much. And that she may have life, I shall die for her, and, lifting her out of the deep, I shall return her to You". (7.10-11).

438 John has the Father saying to the Son: "Surely your bride's delight would greatly increase if she were to see you like her, in her own flesh" (7.6) The same emphasis produces a metaphorical eroticising of the relationship between Mary and the infant Jesus in stanza nine.

439 "Now that the time had come for him to be born, he went forth like the bridegroom from his bridal chamber, embracing his bride, holding her in his arms, he whom the gracious mother had borne in a manger". (9.1-2).

440 See C. S. McCoy, J. W. Baker & H. Bullinger, *Fountainhead of Federalism: Heinrich Bullinger and the Covenantal Tradition,* 1st edition (Louisville: Westminster/John Knox Press, 1991), 37-39. There is some dispute here as to the first proponent of covenantal theology. Other antecedents include Johannes Oecolampadius (1482-1531) – see R. S. Clark, *A Brief History of Covenant*

"covenant (or federal) theology" interprets salvation history through the prism of covenant: there is the covenant of works or law by which Adam's status before God was maintained and lost;[441] then there is the covenant of grace through which God promises and provides redemption to the elect through the cross. Yet there is also often a third covenant; a *pactum salutis* or counsel/covenant of redemption/peace, which involves an agreement freely entered into between the Father and Son, that the Son will come and die for the elect. It is this last covenant which concerns us here.

Belief in some form of intra-Trinitarian agreement (if not in explicitly covenantal terms) appears to have disseminated rapidly and widely within the broad circle of Reformed theology.[442] Early examples (varying in degrees of sophistication) can be found in figures diverse as: English court chaplain Richard Field (1561-1616);[443] Puritan Richard Sibbes (1577-1635);[444] Scottish

---

Theology, (2001) http://www.spindleworks.com/libraryCR/clark.htm, (accessed November, 2007) – and Heinrich Bullinger (1504-1575) – see A. Stewart, "Heinrich Bullinger, The First Covenant Theologian", *British Reformed Journal* 39 (2001): 18-26. The assertion that Coccius is the pioneer in this regard is certainly wrong given that he himself names Olevianus and Cloppenburg as his instructors: see discussion in W. J. van Asselt, *The Federal Theology of Johannes Coccius (1603-1669)*, trans. R. A. Blacketer. *Studies in the History of Christian Thought* (Leiden: Brill, 2001), 227-228.

441 Or, on Vos' reading, the means by which a *further* blessing is promised – a blessing that will ultimately only be fulfilled in Christ: "the Reformed view fixes its gaze on something higher ... the covenant of works is something more than the natural bond which exists between God and man"; G. Vos, *The Doctrine of the Covenant in Reformed Theology*, www.biblicaltheology.org/dcrt.pdf, (accessed October 2010), 7 – originally published in G. Vos, *Redemptive History and Biblical Interpretation: The Shorter Writings of Geerhardus Vos*, ed. R. B. Gaffin (Phillipsburg: Presbyterian and Reformed Pub. Co, 1980), 234-269.

442 Vos notes the simultaneous (and apparently independent) emergence of covenantal theology in both Holland and England; Vos, "Doctrine of the Covenant", 3-4. For a more recent (and extremely helpful) contribution to the discussion of the doctrine's origins see M. Jones, *Why Heaven Kissed Earth: The Christology of the Puritan Reformed Orthodox Theologian, Thomas Goodwin (1600-1680)* (Göttingen: Vandenhoeck & Ruprecht, 2010), 123-143.

443 "When God had the contrary pleas and desires of [... justice and mercy], and there was no other means to give them all satisfaction, it was resolved on in the high council of the blessed Trinity, that one of those sacred persons should become man ..."; R. Field, *Of the Church, Five Bookes. Vol. 5. Eccles. hist. soc.* (Cambridge: J.H. Parker, 1850), 40-41.

444 Therefore bless God for his love for Christ, and Christ for his love to us; for they both join in our salvation. ... Therefore consider the sweet agreement of the Trinity towards the salvation of mankind; and that we come not to heaven, are elect and saved only by the counsel of the Father, or only by the

covenanter David Dickson (1583-1662),[445] and Dutch theologians Johannes Cocceius (1603-1669) and Herman Witsius (1636-1708). Fairly well-developed examples of the *pactum salutis* concept[446] can be observed in the theology of John Owen (1616-1683) and Thomas Goodwin (1600-1680) whom I will now use to introduce the doctrine.

John Owen

Owen's most protracted examination of the covenant of redemption occurs within his anti-Socinian work, *Vindicae Evangelicae*, amid wider consideration of the significance and necessity of the death of Christ. Having just concluded discussion of expiatory and sacrificial aspects of the punishment endured by Christ, he now turns to "the ground of ... Christ's being punished for us" which, he writes, "is that compact, covenant, convention and agreement, that was between the Father and the Son, for the accomplishment of the work of our redemption ..."[447] Or to make it more explicit:

> The will of the Father, appointing and designing the Son to be the head, husband, deliverer and redeemer of his elect, his church, his people, whom he did foreknow, with the will of the Son voluntarily, freely undertaking that work and all that was required thereunto.[448]

The anthropomorphic overtones of this statement might appear suspect. Yet Owen is very aware of the danger of dividing the persons into a collection of conferring individuals. In accordance with orthodox tradition, he hastens to add that the "will of the Father, Son and Holy Ghost is but one" as a "natural

---

> love of the Son, or only by the operation of the Holy Ghost, but all three joining together in our salvation.
>
> R. Sibbes, *The Complete Works of Richard Sibbes, D.D,* ed. A. B. Grosart. *Nichol's Series of Standard Divines. Puritan Period* (Edinburgh: J. Nichol, 1863), 832.

445 See C. R. Trueman, *John Owen: Reformed Catholic, Renaissance Man. Great Theologians Series* (Aldershot: Ashgate, 2007), 81-82. Dickson appears to be the first person to use the expression "covenant of redemption" in a 1683 address; Jones, *Heaven Kissed Earth,* 123.

446 Robert Letham states that Owen is one of the first – "and by far the best" – exponents of the covenant of redemption R. Letham, *John Owen's Doctrine of the Trinity in its Catholic Context and its Significance for Today,* http://www.johnowen.org/media/letham_owen.pdf, (accessed January, 2008), 7-8. See also Trueman, *John Owen,* 93-92.

447 J. Owen & W. Orme, *The Works of John Owen,* ed. T. Russell, 21 volumes (London: Richard Baynes, 1826) (cited hereafter by volume and page) 9.125.

448 Ibid., 9.125.

property",⁴⁴⁹ and that this will must be "appropriated to them respectively; so that the will of the Father, and the will of the Son, may be considered ... in their distinct personality".⁴⁵⁰ Making similar comments in his commentary on Hebrews, he explains that:

> If it be objected, that the will is a natural property, and therefore in the Divine essence, it is but one; and how, then, can it be said that the will of the Father, and the will of the Son, did concur distinctly in the making of this covenant? We reply that ... they subsist distinctly; if such is the distinction of the persons in the unity of the Divine essence, that they act in natural and essential acts reciprocally one towards another, as in understanding, love, and the like; what impropriety to suppose that they act distinctly in those works, which are of external operation? The will of God as to the peculiar actings of the Father in this matter, is the will of the Father; and the will of God, with regard to the peculiar actings of the Son, is the will of the Son; not by a distinction of sundry wills, but by a distinct application of the same will to its distinct acts, in the persons of the Father and Son.⁴⁵¹

But Owen goes beyond connecting subsistence to modes of willing. He also speaks of a " ... distinct acting of the will of the Father, and the will of the Son, with regard to each other"⁴⁵² which makes the decree of God into covenant or compact, and which also transforms the way Father and Son relate to each other:

> Hence from the moment of [the covenant's inception], I speak not of time, there is a new habitude of will in the Father and Son towards each other that is not in them essentially; I call it new, as being in God freely, not naturally. And hence was the salvation of men before the incarnation, by the undertaking, mediation, and death of Christ. ... From hence was Christ esteemed to be incarnate, and to have suffered; or the fruits of his incarnation and suffering could not have been imputed to any; for the thing itself being denied, the effects of it are not.⁴⁵³

The concepts in play here are extremely challenging. Owen insists that the *pactum* is freely entered and non-necessary, yet – God being outside time – also eternal in nature. More surprising, the fact that the incarnation and atonement are retro-active (saving the saints of the Old Testament), means that in some

---

449 Ibid., 9.125.

450 Ibid., 9.125.

451 J. Owen, *Exposition of the Epistle to the Hebrews with the Preliminary Exercitations.* vol. 1, 4 volumes (Boston: Samuel T. Armstrong, 1811), 333-334.

452 Owen & Orme, *Works,* 9.126.

453 Ibid., 9.126.

sense the Son must be esteemed to be Christ and man from all eternity – that is from the (timeless) moment of the covenant's establishment.[454] But the scheme also looks back to the scholastic division between the *potentiae absoluta* and *ordinata,* wherein the God of absolute freedom meets us as the self-constrained God of his own eternal *pactum salutis.* The covenant of redemption merely renders into social language the *pactum* concept of the *via moderna.*[455]

To justify these assertions, Owen next lays out an array of biblical arguments. Briefly, he argues that the eternal aspect of the incarnation/atonement is attested by the past tense of prophetic passages such as Isa 53 and Ps 40:6.[456] At greater length he lays out a five-point test for covenants,[457] contending that all are fulfilled between the Father and the Son as they form a compact to secure the glory of God and salvation of the elect (Heb 2:9-10, 12:2). The expression "counsel of peace" itself is justified from Zech 6:13 with (puzzling) support from Ps 55:14.[458] And there is more support for the "eternal" significance of creation in the life of God found in Prov 8:21-31: Wisdom is held to be rejoicing in an earth that does not yet exist and which must therefore be present by "the counsel of peace, that was between them both, which is the delight of the soul of God and wherein both Father and Son rejoice".[459]

---

454 See too ibid., 12.71-72. Interestingly, Owen here somewhat anticipates the speculations of modern trinitarians such as Barth, Pannenberg and Moltmann, who also make the mission of Christ retroactively determinate of his eternal relationship to God (see more on this in Chapter 7). Of course there is a very significant difference here too, in that Owen regards this achieved status as an entirely separate and additional thing which does not impinge on his ontological status either as God or Son.

455 Thus Mark Beach, in his discussion and defence of Witsius' version of the *pactum salutis,* justly describes the covenant as simply a way of "giving content" to the divine decrees; J. M. Beach, "The Doctrine of the *Pactum Salutis* in the Covenant Theology of Herman Witsius", *Mid-America Journal of Theology* 13 (2002): 101-142, 138. Beach is right here, though we should add that it doesn't simply give content but *form of expression;* it offers a description of *how* the triune God decrees things.

456 Owen & Orme, *Works,* 9.126-127.

457 (i) Two or more persons agree to work toward some common end. (ii) The initiator imposes some condition or requirement on the other party. (iii) The initiator also makes promise of recompense. (iv) The second party performs the requirement and expects the reward. (v) The goal envisaged by the initiator and second party is secured.

458 Ibid., 9.130: "We took sweet counsel together".

459 Ibid., 9.130.

How this proleptic economy in the eternal life of the Godhead relates to the relations which arise from the modes of subsistence is not made completely clear at this point. Nevertheless, here and elsewhere we *do* see the Father's role as initiator of the covenant and the Son as respondent; a pattern which accords with the more ancient principle that *opera ad extra* correspond to the *opera ad intra*. So Owen writes in *A Declaration of the Mystery of the Person of Christ* (or *Christologia*):

> [T]heir order herein [ie. in salvation history] doth follow that of subsistence. Unto this great work there are peculiarly required, authority, love and power, all directed by infinite wisdom. These originally reside in the first person of the Father, and the acting of them in this matter is constantly ascribed unto him. He sent the Son, as he gives the Spirit, by an act of sovereign authority. ... The Son, who is the second person in the order of subsistence, in the order of operation puts the whole authority, love and power of the Father in execution. This order of subsistence and operation is expressly declared by the apostle, 1 Cor. 8.6. ... The Father is the original fountain and spring, ἐξ οὗ, from whom, ... are all these things.[460]

Accordingly, Owen, like the Medieval doctors before him, regards it appropriate that the Son should become human and that the Father should send him. As the Father is first in order of subsistence and the Son receives from him "his personal subsistence, and therewithal the divine nature",[461] hence "it became not the person of the Father to assume our nature ... it was every way

---

460 Ibid., 12.274, In the preface of the same work, Owen adduces a number of quotes to establish the reason why it was "condecent unto divine wisdom that the Son, and not the Father or the Holy Spirit should be incarnate". Notable passages are derived from Ambrose:

> The image of God, that is the Word of God, came into him who was after the image of God, that is man. And this image of God seeks him who was after the image of God, that he might seal him with it again and confirm him, because he lost that which he had received.

(12.xxxviii-xxxix)

And also Augustine:

> The Father did not assume flesh, nor the Holy Spirit, but the Son only; that he who in the Deity was the Son of the Father, should be made the Son of man, in his mother of human race; that the name of the Son should not pass unto any other, who was not the Son by eternal nativity.

(12.xxxix).

461 Ibid., 12.273. Nevertheless, the Son is elsewhere painted (after Calvin) as *autotheos* in terms of his possession of the essence; with the order of operations ascribed to the "external economy and dispensation of persons in reference to the work of our salvation"; ibid., 8.515.

suited unto divine wisdom, unto the order of the holy persons in their subsistence and operation, that this work should be undertaken and accomplished in the person of the Son". [462]

As we saw with John of the Cross, Owen's vision of the persons covenanting an operational dispensation to work *ad extra*, suggests a bold advance toward social trinitarianism and a more thoroughgoing triune conception of redemption. From the very beginning, the persons of the Godhead are *personally* and voluntarily involved – committed *together* to the great plan of salvation history. Other indications of this social consciousness can be seen in Owen's willingness to speak of love between the persons as the source of human love:

> He made the heavens and the earth to express his being, goodness and power. He created man in his own image to express his holiness and righteousness and he implanted love in our natures to express this eternal mutual love of the holy persons of the Trinity.[463]

Owen sees an *analogia relationis* connection between human love and God's.[464] He also sees the love of the Father toward the *incarnate* Son as central to the created order: *this* love for this *man* is the source and recapitulation of God's love toward creatures. Contrasting the two loves, Owen writes:

> The person of Christ in his divine nature is the adequate object of that love of the Father which is *ad intra*, a natural necessary act of the divine essence in its distinct personal existence and the person of Christ as incarnate, as clothed with human nature, is the first and full object of the love of the Father in those acts of it which are *ad extra* or are towards any thing without himself. [465]

But even as Owen depicts the filial bond as central to creation, he also disconnects it. Like the Franciscan exemplarists before him (or, more

---

[462] Ibid., 12.274-5.

[463] Ibid., 12.184.

[464] R. A. Muller observes of the Reformed in general and Owen in particular that while they were cautious about metaphors and similes in general for the Trinity, "they were very much in favour of describing the relation between the Father and the Son in the Godhead in terms of mutual love"; R. A. Muller, *The Rise and Development of Reformed Orthodoxy, ca. 1520 to ca. 1725.* vol. 4. *Post-Reformation Reformed Dogmatics,* 2nd edition (Grand Rapids: Baker Academics, 2003), 266. Of course this: "love" might be taken in a fairly weak sense as an (Augustinian) analogy for self-knowledge.

[465] *Christologia* or *A Declaration of the Glorious Mystery of the Person of Christ* (henceforth *Christologia)*, Owen & Orme, *Works,* 12.183.

immediately, John Calvin),[466] Owen sees the relationship between Christ and God as something separate from the relationship between the Father and Son – indeed its analogy:

> [T]he love of the Father unto the Son, as the only-begotten, and the essential image of his person, ... was the fountain and cause of all love in the creation, by an act of the will of God *for its representation*.[467]

It is not hard to surmise why Owen expresses it like this. In distinguishing the sufficiency and necessity of eternal filiality from the events of salvation history, he forestalls Socinian attempts to *subordinate* the Son to his incarnate work and glory. There can be suggestion of mutability or imperfection and no gift given from the Father to Son since, as God, he already possesses all things. Yet the same cannot be said with regard to the Son as he is man. The *human* nature of the Son *can* experience change and exaltation and thus Owen declares that it is only of the Son *as man*, that the Bible speaks when it says that the Father loves the Son and commits all things to his hand (John 3:35; 5:20);[468] or who receives the name above all names (Phil 2:8-11; John 5:25, 26);[469] or who is wed to the

---

466 For this dichotomy in Scotus see *Reportata Parisiensia* 3.7.9.4.

Calvin's Mediator Christology draws a sharp line between the interests of the eternal Son and the office he occupies vicariously on our behalf. The Reformer argues that the interests and inheritance gained by Christ, hold no value for him as Logos. See: *Institutes* 3.1.1; comments on Heb 1:2 – J. Calvin, *Commentaries on the Epistle of Paul the Apostle to the Hebrews,* trans. J. Owen, ed. J. Owen (Edinburgh: Calvin Translation Society, 1853) 33-34; exegesis of Eph 1:10 – J. Calvin, *The Eighth Sermon on the First Chapter of Ephesians,* http://www.the-highway.com/Calvin_Eph8.html, (accessed March, 2010) taken from J. Calvin, *The Sermons upon the Epistle of S. Paule to the Ephesians,* trans. A. Golding (London: Lucas Harison & George Byshop, 1577). At his most extreme Calvin seems to cast doubt on whether there is any *ad intra* love between Father and Son at all. In his comments on John 15:9, he dismisses the "abstruse inquiry" of love between the divine persons, arguing that it "has nothing to do with the present passage. But the love which is here mentioned must be understood as referring to us ... the Father loves him, as he is the Head of the Church"; J. Calvin, *Commentary on the Gospel According to John,* trans. J. Pringle, 2 volumes, reprint edition (Grand Rapids: Eerdmans, 1956), 2.111. Later references to the Father's love for Christ in John 17:24 are handled similarly: "For thou lovedst me ... agrees better with the person of the Mediator than with Christ's Divinity alone. It would be harsh to say that the Father loved his Wisdom ... Christ, unquestionably, spoke as the Head of the Church"; ibid., 2.187.

467 *Christologia,* Owen & Orme, *Works,* 12.183, my emphasis.

468 Owen & Orme, *Works,* 12.182-183.

469 Ibid., 10.21.

church;[470] or who obeys the Father.[471] In short, the Father has two very different relationships with the Son under his two natures – as do we ourselves.

Thomas Goodwin

At this point it is interesting to compare Owen to a less well-known peer, Thomas Goodwin (1600-1680), who similarly deploys a well-developed theory of the *pactum salutis*.[472] Goodwin is also careful not to compromise God's transcendence. He stresses that God doesn't need creation to make himself glorious: God "was so happy in himself, that he needed not that glory which is manifested in and by the union of the second Person with a human nature".[473] He also makes clear that the union of the triune persons is of such a kind that it "cannot be communicated to any mere creature" but can only be manifested to us by way of imitation: first to Christ, and then to us:

> [O]ur union hath the union among the three persons for its foundation, and pattern, and original ... [it] is let down to the man Christ Jesus first, and in him conveyed to us; to know and behold the union of three persons in one divine nature, Father, Son, Holy Ghost, one God blessed for ever, producing, in imitation of them, an union of the two natures of God and man in the person of Christ Jesus ... then, that occasioning a third ... multitudes of persons united unto one Christ Jesus.[474]

Again, then, what we see in Jesus Christ is not the persons as they are *in se*, but an analogical and partial manifestation. Yet Goodwin's theological centre-of-gravity is more personalist than such a description might imply.[475] He sees

---

470 Ibid., 10.70.

471 Ibid., 10.191.

472 Mark Jones sees it as the centre of his whole Christology; Jones, *Heaven Kissed Earth*, 13. References to the covenant of redemption occur frequently throughout Goodwin's work. The most sustained treatment occurs in Book 1 of *Of Christ the Mediator*; T. Goodwin, *The Works of Thomas Goodwin, D.D., Sometime President of Magdalene College Oxford*, 8 volumes (Edinburgh: James Nichol, 1861), 5.8-31 – yet here the emphasis is on the proximate redemptive aspect of the *pactum*. Elsewhere, as we shall see, he explains a deeper intra-trinitarian agenda.

473 Goodwin, *Works* 1.101.

474 Ibid. 4.371.

475 This shows up, for example, in the way Owen and Goodwin accent the word "God". So, for example, while Owen insists that "God as *primo Veritas* ... is not to be considered ὑποστακικῶς ... but as οὐσιωδῶς, comprehending the whole deity" – Owen & Orme, *Works,* 10.15 – and holds that the "person of any one of them is not the prime object of divine worship"; ibid. 10.22, Goodwin typically thinks of God as the Father. His treatment of 1 Cor 15:28 goes against the Calvinist pattern of rendering "God may be all in all" as a reference to God *as Trinity*;

these contingent manifestations as having value for the persons themselves – salvation history gives rise to a new glory and manifestation. Thus, Goodwin writes of the Son in his exposition of Ephesians:

> Though I know divines say he merited nothing for himself, because all was his due as he was the Son of God, and it is a truth; but I cannot see but he might have a double title to glory, and resurrection, and all, and might purchase it and merit it; it was by the blood of the everlasting covenant.[476]

Goodwin's distinctions concerning the differences between the Son's glory as God, man and Mediator are quite complicated and are beyond adequate treatment here.[477] But it *is* important to note that Goodwin sees that glory accruing to the Son in his human nature, as having eternal and personal significance. From all eternity after the inception of the *pactum salutis,* Goodwin sees the Son as already (proleptically) glorified as God-man.

And this same pattern of personal glory has a very personal dimension. At one point, Goodwin imagines the Father, Son and Spirit conversing over how they will save humanity and glorify one another in the process:

> I will choose him to life, saith the Father, but he will fall, and so fall short of what my love designed to him; but I will redeem him, says the Son, out of that lost estate. But yet being fallen he will refuse that grace, and the offers of it, and despise it; therefore I will sanctify him, said the Holy Ghost, and overcome his unrighteousness, and cause him to accept it. ... [T]hese three glorious persons thus equally share this work, of so much glory to God in the highest, amongst them, and one doth not take upon him all, but each bears his part, that each may be honoured as the other; yea, are jealous of the glory of each other herein as much as of their own ... If there had been contending amongst these persons who should have the glory of all, or who should be the first or second, this work had stood still, and man had not been saved; but they willingly

---

Goodwin, *Works* 1.100, 1.502. Other examples can be found in his comment on the first line of the NCC in ibid, 4.354; and his distinction of the Father from God as applied to the Godhead in ibid, 7.522.

476 Ibid. 1.100. We might note that here it is the atonement, and not simply the incarnation, that seems to be on view as a means to the Son's glory. This (implicitly supralapsarian) perspective will reemerge in Jonathan Edwards (see below). Mark Jones, in forthcoming work, traces this pattern in Goodwin under the rubric "Christological Supralapsarianism".

477 For an extended treatment, see Jones, *Heaven Kissed Earth,* 203-221. Jones highlights Goodwin's attention to the Son's proleptic glory as "God-man" as distinctive aspect of his theology.

share it, according to their order and priority of subsisting, and involve our salvation with their glory.[478]

Of course it might be premature to see this as a theologically rigorous attempt to literally portray triune life – it could be argued that Goodwin's imaginings operate on the same level as those of John of the Cross. Yet there are clues that Goodwin has something more developed and serious in mind. In the same section cited above where he speaks of the divine relations as being available only to us through imitation, he also details that superior reality as including such elements as "communications of mutual love"; "a communication of, and imparting of secrets, a discovery of each other's mind"; and "mutual pleasures in each other".[479] It would seem that despite the "infinite difference and distance between us and him",[480] God can be at least legitimately imagined under the signs and referents of creaturely reality.

This distinctly social take on the *analogia entis*[481] comes into sharpest relief where it comes to the *pactum salutis*. For here, not only is the divine union given an external *manifestation* in the appointment of the Son as God-man, this manifestation itself arises out of actual "events" *within* God which are themselves described under the relational analogies of choice, communication, proposal and acceptance. As Goodwin elaborates it, The Father chooses between an infinity of possible universes and alights on one that will allow his Son [as Christ] to be glorified:

> When God [the Father] went about to choose Christ and men, he had all his plot before him in his understanding, through the vast omnisciency of that his understanding, ... so infinite more frames of worlds which he could have made; and all these he must be supposed to have had in his view at once, afore ever his will concluded all that was ordained to come to pass. Now, he having Christ, and the work of redemption, and us, and all thus before him, the question is, which of all other projects he had most in his eye, and which his will chiefly and primarily pitched upon to ordain it. I say, it was Christ and the glory of his person. God's chief end was not to bring Christ into the world for us, but us for Christ.[482]

Or, again:

---

478 Ibid. 7.540-541.

479 Ibid. 4.368.

480 Ibid. 4.367.

481 Goodwin himself does not use the expression but comes close when he states that "the whole creation was but *Deus explanatus*, so we may truly say that the story of Adam is nothing else but *Christus explanatus*, Christ explained; ibid. 2.415.

482 Ibid. 1.100.

The Father shewed the Son a platform of a world below, in which men should dwell, which Christ calls his Father's "habitable earth", and therein the sons of men, his elect, given to him to be one for ever with him. Now, as he was God's delight, and God his immediately and naturally, so these were made for Christ's delight ... The chain of interest, and of delight [between Father and Son], have the same parallel subordinate links [between Christ and us].[483]

Goodwin here fills out his version of the *pactum salutis* in a way that quite closely corresponds to RITW. The Father chooses between actualities afforded by his nature, and opts for those contingencies that will manifest and adorn the Son. And, it should be noted, Goodwin's scheme also supports the filial corollary of RITW wherein the Son receives and approves the Father's will in accordance with his natural unity and filial subsistence. "[The] Father recommended the business to [the Son], so also he gave especial recommendation of the persons for whom he would have all this done".[484] Whereupon the Son, being of one will and mind, agreed: "as it was his Father's will, he had no reluctancy ... 'I and my Father are one' (saith he), and so have one will and agree in one". [485]

Jonathan Edwards

Thomas Goodwin's interest in the personal glory and relationships of the Trinity, finds even more elaborate expression in the writings of the last puritan, Jonathan Edwards (1703-1758). Edwards' favourite image for the Trinity, as it emerges from his *Unpublished Essay on the Trinity*, comes in the familiar form of Augustine's psychological analogy: the second person is God the Father's perfect self-knowledge, a perfect "representation of the Divine nature" and therefore "the Divine nature and essence again".[486] The Son of God (whether as Word or Wisdom) is the "eternal, necessary, perfect, substantial and personal idea which God hath of himself". In terms of the language of pro-Nicene theology (which Edwards generally avoids),[487] Edwards holds that, "by God's

---

483 Ibid. 4.370.

484 Ibid. 5.25.

485 Ibid. 5.25, 497.

486 Edwards, "Unpublished Trinity". The same idea occurs repeatedly in Edwards' work. See William Danaher's very helpful treatment in W. J. Danaher, *The Trinitarian Ethics of Jonathan Edwards. Columbia Series in Reformed theology*, 1st edition (Louisville: Westminster John Knox Press, 2004), 16-66.

487 A. P. Pauw, *The Supreme Harmony of All: The Trinitarian Theology of Jonathan Edwards* (Grand Rapids: Eerdmans, 2002), 73.

reflecting on himself the Deity is *begotten*".[488] The Son, as the Father's idea, has all that the Father has (including self-consciousness),[489] and an ability to relate to the one who conceives him. This adds a social aspect of the psychological analogy,[490] with the result that the outcome of this begetting is love:

> The Godhead being thus begotten by God's loving an idea of himself ... a most pure act, and an infinitely holy and sacred energy arises between the Father and Son in mutually loving and delighting in each other, for their love and joy is mutual, (Prov 8:30). "I was daily his delight rejoicing always before him". This is the eternal and most perfect and essential act of the divine nature, wherein the Godhead acts to an infinite degree and in the most perfect manner possible. The Deity becomes all act, the divine essence itself flows out and is as it were breathed forth in love and joy. So that the Godhead therein stands forth in yet another manner of subsistence, and there proceeds the third person in the Trinity, the Holy Spirit, viz., the Deity in act, for there is no other act but the act of the will.[491]

But Edwards is not simply Augustinian. Like the Medieval exemplarists he *also* sees the same kind of relationship between God and the created order. In a major treatise on which he was working at the time of his death, *Dissertation*

---

488 *Misc.* 94 (my emphasis). Edwards immediately adds that "though this word 'begotten' had never been used in Scripture, it would have been used in this case: there is no other word that so properly expresses it". Of course Edwards is simply mining the analogy of "idea" for the same concepts (reiteration, continuity etc.) that the Bible and the Nicene Fathers associate with "Son" (protests notwithstanding; cf. *Misc.* 151). As Rhys Bezzant elegantly puts it; "Edwards is able to assert the traditional creedal language of the generation of the Son using the bridging category of repitition"; R. Bezzant, "Trinitarian Strategy", *(draft research paper sent to me, April 2008)*

489 Edwards quotes Chevalier Ramsay's observation that God "contains necessarily the three real distinctions of Spirit conceiving, idea conceived, and love proceeding from both, which in the supreme infinite are not three single attributes or modes, but three different persons or self-conscious intellectual agents". *Misc.* 1180.

490 Though see Studebaker's contention (in contrast to Pauw – and, we might add, Danaher) that Edwards operates with only one model: the "mutual love" model which is a variation on the psychological model. S. M. Studebaker, review of *The Supreme Harmony of All: The Trinitarian Theology of Jonathan Edwards* by A. Plantinga Pauw, *Fides et Historia*. Terre Haute 36.1, (2004): 156.

491 Edwards, "Unpublished Trinity" Note the divergence with Owen over the context of Proverbs 8 – not in this case the *pactum salutis* but simply the life of the Trinity.

Concerning the End for Which God Created the World,[492] Edwards proposes that God's purpose in creation is an overflowing or emanation of his own nature.[493] Pointing to that "disposition in God, as an original property of his nature, to an emanation of his own infinite fullness",[494] this same fullness was what "excited him to create the world",[495] with the prospect that his excellencies should be further esteemed and multiplied.[496] The end in view is that "as God delights in his own beauty, he must necessarily delight in the creature's holiness; which is a conformity to, and participation of it, as truly as the brightness of a jewel, held in the sun's beams, is a participation or derivation of the sun's brightness, though immensely less in degree".[497]

Though Edwards is somewhat coy in explicitly mentioning the Trinity in this dissertation, the connection is clearly there.[498] Given what we have seen in his other writings, this "original property" of God toward self-diffusion can be nothing other than the divine begetting.

> This twofold emanation [via Son and Spirit] or communication of the divine fullness *ad extra* is answerable to the twofold emanation or going forth of the Godhead *ad intra*, wherein the internal and essential glory and fullness of the Godhead consists, *viz.* the proceeding of the eternal Son of God, God's eternal idea and infinite understanding and wisdom

---

492 J. Edwards, *The Works of President Edwards in Four Volumes. A Reprint of the Worcester Edition.*, 4 volumes, 9th edition (New York: Leavitt & Allen, 1856), 2.199.

493 "Surely it is no argument of indigence in God, that he is inclined to communicate of his infinite fullness. It is no argument of the deficiency of a fountain that it is inclined to overflow" ibid. 2.213.

494 Ibid. 2.207.

495 Ibid.

496 Ibid. 2.206.

497 Ibid., 2.210.

498 Holmes surmises that Edwards was reluctant to create confusion by introducing his trinitarian thought when a fuller treatise was planned; S. R. Holmes, *God of Grace and God of Glory: An Account of the Theology of Jonathan Edwards* (Edinburgh: T&T Clark, 2000), 54-55. This argument makes good sense – especially in light of a late aside in the dissertation that Holmes seems to miss where Edwards writes that "the *glory of God* is sometimes manifestly used to signify the second person of the Trinity" – immediately adding that "it is not necessary at this time to consider that matter"; Edwards, *Works*, 2.246. To the same point we might also observe Edwards' reference to the creation as a remanation of the emanation or "refulgence" of God. The last term is applied explicitly to the Son in *Misc.* 144.

and the brightness of his glory, whereby his beauty and ... the proceeding of the Holy Spirit.[499]

In each diffusion the result is the same: the delight of the Son and the Father in each other, corresponds to the enjoyment of God in this *new* reflection and the simultaneous exaltation of the creature that thus participates in God. To this end, Edwards outlines an eschatology built around the idea of *epecstasis*, in which the finite is eternally drawn into the infinite perfections of God.[500] The overarching idea is that there is thus a single and unified movement toward the glory of God wherein God delights to find himself in creation, and creation delights to discover herself in God:

> God's respect to the creature's good, and his respect to himself, is not a divided respect; but both are united in one, as the happiness of the creature aimed at, is happiness in union with himself. The creature is no further happy with this happiness which God makes his ultimate end, than he becomes one with God. The more happiness the greater the union: when the happiness is perfect, the union is perfect. And as the happiness will be increasing to eternity, the union will become more and more strict and perfect; nearer and more like to that between God the Father, and the Son; who are so united, that their interest is perfectly one.[501]

Such a vision as Edwards presents here might suggest that the creation functions as a kind of finite, contingent "brother" of the second Person; just as

---

499 *Misc.* 1266a; cf. 1151. Statements very similar to this occur at the start of Section VI in the *Dissertation*. ibid. 2.246.

500 See discussions in M. J. McClymond "Salvation as Divinization: Jonathan Edwards, Gregory Palamas and the Theological Uses of Neoplatonism" in *Jonathan Edwards: Philosophical Theologian*, ed. P. Helm & O. D. Crisp (Aldershot: Ashgate Publishing Limited, 2003), Holmes, *God of Grace*, 57-58, Danaher, *Ethics*, 6-7.

The idea of ἐπέκτασις – the creature's eternal advance toward the infinite goodness of God – can be found in the mystical writings of Gregory of Nyssa – see Gregory of Nyssa & J. Daniélou, *From Glory to Glory: Texts from Gregory of Nyssa's Mystical Writings*, trans. H. Musurillo (Crestwood: St. Vladimir's Seminary Press, 1979), 56-71 and K. Rombs "Gregory Nyssa's Doctrine of Epektasis: Some Logical Implications" in *Papers Presented at the Thirteenth International Conference on Patristic Studies Held in Oxford, 1999*, ed. W. F. Wiles, E. Yarnold & P. M. Parvis (Leuven: Peeters, 2001). Of course the concept appears elsewhere in Christian writing too – most popularly in the works of C.S. Lewis; cf. C. S. Lewis, *The Last Battle*, reprint edition (Harmondsworth: Penguin Books, 1971), 146-155.

501 Edwards, *Works*, 2.256.

the Father is perfectly and necessarily imaged in the Son, so he is less perfectly seen amongst his created people:

> The world was made for the Son of God especially. For God made the world for himself from love to himself; but God loves himself only in a reflex act. ... When God considers of making any thing for himself he presents himself before himself and views himself as his end, and that viewing himself is the same as reflecting on himself or having an idea of himself, and to make the world for the Godhead thus viewed and understood is to make the world for the Godhead begotten and that is to make the world for the Son of God.[502]

Edwards' logic here, is that because the Son is the way in which the Father knows himself, he must be the archetype of any additional (contingent) expression of God. Edwards also sees the Son as head of the moral part of creation – those creatures which are "capable of knowing their Creator and ... actively complying with his design in their creation and promoting it; while other creatures [do so] only passively and eventually".[503] For Edwards, the essence of virtue and beauty is consensual agreement (or "falling in with")[504] God – for all being exists in and for him[505] – and this is true first for the Son, whether as incarnate man[506] or as eternal Logos.[507] As Amy Plantinga Pauw observes, Edwards' challenge to the Western tendency toward modalism, is that

---

502 Edwards, "Unpublished Trinity".

503 *DisEnd.;* Edwards, *Works,* 2.225. "On the whole I think it is pretty manifest, that Jesus sought the glory of God as his highest and last end; and that therefore [being head of creation], this was God's last end in the creation of the world"; ibid. 2.232.

504 *DisEnd.;* ibid. 2.225.

505 This idea of beauty and virtue comprises the main argument of a second essay Edwards was working on at the time of his death: *The Nature of True Virtue.* Here, ultimate virtue means consenting and loving the One in whom all existence and benevolence comes together: "Virtue, as I have observed, consists in the cordial consent or union of Being to Being in general ... a universally benevolent frame of mind. ... God himself is in effect Being in general"; ibid. 2.301.

506 "On the whole I think it is pretty manifest, that Jesus sought the glory of God as his highest and last end; and that therefore [being head of creation], this was God's last end in the creation of the world"; ibid. 2.232.

507 "Tis peculiar to God, that he has beauty *within himself,* consisting in Being's consenting with its own Being, or the love of himself in his own Holy Spirit. Whereas the excellence of other is in loving others ... "; "On the Mind" (begun in 1723) in S. E. Dwight, *The Life of President Edwards* (New York: G&C&H Carvill, 1830), 701.

if God is *simply* one then there can be no excellence "inasmuch ... as there can be no consent".[508]

The Logos and the Goal of Salvation History

What then is the eternal Son consenting *to* in Edwards' understanding? According to the pattern above it is simply to be *what he is* – a perfect reflection of the Father. But in the *opera ad extra*, the Son's consent is also to the Father's plans for his (the Son's) glory. Edwards' scheme is not simply exemplarist – pointing to a congruence between the inner life of God and that between God and creation (Christ/creation, as mirror of the Logos). Rather creation is for the eternal Son himself. And Jesus *is* the Son himself – the same acting, thinking, loving subject in a new context.

Thus Edwards here aligns with Goodwin in distinction from Owen. While Owen is at pains to distinguish God (and particularly the Logos) from the world – almost to the point of dividing the person of the Son – Goodwin and Edwards are prepared to draw *positive* connections between God and the world and show the personal continuity between the Logos and Jesus. Like Goodwin Edwards is clear that the Mediator comes for *us*, but he wants us also to understand that the Mediator comes to do something for God. The Christ is the Logos *continuing* his relationship with the Father in a new context:

> The infinite love which there is from everlasting between the Father and the Son is the highest excellency and peculiar glory of the Deity. God saw it therefore meet that there should be some bright and glorious manifestation made of [it] to the creatures, which is done in the incarnation and death of the Son of God. Hereby was most clearly manifested to men and angels the distinction of the persons of the Trinity. The infinite love of the Father to the Son is thereby manifested, in that for his sake he would forgive an infinite debt, would be

---

[508] *Misc.* 117 cited in A. P. Pauw "'One Alone Cannot be Excellent': Edwards on Divine Simplicity" in *Jonathan Edwards: Philosophical Theologian,* ed. P. Helm & O. D. Crisp (Aldershot: Ashgate). 57. Pauw's ensuing line of discussion is that Edwards prescinds from the Western and Reformed commitment to divine *simplicity* by this elevation of consent. But this is not entirely true. Edwards' *emphasis* on consent is certainly new but we have already seen that as early as Athanasius there was an insistence that the natural and necessary processions are *also* be accompanied by the desire (or enjoyment) of the persons involved. Nor is it fair for Pauw to treat Edwards' as if he were presaging a Western individualistic vision of the persons; ibid., 77. On the contrary, his Augustinian self-love analogy, together with his compatibilistic (deterministic) understanding of free will, mean that he is talking about something entirely different. The persons may well "choose" and "consent" but they will always be as one, simply because they share the one nature.

reconciled with and receive into his favor and to his enjoyment those that had rebelled against him and injured his infinite majesty, and in exalting of him to that high mediatorial glory; and Christ showed his infinite love to the Father in his infinitely abasing himself for the vindicating of his authority and the honour of his majesty. When God had a mind to save men, Christ infinitely laid out himself that the honour of God's majesty might be safe and that God's glory might be advanced.[509]

Again, the love between the persons of the Trinity directs the shape of salvation history but not simply as (creation) archetype for human relations but as *actually played out* before our eyes in the event of the Cross. The salvation wrought by Christ's death is not first about God loving us – or even loving the perfect creature who is Christ – but it is the Father loving his Son and saving us for the Son's sake and for his ultimate glory. At the same time, Christ shows his "infinite love" for the Father, abasing himself so the Father will be honoured. Like John of the Cross, Edwards magnifies salvation history as an adjunct chapter in the life of the Trinity – a new opportunity for the Father and Son to love each other. Or, in Edwards words, a "bright and glorious manifestation" of triune relations leading to a "peculiar glory" arising out of the "distinction of the persons".[510]

Edwards' use of the nuptial motif in this connection, provides another point of connection to his unexpected Spanish forerunner. In the relationship between the Son and his people, Edwards sees the perfect archetype alluded to by Paul in Eph 5:25-33.[511] The world is "made to gratify the love that is in Christ's

---

509   *Misc.* 327[a]. Very similar summaries are to be found elsewhere:

It shews the infinite excellency of the Father thus: That the Son so delighted in him, and prized his honour and glory, that when he had a mind to save sinners, he came infinitely low, rather than men's salvation should be the injury of that honour and glory. It shewed the infinite excellency and worth of the Son, that the Father so delighted in him, that for his sake he was ready to quit his own; yea, and receive into favour those that had deserved infinitely ill at his hands.

J. Edwards, *Treatise on Grace*,
http://www.ccel.org/ccel/edwards/grace/files/grace.html, (accessed March, 2008).

And again,

It showed the infinite excellency and worth of the Son that the Father so delighted in him that for his sake he was ready to quit His anger and receive into favor those that had [deserved?] infinitely ill at his Hands ...

Edwards, "Unpublished Trinity".

510   *Misc.* 327[a].

511   See Edwards, *Works,* 2.219, cf. 2.243.

Can We Find Positive Examples of Intra-Trinitarian Willing?

heart" as it flows forth *ad extra*, it is made "to provide a spouse for Christ".[512] Edwards depicts the Father's intention in creating as to "present his Son a spouse in perfect glory from among sinful miserable mankind", insisting that the "the principal means by which God glorifies his Son in the world is by providing him a spouse".[513] Edwards writes again and again of the centrality of the betrothal of Christ to the church, insisting that it is the chief scriptural image to describe the church[514] and the very reason why there is a creation in the first place:

> The end of the creation of God was to provide a spouse for his Son Jesus Christ that might enjoy him and on whom he might pour forth his love. And the end of all things in providence [is] to make way for the exceeding expressions of Christ's love to his spouse and for her exceeding close and intimate union with, and high and glorious enjoyment of him ... And therefore the last thing and the issue of all things is the marriage of the Lamb. ... The wedding feast is eternal; and the love and joys, the songs, entertainments and glories of the wedding will never be ended. It will be an everlasting wedding day.[515]

In this vein, Edwards remarkably manages to elide the Maximian theory of united willing with the Bible's marriage typology: "They shall sit with him in his throne and reign over the same kingdom, as his spouse, ... for the will of the Head will be the will of the whole body ... they shall have no other will"; *Misc*. 1072. For a fuller discussion of this point (and many other points) of connection between the Edwards and Maximus see Michael Gibson's outstanding essay: M. Gibson, "The Beauty of the Redemption of the World: The Theological Aesthetics of Maximus the Confessor and Jonathan Edwards", *Harvard Theological Review* 101.1 (January 2008): 45-76.

512 Edwards, "Unpublished Trinity", final paragraph.

513 *Approaching the End of God's Grand Design* (1744 sermon) in , *Works of Jonathan Edwards Online,* (Jonathan Edwards Center at Yale University) http://edwards.yale.edu/archive/, (accessed from February, 2008), Vol 25.768. At the time of citation this work has still not been edited by Yale. I have cleaned it up a little to make Edwards' abbreviations and note-form clearer.

514 The relation or union between Christ and his Church is compared to many earthly relations and unions. Sometimes to that which is between Father and Children, sometimes friends and companions, sometimes brethren, [sometimes] head and members, [sometimes] stock and branches. But none is so commonly made use of as that of espousal or marriage. Above all, the Holy Ghost [seems to find] peculiar delight in this relation above all others [as] a similitude and representation of the between Christ and his church.

The Wise and Foolish Virgins: The Church Espoused to Christ, (1737 sermon), ibid., Vol 52.448 (my editing).

515 *Misc*. 702. See very similar statements in: *Misc*. 271 – J. Edwards, *The Miscellanies: a - 500*, ed. T. A. Schafer. vol. 13. *The Works of Jonathan Edwards*

As we can see here, Edwards promotion of the marriage image leads to the most exalted conception of God's people and their glorious future. Just as John of the Cross depicts the bride of Christ being being caught up into the exchange of love between the Father and Son, so Edwards envisages the church being brought into the very family life of the Trinity by marriage and adoption.

> It seems ... to have been God's design to admit man as it were to the inmost fellowship with the Deity ... into the divine family as his Son's wife.[516]

> The church is the daughter of God not only as he hath begotten her by his word and Spirit but as she is the spouse of his eternal Son. So we, being members of the Son are partakers in our measure of the Father's love to the Son and complacence in him.[517]

> The Church is now, as it were, brought into this family; adopted into it though naturally far off [from] the household of God. ... In this heavenly family there are first the persons of the Trinity – the natural members of the family. ... And there is the church – the adopted child.[518]

Occurrences of this kind of language in Edwards' *Miscellanies* and sermons are so common as to make selection of examples almost completely arbitrary. Edwards' understanding of the strong connection between the Son and the creation encourages him to promote a vision of union that reaches beyond the normal bounds of Reformed theology and often sounds like something from the Eastern or mystic traditions.

The Cross as Bride-Price

Yet we should hasten to observe, however, that there are crucial elements of Reformed theology at work here too. In contrast to modern theologians who would see union or deification language in *opposition* to juridical theories of the atonement,[519] Edwards builds his mysticism on the foundations of Christ's

---

Series ed. P. Miller (New Haven: Yale University Press, 1994), 374 (this work is not in Yale's online collection); *Misc.* 1245 – *The Church's Marriage to Her Sons, and to Her God*, (1746 sermon); and *Approaching the End of God's Grand Design* (1744, sermon) in , "WJE Online", Vol. 25.768.

516 *Misc.* 741.

517 *Jesus Christ is Transcendently Excellent and Lovely*, (1734 sermon), ibid. Vol. 19.593.

518 *God the Father* (1746 sermon), , ibid., Vol. 24.147-148.

519 A clear example of this kind of approach can be seen in S. Finlan, *Problems with Atonement: The Origins of, and Controversy about, the Atonement Doctrine* (Collegeville: Liturgical Press, 2005), 117-124. But of course the elevation of

love for sinners. In one of his major sermons on the topic, *The Wise and Foolish Virgins: The Church Espoused to Christ*,[520] Edwards highlights both the church's initial abjection and her final glory. He speaks of how, in her "rags" and "filth", "Christ found the Church in most disgrace ... nothing but mere grace that could induce Christ to espouse such an one".[521] "Christ loved her when she had none but was in the grossest deformity and filthiness a sordid odious Creature", such that "he could not come to unite her to him without wading through a sea of blood, without himself descending from heaven and as it were leaving the bosom of his Father".[522]

> [A]ll that Christ has bestowed upon her has cost Jesus Christ his blood. Nothing could be obtained for her at any other price than that of his blood. It was at this price he procured that holy and heavenly beauty which he puts upon her to fit her for his presence and cohabitation it was it was by the price of this blood that he purchased those excellent ornaments which he adorns her that he might present her to himself a pure beautiful and glorious church: Ephesians 5:25-27.[523]

This emphasis on the poverty of the church is not simply due to the fact that Edwards holds to the Reformed doctrine of depravity which necessitates a gracious salvation (though he certainly does). Going deeper, Edwards also sees that creation is set up so that Christ would *have opportunity* to "exercise the benevolence of his nature" and that thus "God might be glorified". Or, to put it another way, "the work of creation is subordinate to the work of redemption".[524] Thus the old Anselm/Scotus dichotomy over whether there

---

    incarnation *to the neglect* of atonement is something we have already witnessed in John of the Cross.

520 *The Wise and Foolish Virgins: The Church Espoused to Christ*, (1737, sermon); , "WJE Online", Vol. 52.448.

521 Ibid.

522 Ibid.

523 Ibid.

    Thus another difference between John of the Cross and Edwards is that, for the latter, the body of redeemed *humans* rather than creation is held to be the bride of Christ: "As the bridegroom chooses the bride for his peculiar friend, above all others in the world; so Christ has chosen his church for a peculiar nearness to him ... rather than the fallen angels, yea, rather than the elect angels". From *The Church's Marriage to Her Sons, and to Her God;* Edwards, *Works,* 3.567, cf. *Misc.* 824.

524 Ibid. 3.573. We can detect here another divergence from Calvin who, in *Institutes* 12.5-7, denounces Osiander's view that the incarnation would have occurred even without the fall since man's image was actually proleptic of Christ's future incarnation. In contrast, Calvin refuses to see either the fall or the incarnation as necessary to God's plans for humanity and maintains that humans would have been

would have been an incarnation apart from the fall,[525] is set aside; creation is set up with a view to the glorious atoning work of Christ.[526]

The Edwardsean *Pactum Salutis*

The rubric under which Edwards typically contemplates this grand scheme is a form of the *pactum salutis* that is somewhat more detailed than that delineated by his predecessors. In his most protracted discussion of the covenant of redemption, *Miscellanies* 1062,[527] Edwards unveils a three-stage scheme of trinitarian life. At the most fundamental level there is the procession of the Son and Spirit from the Father which simultaneously signifies an equality of glory yet also dependence: "everything in the Father is repeated or expressed again, and that fully: so there is no inferiority".[528] This order of procession does not, by itself, indicate any kind of subordination for Edwards: the procession is not voluntary but necessary and so "infers no proper subjection of one to the will of another". But these primordial actions do, nonetheless, *fit* with some kind of responsive intra-trinitarian willing.[529] Edwards identifies an order of operation within the Godhead – separate from the *pactum salutis* but congruent also with it – to which the persons agree voluntarily.

---

    as much in God's image if they had never fallen. Though even Calvin, it seems, recognizes some necessity in the incarnation, observing that "Even if man had remained free from all stain, his condition would have been too lowly for him to reach God without a Mediator"; *Institutes* 2.12.1. See further discussion in Helm, *Calvin's Ideas,* 139-141.

525 For an excellent overview of this question see J. Sheppard, *Christendom at the Crossroads: The Medieval Era* (Louisville: Westminster John Knox Press, 2005), 66-76.

526 Such a view may strike modern readers as distinctly Calvinist (and perhaps distastefully supralapsarian). I will return this matter in Chapter 5.

527 This work was a source of scandalized rumour up until its publication in 1880: J. Edwards, *Observations Concerning the Scripture Oeconomy of the Trinity and Covenant of Redemption,* ed. E. C. Smyth (New York: C. Scribner's Sons, 1880).

528 Ibid., 22-23.

529   As he writes in *Misc.* 1349, 50.

    That the eternal Logos should be subordinate to the Father, though not inferior in nature-yea that Christ, in his office, should be subject to the Father and less than he, though in his higher nature not inferior, is not strange. 'Tis proper among mankind [that] a son should be subordinate to his Father, yea subject in many respects, though of the same human nature, yea though in no respect inferior in any natural qualification. It was proper that Solomon should be under David his father, and be appointed king by him, and receive charges and directions from him, though even then in his youth probably not inferior to this father.

> [T]here is a natural decency or fitness in that order and economy that is established. It is fit that the order of the acting of the persons of the Trinity should be agreeable to the order of their subsisting. That as the Father is first in the order of subsisting, so he should be first in the order of acting. That as the other two persons are from the Father in their subsistence, and as to their subsistence naturally originated from him and are dependent on him, so that in all that they act they should originate from him, act from him and in a dependence on him. That as the Father with respect to the subsistences is the fountain of the deity, wholly and entirely so, so he should be the fountain in all the acts of the deity. This is fit and decent in itself. Though it is not proper to say, decency *obliges* the persons of the Trinity to come into this order and economy. Yet it may be said that decency requires it, and that therefore the persons of the Trinity all consent to this order, and establish it by agreement, as they all naturally delight in what is in itself fit, suitable and beautiful.[530]

Edwards' reasoning here thus seems to be a more explicitly personalist version of the scholastic theory of the divine missions. Just as the Medievals insisted that *any* of the persons might have become human but it was most appropriate for the Son, so Edwards insists that any of the equal persons might take the lead but that it most fit for that to fall to the Father.[531]

Edwards' eagerness to demonstrate this distinction between the economical agreement and the *pactum salutis* affords us insights into his trinitarian eschatology. Subsequent to the arguments just cited, he adduces another piece of supporting evidence which is that, by the covenant of redemption, the "Son of God is advanced into the economical seat of another person, viz. the Father, in being by this covenant established as the Lord and Judge of the world in the Father's stead".[532] The covenant of redemption delineates a pattern of subordination between the Father and the other two persons that is at once similar but different to that already arising from the processions and economy. For while the Father "merely by his economical prerogative can direct and prescribe to the other persons of the Trinity in all things not below their economical characters", he requires further mandate to ask the Son to stoop and serve him as he does in the incarnation: "the Father has no right to prescribe ...

---

530 *Misc.* 1062, 2.

531 Of course, in both cases, the insistence on divine freedom rings a little hollow when we realize that the alternative is that the persons *don't* act in accordance with what is "fit, suitable and beautiful".

532 Ibid., 35.

these things, unless invested with a right by free covenant engagements of his Son".[533]

At the same time there are gains and rewards received by the Son in this. While it is the "Father that is economically the King of heaven and earth", under the terms of the covenant, the Son is installed as regent "by having the Father's authority committed unto him" – a "reward for the aforementioned subjection".[534]

This newly delegated prerogative also involves the Holy Spirit. Whatever the original processional relationship between the Son and Spirit, there is a new state of affairs instigated under the covenant of redemption wherein the Father gives the Son "dispensation and disposal" of the Spirit which is the Father's own "divine infinite treasure". Though this dispensational authority will be "resigned at the end of the world ... that God may be all in all"[535] – along with all the delegated authority that the Son receives under *pactum salutis* – nevertheless there remains an aspect wherein it continues forever. In a final complication to the scheme, Edwards observes that there is a difference between the authority possessed by the divine Son and the mediatorial God-man, husband of the church. With regard to the former there will come a time when the work of redemption is complete and things revert back to the *status quo* of the economy. Yet the latter will go on; "the inheritance he purchased and received is an eternal inheritance":

> He then was invested with a two-fold dominion over the world: one vicarious, or as the Father's vicegerent, which shall be resigned at the end of the world, and the other, as Christ, God-man and Head and Husband of the Church, and in this latter respect he will never resign his dominion, but will reign forever and ever, as is said of the saints in the new-Jerusalem, after the end of the world, Rev 22:5.[536]

Here, finally, is the strength of Edwards' form of the covenant of redemption. By making the Son's role as mediator more about *relationship* and less about ontology, he avoids the sense we get from Owen that the *pactum* is a way of protecting the Son from creation.[537] Rather, it becomes a legitimate means by which the Father can "give to" or "reward" his Son without thereby implying a former insufficiency in the Son's divinity. The Logos is not changed by

---

533 Ibid., 39.

534 Ibid., 45-46.

535 Ibid., 48.

536 *Misc.* 1062, 10.

537 Or the same sense conveyed by "nature" or "Mediator" Christologies in general – see recent discussion of the distinction in Edmondson, *Christology*, – that the Son's activity *qua* Christ is purely vicarious.

salvation history, yet he does change *with regard to us* in that redemption creates a new bond between him and us. Thus he *does* gain from creation and redemption. While his innate character and glory is unchanged, his glory is now manifest and given expression in a way it was not before. Creation represents a wholly new context for the Son's glory as history moves toward perfection and completion in his redemption of sinners. Thus, though "there are but three in the [divine] society, the Church is brought in as belonging to one of the eternal members of the society *to render him complete in his station ... the fullness of him that filleth all in all"*.[538]

Some Final Observations Concerning the Pactum Salutis

At this point it may be opportune to stand back for a moment and ask some more basic questions about the *pactum salutis*. Although the idea has certainly survived into the modern era,[539] it has by no means gone without criticism. Among other charges, it has been labelled speculative, scholastic and inherently tritheist.[540]

Thus Karl Barth devotes several pages to a refutation of the doctrine in his *Church Dogmatics*,[541] suggesting that the idea of "two divine subjects ... who can have dealing and enter into obligations one with another" is "mythology, for which there is no place in a right understanding of the Trinity".[542] To Barth's way of thinking, the psychological monism of God means that the only

---

538 *God the Father* (1746, sermon), "WJE Online", Vol. 64.813 (my editing and emphasis). Here is Augustine's doctrine of *totus Christi* reworked with an emphasis on the Son's final situation as Christ – not simply our completion in him.

539 A few examples of *pactum salutis* theology from the modern era can be found in: L. Berkhof, *Systematic Theology* (Edinburgh: Banner of Truth, 1959), 265-271; J. I. Packer, *Introduction, On Covenant*, http://www.gospelpedlar.com/articles/Bible/ cov_theo.html, (accessed May, 2008) – originally published as a foreword piece for H. Witsius, *The Economy of the Covenants Between God and Man: Comprehending a Complete Body of Divinity* (Phillipsburg: P&R Publishing, 1990); M. S. Horton, *Lord and Servant: A Covenant Christology* (Louisville: Westminster John Knox Press, 2005); and R. A. Smith, *The Eternal Covenant: How the Trinity Reshapes Covenant Theology* (Moscow: Canon Press, 2003).

540 Such criticisms have even come from within the Reformed fold. For assessments by Herman Bavinck and Abraham Kuyper see G. C. Berkouwer, *Divine Election. Historical Studies in Dogmatics* (Grand Rapids: Eerdmans, 1960), 162-163. For a broader (and excellent) survey of modern critiques: Beach, "Pactum Salutis", 104-115.

541 CD 4/1:63-66

542 CD 4/1:65.

inter-subjective covenant can be between God and humanity; any intra-trinitarian compact will have to be proleptic of the Son's role as Mediator.[543] To imagine a prior (triune) reality or covenant (or works) behind this single decision hints at a *determining reason* for God's actions in Christ which truncates God's absolute freedom.[544]

Much more recently, Jonathan Edwards' *pactum* theory has come in for sustained and less-than-sympathetic attention from Amy Plantinga Pauw. Pauw contends that Edwards' development of the doctrine contradicted the relationality inherent in his psychological model and "fell prey to [an] atomistic view of personhood".[545] While commending the covenant of redemption for trying to address the gap between the "ontological parity" and the subordination and difference that is obvious in the economy,[546] she also sees in such federalism a (paradoxical) tendency that "threatened the orthodox confession of the immanent parity of the persons".[547] Because Edwards specifically rejected those schemes which made a sharp division between the immanent and economic Trinity and insisted that there "had to be an eternal fittingness"[548] to the way the covenant was instituted, Pauw sees him as attempting to retranscribe human hierarchical norms over the Trinity:

---

543   God is one God. If He is thought of as the supreme and finally the only subject. He is the one subject. And if, in relation to that which He obviously does amongst us, we speak of His eternal resolves or decrees ... then we do not regard the divine persons of the Father and the Son as partners in this contract, but the one God – Father, Son and Holy Spirit – as the one partner and the reality of man as distinct from God on the other. ... [As Mediator] the Son of the Father is no longer just the eternal Logos, but as such, as very God from all eternity He is also the very God and very man He will become in time.

    CD 4/1:65-66

544   Barth's real issue here seems to be the Coeccian distinction between the Covenant of *Grace* and Law which, he argues, made it impossible for its adherents to make an "unequivocal" affirmation that it was "the eternal divine decree [that is] the beginning of all things"; CD 4/1:66.

545   Pauw, *Supreme Harmony*, 77.

546   Ibid., 93. Pauw's assessment here corresponds to that of Berkouwer who states that the question addressed by the doctrine was "how we must understand that testimony of Scripture which speaks of the submissiveness of the Son to the Father, the Servant of the Lord"; Berkouwer, *Divine Election*, 167.

547   Pauw, *Supreme Harmony*, 99.

548   Ibid., 104.

The notions of a son agreeing, at great personal cost, to a father's plan, and of another member of the society [the Spirit] being excluded from the covenant altogether, mirrored familiar social arrangements.[549]

Pauw finally accuses Edwards of promulgating both nascent tritheism and subordinationism. In regard to the former, the *pactum* makes it look like the three persons are simply three "friends" who form a committee to work on salvation.[550] Pauw exclaims that "anthropormorphism doesn't get much cruder" than it does in Edwards' insistence that the Son must have his own volitional capacity (*sui juris*).[551] On the other hand, Pauw is more personally deeply offended by the anti-egalitarianism implicit in Edwards' *style* of social covenant. Switching hermeneutical approaches she offers a feminist critique of such "narratives within the Godhead" which:

... shore up subordinationist schemes within human communities. In societies still battling the injustices of deferential and exclusive social arrangements, the social presuppositions of Edwards' covenantal scheme are deeply troubling.[552]

Defending the *pactum salutis*

Before I offer any response to these critiques, I should clarify that it is not my intention to offer a general defence of covenantal theology insofar as it envisages a two- or three-stage covenantal scheme as the basis of all salvation history. I am sympathetic to the charge that some of the theory's putative proofs are very weak.[553] I find many of its refinements – for example Edwards' delineation of temporary and permanent covenants and multi-tiered relationships between the Son and Spirit – reminiscent of Ptolemaic epicycles designed to rescue a paradigm in crisis.

---

549 Ibid., 116.

550 Ibid., 114.

551 Ibid., 115.

552 Ibid., 116. See also Danaher's references to other anti-hierarchical commentary on Edwards from Ola Winslow, Patricia Tracy and Ava Chamberlain. Danaher is quick to add his name to the list, stating that these aspects of Edwards theology are "without defence and must be resisted". Displaying the very willingness to reshape theology for the sake of anthropology that Pauw decries, Danaher writes that "Edwards' acceptance of gender hierarchies as part of the created order indicates the vulnerability of his theological scheme to the unwitting perpetration of systemic injustice" and "raises the question as to whether the 'economy of the Trinity' ... can provide a viable social model for fallen human beings"; Danaher, *Ethics*, 111.

553 If this is not already clear from John Owen then see Berkhof's concession that to use Zech 6:13 as a justification for the expression "counsel of peace" was "clearly a mistake". Berkhof, *Systematic Theology*, 266.

But I do want to suggest that there are real attractions in a modest version of the *pactum salutis* – or at least a *relational dynamic* which is in broad agreement with the *pactum*-based scheme laid out by Edwards (shorn of its more extravagant elements). The scheme I have in mind is similar to that which I proposed at the end of my examination of Maximus in Chapter 2.

- That God makes free choices and that these decisions are chosen from among the multitude of good possibilities available to him as defined by his essential nature.

- That these decisions must be made at the level of the persons, and that, in the case of the Trinity, they are made by the Father and subsequently (in eternity) actively embraced by the Son (and Spirit).

The chief merits of this scheme are as follows:

1. A *pactum salutis* which portrays the possibilities available to the persons as expressions of the divine essence, is able to maintain an orthodox commitment to the one essential will (since everything that the Father and Son choose is in accordance with their common essence), without compromising the genuine agency of the divine persons themselves.

2. If the "possibilities" made available by the essence are identified with the *logoi* of Maximus or the *rationes* spoken of by the Western Medieval schoolmen, then the *pactum* can be seen as an elegant interpolation of mainstream logos-theology: the transmission of the *rationes* from Father to Son (as per Anselm etc.) is followed by an interpersonal communication as to which should be actualised.

3. In attributing consenting will to the Son in contingent matters, we acknowledge the equality of the persons and honour the traditional distinction between nature and *hypostasis/tropos*, while offering a more plausible rendition of how the personal expressions of divine willing operate in the context of contingent decision. The Scotist (and Thomist) implication that the Son is born with the Father's decisions already set (meaning that only the Father is truly free) is avoided.

4. The scheme represents an advance on nominalist *pactum* theory without the extreme voluntarism inherent in the idea of an unbounded *potentia absoluta* beyond the *rei ordinata*.[554]

---

[554] In other words we are dealing not with a *potentia absoluta/ordinata* dichotomy but rather one of *potentia essentiae* vs. *potentia ordinata*. As per Calvin, we reject absolute voluntarism in favour of an "infinite" power which is already circumscribed by God's character. See Helm, *Calvin's Ideas*, 312, also D. C. Steinmetz, *Calvin in Context* (New York: Oxford University Press, 1995), 40-52.

5. Seeing the Father as initiator (with the Son accepting his decisions) accords perfectly with the universally held processional order of the persons. Here, the Father is *principium* as to essence *and* as to decree, while the Son shares in that essence and those decrees in different (but congrent) ways. He partakes of the essence by filial procession (begetting); he actively shares in the second by responsive intra-trinitarian willing.

6. The scheme allows us to see the persons as loving agents in a true sense. The filial love of the Son for the Father will ensure that the latter's choices will be embraced – not simply because they are in accordance with the divine nature[555] – but because the Son delights in the opportunity for further responsiveness. Conversely, the Father's love for the Son means that the decisions he makes will be such that the Son will be honoured and glorified – in other words he will use his prerogative for the sake of the Son.

7. The *pactum*, insofar as it shows us the Father and Son serving each other, reorients our perspective on the divine aspirations for salvation history. Advancing on Medieval (or modern) aesthetic theories, the *pactum salutis* pictures the divine plans as primarily inter-personal: the conformity and convergence of contingent beings toward the eternal exemplar is first for the sake and glory of that *other eternal person*.

I would suggest that a *pactum* dynamic configured in the manner just described largely evades the objections mentioned above.[556] Barth, in his radical voluntarism, protests that the *pactum salutis* implies some determining foundation below grace and election: but of course we have seen that part of the very attraction of the *pactum* for Edwards and (especially) Owen is that it facilitates divine freedom. By interposing a free act of choice between God's essential nature and the *opera ad extra* both God's unchanging character *and* original freedom is secured.

Similarly forestalled are the warnings of tritheism. It is too simple to complain that under such a scheme the persons have "different wills" – especially given the range of meanings for the word "will". In the scheme I am suggesting, each person equally partakes of, and delights in, the *rationes* (*logoi*) from which the Father makes his choice. As long as the *pactum* arises out of that common essence and is seen to operate in accordance with the orthodox modes of subsistence, the *pactum* illuminates the oneness/threeness in exactly

---

555 And thus already "his" *in potentia*.

556 At least those which are orthodox; Barth's collapse of the immanent Trinity into God's eternal decree robs the Son and Spirit of real personhood and raises the spectre of a Modalistic entity (*deus absconditus*) "behind" the persons who does the deciding.

the same way that the doctrines of begetting and procession elucidate the unity of essence.

At this point the charge of subordinationism is also misdirected. If the objection arises out of the fact that the Father is first and the Son is seen to be derivative – well, we have seen again and again that this is simply what orthodox trinitarian theology *is* and has always been since (at least) the fourth century.[557] If the priority of the Father and the responsiveness of the Son is criticised as validating oppressive human power structures, the response can only be that any such enlisting of the *pactum salutis* is a wilful misunderstanding. The true Patriarch uses his priority for the glory of the Son – not to exploit him. [558]

Finally, what can we say about the charge that the *pactum salutis* is mythological – that it projects anthropomorphic categories onto the ineffable and transcendent persons of the Godhead? Of course the objection is partly correct. It *is* problematic to speak of the persons of the Trinity as "people" having "conversations" and "coming to conclusions". But such difficulties here are already with us when we declare that the Son is "begotten" of the Father or that God "answers prayer", or that the persons of the Trinity "love one another". Surely we handle all such ideas as these apophatically – not because we *really* understand what they mean – but because Scripture uses them and we trust that God (as creator and revealer) has given us adequate symbols to tell us what we need to know.[559]

Moreover some such "mythology" is simply unavoidable. The moment the question is raised about whether creation is eternal (*á la* Origen), we *have to* say that God "freely decided", or slide into some form of pantheism. The fact that we have no clear idea how or "when" this decision took place, is beside the point. And once we say that God has decided things, then it is also legitimate to

---

557 Pauw's own critique of the *pactum salutis* is also tellingly accompanied by a sideswipe against orthodox trinitarianism itself – echoing Mary Rose D'Angelo's complaints against subordinationism in the "metaphorical" language of "Father" and "Son"; Pauw, *Supreme Harmony,* 115-116, cf. 77 n. 73.

558 Pauw herself is quite sanguine about the idea of personal consent within the Trinity when it is associated with love. In her essay "One Alone Cannot be Excellent" she repeats the "crude anthropomorphism" charge before moving on to commend the "aesthetic dimensions of Edwards' theology derived from the more basic category of loving consent" which is, in the words she takes from Edwards, the "original beauty or excellence ... among minds"; Pauw, *One Alone,* 121-122.

559 Here of course I am invoking an analogical theory of revelation founded on the idea that God has created human beings in such a way that they can know and speak about God. This is neither a claim for univocal knowledge nor a defence of natural theology, simply the observation that *analogia fidei* and *analogia entis* must work together.

ask *who* does the deciding – the divine "being" or the persons? How do we avoid modalism and tritheism here?[560] And what defines God's ends in making such "decisions"?

I believe that the answers which work best with these questions are those envisaged by the likes of John of the Cross, Thomas Goodwin and Jonathan Edwards. And, in the next chapter, I will endeavour to show that these answers might also be seen to accord with the great themes of the Bible.

---

560   The point is that once we press the question of divine decision, the alternatives are limited. Barth's solution is to deny the Son and Spirit any distinct subjectivity at all – a dangerous lurch toward modalism. The only alternatives that we have discovered to this which resist modalism (Aquinas and Scotus) still end up with one person deciding and the others passively following – scarcely an improvement. Modern *perichoretic* theology (see Chapter 6) avoids the problem by fudging it – each person relies on the others so nobody can be distinguished as the decider. Perhaps in the light of this it is interestingly, Pauw herself finally refuses to be drawn on the question and retreats into mystery: cf. Pauw, *Supreme Harmony,* 117-118.

Chapter 5

Does Responsive Intra-Trinitarian Willing Fit with Scripture?

...but in these last days he has spoken to us by his Son, whom he appointed heir of all things, and through whom he made the universe.

– Hebrews 1:2

It is not to angels that he has subjected the world to come, about which we are speaking. But there is a place where someone has testified: "What is man that you are mindful of him, the son of man that you care for him?"

– Hebrews 2:5-6

Introduction

My ultimate goal in writing this thesis is to propose a certain model of divine relations that might inform a unified and coherent vision of salvation history, incarnation, atonement and trinitarian orthodoxy. I will argue that the life and obedience of Jesus is a real expression the life of the eternal Son and this dynamic might be seen as the structuring principle for salvation history itself.

All this will require hard work at the historical and systematic level. Any theology which seeks a close identification of the Trinity *ad intra* and *ad extra* will have to negotiate its way through a thicket of heresies and controversies, both ancient and modern.

And yet, with these matters still ahead of us, I would open my case by making the, obvious observation that if the eternal relationship between the Father and Son is anything like that revealed between the Father and Jesus then some form of responsive intra-trinitarian order would seem to be inevitable. The Jesus of the gospels speaks words that are given by the Father and does the work the Father gives him to do. When the Father does not reveal something to him he doesn't know it. When the Father's will is different from his, it is his Father's will that is done.[561] Clearly, whatever equality Jesus might possess

---

561 Thus in the Fourth Gospel alone, for example:

with God, it is communicated to us in the context of his being functionally subordinate and dependent on the Father.

The very language of "Father" and "Son" used by Jesus must, if we take the social-historical context of the Bible seriously, connote some kind of paternal priority.[562] Rabbinic teachings criticise the bad son who thereby "makes himself equal to his father".[563] Cultural studies by Kenneth Bailey reveal a consistent authority enjoyed by the Near Eastern patriarch: "An oriental father is never his son's equal".[564] Bruce Malina also stresses the importance of appreciating Mediterranean patriarchy. He explains how the honour of a father in such cultures depends on the deference shown him by his children,[565] and

---

1. The Son's words actions and judgments are delivered in conformity to the Father.
   (3:34; 4:34; 5:19, 30; 6:38; 7:16, 18; 8:16, 28, 29, 40; 12:49, 50; 14:11, 31; 15:10, 15; 17:8, 14)

2. The Son's works and miracles testify to the power of the Father.
   (5:36; 9:3, 32; 10:25, 31; 14:11; 17:2)

3. It is *the Father* who gives the Son all things
   (3:35; 6:37; 10:29; 13:3; 16:15; 17:2, 7).

[562] Thus the exigence implicit in "Father" comes through explicitly in the parable of the two sons (Matt 21:28-30), and implicitly in the parable of the prodigal son. This is not to argue that God's fatherhood can just be "read off" near-eastern patriarchy – the humiliating sprint of the prodigal's father is often justly cited here. But whatever elements of the paternal analogy are discontinuous between divine and human patriarchy, authority and honour-due would not appear to be among them. The running father of Luke 15:20 *remains* a patriarch – his alarming compassion simply tells us what kind of ruler he is with regard to his family.

[563] See R. H. Strachan, *The Fourth Gospel: Its Significance and Environment,* 3rd & revised edition (London: SCM, 1941), 168 and R. H. Lightfoot, *St. John's Gospel: A Commentary,* ed. C. F. Evans, revised edition (Oxford: Clarendon Press, 1956), 149.

[564] K. E. Bailey, *Poet & Peasant; and, Through Peasant Eyes: A Literary-Cultural Approach to the Parables in Luke,* Combined edition (Grand Rapids: Eerdmans, 1983), 182-183. Bailey here is rebutting the idea that the father's kissing of the prodigal signifies equality; "it would be unthinkable for any father publicly to assert that his son was his equal!" (ibid.). Elsewhere in the same volume he also cites the observations of Egyptian scholar Ibrahim Sa'id who also notes the *elder* son's shocking "failure to offer the esteem of a son to his father"; ibid., 197. If these observations trigger the same recoil in the Western mind as RITW itself, then it should perhaps be explained that this is not an inequality of nature (see Bruce Malina's comments in the next note) but a relational modality which subsists within the familial bond.

[565] "When a father commands his children to do something, and they obey him, they treat him honourably ... [otherwise] the father's peers would feel free to ridicule him, thereby acknowledging his lack of honour as a father" B. J. Malina, *Windows*

that it is the special duty of the firstborn son to defend the honour of the father.[566] Elsewhere he introduces a slightly different concept – the idea of a patron "father" – to throw light on Jesus' customary way of describing the relationship between God and his people – again with the same stress on due honour.[567]

But does this subordination extend beyond Jesus' years on earth? The scant glimpses we have of how the Son and Father relate before the incarnation consistently express the idea that Jesus *was sent* into the world.[568] Other passages seem to indicate that Jesus seems to *remain* functionally subordinate to the Father after the ascension: his disciples speak of him as God's ἅγιος παῖς (Acts 4:27; 30):[569] Revelation 1:1 depicts the exalted Jesus Christ

---

on the World of Jesus: Time Travel to Ancient Judea, 1st edition (Louisville: Westminster/John Knox Press, 1993), 2, cf. 171. We should note that this paternal "superiority" does not mean the son is inferior in other respects. Indeed Malina explains that "children bear the acquired and inherited status of their parents and ancestors". From outside the parent-child relationship "parents and children are at the same level of their in-group"; ibid., 79.

566 Ibid., 4-7. The (distractingly abhorrent) example he gives is of a son murdering his sister to remove the stain of her elopement. Despite this, the general concept of the firstborn securing the family honour fits well with the pattern of filial honour running through John's gospel (eg. John 8:49) and also the dynamic associated with the defence of "my father's house" which elicits the demand for a proof of authority (cf. John 2:15-17). We might observe in passing that this concept also forestalls the "divine child abuse" charge lately levelled against penal views of the atonement. If the firstborn son is the guardian and champion of the father's honour (which is ultimately his own honour as heir) then he is far from the Father's reluctant or passive victim. Their interests and roles in the transaction are rather in perfect alignment. "Males attempt to gain honour for the family on the outside; they represent the family and its interests on the outside"; ibid., 87 (cf. John 14:13, 17:4).

567 B. J. Malina, *The Social World of Jesus and the Gospels* (New York: Routledge, 1996), 147-149. I am not entirely convinced by Malina's argument that the relationship between Jesus and the Father fits this latter form rather than that of natural father; though it may well be closer to the mark in the case of the relationship that he describes between his followers and Jesus ("your father" as opposed to "my father" cf. John 20:17).

568 So in John: 3:17, 34; 4:34; 5:23, 24, 30, 36, 37, 38; 6:29, 32, 38, 44, 57; 7:16, 18, 28, 29, 33; 8:16, 18, 26, 29, 42; 9:4; 10:36; 11:42; 12:44, 45, 49; 13:20; 14:24; 15:21; 16:5; 17:3, 8, 18, 21, 23, 27; 20:21.

569 Obviously we are not meant to regard Jesus as just *any* servant here. The contrast with δούλοις in v. 29 and the association with Ps 2 where David is God's παῖς (Acts 4:25) ensure this – see. W. Arndt, F. W. Gingrich & W. Bauer, *A Greek-English Lexicon of the New Testament and other Early Christian Literature* (Chicago: Cambridge University Press, 1957), 609. Nevertheless the fact remains that the disciples here pray *to* God *for* God's chosen and exalted servant/king.

receiving a revelation to pass on to his servants;[570] Rev 3:12 has him calling the Father "my God".[571] First Corinthians 15:24-28 describes a pattern wherein the Father brings all things under the feet of the Christ so that all things are subject to him – except, he adds hastily, the one who subjects all things to him (ἐκτὸς τοῦ ὑποτάξαντος αὐτῷ τὰ πάντα; v. 27b). "Then the Son himself will also be subjected to the one who put all things in subjection under him, so that God may be all in all" (v. 28).

None of this is to deny that there is *no* new service that is embraced in the incarnation (eg. Phil 2:6-8; Heb 5:8), nor to overlook the glory relinquished in

---

570   So G. E. Ladd observes of the passage that:

> God the Father is the ultimate source and fountainhead of all revelation; God the Son is the agent through whom this revelation is imparted to men. This is true even of the exalted Christ. That the Son receives what he is and has from the Father is a New Testament truth in general which is particularly emphasized in the Gospel of John (John 3:35; 5:20ff., 26; 7:16 and 8:28). We are reminded of our Lord's saying, "But of that day or that hour no one knows, not even the angels in heaven, nor the Son, but only the Father" (Mark 13:32).

> G. E. Ladd, *A Commentary on the Revelation of John* (Grand Rapids: Eerdmans, 1972), 21.

> Bruce Malina makes complementary observations from a social-historical perspective:

> Writing in this historical period was essentially aural ... Official documents were read by personal representatives of the emperor or king, while documents of revelation were directed to prophets and royal personages alone. ... Sacred documents were to be read and interpreted by personal representatives of the deity ...

> B. J. Malina & J. J. Pilch, *Social-science Commentary on the Book of Revelation* (Minneapolis: Fortress Press, 2000), 29-30.

> Meanwhile, Robert Mounce connects the pattern seen here in the prologue with that seen in Revelation 5 where Jesus is the one who has the right to unseal the scroll of history which, again, comes from the Father. Jesus is thus not a (passive) messenger like an angel but the mediator who reveals by *what he achieves*; R. H. Mounce, *The Book of Revelation,* revised edition (Grand Rapids: Eerdmans, 1998), 40-41. This is a very helpful observation and – though Mounce does not make the connection – fits with Jesus' own comments in John 5:19-23 about the Son doing what the Father *shows* him. Clearly in the Johannine framework, revelation that takes place through Jesus is not merely informative but effective. Jesus is thus also the *source* of revelation in the Father's economy, for it is given to him to be the key to history.

571   Kevin Giles suggests that "exegesis cannot harmonise" such passages as Rev 1:1; 3:12 and 12:10 – Giles, *Jesus*, 126. This is puzzling given that he is able to see the *shaliach* dynamic as establishing Jesus equality five pages earlier – ibid., 119-120.

the Son's earthly appearance (cf. John 17:5). But there is little indication that Jesus' original glory or existence ἐν μορφῇ θεοῦ connotes a peer-relationship with the Father. Even if we choose to associate all the data mentioned in the previous paragraph with the temporary provisions of redemption,[572] the fact remains that *every* symbol that might be taken to depict the second person's eternal relation to the Father – word, image, stamp, radiance, son – trades on a "from-ness" and paternal priority that is at least congruent with the responsiveness and dependence of the Son-as-man.[573]

Equal is as Equal Does

Yet if there is little textual warrant for trying to avoid RITW this does not mean that there are no *other* reasons. For many modern theologians, as we will soon see, such passages as those just adduced are *logically* incommensurable with the Son's divinity. Since God is the uncaused cause of everything we cannot think of the Son receiving anything from the Father without threatening his *aseity*.[574] To see him as below or from the Father in any sense (whether in terms of subsistence or will) is to introduce a "gradation" within the Godhead[575] – something that other passages in the New Testament explicitly rule out.[576]

There is no need to go preempt the historical discussion at this point – except to reiterate that it is more complicated than that. But the logic of the point is important for us here because it is directly addressed for us in two crucial passages of the New Testament.

---

572 In other words, his human nature or mediatorial office.

573 I stress that this refers to those symbols that depict the Son *in relation to the Father* – not to deny that they are also *one* Lord and God from an external frame of reference.

574 In passing it should be noted that there is nothing new in this confusion of the (Father's) personal property of innascibility with the essential property of aseity. In *DeTrin.* 5.3, Augustine identifies the demand that "unbegotten" be taken in a substantial (essential) sense as the *maxime calidissimum machinamentum* (most cunning device) of the Arians to divide the persons. See Brown, *Trinity,* 281.

575 I refer here to Millard Erickson's nomenclature which contrasts *equivalentism* ("eternally the Father and the Son have equal authority") with *gradationism* ("the Father eternally has supreme authority"); Erickson, *Tampering,* 21.

576 So Erickson cites passages which show Jesus sharing the Father's rule/throne (Rev 3:21, 7:17, 12:5, 22:3 and Matt 25:31-36) as a counter to gradationism; ibid., 114, 118.

1 Corinthians 8:6

The first passage occurs in the early verses of First Corinthians 8 where Paul seeks to lay out the principles for dealing with food offered to idols. As Paul elaborates, idolatory and its practises are founded on an illusion, since in reality there is only one God (vv. 4-6). But it is not enough to simply *know* this fact, we must also be careful of the consciences of weaker brethren (vv. 1-3, 7-13). As an aside, in the midst of this, Paul contrasts true Christian monotheism with polytheism:

> Indeed, even though there may be so-called gods in heaven or on earth – as in fact there are many gods and many lords, yet there is one God, the Father, from whom are all things and for whom we exist, and one Lord, Jesus Christ, through whom are all things and through whom we exist. (vv. 5-6)

The reason for the interjection in verse six seems to be that Paul has just spoken of the idea of there being many gods and many lords as error. But doesn't Christianity immediately contradict this with its devotion to God *and* the Lord Jesus? Some response would seem to be in order; both to buttress the point about polytheism, and to head off any misconceptions in the minds of the factious Corinthian church.[577]

In response to this, Paul proclaims Christian monotheism. As a number of scholars have observed,[578] the stress on "one God" and "one Lord" found in 1 Cor 8:6 seems intended as a parallel to the *Shema* of Deut 6:4; "Hear, O Israel: the LORD [Yahweh] is our God, the LORD is One". If this is correct, Paul is signifying that the Father and Son together are Yahweh, the God of the OT.

And yet if "Yahweh" is inclusive of the Son here, "God" applies first and most properly to the Father.[579] The Father "God" (ἐξ οὗ τὰ παντα) is clearly made the fountainhead (*arché* or *principium* in systematic language) of divine life and action. The Son (δι' οὗ τὰ παντα) is the Father's agent. Paul makes

---

[577] There is some value, at this point, in James Dunn's argument that Paul has his eye on the Corinthian tendency to break apart into competing fan clubs (Paul, Apollos, Christ); Dunn, *Christology*, 181-182. What Dunn misses, however, in his desire to avoid any early reference to Christ's divinity, is that Paul is not simply speaking of Christ as the unifier and *telos* of Christian faith, he must also be explained *at the level of divinity* – otherwise there would be no logical connection to the denunciation of polytheism. In other words the immediate context is not primarily existential or teleological, rather protological/ontological.

[578] See for example R. Bauckham, *God Crucified: Monotheism and Christology in the New Testament* (Grand Rapids: Eerdmans, 1999), 37-40 or L. W. Hurtado, *How on Earth did Jesus Become a God?: Historical Questions about Earliest Devotion to Jesus* (Grand Rapids: Eerdmans, 2005), 49.

[579] Cf. John 8:54.

clear that this is not the agency of an exalted creature. His action is *completely coextensive* with that of the Father; so fully, that his lordship must be included in any understanding of God the Father. We are to see "God" and "Lord" neither as coordinate entities, nor *simply* as one. Christian monotheism, as Paul depicts it here is the Son *included* in the divinity of the Father. As Larry Hurtado observes:

> Paul's phrasing here certainly affirms an exclusivist monotheism ... Yet we must also notice that the bold inclusion of Jesus here as the "one Lord" is expressed in a way that maintains a clear distinction between him and "the Father". More specifically, this distinction involves a functional subordination of the "Lord" (Jesus) to the one God.[580]

In this light, simple assertions that the persons are "equal" or "subordinate" (not to mention labels such as "gradationist") are revealed as thoroughly inadequate. The Son is equal with the Father – because he is the perfect *sine qua non* mediator of the Father. His derivative status with regard to the Father in everything, leads to *absolute equality* in any "external" frame of reference, for the Father is perfectly and wholly re-presented in the Son. The result is that there is only one divinity for us to worship; that of the Father, in and through the Son.

John 5:18-23

Similar issues emerge out of Jesus' interaction with the hostile Jews of John 5:18. Here Jesus has just healed a man on the Sabbath and justified the action by associating himself with the Father who is also always working. The result is a compounded offense for, as John puts it, "not only was he breaking the Sabbath, but he was even calling God his own Father, making himself equal with God" (v. 18).

This preliminary, interpretive statement is crucial to understanding both the objection of the Jews and the response of Jesus. In the first place we might observe that there was not necessarily anything offensive about Jesus calling himself the Son of God if the title simply connoted the special relationship and authority given to the heir of David (eg. 2 Sam 7:14; Ps 89:26-27) – it need be neither more nor less than a claim to be the Messiah (cf. Matt 26:63). But John's commentary makes it clear that Jesus meant more than this – and that his Jewish interlocutors *knew* he meant more than this.[581] Jesus was speaking

---

580 Ibid., 49.

581 Thus, I am not convinced that the problem is simply that Jews considered it blasphemy to *claim* (or falsely claim) to be the Messiah – eg. E. W. Hengstenberg, *Commentary on the Gospel of St John.* vol. 5, 7. *Clark's Foreign Theological Library ser. 4* (Edinburgh: T&T Clark, 1865), 392. Jesus' statements are taken correctly as claims to equality (5:18) even if the mode of that equality is mistaken

apparently about a kind of literal sonship that would connote *equality* with God, and in terms that might approximate a pagan theogony wherein Jesus has been sired by God and now stands before them as a competitor (*deuteros theos*) to their monotheistic faith.[582]

In this context Jesus immediately seeks to outflank the misunderstanding by explaining what his Sonship and equality looks like: conformity, dependence and unity of action. His claims about himself take nothing away from God, since the Father is the enabler and source of his actions:

> Jesus said to them, "Very truly, I tell you, the Son can do nothing on his own, but only what he sees the Father doing; for whatever the Father does, the Son does likewise. The Father loves the Son and shows him all that he himself is doing; and he will show him greater works than these, so that you will be astonished. Indeed, just as the Father raises the dead and gives them life, so also the Son gives life to whomever he wishes. The Father judges no one but has given all judgment to the Son, so that all may honour the Son just as they honour the Father. Anyone who does not honour the Son does not honour the Father who sent him. (vv. 19-23).

Here again, then, is a defence of Christian monotheism[583] that employs the same basic structure as 1 Cor 8:1-6. Jesus wants his hearers to be clear that he is dynamically and relationally subordinate to the Father.[584] Emphatically (ἀμὴν ἀμὴν), the Son has no ability to do anything by himself (οὐ δύναται ... ἀφ' ἑαυτοῦ) – surely not meaning that he is *powerless* given what follows, but that his power is not independent of, nor coordinate with that of the Father.[585] The

---

by his Jewish hearers. In John 10:30 (cf. v. 36) he associates being "Son of God" with being "one" with God. In the trial, where the connection between "Son of God" and Messiah is made most explicit (cf. Matt 26:63; Mk 14:61) he heightens+ the claim with apocalyptic language of coming on the clouds.

582 See F. F. Bruce, *The Gospel of John,* 1st paperpack edition (Grand Rapid: Eerdmans, 1994), 128 and C. H. Dodd, *The Interpretation of the Fourth Gospel* (Cambridge: Cambridge University Press, 1953), 327.

583 Lightfoot, *John,* 141.

584 By "dynamically" here I mean both: (1) that connection between the persons is shown to be living and active (more like *radiance* than *genericism* in the language of subsequent history); and (2) that it involves power (δύναμις).

585 Thus, *pace* Torrance, Calvin or Lonergan – Torrance, *Trinitarian Faith,* 28-29; *Institutes* 1.8.19, 1.13.25; B. J. F. Lonergan, *The Triune God: Systematics,* trans. M. G. Sheilds, ed. R. M. Doran & D. Monsour (Toronto: Lonergan Research Institute/University of Toronto Press, 2007), 127-129 – the Son is not *autotheos* (if, by that term, we mean *Deus a se ipso* rather than *Deum verum*). He possesses divinity *from* the Father and *as* the Son of the Father; thus sharing the Father's essence dynamically and without separation. For an outstandingly nuanced

Son follows the lead of the Father and does whatever he sees the Father doing (v. 19).[586] The Father, because he loves the Son, does *everything* through him, including the great prerogatives of judging and life-giving (vv. 21-22), so that the Son will receive exactly *the same honour* (... καθὼς τιμῶσι τὸν πατέρα) that is accorded to the Father.[587]

Once again, then, the conclusion to this ordered pattern of operation is the same as that seen in 1 Cor 8:1-6. Because the Father does *everything* through the Son, and because the Son always acts in accordance with the Father's lead (cf. v. 30), there is no way to separate them doxologically. Indeed to try to do so can only result in apostasy (v. 23b) for in that the Father's work is revealed in the Son, and the Father's purpose is focussed on the Son, to reject the Son is to reject the one who sent him. C. H. Dodd offers a helpful summary overview of the scheme:

> [The] unity between Father and Son is so close that to see the Son is tantamount to the *visio Dei*; ... [It] is conceived as a dynamic and not a static relation; it consists in an activity originating with the Father and manifested in the Son. It may be described as obedience to the word of the Father, or imitation of his works, but at bottom it is nothing so external as obedience or imitation. It is the sharing of one life ... and

---

discussion of this matter see S. W. P. Hampton, *Anti-Arminians: The Anglican Reformed Tradition from Charles II to George I. Oxford Theological Monographs* (Oxford: Oxford University Press, 2008), 167-170.

586 Of course qualifications must abound. The dynamic is not so much one of copying, for that would create two sets of work. Rather the Father reveals *by acting through* the Son – cf. L. Morris, *The Gospel According to John. New International Commentary on the New Testament,* revised edition (Grand Rapids: Eerdmans, 1995), 277. Nor can it quite be that the Son doesn't know what the Father is about to do, such that this revelation takes him by surprise – his apprehension of what the Father is going to do through him is far too clear for that. This must, then, be an analogical expression of the Father's initiative toward him and through him; perhaps Dodd is correct to see it as an image (parable) drawn from the days of Jesus' apprenticeship with his earthly father C. H. Dodd, *More New Testament Studies* (Manchester: Manchester U.P, 1968), 30-40.

587 An alternative perspective here is afforded in R. G. Gruenler, *The Trinity in the Gospel of John: A Thematic Commentary on the Fourth Gospel* (Eugene: Wipf & Stock, 1986). Gruenler, in stressing the voluntary and temporary nature of the Son's earthly subordination (cf. ibid. xiv-xvii), sees the Father as "deferring to" or "subordinating himself" to the Son in the context of John 5:22-27(ibid. 37-38). The observation that the Father uses his position on the Son's behalf is unquestionably correct, but this language obscures the prerogative that the Father uses to "serve". Overall, it seems uncertain for Gruenler whether the relationship revealed between the Father and Jesus is an apt *expression* of the Godhead *in se* or temporary distortion.

activity [which] is rooted in the love of God. "The Father loves the Son, and shows him what he himself does".[588]

The Harmony of Function and Ontology

An obvious concern at this point might be that what I am describing could be affirmed by many who would deny the divinity of the Son.[589] A devotion to Christ that is predicated on the manner in which he represents the Father, does not necessitate him sharing the Father's *nature* nor preclude him from being the most exalted of created agents. Even if this agency is held to extend backward in time through all of salvation history, we have still not described Jesus in terms that would exclude ancient or modern Arianism.

Here several responses can be offered. In the first place, there is sufficient biblical data that *does* point to Jesus being a co-sharer in the divine nature at an ontological level. At the very least we might observe that:

- Jesus' own use of "Sonship" language was seen by Jesus' opponents as connoting "equality with God" (John 5:18). Other uses (eg. Mk 12:1-8; Rom 8:32; Heb 1:2) rely on the qualitative distinction between Jesus and created servants and would lose their force if Jesus' sonship were not "natural".[590]

---

588 Dodd, *Interpretation*, 194.

589 Dodd's careful treatment of the equality question reveals the potential danger and delicacy of the issue. Concluding that Jesus is not trying to present himself as a "second God" or "second principle": Dodd states that Jesus is *not* claiming equality. Yet, as he immediately observes: "it is difficult to deny τὸ ἰσόθεον in some sense, to one who exercises the supreme divine δυνάμεις ... ἴσος, whether affirmed or denied, is not a proper term to use in this context"; ibid., 327-328. We might say otherwise that ἴσος *is* a perfectly proper term as long as it is simultaneously affirmed *and* qualified in the way Jesus does it.

590 In the parable of the tenants, the final messenger clearly has a differentiating *natural* right to the vineyard which both the sender and the tenants recognise. In Romans 8:32 the *personal* sacrifice of God seems predicated on the fact that Jesus is in some sense his *actual* son. In Hebrews 1:2 God's *final* revelation is different because it is a communication ἐν υἱῷ. This last argument takes us close to a point laboured in the fourth century struggle against Arianism; that a created "son" could not adequately reveal God because he would not know God's essence: "God himself, in so far as he is incomprehensible for all ... is incomprehensible for the Son ... it is impossible for him to search out the Father who is in himself"; Arius' *Thalia* quoted in Grillmeier, *Christ (vol. 1)*, 228.

- Hebrews 1:3 describes Jesus as "reflection/radiance" (ἀπαύγασμα τῆς δόξης) and "exact impression of God's nature" (χαρακτήρ τῆς ὑποστάσεως). This leads to the conclusion that the Son's revelatory capacity is underpinned by his ontology (and teleology – "heir"). Indeed the argument loses force if Christ if these are not ontological statements;[591] Christ is not here Son, image and radiance *because* he reveals.[592] Rather the logic is that he more fully reveals *because* he is son, image and radiance.

- The depiction of John 1 presents the Word as both functionally united with God (as revealer and creator) but *also* ontologically one (θεὸς ἦν ὁ λόγος) and naturally derived (μονογενοῦς παρὰ πατρός – v. 14; ... μονογενὴς θεός – v. 18).[593] Even a functionalist such as Oscar Cullmann

---

591 What *kind* of ontological statement is, of course, a harder question. The danger is that the reiterative nature of χαρακτήρ might signify the creation of a purely generic relationship between the persons – the very polytheism that looms for the Jews in John 5:18ff. This is mitigated, however, if ἀπαύγασμα is taken to mean "radiance" rather than "reflection": then we have the reiterative image counterbalanced with a dynamic process-type image. If that is the case, then the overall effect is very close to the picture painted by the NCC; not *quite* the same, for here the Son is the radiance of the Father's *glory* not his self ("light from light"), but the distinction is not significant; see Thiselton's comments to the same effect in A. C. Thiselton, *The Hermeneutics of Doctrine* (Grand Rapids: Eerdmans, 2007), 394.

592 A transposition of Bultmann's question: "does he help me because he is God's Son, or is he God's Son because he helps me"? See ibid., 381.

593 I have generally avoided the exegetical question of the Son's "begottenness" (cf. John 1:14, 18; 3:16) on the grounds that the (more significant) fact of *real* divine sonship can be inferred from other contexts (for an early post-biblical deliberation on divine begetting see Irenaeus' *Demonstration of the Apostolic Preaching*, 47) regardless of whether μονογενής means "unique" or "begotten". Nevertheless, given that I have made much of the fourth century Fathers and their understanding of the Son's begottenness, it is worth making a brief comment against the recent "unique" rendering.

In the first place, it is *not* true that the construal of μονογενής as *unigenitus* is a fourth century (anti-Arian) invention as suggested by Dale Moody; D. Moody, "God's Only Son: The Translation of John 3:16 in the Revised Standard Version", *JBL* 72 (1953): 213-219. The association of μονογενής with begetting can be found explicitly in Tertullian's recitation of Valentinian cosmogony where he speaks of the *"Monogenes"* (the Greek is transliterated) who would be better dubbed *"Protogenes"* on account of his *"prior genitus"*; *Adversus Valentinianos* 7; Tertullian, *Qu. Sept. Flor. Tertulliani Opera ad Optimorum Librorum Fidem Expressa, Pars IV,* ed. E. F. Leopold. vol. 4. *Bibliotheca Patrum Ecclesiasticorum Latinorum Selecta: Ad Optimorum Liborum Fidem,* 7 volumes ed. Gersdorf, E. G. (Lipsiae: Tauchnitz, 1841), 42. In *Adversus Praxean* 15 and 21 he uses *"unigenitus"* to translate John 1:14. John Dahms also finds other significant uses of

acknowledges that here we have a statement concerning the being of the Word.[594]

High Christology from Below

However a less defensive response to the arguments of those who analyse the Christ in terms of his earthly and functional aspects, is to argue that they are not wrong in what they affirm, but rather in what they deny.[595] To make the observation that Jesus can be understood in functional or human terms is only a problem if we see him as wholly constrained or limited by those terms – that is to capture and subordinate him to creaturely categories.

The alternative possibility is that these functional/human categories are themselves supposed to be preparative for *him*; that they are types and signs of what he is (the same pattern observed above in the Irenaean or exemplarist tradition). Or even more radically, *they are pointers to what he himself will become in the context of salvation history*. In place of the protracted study of Christological names and typology required to do justice to these ideas, two brief passages might provide helpful hermeneutical windows.

---

the term in Justin's *Dialogue with Trypho* 105; J. V. Dahms, "Johannine Use of Monogenés Reconsidered", *New Testament Studies* 29 (1983): 222-232, 227.

Thus while Moody may well be correct insofar that *unicus* may *also* be a legitimate meaning for the word (cf. Moody, "God's Only Son", 214-215), the connotation of begetting cannot be excluded. This generally accords with later studies of both D. A. Fennema and John Dahms: Fennema argues that the "unique" vs. "begotten" dilemma is a false antithesis – D. A. Fennema, "John 1.18: 'God the Only Son'", *New Testament Studies* 31 (1985): 124-135, 126 – while both he and Dahms note the strong association between μονογενής and filiality. Dahms' observation that there are no occurrences of constructions like μονογενής ἀδελφος is telling; Dahms, "Monogenés", 227.

594 O. Cullmann, *The Christology of the New Testament,* revised edition (Philadelphia: Westminster Press, 1953), 265. Of course Cullmann doesn't mean it in the same sense that I do; his opinion is that the Words' action *is* his being and that further speculation about "nature" is improper and useless (ibid., 266). But Cullmann's functionalism fails to see that the fundamental datum in John 1 is not creation or revelation but the God with whom he is (and whose identity he shares) in the beginning (cf. John 17:24).

595 Indeed the real weakness of functionalist Christology is that in its reactionary campaign against ontological (Chalcedonian) speculation, it finds itself doing exactly what the New Testament *never* does, drawing limits on the degree to which he re-presents the Father. Even if mere functionalism were true (which it isn't) its intellectual project is entirely against the *grain* of the New Testament.

The Functional Christology of Jesus: John 10:22-36

The first example comes from another passage in the Fourth Gospel which has some fascinating similarities to (and differences from) John 5:18ff. In John 10:22, Jesus again creates a flashpoint with the Jews over his divinity. While in John 5, Jesus is heard by his accusers to be saying that he is a competing divinity, here they seem to interpret his assertion that "I and the Father are one" (v. 30) as a claim to *be* God; a blasphemous pretense to be divine ("you, though only a human being, are making yourself God;" v. 33). To put it anachronistically, the Jews of John 5 think he is being ditheist, those in chapter 10 suspect him of something like modalism.

In response to this charge, Jesus again elaborates an agent-type relationship – with his proximity to the Father confirmed by the works that the Father does in and through him (vv. 32, 37-38). Yet his main strategy for proving that he is worthy of the title "Son of God" is, somewhat shockingly, to prove that this participation in divine authority applies to humans (or at least created agents) too:

> "Is it not written in your law, 'I said, you are gods'? If those to whom the word of God came were called 'gods' – and the Scripture cannot be annulled – can you say that the one whom the Father has sanctified and sent into the world is blaspheming because I said, 'I am God's Son'"? (vv. 35-36).

Of course exegetical debates swarm around the passage. Are the "gods" here angelic beings, or human judges, or the people of Israel?[596] Is Jesus arguing from the greater to the lesser ("son of God" *must be* permissible if "god" is okay!) or the lesser to the greater (if humans can be so dubbed, how about *me*)?[597]

But these issues need not detain us too long. Whatever the original context of Ps 82, the interesting thing from our perspective is that Jesus seems to be clearly applying it *now* to humans ("those to whom the Word of God came"). Whether he thereby means the rulers of Israel or the whole assembly, the general point is clear: *people* can be called "gods"; the OT depiction of created agents is subject to the same charge of blasphemy that Jesus is facing.[598]

---

596 See discussion in D. A. Carson, *The Gospel According to John: An Introduction and Commentary. Pillar New Testament Commentary* (Grand Rapids: Eerdmans, 1991), 297-298 and L. Morris, *The Biblical Doctrine of Judgment*, 1st edition (London: Tyndale Press, 1960), 34-36.

597 For an excellent survey of the complexities of this question see W. G. Phillips, "An Apologetic Study of John 10:34-36", *Bibliotheca Sacra* 146 (1989): 405-419.

598 It will not do to interpret this argument as simply negative (as some commentators do), as if Jesus were *merely* attempting to confound his opponents without endorsing the premises of the syllogism (cf. Matt 12.27). Such cynical use of

Putting it positively, Jesus is pointing out that the Bible *already* allows for a high description of entities who stand in some special relationship with God. How much, more, then is *he* entitled to such claims, whose status as the one ὁ πατὴρ ἡγίασεν *prior* to his being sent into the world.[599] Although he clearly sees himself in a different league, he is not ashamed to endorse the exalted status of human agency as a means of understanding his own.

If Jesus' logic is taken seriously here, the modernist quest for Christology "from below" begins to look simply like a misapplication. Jesus *wants* us to reflect on earthly and creaturely categories so we can begin to understand him. To observe that he can be understood through the lens of function and creation and thence reduce him to that, is to commit exactly the same error as those (Judaizers) who would subordinate him to the Jewish categories of king and prophet. If he *is* those things it is not because they are the primary reality which define and give him significance; rather he is the reality to which they gesture. "These are only a shadow of what is to come, but the substance belongs to Christ" (Col 2:17).

Agency and the Development of Christology

This theory, that an understanding of the Son's eternal filiality arises out of reflection upon OT agency-types, accords with a crucial insight that has emerged from many recent studies of early Christology. The reason why the church was able to move from monotheism, to seeing Jesus as divine, was

---

Scripture would be completely uncharacteristic, especially in the light of v. 35 – "and the scripture cannot be annulled".

599 I find W. Gary Phillips "polysyllogistic" rendition of Jesus argument (ibid., 418) persuasive here:

Major premise:	The assertions of Scripture are not blasphemous.
Minor premise:	Scripture asserts the principle that individuals who are divinely commissioned can be called by divine title (general).
Conclusion:	The principle (that individuals who are divinely commissioned can be called by divine title [general]) is not blasphemous.

The conclusion of the first syllogism becomes the major premise of the second [thus].

Major premise:	The principle (stated above) is not blasphemous.
Minor premise:	That Jesus may rightly be called by His (specific) divine title (Son of God) is included in the principle, a fortiori.
Conclusion:	That Jesus may rightly be called by His (specific) divine title (Son of God) is not blasphemous.

because Judaism already possessed a range of motifs that prepared the way for divine agency:[600]

- the figure of the *shaliach*/messenger who stood before a third party *as if* he were the one who sent him;[601]

- the king (or Israel) as God's son;

- the apocalyptic Son of Man; the angel of the Lord;

- principal angels and patriarchs;

- the personified categories of Word or Wisdom.[602]

As Larry Hurtado summarises:

> At the earliest stages, Christian experience of, and reflection upon, the risen Jesus were probably influenced by, and drew upon, the divine agency category. Jesus was experienced and understood as exalted to the position of God's chief agent. The divine agency tradition was important in providing the resources for accommodating a heavenly figure second only to God in authority and glory[603]

In a later work Hurtado also notes the similarity between this "mutated Jewish"[604] approach to Jesus and even more developed forms of Christian devotion to Jesus in its creedal stages. As he rightly notes, the Nicene Creed's "light from light, God from God" works in just the same way:

---

600 See A. W. Wainwright, *The Trinity in the New Testament,* 2nd, corrected edition (London: SPCK, 1962), 29-37. Of course, as Ben Witherington notes, *agency alone* is not sufficient – representing a kind of legal fiction; B. Witherington, *John's Wisdom: A Commentary on the Fourth Gospel,* 1st edition (Louisville: Westminster John Knox Press, 1995), 141. Nevertheless as Witherington *also* observes, (and this fits with Malina's observations above) the situation alters if the agent is a son. See the same observation in A. E. Harvey "Christ as Agent" in *The Glory of Christ in the New Testament: Studies in Christology in Memory of George Bradford Caird,* ed. L. D. Hurst, N. T. Wright & G. B. Caird (New York: Oxford University Press, 1987), 243.

601 See ibid..

602 See Hurtado's brief survey of the main categories in L. W. Hurtado, *One God, One Lord: Early Christian Devotion and Ancient Jewish Monotheism* (Philadelphia: Fortress Press, 1988), 17-18.

603 Ibid., 123-124. We might note again the inadequacy of this last statement. As we have seen in 1 Cor 8:6, the early thrust of Christological understanding was that the Son was included in the Christian understanding of God *as well as* and *because of* the way he was "second only to God".

604 This is Hurtado's own mode of expression.

In short, in the proclamation and the religious practice reflected in the New Testament and characteristic of "mainstream" Christian traditions down through the centuries, the significance of Jesus' redemption and revealing work is seen and celebrated as deriving from his status as the unique agent of God's will. That is, the meaning of Christ is always expressed in terms of his relationship ...that derives from God. Even in the notion of Christ as the divine Son from all eternity, this definition of Christ in relation to God (the Father) remains clear.[605]

Agency as the key to Anthropology: Hebrews 2

The application of Jewish agency theory to Christology is a welcome and enormously fruitful development. And it can be taken further. The earliest expression of the Old Testament's agency category – and one which has been largely neglected in the context of modern Christological discussion – is humanity itself. In accordance with the now widely preferred interpretation of Genesis 1:26-28; the very idea of humans being made "in the image of God" is that they are thereby *designated* as God's representatives on earth, just as an idol (graven image) might represent the presence of a deity; or a statue or coin might represent a king; or the king himself might be held to be an image of *his* sponsoring god.[606] It is this functional designation of humanity as divine viceroy or ambassador that is the reason and basis for its "dominion" (cf. Gen 1:26).

This theory of humans as God's representative agents makes good sense of the historico-cultural context. It also makes sense of the debt of respect owed to humans. Since humans represent God, an attack on humanity signifies an attack on him *via proxy*: "Whoever sheds the blood of a human, by a human shall that

---

605 L. W. Hurtado, *At the Origins of Christian Worship: The Context and Character of Earliest Christian Devotion* (Grand Rapids: Eerdmans, 2000), 104.

Of course there are a host of scholarly debates in our wake here. There remains the question of how this agency fits with early notions of Jesus' pre-existence (it clearly does for Jesus in John 10:36) or how the *worship* of Jesus arises out of Jewish monotheism. These issues should not distract us from Jesus' central strategy of seeing human "gods" as limited expressions of his far greater sonship.

606 For helpful overviews of the issues see D. J. A. Clines, *On the Way to the Postmodern: Old Testament Essays, 1968-1998. Journal for the Study of the Old Testament - Supplement Series* (Sheffield: Sheffield Academic, 1998), 447-497; E. H. Merrill "Image of God" in *Dictionary of the Old Testament: Pentateuch*, ed. T. D. Alexander & D. W. Baker (Downers Grove: IVP, 2003), 443-444 and, and especially, J. R. Middleton, *The Liberating Image: The Imago Dei in Genesis 1* (Grand Rapids: Brazos Press, 2005). According to Middleton (also quoting James Barr), the "royal" interpretation of the *imago* is now the dominant one; ibid., 29.

person's blood be shed; for in his own image God made humankind" (Gen 9:6, cf. Jas 3:9).[607] "Those who mock the poor insult [his or her] Maker" (Pr 17:5a).

The theory does a better job of explaining the *Imago Dei* than the search for attributes (rationality, free-will, moral uprightness etc.) that has typically characterised the attempt to exegete Gen 1:26-28. If humanity is primarily "representative rather than representation",[608] then such discussions are essentially beside the point. Whatever intrinsic qualities humans might *also* possess (or lose) that make them *like* God,[609] their installation as his stewards is an act of grace. From the point of view of Psalm 8 it is a deliberately perverse appointment made *despite* their intrinsic qualities so that God's enemies are shamed and silenced:

From the lips of children and infants you have ordained praise

> because of your enemies,

> to silence the foe and the avenger.

When I consider your heavens,

> the work of your fingers,

> the moon and the stars, which you have set in place,

what is man that you are mindful of him,

> the son of man that you care for him?

You made him a little lower than the heavenly beings (elohim)

> and crowned him with glory and honour.

You made him ruler over the works of your hands;

> you put everything under his feet. (Ps 8:2-6 NIV)[610]

---

607 "The murderer has committed an act of *lèse majesté* against God himself since he has attacked God's image"; Clines, *On the Way,* 474 n. 121.

608 Ibid., 495.

609 And at this point we might reopen the door to the old distinction between "image" and "likeness" – at least in systematic terms; "'likeness' is an assurance that humanity is an adequate and faithful representative"; ibid., 495.

610 Here the non-inclusive translation is preferred where neutering or generalising the language of the text obscures the typological fulfilment in *one man*. The crucial expression "Son of Man" is lost in both the NRSV and TNIV translations. Thomas G. Long would seem right to describe this as an otherwise laudable attempt that here produces a "seriously misleading" reading of Hebrews 2; T. G. Long,

To the writer of Hebrews, the unexpected nature of human preferment is an antidote to angelolatry and a left-of-field proof of the Jesus' superiority; Jesus is greater than angels *because he is a human,* and because it is *humanity* – not angels – that occupies the highest place in God's ultimate economy:

> It is not to angels that he has subjected the world to come, about which we are speaking. But there is a place where someone has testified: "What is man that you are mindful of him, the son of man that you care for him? You made him a little lower than the angels; you crowned him with glory and honour and put everything under his feet? In putting everything under him, God left nothing that is not subject to him. Yet at present we do not see everything subject to him. But we see Jesus, who was made a little lower than the angels, now crowned with glory and honour because he suffered death, so that by the grace of God he might taste death for everyone. (Heb 2:5-9 NIV)

Here the writer's approach to Psalm 8 is akin to what we would now call deconstruction – a wedging open of the fault lines and cracks in the text. In the original, David marvels that tiny inglorious humans should be exalted over the works of God's hands, being elevated to a status only slightly below that of the heavenly *elohim.* Here the Hebrews exegete observes a further anomaly: humans are appointed to have all things and be crowned with glory and honour (v. 8a), yet they are *still* subordinate (v. 8b).[611] The caveat concerning the angels appears to abrogate the anointing.[612]

The solution for the writer of Hebrews 2 is that humanity in its present state is a contradiction, an *aporia,* which only finds fulfillment in Christ. He is the one who, having been made like us in our deficient humanity (slightly lower

---

Hebrews. Interpretation Commentary Series (Louisville: John Knox Press, 1997), 35.

611 I am following here the (now) majority interpretation that would make the αὐτῷ of v. 8 apply to humanity rather than Christ – see survey of discussion in P. Ellingworth, *The Epistle to the Hebrews: A Commentary on the Greek Text. NIGTC* (Grand Rapids: Eerdmans, 1993), 150-152. Of course, as J. Kögel notes (cf. ibid., 151) the *ultimate* meaning of the human is fulfilled in Christ.

612 Philip Edgecumbe Hughes sees the situation thus:

> Man, as we have seen, was made lower than the angels only *for a little while;* his true destiny was always intended to be higher than the angels, in union with Christ, the true Image of his being, crowned with glory and honour, "far above all rule and authority and power and dominion", participating in his lordship over all the works of God's hands (Ps 8:5ff.; Heb 2:5-9; Eph 1:19-23).

P. E. Hughes, *The True Image: The Origin and Destiny of Man in Christ* (Grand Rapids: Eerdmans, 1989), 411.

than the angels), now reigns far above them as the glorious fulfilled man. Here is the true man of Psalm 8 who fulfils human destiny: lower than the angels and *finally* crowned with glory and honour above all.[613] While John 10 elevates human agency as a pointer to the greater sonship of Jesus himself, Hebrews 2 depicts an incompleteness to human agency that is only fully realised in the death and ascension of Christ. In the first, human nature is congruent with divine filiality; in the second, the Son as man (and Mediator) completes human nature.

Much more could be made of this and, space permitting, it would be fruitful to explore the ways in which the eternal Son is archetype, true type, and antitype in regard to humankind.[614] According to the pattern here, humanity is at once an *echo* of what the Son is (eg. Col 1:15, cf. Gen 1:26) and a *shadow* of what he will be. Because human nature only finds its destiny in him, *his* own achievement is also shared with us. So we are already raised up with him in heaven (Eph 2:6); already priests as sharers in his priesthood (1Pet 2:9); already his "sons" (Gal 4:4-7); being inwardly transformed (2Cor 3:18). We will one day share his authority over angels (1Cor 6:3) and receive the full rights of our adoption (Rom 8:23). We will sit down on his throne – just as he overcame and now sits on his Father's (Rev 3:21).

The Logos and the Mediator

But this last sentence returns us to a problem glimpsed in the last chapter. While it surely makes sense to imagine us sharing in the benefits won for us by Christ, it is more difficult to work out how those things apply to *himself.* How do we read those passages which seem to speak of Christ becoming something

---

613   As James Dunn argues:

> Jesus was being described as one who had fulfilled the complete divine plan for humankind. His work could be seen through the lens not only of Ps 8:6b but also of the whole passage (Ps 8:4-6). Jesus only fulfilled the role of Ps 8:6b, because he could be said to have come to it via Ps 8:4-6a ... [In Heb 2:5-9] the point is very clear. It was not to angels that the coming world was subjected (2:5). Nor was it yet at this stage to humans. ... humankind was not exercising the intended dominion over the rest of creation. But in Jesus God had "run the programme through again". And in him it had achieved its goal: all things were at last under the feet of God's man.

J. D. G. Dunn, *The Theology of Paul the Apostle* (Grand Rapids: Eerdmans, 2003), 201.

614   We should add that it is not just humanity that this applies to, but particular aspects of redeemed humanity; such as Israel or the temple – prophet, priest, king and so on, that follow a similar pattern. In most of these the place of Christ as antitype is more pronounced than that of archetype.

or achieving something through his work? What, for instance, should we do with those passages which speak of him being *adopted* or *appointed* as Son of God:

- "You are my son; today I have begotten you" (Acts 13:33; Heb 1:5; 5:5, cf. Ps 2:7).

- "... predestined [ὁρισθέντος] to be Son of God with power according to the spirit of holiness by resurrection from the dead" (Rom 1:4).

... or him being somehow exalted or glorified by his saving work:

- " ... he has spoken to us by a Son, whom he *appointed heir* of all things ... [Jesus] having become as much superior to angels as the name he has inherited is more excellent than theirs" (Heb 1:1, 4).

- "Therefore God also highly *exalted him* and gave him the name that is above every name, so that at the name of Jesus every knee should bend, in heaven and on earth and under the earth" (Phil 2:9).

If Jesus is the eternal Son, how can he *become* God's son or *earn* the "name above every name"? If he is God, how can he *inherit* what is already his as Creator?

Of course, the problem might be resolved by taking a kenotic view of the incarnation, or a somewhat fallibilist view of Scripture. In the first, the Son's achievements would simply be a restoration of that which he kenotically surrendered by becoming human. The second simply accepts that the Christology of the early church (and NT) *was* functionalist or adoptionist. In Dunn's words: "primitive Christian preaching seems to have regarded Jesus' resurrection as the day of his appointment to divine sonship – as the event by which he became God's son".[615]

But the standard interpretation of classical theology is that such verses which indicate some gain in glory or status for the Son, apply to him as our representative or *plerosis*.[616] While his glory, his inheritance, his rule, the name above every name and so on – have absolutely no meaning for the unchangeable Word, they are significant *for us* as vicarious or federal gains that he secures on our behalf as the Son of Man: the Mediator of our salvation. Thus, for example, Athanasius explains that the exaltation and naming of Christ in Phil 2:9-10 does not indicate that he received –

---

615 J. D. G. Dunn, *Christology in the Making: A New Testament Inquiry into the Origins of the Doctrine of the Incarnation,* 2nd edition (London: SCM Press, 1989) 36.

616 Whether that concept is understood in terms of nature, moral character or relationship.

... promotion from his descent, but rather himself promoted the things which needed promotion; ... he did not receive in reward the name of the Son and God, but rather he himself has made us sons of the Father, and deified men by becoming himself man. ... he alone is very God from the very God, not receiving these prerogatives as a reward for ... after the resemblance of the unalterable Father, he the Word also is unalterable.[617]

Theodoret of Cyrrhus reads Acts 2:34-35 the same way:

The words "sit on my right hand" he speaks as to a man, for they are not spoken to him that sits ever on the throne of glory, God the Word after his ascension from earth, but they are said to him who has now been exalted to the heavenly glory as man ... [618]

As does Gregory of Nyssa:

Who then was "exalted"? He that was lowly, or he that was the highest? ... Surely, God needs not to be exalted, seeing that he is the highest. It follows then, that the apostle's meaning is that the humanity was exalted: and its exaltation was effected by its becoming Lord and Christ.[619]

John Chrysostom takes the same line with Hebrews 1:

Henceforward then he treats here of that which is according to the flesh, ... For this Name, God the Word ever had; He did not afterwards "obtain it by inheritance"; nor did He afterwards become "better than the Angels, when He had purged our sins"; but He was always "better", and better without all comparison.[620]

As does Calvin twelve hundred years later:

But the word heir is ascribed to Christ as manifested in the flesh; for being made man, he put on our nature, and as such received this heirship, and that for this purpose, that he might restore to us what we had lost in Adam. For God had at the beginning constituted man, as his son, the heir of all good things; but through sin the first man became alienated from God, ... the Apostle now adorns [Christ] with this title, that we may know that without him we are destitute of all good things.[621]

---

617 *CA* 1.38-39; NPNF 2.4.328-329.

618 From *Dialogue 2* quoted in F. Martin & T. C. Oden, *Acts.* vol. 5. *Ancient Christian Commentary on Scripture* ed. Thomas C. Oden (Downers Grove: IVP, 2006), 34.

619 *CE* 5.3 in ibid., 35.

620 *Homily* 1; NPNF 1.14.368.

621 Calvin, *Commentaries on the Epistle of Paul the Apostle to the Hebrews*, 33-34.

Does Responsive Intra-Trinitarian Willing Fit with Scripture?

The theological reasoning behind these readings is clear enough. Divinity is immutable and without potentiality, so to acknowledge the promotion of the Son is tantamount to an own-goal in the face of Arianism. And we have just seen above – there is an important truth here. Humanity *is* exalted in Christ. He *is* our mediator in whom we are raised up and adopted and so on.

But this approach of dividing Christ's relationships and achievements from those of the Word is not without its problems. Certainly the sharp distinction between Christ's eternal and achieved sonship seems necessary to guard his divinity but if there is no *personal* stake in the achievement for the Logos then "the Mediator" becomes an act or role he plays purely for our benefit. This is at once too anthropocentric – "Christ" only exists for our benefit[622] – and alienating, for now it is difficult to see whether we have any stake in the Son at

> The same insistence that the Logos gains nothing personally from his mission is repeated elsewhere: for example in Calvin's commentary on Ephesians 1 – see Calvin, "Eighth Sermon on Ephesians", taken from Calvin, *Ephesians Sermons,* – and *Institutes* 3.1.1.
>
> Perhaps the most disturbing application of the same principle, however, is Calvin's belief that passages which speak of *love* between the Father and Christ should only to be taken officially. In expounding John 15:9 he dismisses the "abstruse inquiry" of those who would speculate on love between the first and second persons of the Godhead, arguing that "the love which is here mentioned must be understood as referring to us ... the Father loves him, as he is the Head of the Church"; Calvin, *John,* 2.111. Similar observations occur in the case of John 17:24; "You loved me before the foundation of the world", writes Calvin:
>
> > ... agrees better with the person of the Mediator than with Christ's Divinity alone. It would be harsh to say that the Father loved his Wisdom; and though we were to admit it, the connection of the passage leads us to a different view. Christ, unquestionably, spoke as the Head of the Church ... he was beloved, in so far as he was appointed to be the Redeemer of the world. With such a love did the Father love him before the creation of the world, that he might be the person in whom the Father would love his elect.
>
> Ibid., 2.187.

---

622 Thus Geerhardus Vos distinguishes the Reformed vision of salvation (which terminates in the glory of God) from the Lutheran scheme which begins and ends with human beatitude: Vos, "Doctrine of the Covenant". This point is well made, though I would observe that Vos' own theology risks the same anthropocentrism. If the work of Christ is *simply* a post-facto accomplishment of that which Adam might otherwise have rendered by himself then the work of the second person of the Godhead is made more or less incidental to the achievement of human perfection (even though that perfection is defined in terms of doxology). I would suggest that if God is more glorified by the Son doing humanity's work – and Vos would surely not disagree with this – then history was always going to include this according to the secret and decretive will of God.

all, or merely in the humanity that he represents and repairs. In the case of Reformed theology after Calvin,[623] this problem is compounded by the declaration that the Mediator's role is temporary:

> But when as partakers in heavenly glory we shall see God as he is, Christ, having discharged the office of the Mediator, will cease to be the ambassador of his Father and will be satisfied with that glory which he enjoyed before the creation of the world ... Then he returns the Lordship to his Father so that – far from diminishing his own majesty – it may shine all the more brightly.[624]

This seems a terribly sad way to see our final state, and leaves us very much on the outside. The Son, having brought his bride home and bid her welcome, goes back inside to where he *really* lives with his Father, while she gets to stand out on the porch looking in through the window.[625]

More generally, there are problems with this nature – or office-Christology[626] from an exegetical perspective too. When we read that the Father "has spoken to us by his Son, whom he appointed heir of all things, and through whom he made the universe;" (Heb 1:2) the most natural way to understand it, is that the Father wants his Son made the focus of creation and salvation history. It is decidedly perverse to read this as a plan to bless an "office" or a "nature" – apart from any regard for his Son who occupies that office or nature. The same question might be raised concerning Ephesians 1:1-14. Paul heaps up volitional terminology (ἐξελέξατο προορίσας εὐδοκίαν προθεσιν θελήμα βουλὴν) to describe the plans and purposes of "the God and Father of our Lord Jesus Christ" (v. 3) which are to be achieved in "the one he loves" (v. 6), culminating in the ultimate mystery of his will (μυστήριον τοῦ θελήματος

---

623 Though as far as I can the idea orginates with Martin Bucer – see W. v. t. Spijker, *The Ecclesiastical Offices in the Thought of Martin Bucer,* trans. J. Vriend. vol. v. 57. *Studies in Medieval and Reformation Thought* (Leiden: Brill, 1996), 40.

624 *Institutes* 2.14.3

625 And such an abandonment surely contradicts the idea of permanence and mutual delight inherent in the image of the Lamb as groom (Rev 21, cf. Is 62:4). The idea that our salvation might one day no longer be "in Christ" is hard to justify either from the Bible or tradition and, interestingly, jars with the "union with Christ" theme expressed elsewhere in Reformed theology; see for example, L. Gatiss, "The Inexhaustible Fountain of All Good Things: Union with Christ in Calvin on Ephesians", *Themelios* 34.2 (2009): 194-206.

626 That is, opposed to a more Alexandrian person-Christology. The distinction made by Heiko Obermann, and lately elaborated by Stephen Edmondson – Edmondson, *Christology,* – that Calvin's theology represents a transition from a nature-Christology to a (person-centred) office or Mediator-Christology is of limited significance here given that *neither* system envisages any personal stake for the Logos in his mission.

αυτοῦ) to recapitulate all things in Christ (ἀνακεφαλαιώσασθαι ...ἐν τῷ Χριστῷ). Are we really to exclude the person of the Logos from these blessings and ascribe them only to the humanity he mediates?

If this is where our systematic commitments takes us then perhaps it is time to revisit their assumptions and try to work out a framework that is less injurious to the plain sense of Scripture and the unity of the person *who is* the Mediator.[627]

Jesus Christ: The Logos Made Manifest

I would further suggest that such a framework is actually not hard to find. If we stop thinking about Jesus' achievements as pertaining to changes in his *nature*, and start thinking about them in terms of relationship toward creation then it is quite obvious that there *are* ways in which the Son "becomes" and "achieves" and is "promoted" by the course of salvation history.

In the first place, the mission of the Son amongst us reveals him to us as a distinct object of worship. It is an obvious fact that although the Son may be *foreshadowed* in the Old Testament – and is certainly at work therein (cf. John 1:3, 10; Col 1:16-17; 1 Cor 8:6, 10:3-4 etc.) – his personal identity remains obscure (μυστήριον eg. Col 1:26) until his advent. What is the significance of this? Why, given that he *too* is creator, is he not made known as such until the New Testament? According to the doctrine of *appropriations* thematised in the West,[628] the answer has to do with the way the persons work. Although the whole Trinity is involved in the act of creation, it is nonetheless most appropriately ascribed to the Father who is the source of the works both *ad intra* and *ad extra*. Aquinas refers to the Nicene Creed which calls the Father "creator of all things visible and invisible" explaining that as an artist

> ... works through an idea conceived in his mind and through love in his will bent on something. In like manner God the Father wrought the

---

627 It is enlightening to read Stephen Edmondson's observation that Calvin works with a classical Latin (vs. Boethian) definition of person wherein "*persona* designated principally one's role or character in a play or one's role or office within the fabric of society ... and then, only secondarily, one's status as a substantial self or personage who fills this role"; ibid., 186. This might well give us insight into the rather problematic expression "*person* of the Mediator" who seems to arise "*ex duobus connexis compositam*"; Institutes 2.14.1 cf. J. Calvin & A. Tholuck, *Ioannis Calvini Institutio Christianae Religionis* (Berolini: G. Eichler, 1834), 314.

628 The theological framework expressed by "appropriation" however is scarcely confined to the West – the same pattern is implicit in the NCC's designation of Father as "creator of heaven and earth".

creature through his Word, the Son and through his Love, the Holy Ghost ... [T]he comings forth of the divine persons can be seen as types for the coming forth of creatures.[629]

A similar taxonomy persists in Reformed theology. In Article 9 of the Belgic Confession we read that:

> ... we must observe the particular offices and operations (*offices et effets*) of these three persons toward us. The Father is called our creator, by his power; the Son is our saviour and redeemer, by his blood; the Holy Ghost is our sanctifier, by his dwelling in our hearts.[630]

Thus in relation to creation itself, the Father is *especially* to be considered creator in that the Son and Spirit are from him. And this, it seems, does align with what we have witnessed in 1 Corinthians 8. The Father is God "from whom" while the Son is the Lord "through whom" are all things. Together they are the one God of Deuteronomy 6, but not in a way that is opaque or modalistic. Considered in relation to each other, the Father is first.

Yet the mode of the Son's instrumentality in redemption is very different. In the NT, the invisible "transparent" mediation gives way, as he is set forth as the *object* of revelation and faith. He himself *is* the revelation: "the Word became flesh and *tabernacled* (ἐσκήνωσυεν) among us" (John 1:1); in these last days God has spoken to us by a Son (ἐν υἱῷ)" (Heb 1:1). With the incarnation, the medium becomes the message, not simply because he perfectly embodies the Father's nature and thus shows us the Father (though that is certainly true), but because the Father's will is that the Son himself become the object of our

---

[629] Thomas Aquinas, *Creation, Variety, and Evil (1a.44-49)*, trans. T. Gilby. vol. 8. *Summa Theologiae*, 61 volumes, paperback edition (Cambridge: Cambridge University Press, 2006), 52-53. We should note that this rendition stands in contrast to some caricatures of the doctrine of appropriations wherein the impression is given that the ascription is basically arbitrary – a form of words superficially pasted over Western modalism – see, Torrance, *Doctrine of God*, 200 or LaCugna, *God for Us*, 99-102. Here, once again, the appropriations *ad extra* are thoroughly connected to the *opera ad intra*.

[630] P. Schaff, *The Evangelical Protestant Creeds, with Translations*. vol. 3. *The Creeds of Christendom with a History and Critical Notes*, 3 volumes, 6th edition (New York: Harper & Brothers, 1877), 392. Calvin has the same structure: " ... to the Father is attributed the beginning of action, the fountain and source of all things; to the Son wisdom, counsel, and arrangement in action, while the energy and efficacy of action belong to the Spirit". *Institutes*, 1.13.18. This takes Calvin closer to the scholastic characterisation of the Father as *efficient* cause, Son as *exemplary* cause and Spirit as *final* cause; see G. Sauvage "Appropriations" in *The Catholic Encyclopedia*, (New York: Robert Appleton Company, 1907); http://www.newadvent.org/ cathen/01658a.htm, (accessed February, 2010).

worship: "so that all may honour the Son just as they honour the Father;" (John 5:23).

A New Relationship to Creation

Intimately connected to this pattern of Jesus as the manifest content of the Father's revelation, is the achievement he wins for *himself* through his mission – to be *the person* who effects and secures our redemption. In the incarnation he becomes the one who actively fulfils all that we should have been,[631] atones for our sins, and finally shares with us his ascended life. Thus in his life, death and resurrection he recapitulates humanity, remaking us and redefining us in relation to him, becoming the new Adam, Moses, Passover, temple, David and so on.

It must be immediately granted, of course, that this saving act is also the work of the Father. At every stage Jesus' life, mission and message is governed by the Father; the cross most especially is the cup *given to* the Son (John 18:11; Matt 26:39).[632] But again, the way in which the Father and Son work together here is very different from the way they work in the act of creation. It is *only* the Son who comes to earth as a man; *only* the Son who bears our humanity into heaven as our priest and representative. Most strikingly, it is *only* the Son who dies for us on the cross[633] – and indeed apparently saves us here *by* being alone as he cries "*Eloi Eloi, Lama Sabacthani*".[634]

---

[631] By this I refer to the Gospel depictions of him reliving the Exodus (Matt 2:16; John 6:30-33); the Adamic temptation (Luke 4:1-13); sharing in the penitential baptism of Israel (Matt 3:13-17); and generally depicting himself as the centre and fulfilment of the Jewish cultus (John 2:19-22) etc. Aspects of this massive theme are picked up by Irenaeus who speaks of Jesus passing "through every stage of life, restoring to all communion with God" (*Adversus Haereses* 1.18.6; *ANF* 1.448), and also in the Reformed doctrine of active obedience:

> When it is asked then how Christ, by abolishing sin, removed the enmity between God and us, and purchased a righteousness which made him favourable and kind to us, it may be answered generally, that he accomplished this by the whole course of his obedience ... from the moment when he assumed the form of a servant, he began, in order to redeem us, to pay the price of deliverance.
>
> *Institutes* 2.16.5.

[632] Tom Smail helpfully observes the perichoretic structure: "as he obeys the Father, the Son participates in the authority of the Father; as he sends the Son, the Father participates in his self-offering on the cross"; T. A. Smail, *Like Father, Like Son: The Trinity Imaged in Our Humanity* (Grand Rapids: Eerdmans, 2006), 157.

[633] Thus the Chalcedonian (and Cyrillian/Alexandrian) pattern affirmed amid the Monophysite controversies in the sixth century. As declared by the 5th Ecumenical Council (Constantinople II) of 553:

In John 5, after explaining the Father's intention to have the Son receive equal honour (v. 23), Jesus speaks of his ministry as one that brings life in a new way: "For just as the Father has life in himself, so he has granted the Son also to have life in himself". What does this mean? While commentators find it easy to agree on the intent of this "gift", what it actually *is* seems less obvious – many positing that Jesus here designates the paradox of *derived aseity* given him by the Father.[635] But it is unlikely that Jesus has anything so rarefied in mind here.[636] The context of his statement is the Son's status as the key to history's consummation, both in the present and the future: "Very truly, I tell you, the hour is coming, and is now here, when the dead will hear the voice of the Son of God, and those who hear will live" (v. 25); "the hour is coming when all who are in their graves will hear his voice and will come out – those who have done good, to the resurrection of life, and those who have done evil, to the resurrection of condemnation" (vv. 28-29). Thus Jesus' comparison is not

---

> If anyone shall say that the wonder-working Word of God is one [Person] and the Christ that suffered another; or shall say that God the Word was with the woman-born Christ, or was in him as one person in another, but that he was not one and the same our Lord Jesus Christ, the Word of God, incarnate and made man, and that his miracles and the sufferings which of his own will he endured in the flesh were not of the same [Person]: let him be anathema.

Capitula 3; NPNF 2.14.312

Or again

> If anyone shall not acknowledge that God the Word, of the same substance with the Father and the Holy Ghost, and who was made flesh and became man, one of the Trinity, is Christ in every sense of the word ... let him be anathema.

The Anathemas Against Origen 8; NPNF 2.14.319

634 This is not to deny that the Father too, in some sense, suffers by surrendering his Son (cf. Rom 8:32).

635 So F. L. Godet, *Commentary on the Gospel of St. John with a Critical Introduction,* trans. M. D. Cusin & S. Taylor. *Clark's Foreign Theological Library,* 3rd edition (Edinburgh: T&T Clark, 1889), 2.178-178; C. K. Barrett, *The Gospel According to St. John: An Introduction With Commentary and Notes on the Greek Text* (Louisville: Westminster John Knox Press, 1978), 262; Carson, *The Gospel According to John: An Introduction and Commentary,* 256-257. See a brief survey of ancient commentary in J. C. Elowsky, *John 1-10.* vol. 4. *Ancient Christian Commentary on Scripture* ed. Thomas C. Oden (Downers Grove: IVP, 2006), 198-199. Of course this would correspond to the contraverted theory that Jesus is begotten before the ages in *contradistinction* to the idea of eternal generation. See Jung S. Rhee; Rhee, "Eternal Generation".

636 Which is not to say that the concept is untrue or unbiblical. Something like this would seem to be implicit in the presentation of the Son who both *is* the Father's Word and *has* a powerful word (John 1:1, cf. Heb 1:3).

between the Father's aseity and his own, but the Father and Son's respective *roles in creation and salvation*.[637] As the Father gives life (as creator) so the Son gives life as incarnate saviour (cf. v. 21). History, once again, is designed for the manifestation of the Son's glory and honour, alongside that of the Father – for him to *become* lifegiver in relation to us.[638]

If this reading is correct then John 5 aligns very closely with another passage from the Johannine corpus – Revelation 4-5. In chapter four, John's door into heaven opens to reveal a view of God enthroned at the centre of all glory and creation. Around him the four living beasts representing the orders of creation endlessly praise him while, further out, the twenty-four elders representing the full complement of God's elect respond to the hymns of the creatures by surrendering their authority and proclaiming:

"You are worthy, our Lord and God, to receive glory and honour and power, for you created all things, and by your will they existed and were created" (v. 11).

---

637 So Raymond Brown: "'life' here does not refer primarily to the internal life of the Trinity, but to a creative life-giving power exercised toward men"; R. E. Brown, *The Gospel According to John*, 2 volumes (Garden City: Doubleday, 1966), 1.215. See too M. M. Thompson, *The God of the Gospel of John* (Grand Rapids: Eerdmans, 2001), 77-80. Both Brown and Thompson observe the transitive nature of the "life" being discussed, but miss the differentiation in mode of life-giving that seems to be implicit.

638 In responding to the quandary of divine immutability, Benedictine John Farrelly dissects the matter well. If we ask whether God is changed in *perfection* by history then the answer is "no". Yet if we speak of relationships, the matter is different – God changes *in relation to us* by entering into new relations with us: "The Son has a real and new relationship with us, and the Father takes a real and new initiative with us; they are involved with us in a new way"; Farrelly, *Trinity*, 134.

Along the same lines Thomas Aquinas distinguishes between the worship due to God as God (*adoratio latriae*) and that occasioned by God's contingent acts – whether creation or incarnation – (*adoratio duliae*); Summa Theologiae 3a.25.2. The seventeenth century Anglican Daniel Waterland puts it more helpfully:

Though the absolute, essential dignity of our blessed Lord was always the same, and in respect of which he was ever equal with God, yet his relative dignity towards us, founded in the obligations we have received from him, never so signally appeared as in that amazing and astonishing instance of condescension and goodness, his becoming man, and dying for us. We were hereby "bought " with a price", becoming servants to Christ, and Christ a Lord to us, in a peculiar sense, and under a new and special title.

Equality of Christ with the Father: Sermon V, Jan 6, 1719 in D. Waterland, *The Works of the Rev. Daniel Waterland: Now First Collected and Arranged*, ed. W. Van Mildert (Oxford: Clarendon Press, 1823), 104.

The Will of Him Who Sent Me

But in chapter five the theme of the praise switches from creation to redemption. In answer to the vain search for someone worthy to unseal the scroll of history, the Lion of Judah appears as a slain Lamb in the middle (ἐν μέσῳ)[639] of the throne amidst the living creatures, and the elders[640] initiate a *new* song that is at once very similar and yet significantly different from 4:11. Falling to worship, they declare:

> "You are worthy to take the scroll and to open its seals, for you were slaughtered and by your blood you ransomed for God saints from every tribe and language and people and nation; you have made them to be a kingdom and priests serving our God, and they will reign on earth" (vv. 9-10).

The proclamation of the gospel of the Lamb's redeeming death is thus the ostensible reason he is praised, just as the Father is honoured as creator in the previous chapter. This is significant for our discussion, for while there is no denial that the Son is also creator, nor that the Father is also saviour, there *is* the clear implication that the persons are relatively responsible for these achievements in different ways. In the cross event the Son becomes worthy of praise (ᾠδὴν καινὴν) in a *new* way and in his own right even though he is with the Father and shares in the Father's divinity from eternity. In space and time the Son dies and wins a new reputation for *himself* to be accorded a *distinct* worship which is different from, but equal with, that accorded to the Father.[641] As the cycle of Revelation 4-5 concludes, the Father and Son are hymned together as one, the creator and redeemer (alpha and omega) together:

> Then I heard every creature in heaven and on earth and under the earth and in the sea, and all that is in them, singing, "To the one seated on the throne and to the Lamb be blessing and honour and glory and might forever and ever!" And the four living creatures said, "Amen!" And the elders fell down and worshiped. (vv. 13-14)

---

639 The phrase here might either mean in the centre of the throne and creatures or *in between* the throne and creatures. The first reading is adopted here in light of chapter 3:21 where Jesus speaks of sitting with his Father on his throne.

640 Presumably it is the elders here and not the beasts, because the latter signify creation while the former represent the redeemed.

641 The same might be seen in Jesus' declaration that he has overcome and sat down with his Father on his throne (Revelation 3:21), or in the elevation of Jesus and his receipt of the name above all names (Philippians 2:9). The point in each case is not that he was previously unworthy of being known as God (cf. Revelation 22:13, Philippians 2:6), but that he has now, by his work, won the right to be manifest in his own right as the one who " ... loves us and freed us from our sins by his blood, and made us to be a kingdom, priests serving his God and Father, to him be glory and dominion forever and ever. Amen" (Revelation 1:5b-6).

Assembling the Pieces

At this point I believe we are ready to draw up a broad outline of the kind of Biblical theology that I am trying to commend. It includes the following elements:

1. The work of Creation and Redemption begins with the plan of the Father with the formal cause of bringing glory and honour to himself and his Son. This plan is for the Son to be manifest as the mediator of the Father's rule and glorified as the one through whom the plan is achieved.

2. The plan begins with installation of humans as stewards of God's creation. With the fall they become self-thwarted rulers but remain ectypal anticipations of the Son's own rule (though this is not made clear until his advent). This pattern is retranscribed again and again through the course of salvation history as fresh expressions of agency and failure propagate in the life of Israel.

3. Meanwhile, in accordance with his divine and filial nature, the Son willingly receives the free decision of the Father and effects the plan in time. Uniting himself with Adamic humanity, he at once subjects it to judgment and recapitulates it afresh in himself[642] – thus becoming the new Adam and true "man".

---

642 Thus the motif of union, which underlies all ancient soteriology, is also the basis for "substitution". Death of the representative *in whom* we died (eg. Col 3:3) explains why we are *personally* able to avoid condemnation. Cyril of Jerusalem (c.313-386) puts it thus in *Catechetical Lecture* 13:

> He stretched forth human hands, who by His spiritual hands had established the heaven; and they were fastened with nails, that his manhood, which bore the sins of men, having been nailed to the tree, and having died, sin might die with it, and we might rise again in righteousness. For since by one man came death, by one man came also life; by one man, the Saviour, dying of his own accord.

Catechetical Lecture 13.28; NPNF 2.7.89.

And again.

> For we were enemies of God through sin, and God had appointed the sinner to die. There must needs therefore have happened one of two things; either that God, in his truth, should destroy all men, or that in His loving-kindness He should cancel the sentence. But behold the wisdom of God; He preserved both the truth of His sentence, and the exercise of His loving-kindness. Christ took our sins in His body on the tree, that we by his death might die to sin, and live unto righteousness.

Ibid. 33; NPNF 2.7.91.

The Will of Him Who Sent Me

4. The Son is raised to life again and presented to the cosmos as the supreme agent of God – the fulfilment of humanity.[643] He is given power from the Father through the Spirit to call a people (bride) to share in his conquest over sin and the glory of his eternal rule.

5. In the final consummation of his rule on the Father's behalf,[644] the Son judges the world, exiling his enemies and restoring the creation into alignment with the Father in him.[645]

Some Potential Objections

Too Theocentric?

But does this theo/filiocentric vision of salvation make us mere objects or pawns of God's own self-glorification? A very appropriate concern might be that what we are looking at here is a kind of distasteful hypercalvinist supralapsarianism that demands humans fall so that they can be saved by the incarnate Son.[646] If God makes the world's disaster part of a prior plan it seems

---

643 Thiselton sees the final fulfilment of Ps 8:6-7 as occurring at the *parousia*; A. C. Thiselton, *The First Epistle to the Corinthians: A Commentary on the Greek Text. NIGTC* (Grand Rapids: Eerdmans, 2000), 1236.

644 That is, the final act presented to us in Scripture. Of course if eternity has a history then we might surmise an eternal (*epecstasic* – see above) transformation of the creation as its human rulers venture further into the infinite perfection of God in Christ. But that is beyond us now.

645 This, I take it, is the meaning of 1 Cor 15:27-29 as it speaks of all things being subjected to the Son, and the Son also being subjected to the Father: the Son – having brought all things under his sway – makes presentation of himself and his kingdom to the Father as the reciprocal gift to the one who has given him everything. This dynamic, corresponds to that perichoretic reciprocity seen in Revelation, wherein humanity simultaneously surrenders its rule to God (Rev 4:10) and yet rules in Christ (5:10), who in turn sits on his Father's throne (3:21). For the same interpretation as just given, see Pannenberg, *Systematic Theology*, 312-314; Jonathan Edwards, *Miscellanies* 1062.

646 For examinations of this question from an historical perspective see forthcoming contributions from Mark Jones and Richard A. Muller. Meanwhile the issue of supralasarianism has featured in a number of recent discussions of Jonathan Edwards. Oliver Crisp, for example – O. Crisp, *Jonathan Edwards and the Metaphysics of Sin* (Aldershot: Ashgate, 2005), 5-24 – makes the case that Edwards *is* a supralapsarian, although he inconsistently speaks of God permitting sin whilst *also* implying that God determines all things; ibid., 18-19. Crisp's argument against Edwards probably stands, given the latter's well known determinism (compatibilism) – see *Freedom of the Will* in Edwards, *Works,* 2.1-183. Nevertheless, it should also be noted that Edwards (even if he fails) is

bad enough, but for him to instigate human sin and suffering for his own (and Son's) glory seems utterly abhorrent.

Without question this is a very deep problem, which cannot be answered adequately here.[647] Yet I would hasten to add that it is not a problem raised exclusively for this scheme. Jesus himself proclaims that there is greater joy in heaven "over one sinner who repents than over ninety-nine righteous persons" (Lk 15:7), raising the question of whether sin itself is a necessary element in the greater plan of God. The insistence of Paul and the writer of Hebrews that the world was made for Christ (Col 1:16) as his inheritance (Heb 1:2) by the one who works out all things in accordance with his will (Eph 1:10-11), forces us to ask whether this recapitulation was *always* intended to come via the fall or was there some extra-lapsarian possibility?[648] If we prefer the idea that God was not taken by surprise by human evil, but foreknew and (somehow) even planned it, this is scarcely much different from the NT presentation of God's relationship to the cross (Luke 20:13, cf. Acts 2:23) or Joseph's complex account of his betrayal (Gen 50:20).

Nor is the problem raised here simply "Calvinist". Trading on an implicitly supralapsarian theology the ancient Western paschal *Exultet* proclaims:

O certe necessarium Adae peccatum, quod Christi morte deletum est!
O felix culpa, quae talem ac tantum meruit habere Redemptorem![649]

(O surely necessary sin of Adam,[650] that is erased by the death of Christ!
O happy blame that was so great as to merit so great a Redeemer).

---

nonetheless still trying to avoid the hyper-calvinistic conclusion that God is responsible for human sin *in the same way* that he is responsible for salvation and predestination. This is the same argument I am making here (see below).

647 Principally because a major aspect of the problem is the most hoary of questions – how divine sovereignty relates to human freedom and sin.

648 This is to return us to the Medieval debate over the incarnation already mentioned above. See relevant discussion in V. Y. Haines "Felix Culpa" in *A Dictionary of Biblical Tradition in English Literature*, ed. D. L. Jeffrey (Grand Rapids: Eerdmans, 1992), 274-275.

649 Latin text: A. W. Godfrey, *Medieval Mosaic: A Book of Medieval Latin Readings*, ed. L. H. Keenan (Wauconda: Bolchazy-Carducci Publishers, 2003), 36. The liturgy is often ascribed to Ambrose, but for more detailed discussion see G. Lukken, *Original Sin in the Roman Liturgy. Research into the Theology of Original Sin in the Roman Sacramentaria and the Early Baptismal Liturgy* (Leiden: Brill, 1973), 218.

650 If *necessarium* is rendered "useful" or "profitable", as it may be, the meaning becomes " ... sin, which is really to our advantage"; ibid., 392-393.

Speaking along the same lines, Franciscan theologian Thomas Weinandy diverges somewhat from his Medieval forebears, directing our attention to the significance of sin and redemption – and not simply in relation to *us* (as we see in the *Exultet*), but in relation to the Father and Son:

> [T]he primacy of Christ cannot be separated from the condition of sin. Rather, the primacy is actually manifested from within our situation for the sake of our healing ... The Father sent his Son into the world for our salvation, but inherent in this salvific plan was the Father's desire to reveal the Son's glory ... the exaltation of Jesus is logically prior to and the cause of our redemption.[651]

Of course all theology that would defend God's transcendence and sovereignty must also face the difficult question of God's relationship to the fall. The contention that God is sovereign here – *without* that sovereignty signifying a violation of human free will – is a part of the Catholic tradition just as much as the Reformed.[652] And if this antinomy is possible (or even necessary) then we might also allow that God is *both* sovereign over the fall *and* simultaneously grieved in different ways according to fullness of his will.[653]

A further observation here is that if God's *ultimate* purpose in the incarnation and atonement is our salvation, then we must either embrace universalism or declare that in the end his purposes have failed. This is a manifest danger,[654] not just for modern liberalism, but also for all exemplarist/participationist Neoplatonism where the focus falls on (filiomorphic) harmony rather than filiocentric doxology (see Chapter 7). The Bible will not allow this. Certainly there is *some* sense in which God is thwarted by our unresponsiveness (Eze 33:11; Luke 13:34), but there is no hint

---

651 T. G. Weinandy, *In the Likeness of Sinful Flesh: An Essay on the Humanity of Christ* (Edinburgh: T&T Clark, 1993) 139-140.

652 Thus Aquinas insists that even reprobation must be considered part of divine providence (and thus infallible) despite the fact that it takes place through acts of contingence and free will; *Summa* 1.23.3, cf. 6. Similarly Calvin maintains that the fall was a free act that came from Adam, though it was also God's will; *Institutes* 3.23.8. This depiction of divine sovereignty, it must be noted, is not uniform – putative foreknowledge vs. fore-ordination distinctions can be found in both Catholic and Reformed theology.

653 The terminology in Reformed doctrine is preceptive vs. decretive will; Berkhof, *Systematic Theology*, 78-80. Weinandy, pursuing a somewhat similar distinction, speaks of the Father "allowing the world to see under the most severe conditions of sin how obedient and loving his Son is"; Weinandy, *Likeness*, 142.

654 Danger, of course, both because the doctrine of universal salvation is a heresy after Constantinople II; and, far worse, because it treats "the wound of my people carelessly"; (Jer 6:11) and invites a perilous dereliction of duty on the part of the church (cf. Eze 3:17-19).

that this means God is *finally* confounded. In the end, even rebellion serves the deeper purpose – which is the manifestation of the glory of God and of his Son revealed both in redemption *and* in judgment (Isa 66:22-24; John 5:22-23; Rom 9:22-23; Rev 11:17-18, cf. 19:11-16).[655]

The final point to make here, is that seeing our salvation as subordinate to the inter-personal plans of the Godhead should not detract from our sense of significance,[656] but rather infinitely enhance it. For as those given *to* the Son by the Father and purchased by the Son *for* the Father, we are not simply an external analogy of an infinitely other filiality (though we are that), nor are we simply forgiven (though that is also the case); we are, as it were, written into the life of God as a new chapter as the means by which the Father and Son love and glorify each other. Henceforth the Father and Son love each other *by loving us*.[657] The Father loves us *for the sake of his Son*, giving us to him. The Son loves us as a response to the Father, offering us back to the Father.[658]

He Learned Obedience

One very reasonable objection that might be raised to an RITW perspective on divine relations, is that it fails to do justice to the clearly expressed relational changes and humiliations associated with the incarnation. Jesus' coming resulted in him being *temporarily* "made a little lower than the angels" (Heb 2:9, cf. v. 9b). In Hebrews 5:8 we are clearly taught that "although he was a Son, he learned obedience through what he suffered". Meanwhile in Philippians 2:6-8 that he "emptied himself, taking the form of a slave, being born in human likeness". In 2 Corinthians 8:9 Paul says that Jesus "was rich, yet for your sakes

---

655 This reveals a slightly different emphasis from the exemplarist model where the focus is primarily on the changes wrought in (1) humanity's volitional nature and (2) creation in general. Christ does certainly bring transformation by uniting himself to humanity (and thus creation cf. Rom 8:18ff.), but the focus here is first on the realignment of relationships. In contrast to aesthetic theology which tends toward universalism (*apocatastasis*), the goal of this approach is that Jesus should be saviour, king and judge; the one with the right to include and exclude.

656 Nor is this to deny that it is also appropriate to speak of God's love and compassion toward us outside the context of Trinitarian relations. Both perspectives fit together in the same way that Is 49:14-18 and Eze 36:22ff (respectively) present the God who deeply loves, and the God who loves for a theological reason. The second is deeper, but it certainly does not negate the first.

657 Without, of course, ceasing to be sufficient in their own life and love beyond creation. Salvation history remains a contingent expression of their relationship.

658 This of course is a massive theme in John's Gospel emerging in all the ways the Father and Son act for each other in acting for us: eg. 6.37; 7.18, 10.17-18; 10.27-29; 12.27-28; 13.31-32; 14.12-13; 14.21-23; 15.8; 16.27; 17.1-5.

he became poor"; and in John 17:5 Jesus himself prays that God would restore him to "the glory that I had in your presence before the world existed".

Clearly these passages *do* signify an alteration to the pattern of the Son's circumstances: the eternal Son enters the world ignominiously with his glory veiled. He lives as a human (μορφὴν δούλου) and thereby occupies the same place in the order of creation that goes along with that (βραχύ τι παρ' ἀγγέλους). He neither uses nor displays the prerogatives of his divine sonship in the face of his doubters and persecutors (eg. Matt 26:53; Lk 4:9-12) but endures privation, ignominy persecution and death.

But does Jesus' adoption of the nature of an obedient slave mean that his filiality itself has *no* connotations of obedience or conformity? Not necessarily. Jesus himself distinguishes between different kinds of service in the case of his disciples in John 15:15:

> I do not call you servants (δούλους) any longer, because the servant does not know what the master (κύριος) is doing; but I have called you friends, because I have made known to you everything that I have heard from my Father.

Jesus is clearly not saying here that there is *no sense* in which his followers are his servants.[659] Rather he is making the point that the servanthood experienced by believers is henceforth a kind which includes knowledge, trust and responsibility to the degree that it can also be called friendship. Paul makes a similar distinction in Galatians 4:6-7: "And because you are children, God has sent the Spirit of his Son into our hearts, crying, 'Abba! Father!' So you are no longer a slave (δοῦλος) but a child (υἱός), and if a child then also an heir, through God". Once again, it is clear that the intention here is not the denial of all subordination in our relationship toward God, but simply that our participation in Jesus' sonship creates a decisive difference in our relationship to the one we serve.

It is quite possible to understand the distinction between "son" and "obedience" (ὑπακοήν) (Heb 5:8) or the "form of a slave" in the same way. We have already noted that the first recipients of the NT would certainly have expected sons to honour and obey their fathers. And they would also have understood the difference between the obedience of a son and that of a slave. Whereas a son's interests would be aligned with those of his father,[660] and his

---

659 If that were the case then he contradicts himself five verses later when he implicitly calls them servants (v. 20); and John fails to take Jesus seriously for he calls himself δοῦλος in Revelation 1:1.

660 Bruce Malina explains the concept of the "in-group" where the status of the whole unit will be affected by the actions of individuals. This is particularly strong in

obedience is seen as bringing honour to both his father and thereby himself,[661] the slave must receive instruction as heteronomous, with obedience being simply an expected obligation. Slavery is a burden predicated on a conflict of interest.[662]

And surely it this conflict – which so marks humanity – that Jesus takes upon himself. In a fallen world obedience is painful because our interests and *even legitimate* creaturely desires are in constant tension;[663] we (sometimes!) want to serve God but we *also* want pleasure, esteem, comfort, peace, relief and so on. We want to approach God but we are guilty, and such proximity can only mean death. And Jesus, as full participant in our humanity, experiences this conflict too. As a man, the eternal Son discovers what it is to be required to do something he doesn't *want* to do, crying out in the garden "not my will but yours" (Luke 22:42). On earth his agency is met with mocking and rejection instead of glory, so that he must "entrust himself to him who judges justly" (1 Pet 2:23) and endure the cross "disregarding its shame" (Heb 12:2). And, in surrendering to the cross, he submits himself to the ultimate conflict between faith and humanity, surrendering himself to the full implication of what we have made ourselves before God.

The alteration that takes place in the Father/Son relationship need not be seen then as absolute transformation from *égalité* to hierarchy. Rather, the sufferings of Gethsemene and Golgotha torture, test and prove the devotion of the Son to his Father's will – entitling him to be the priest and mediator of a struggling and suffering humanity. Only in the context of the Father and Son's separation do we see that the glory of the Son is not simply proximate and mediatorial, but that he himself is an active source of will and grace *a se* as well as *ex Patre*. That the incarnation and cross represent an *in extremis* expression of the filial bond, does not nullify its basic order, but allows us to see its dynamic in stark clarity.

---

relationships between children and parents who are regarded externally as being at equivalent levels of the in-group. Malina, *Windows,* 79.

661 A father rises in the estimation of his peers and neighbours according to the honour accorded to him by his sons; ibid., 2.

662 I am speaking generally here, not denying the fact that slavery might also encompass or give rise to more complex and positive benefactor relationships in first century society. See Malina's helpful explanations concerning the expectation (from the served as well as the servant) that servants be treated as inferiors in Mediterranean culture; ibid., 39-41.

663 Cf. our discussion of Maximus the Confessor above.

Changes to the Order of Names

For some theologians, the traditional prioritising of the Father in relation to the Son fails to do justice to the way the Scriptures treat the order in which "Father, Son and Spirit" are listed.[664] Certainly there are texts which preserve the order just observed (eg. Matt 28:19; 1 Pet 1:2),[665] but there are others which seem not to. The benediction of Second Corinthians 13:14 places "the grace of the Lord Jesus Christ" ahead of "the love of God". 1 Cor 12:4-6 actually reverses the order:

> Now there are varieties of gifts, but the same Spirit; and there are varieties of services, but the same Lord and there are varieties of activities, but it is the same God who activates all of them in everyone.

Kevin Giles examines the variation in passages such as these and draws the quite appropriate conclusion that "Paul did not believe the three divine 'persons' are ordered hierarchically ... in precedence and power".[666] But, as Giles immediately adds, this does not mean there is no *order*:

> For Paul there is nothing arbitrary or random in how God the Father and God the Son work or function. There is a given disposition. God the Father creates through the Son (Col 1:16); judges through the Son (Rom 2:16) [etc.] ... Such order does not imply the subordination of any party. Rather, it envisages harmonious and agreed ways of cooperatively working together.[667]

This is basically in line with my claim here. The Bible does not proclaim subordination if we mean by that the Son and Spirit are to be considered less *divine* than the Father. As far as we are concerned each person is equally "our God". The intra-trinitarian *taxis* and functional order must not be allowed to signify ontological subordination.[668]

---

[664] Millard Erickson provides a survey of opinions on this topic, identifying B. B. Warfield, Arthur Wainwright (misidentified as Geoffrey), Gerald Bray and Kevin Giles, as those prescinding from the traditional view; Erickson, *Tampering*, 117-118.

[665] For a helpful table which tabulates the variations in order see Giles, *Jesus*, 109-110.

[666] Ibid., 110.

[667] Ibid., 110.

[668] Of course whether Giles connects the processions with the missions in this way is more difficult to say. While he states that there is "nothing arbitrary" here, he also connects the order of operations to "agreed ways of working". Here we are brought to the Warfieldian *pactum salutis* where the persons simply agree to act on a certain order for the duration of salvation history. But if this covenant is not based in any way on the processional order of the persons then it *can only be* arbitrary.

Does Responsive Intra-Trinitarian Willing Fit with Scripture?

Further to this, I would add that if my interpretation of creation's *telos* is correct then we should not be at all surprised if the Son's name is brought forward. If the Father's objective is to manifest his Son as a distinct agent and set him forth as our saviour and head, then it would be quite appropriate for us to begin with Christ and then praise the Father through him (as we see repeatedly with Paul). The fact that the Son is made the visible symbol of the Father and the effective agent of the Father in our salvation, means that he is the first in our perception – just as the Spirit, who enables us to grasp this revelation and salvation (1Cor 2:12), is *instrumentally* prevenient in all that the Son and Father achieve (cf. 1 Cor 12:4-6). None of this contradicts the priority of the Father but rather arises out of his very fatherhood. Thus as Gerald Bray concludes:

> [I]n spite of [the variation in order], the pattern of personal operation is remarkably stable. God the Father is the person who ordains, establishes, judges and appoints; he is also the person to whom worship is chiefly directed. The Son Jesus Christ appears as the Redeemer, the sacrificial victim and the mediator; he is the guarantor of our salvation and the person in whose likeness we are being moulded.[669]

---

669 G. L. Bray, *The Doctrine of God.* vol. 1. *Contours of Christian theology* (Leicester: IVP, 1993), 146-147.

Chapter 6

Does Prioritising Divine Filiality Mean Neglecting the Holy Spirit?

The union between Father and Son is such a live concrete thing that this union itself is also a person. ... It is as if a sort of communal personality came into existence. Of course, it is not a person; it is only rather like a person. But that is just one of the differences between God and us. What grows out of the joint life of the Father and Son is a real Person, is in fact the Third of the three Persons who are God.

– C. S. Lewis[670]

Introduction

Up to this point my focus has been resolutely fixed on the relations and glory of the first two persons of the Godhead – a product largely of the purview of my chosen topic. Yet as the scope and claims of the thesis dilate, questions surrounding the status of the Spirit become more pregnant. Is the scheme I am depicting here effectively, or at least doxologically, *binitarian* rather than trinitarian? How does my case that East and West preserve a common account of paternal priority fare in the light of the *filioque* which ostensibly turns on this very question? And how does my attempt to discern congruence between the Son's relations *asarkos* and *ensarkos* account for the apparent changes in his relationship with the Holy Spirit? Can this thesis account for the transition from Spirit-sent Christ to Spirit-sending Christ?

My strategy here will be to first make some general observations about the *filioque* in the light of historical and contemporary discussion, and then proceed to sketch out the elements of a biblical pneumatology that might begin to address these questions.

Before I begin, however, I would like to propose two principles and one caveatwith regard to this discussion.

The first principle is that we should try, insofar as it is possible, to find a model for the *immanent* workings of the Spirit that can best harmonise the

---

670 C. S. Lewis, *Mere Christianity*, 1986 edition (Glasgow: William Collins & Sons, 1952), 149.

biblical revelation of his operations in the economy. The disagreement between East and West on the matter of the *filioque* arises out of the attempts to develop pneumatology from different *moments* in the economy (respectively, the baptism of Christ and Pentecost)[671] but the divergence does not mean that the quest itself is misguided. I will attempt to suggest (or at least gesture toward) a model that can make sense of both moments.

The second principle is that we should be wary of trinitarian models which break the Trinity down into redundant or replaceable persons. Whatever the coming of the "other counsellor" means, it should not be taken to mean that the second person of the Trinity is now wholly *absent* or has been "replaced" by another. Such a view of the Trinity looks dangerously like a decay into tritheism and a multiplication of aseity. If the Trinity is really one God then we must work harder to see how each person is involved at each stage of the divine enterprise. This does not mean there are no changes or developments in the way the persons work, but it is to assert that models which can show the involvement of all three persons should be preferred.

The caveat is that I do not think we should presume that it will be possible to develop a theology of the *person* of the Spirit in the same way that we can with regard to the Father and Son. As I shall argue below, the Bible most usually presents the Spirit to us in the context of his mediation of other persons: his purpose is not to "speak on his own" but to glorify the risen Christ (John 16:13-14). The does not mean that he is not revealed to us at all; nor that we cannot say anything true about him; nor that his personhood should be denied. But if he is not the object of revelation in the same way as the first two persons, the *prima facie* charge of neglect cannot stand on its own.[672]

With these qualifications in place we are ready to begin. I will attempt to work toward a provisional (and unashamedly incomplete) integrated pneumatology and Christology.

---

[671] To unpack this briefly, in the baptism of Jesus the Son and Spirit are both seen in relation to the sending Father with the Spirit alighting on (and thus manifesting) the Son – a picture which resonates strongly with Irenaean "two hands" theology and appears to affirm the distinction between immanent procession and immanent manifestation. Alternatively, the Pentecost tableau with its depiction of Christ being given the Spirit and pouring him out seems to lend support to Augustinian theories of the Spirit as *donum*; and the *filioque*.

[672] Although we might express caution about the implication of post-canonical revelation, Gregory Nazianzen's comments on the relative clarity with which the persons are revealed seems apposite: "The Old Testament proclaimed the Father openly, and the Son more obscurely. The New manifested the Son, and suggested the deity of the Spirit. Now the Spirit himself dwells among us, and supplies us with a clearer demonstration of himself;" *Or.* 31.26; NPNF 2.7.326.

Some Observations Concerning the Filioque

It is of course brave to the point of foolhardiness to even trespass onto this well-mined territory. Discussion of the history and interpretation of the *filioque* clause has been complex, fraught, and frequently acerbic – and thus I hastily add that it is certainly not my intention to enter the debate, nor to make any presumptuous adjudication concerning its rights and wrongs. Rather, I will observe that, despite the heat and dust generated by the *filioque*, there are some important points of agreement between East and West concerning the processions of the Spirit and Son. My case will be that there are ways to render the matter that support the insights of both East and West and which simultaneously tend to support the notion of agreement between the economic and immanent Trinity.

Filioque and the Monarchy

The first point to be made here is that the *filioque* has never been used to deny the priority of the Father *as regards the Son* (or the Spirit, for that matter). The contested notion that the Son should also identified as the source of the Spirit is not to be (and has not been by any major theologian) set against the idea that the Father is the *arché* or *principium*.[673] If this is not sufficiently clear from our previous examination of Western trinitarianism then the point is readily demonstrated. Augustine, the theologian most directly responsible for the *filioque*, explains that the reason why the Spirit *also* proceeds from the Son is because he *is* a son – and thus does just what the Father does:

> God the Father alone is he from whom the Word is born, and from whom the Holy Spirit principally proceeds. And therefore I have added the word principally, because we find that the Holy Spirit proceeds from the Son also. But the Father gave him this too, not as to one already existing, and not yet having it; but whatever he gave to the only-begotten Word, he gave by begetting him. Therefore he so begat him as that the common Gift should proceed from him also, and the Holy Spirit should be the Spirit of both.[674]

The pronouncements of the seventeenth session of the Council of Florence, despite their generally western tenor, labour to make the same point:

> The Latins asserted that they say the Holy Spirit proceeds from the Father and the Son not with the intention of excluding the Father from

---

673 See R. Letham, "East is East and West is West? Another Look at the Filioque", *Mid-America Journal of Theology* 13 (2002): 71-86, 77.

674 *DeTrin* 15.29; NPNF 1.3.216.

being the source and principle of all deity, that is of the Son and of the Holy Spirit, nor to imply that the Son does not receive from the Father, because the Holy Spirit proceeds from the Son, nor that they posit two principles or two spirations; but they assert that there is only one principle and a single spiration of the Holy Spirit, as they have asserted hitherto.[675]

The same position was maintained in modern times by the important Klingenthal Colloquia, sponsored by the World Council of Churches in 1978 and 1979. There too, delegates from East and West were able to achieve a remarkable level of agreement on the issue of the Father's monarchy – observing in their joint memorandum that:

> From a western point of view ... it may be said that neither the early Latin Fathers, such as Ambrose and Augustine, nor the subsequent medieval tradition ever believed that they were damaging the Father's "monarchy" by affirming the *filioque*. The West declared itself to be as much attached to this principle as were the eastern Fathers.[676]

Pope John Paul II's *Pontifical Council for Promoting Christian Unity* (1995) adopts the same stance in its section entitled "The Father as the Source of the Whole Trinity":

> The doctrine of the Filioque must be understood and presented by the Catholic Church in such a way that it cannot appear to contradict the Monarchy of the Father nor the fact that he is the sole origin (*arché, aitia*) of the *ekporeusis* of the Spirit. The Filioque is, in fact, situated in a theological and linguistic context different from that of the affirmation of the sole Monarchy of the Father, the one origin of the Son and of the Spirit. Against Arianism, which was still virulent in the West, its purpose was to stress the fact that the Holy Spirit is of the same divine nature as the Son, without calling in question the one Monarchy of the Father.

These quotes are not intended to trivialise differences between East and West, yet they remind us that the *filioque's* depiction of the Son as source of the Spirit is not *supposed to* be seen as detracting from the monarchy of the Father (even if the East is right in arguing that it does so implicitly). Whether the Son is seen as a coordinate source of the Spirit or a single source along with the

---

675 N. P. Tanner (ed), *Decrees of the Ecumenical Councils*, 2 volumes (London Washington: Sheed & Ward Georgetown University Press, 1990)

676 L. Vischer (ed), *Spirit of God, Spirit of Christ: Ecumenical Reflections on the Filioque Controversy* (London: SPCK World Council of Churches, 1981), 13.

Father (both highly contested propositions!)[677] the relational *taxis* of the Father and Son itself remains unchallenged. At this level, the *filioque* does not threaten this thesis.

Yet this is not to deny that the *filioque* and its attendent controversies have nothing to say here. As mentioned above, if the eternal Logos is author of the Spirit in eternity and yet is also sent *by* the Spirit in the economy, then complications arise for my argument that the incarnation appropriately expresses the relationships with the Trinity. For while, as just observed, a temporary (or ultimate) reversal of the Son-Spirit order would not necessarily negate the consistency of the *Father-Son* relationship, it would make things less neat overall.

Here again, however, things are less straightforward than the standard account might lead us to believe. For a start, the hostile reaction of eastern theology to the western designation of Son as ontological "cause" should not necessarily be taken to mean that Orthodox theologians believe that the Son and Spirit have *nothing* to do with each other in eternity – as if the Father's "two hands" were held out at opposite extremities until the moment of the incarnation. In actual fact there are ancient traditions – both in the East and the West – which observe that the Son and Spirit condition each other's eternal subsistence in ways that align well with the patterns seen in the economy. Here, very briefly I will survey some of these approaches, making observations where appropriate.

Son & Spirit: Mutual Manifestation

In one important theme found in eastern theology, the Son and Spirit relate to each other in eternity by "manifesting" each other. Maximus the Confessor, for example, defends the Latin use of *filioque* on the basis that it does not speaks of causation or procession, but only speaks of the Son as being the one through whom the Spirit's going-forth is manifested (τό δι' αὐτοῦ προϊέναι δηλώσωσι).[678] Conversely John of Damascus speaks of the Spirit as the companion (συμπαρομαρτοῦν) of the Word and the shining-forth (φανεροῦν) of His energy ... proceeding (προερχομένην) from the Father and resting (ἀναπαυομένην) in the Word, as his declaration (αὐτοῦ οὖσαν ἐκφαντικήν).[679] Although later theology would wrangle over how "deep" this manifestation goes – whether it reaches beyond the created order or past the

---

677 T. Stylianopoulos, "The Filioque: Dogma, Theologoumenon or Error?", *The Greek Orthodox Theological* 3.4 (1986): 255-288.

678 PG 91.136.A-B.

679 *FidOrth.* 1.7; PG 94.805B-C.

eternal "energies"[680] – John makes it clear that he believes this manifestation to be on a par with the Father's begetting of the Son: "for never was the Father at any time lacking in the Word, nor the Word in the Spirit.[681]

Through the Son

The procession of the Spirit from the Father "through the Son" is often regarded as a potential point of compromise for easterners who want to preserve the absolute monarchy of the Father, and for westerners who are looking to align their *filioquism* with the scriptural pattern. Depending on how the scheme is rendered,[682] the compromise might be successful. Yet where "through" (διά/*per*) is taken in a way that clearly distinguishes the Father's causation – then this model also requires us to consider that the Spirit is simultaneously "prior" to the Son, such that he can be received and passed-on by the Son. Thus John Damascene writes "the Holy Spirit is God, being between the unbegotten and the begotten (μεσόν τοῦ ἀγεννήτου καὶ τοῦ γεννητου), and united to the Father through the Son (δι Υἱοῦ τῷ Πατρὶ συναπτερον)."[683] Or, as Thomas explains it using western terminology, if we look to the persons (rather than their common *virtus*) we find that the Spirit proceeds immediately from the Father (*immediate a patre*) and mediately *a filio* in the same way that Abel came forth immediately from Adam and mediately through Eve.[684]

---

680 The Palamite thematising of the idea of divine energies which sit conceptually between divine essence and created economy adds a complicating factor to this whole discussion which cannot be adequately explored here. Nonetheless it is worth observing that the effect of the innovation depends on how it is used. The idea of an "eternal economy" can be taken to buttress a strongly apophatic theology which renders all knowledge of the immanent Trinity doubtful (or at least provisional). In other words, the energies can be invoked to "screen-off" the real God from us (see protests along this line in A. I. C. Heron "The Filioque Clause" in *One God in Trinity*, ed. P. Toon & J. D. Spiceland (London: Bagster, 1980), 74-75; and Letham, "East is East", 79, 81). Yet if the stress is laid on "eternal" rather than "economy", the same concept might be taken to show that the economy is eternally important to God – indeed *defining* of God, even though not essential.

681 *FidOrth*. 1.7; NPNF 2.9.5.

682 For as Boris Bobrinskoy observes, the expression means something very different when used by John of Damascus and at the Council of Florence. While the first intends to secure the hypostatic priority of the Father as cause, the second uses the *per* as connoting a joint causation – which the East utterly rejects; B. Bobrinskoy "The Filioque Yesterday and Today" in *Spirit of God, Spirit of Christ: Ecumenical Reflections on the Filioque Controversy*, ed. L. Vischer (London: SPCK World Council of Churches, 1981) 145-146.

683 FidOrth. 1.13; NPNF 2.9.16.

684 *Summa* 1.36.3

The Spirit as the Bond

In Augustinian pneumatology (though the idea is also found in the East)[685] this inter-filial aspect of the Spirit's subsistence is expressed through his characterisation as gift or bond of love.[686] As Augustine writes:

> Through him the two are joined, through him the Begotten is loved by the Begetter, and loves him that begat him ... they are "keeping the unity of the Spirit in the bond of peace;" which we are commanded to imitate by grace, both towards God and towards ourselves ... And therefore they are not more than three: One who loves him who is from himself, and One who loves him from whom he is, and Love itself. And if this last is nothing, how is "God love"? If it is not substance, how is God substance?[687]

The Spirit Rests on the Son

Another vision of filial/pneumatological relations comes with descriptions of the Spirit's resting on the Son. This description can be found in Cyril of Alexandria and, more prominently in John of Damsacus and Thomas Aquinas.[688] In modern discussion, Boris Bobrinskoy declares that "the descent

---

685 As David T. Williams notes, depictions of the Spirit as *koinonia* can also be found in Athanasius, the Cappadocians, Athenagoras and Epiphanius; D. T. Williams, *Vinculum Amoris: A Theology of the Holy Spirit* (Lincoln: iUniverse, 2004), 15. Indeed the same expressions concerning the Spirit as bond can even be found in Gregory Palamas; see Bobrinskoy, *Spirit of God*, 142. Amazingly, Rheinhard Flogaus argues that Palamas is drawing on a Greek translation of *De Trinitate*! See R. Flogaus "Inspiration-Exploitation-Distortion: The Use of St Augustine in the Hesychast Controversy" in *Orthodox Readings of Augustine,* ed. G. E. Demacopoulos & A. Papanikolaou (Crestwood: St. Vladimirs Seminary Press, 2008), 63-80.

686 Although Augustine does not use the terminology of *vinculum amoris/caritatis* which is sometimes credited to him, the concept signified by the expression is certainly Augustinian and can be found in *DeTrin* 15.29-37 where the Spirit is both God's gift to us and that given to the Son by the Father such that he too is its source.

> *DeTrin* 6.6; NPNF 1.3.100 (translation altered using Augustine, *S. Aurelii Augustini Opera Omnia* iat-tead ition Nudauai)n a, http://augustinus.it/latino/index.htm, (accessed June, 2011)).

688 For Cyril and John see NPNF 2.9.5. Damascene also writes:
> Likewise we believe also in one Holy Spirit, the Lord and Giver of Life: Who proceedeth from the Father and resteth in the Son: the object of equal adoration and glorification with the Father and Son, since he is co-essential and co-eternal.
> *FidOrth*. 1.8; NPNF 2.9.9.

of the Spirit on Jesus at the Jordan therefore appears in the Orthodox Trinitarian vision as an icon, a manifestation of the eternal resting of the Spirit of the Father on the Son."[689] Dumitri Staniloae makes a similar point, relating the temporal reception and sending of the Spirit by the Son to that which occurs in the eternal economy. For him the Spirit's descent on the church as part of Christ continues the eternal resting of the Spirit in him: "the sending of the Spirit to men rather signifies that the Spirit rests in those who are united with the Son, since ... the Son is the only and ultimate resting place place of the Spirit."[690]

Son & Spirit: Word and Breath

Perhaps the most evocative image for the interdependence of the second and third persons comes with the analogy of word and breath. Gregory of Nyssa (in a passage reproduced by John Damascene)[691] suggests that we might be helped in our understanding of the Spirit by considering certain shadows and resemblances (σκιάς τινας καὶ μιμήματα)[692] between the Word and Spirit and *our* words and breath. As he writes in his second theological oration:

> Now in us the spirit (or breath) is the drawing of the air, a matter other than ourselves, inhaled and breathed out for the necessary sustainment of the body. This, on the occasion of uttering the word, becomes an utterance which expresses in itself the meaning of the word. ... The like doctrine have we received as to God's Spirit; we regard it as that which goes with the Word and manifests his energy (φανεροῦν αὐτοῦ τὴν ἐνέργειαν), and not as a mere effluence of the breath ... But we conceive of it as an essential power, regarded as self-centred in its own proper person, yet equally incapable of being separated from God in Whom it is, or from the Word of God whom it accompanies.[693]

> Aquinas strikes a less certain note, but connects the resting with love:
>> To say that the Holy Spirit rests or abides in the Son does not rule out his proceeding from the Son, for we say that the Son abides in the Father even though he proceeds from the Father ... [either] as the love of a lover rests in the beloved or [according to] the human nature of Christ.
>> *Summa* 1.36.2.

689 Bobrinskoy, *Spirit of God*, 144.

690 D. Staniloae "The Procession of the Holy Spirit from the Father and his Relation to the Son, as the basis for our Deification and Adoption" in *Spirit of God, Spirit of Christ: Ecumenical Reflections on the Filioque Controversy*, ed. L. Vischer (London: SPCK World Council of Churches, 1981), 179.

691 *FidOrth.* 1.6.

692 *Oratio Catechetica* 2; PG 45.17.

693 *Oratio Catechetica* 2; NPNF 2.5.135 cf. PG 45.17.

Here then, the Spirit and Son come forth together *and indeed must* come forth together. Without the Spirit, the Word has no moving energy; without the Word the Spirit has no form.[694] D. B. Knox, a contemporary exponent of the same notion, put it even more strongly with regard to the economy:

> The Son is the Word of the Father. Our words are us. They are the expression of our minds, and our words are conveyed to others by our breath. Now the Spirit is the breath of God. It is by God's Spirit or breath that we are related to God through his Word. Breath is movement from God to us; we know God through his Word by means of his Spirit. But breath in itself is nothing; it must carry words to be means of relationship, so the Spirit of God does not testify of himself but takes of the things of Jesus, who is the Word and expression of God, and shows them to us.[695]

Ex Patre Spirituque Natum

A more radical counterpoint to the *filioque* in the light of these perceived patterns of interdependence is the suggestion that, if the Son is seen as implicated in the Spirit's procession, then the Spirit should also be seen as involved in the Son's begetting. Thus Jürgen Moltmann, protesting against the Spirit-subordinating tendencies of filioquist theology, observes that the coming of Christ by the Spirit and the later mission of the Spirit in the Son's name indicates a mutuality in the procession:

> the Spirit proceeds from the Father and determines the Son, rests on the Son and shines through him. The Son proceeds from the Father and has the impress of the Spirit. We might say that Christ comes *a patre spirituque* ... the eternal birth of the Son from the Father and the eternal issuing of the Spirit from the Father are ... not successive to one another, but *in* one another.[696]

---

694 In the Klingenthal agreed statement, the *filioque* is defined, not as the means by which the Spirit proceeds, but the basis for his "personal form" or "*Gestalt*" which he receives from his relationship with the Father and Son; Vischer, *Spirit of God,* 167.

695 Knox, *Everlasting God,* 65. The significance of the economic connection between breath and word also finds patristic precedent in the exegesis of Ps 33:6. For example, in *DeSpir* 16, Basil of Caesarea uses the Psalm to depict the Son and Spirit as creative and perfecting causes to the Father's originative causation.

696 Moltmann, *Spirit of Life,* 71-72. Similar comments can be found in Leonardo Boff who paraphrases Moltmann and Boris Boltov to the effect that the Father "breathes out the Holy Spirit through being Father of the Son ... [while, conversely] the existence of the Holy Spirit is received from the Father alone, but the specific configuration of the Spirit's existence is received from the Son of the Father." Boff

In recent years this same approach has received a more developed treatment in the hands of Thomas Weinandy and, more recently still, Myk Habets. For Weinandy, seeking to cut the *filioque* Gordion, and give the third person a duly active role, the Spirit is not simply the one through whom *the Son* is begotten, but also thereby the one that "conforms the Father to be Father for the Son and conforms the Son to be Son for (of) the Father."[697] Myk Habets, applying the same solution to Christology, sees it as a way past the dichotomy of Logos Christology vs. Spirit Christology (potentially Apollinarianism vs. adoptionism). Christ is the man of the Spirit because the Son is the *also* of the Spirit in eternity: Spirit Christology *enables* Logos Christology because "the giving of the Spirit by the Father constitutes the basis of both Jesus' mission in the world and his filiological relation to the Father."[698]

The Spirit as Essence

The suggestion that the Spirit might be seen as somehow constitutive of the Son, or that he *enables* the Father-Son relationship, take us very close to the notion that the Spirit actually *is* the divine essence. The defining motif of pro-Nicene theology is the equality and oneness of the Son with the Father, predicated on the communication of the Father's own *ousia*. Might it be that the essence which goes forth from the Father in the generation of the Son *is* the Spirit?

Such a view, if taken seriously has the potential to both illuminate and correct the typical Western account of the Trinity.[699] And in fact the idea does appear in an undeveloped form in the West: both Tertullian and Marius Victorinus speak explicitly of the Spirit as the substance of the Father and Son.[700] More importantly, Lewis Ayres argues that this understanding is

---

& Burns, *Trinity and Society*, 205. And the same interest in the simultaneity of the procession/begetting can also be detected in the Klingenthal Memorandum (in which Moltmann was participant); see Vischer, *Spirit of God*, 14-16.

697   Weinandy, *Spirit of Sonship*, 17

698   M. Habets, *The Anointed Son: A Trinitarian Spirit Christology* (Eugene: Pickwick Publications, 2010), 221. Habets' extensive survey of the rise of Spirit Christology in both its orthodox and unorthodox forms is a very instructive support for his argument, and reveals a broad consensus that something has been missed in traditional Logos Christology.

699   By this I mean that a view of the Spirit as essence (provided the Spirit can be maintained as personal in this – see below) might forestall the incipient materialist tendencies in pro-Nicene essentialism and also a corrective to the western tendency to hypostasise the being of God (*simpliciter*) as a *quaternum quid* (or *persona*).

700   See respectively *Adversus Praxean* 26.3-4, *Adversus Arium* 1 A.17. Mark Weedman argues (*contra* Hanson) that Victorinus is directly influenced by

implicit in Augustine's own trinitarianism. For Augustine, the Spirit is the very substance of God – not in the sense of an impersonal stuff which signifies the indefineable divinity,[701] but because the substance of God is the communion that is established in the Son's generation (and in the Son's loving response):[702] "The Spirit comes from the Father to the Son as the fullness of divinity ... [the Son] in some sense has the Spirit as his essence"[703] Or, in Augustine's own words:

> If, then, any one of the three is to be specially called Love, what more fitting than that it should be the Holy Spirit? ... [T]hat substance itself should be love, and love itself should be substance (*substantia ipsa sit caritas, et caritas ipsa sit substantia*).[704]

Certain modern westerners have put the matter more boldy. Wolfhart Pannenberg drawing on Hegel (and scriptural passages such as John 4:24 and 1John 4:8, 16), speaks of the Spirit as the "essence" and "dynamic field" by which the Father lovingly brings forth the Son,[705] and as a distinct hypostasis that "stands over against" the Father and Son.[706] Stanley Grenz, following a similar track to that of his doctoral supervisor writes that the Holy Spirit, as "the dynamic that binds together the Father and the Son ... [is] the essence of

---

Tertullians here; M. Weedman, *The Trinitarian Theology of Hilary of Poitiers* (Leiden: Brill, 2007), 70-71.

701 See L. Ayres "Sempiterne Spiritus Donum: Augustine's Pneumatology and the Metaphysics of Spirit" in *Orthodox Readings of Augustine*, ed. G. E. Demacopoulos & A. Papanikolaou (Crestwood: St. Vladimirs Seminary Press, 2008), 143-146; also L. Ayres, *Augustine and the Trinity* (Cambridge: Cambridge University Press, 2010), 251-272. It is interesting to note, in the first reference, Ayres' sympathy for Weinandy's proposal. In the second, Ayres himself draws forth the same conclusion, believing that the Spirit's involvement is implicit in Augustine's scheme: ibid., 265-266.

702 The Holy Spirit, whether he is that supreme love that joins [Father and Son] or sub-joins us, is, he of whom it is justly written, "God is love." (*Spiritus quoque Sanctus sive sit summa caritas utrumque coniungens nosque subiungens, quod ideo non indigne dicitur quia scriptum est: Deus caritas est*) *DeTrin* 7.6, my translation.

703 Ibid., 266.

704 *DeTrin* 15.29, translation from NPNF 1.3.216. Augustine also defends the idea without explicitly owning it for himself in *De Fide et Symbolo*, 19.

705 Pannenberg, *Systematic Theology*, 1.427-429.

706 Ibid., 1.383-384. For a helpful overview and critique of Pannenberg here, see A. K. Min, "The Dialectic of Divine Love: Pannenberg's Hegelian Trinitarianism", *IJST* 6.3 (July 2004): 252-269.

God, namely love."⁷⁰⁷ In terms that resonate with the exemplarism of Bonventure, he also sees the Spirit's role *ad extra* as an

> ...outworking of his role in the eternal trinitarian relationship. As we have noted, the act of creation flows out of the inner life of God. The creation of the world comes as the outflowing of the eternal love relationship ... the Father who eternally loves the Son creates the world in order that it might share in his existence and ... reciprocate his love after the pattern of the Son's love for the Father.⁷⁰⁸

Biblical Resonances

My reason for briefly citing these various approaches is not to argue that any one of them provides the "correct model" for us to understand the relations between the second and third persons.⁷⁰⁹ Yet the general complementarity of their insights does seem to create a cumulative case that conciliar trinitarianism has missed something with regard to the third person.

They also resonate with the patterns of Scripture. For if the life of Christ is to be our guide in these matters,⁷¹⁰ then the Spirit and Son *always* go together.

---

707 S. J. Grenz, *Theology for the Community of God* (Grand Rapids: Eerdmans, 2000). 105.

708 Ibid., 105-106. Once again, this is similar to, but also short-of, what I am arguing in this thesis: which is that the *opera ad extra* do not merely copy the divine love (for our sake) but give it a new expression. That is, the Spirit's action ad extra is *actually* the loving of the Father and Son in a new context.

709 And, indeed I have some reservations concerning those which seek to give the Spirit a more *personally active* role than he seems to have in Scripture. Moltmann's claim, for example, that the Son has the "impress of the Spirit" verges on a displacement of the Father's relation with regard to the Son (cf. Heb 1:3), despite the helpful point that the this paternal relation comes *through* the Spirit. Ralph del Colle's similar hesitations regarding Weinandy's model also seem appropriate; R. del Colle, "Reflections on the Filioque", *Journal of Ecumenical Studies* 34.2 (Spring 1997): 202-217.

710 And this, of course, is the central question. The eastern objection to the *filioque*, as well as the modern objections to paternal priority all turn on the belief that at key points the analogy between the economic Trinity and immanent Trinity breaks down. Nevertheless, it is also true that it is the desire to derive trinitarian theology from the *economic* mission of Christ that produces the divergent approaches of East and West. As I mentioned in the introduction to this chapter, the East looks to the moment of Jesus' baptism as its dominant icon; the West to Pentecost. If both traditions *also* state that the economy obscures the immanent Trinity at key points, then this is perhaps better interpreted as a sign that their respective paradigms are incomplete.

In the first place, it is the Spirit that seems to facilitate (or at least accompany) the manifestation of the Son's sonship. From the very start of Christ's mission, it is the Spirit who comes upon/overshadows Mary (Luke 1:34): such she is described as "having from the Spirit" (ἔχουσα ἐκ πνεύματος) in her womb (Matt 1:18); and her child is called "the son of God" (Luke 1:35).[711] To Thomas Weinandy, this temporal intervention provides a crucial insight into the eternal begetting:

> The depiction of the Father begetting the Son in the womb of Mary by the Holy Spirit becomes, I believe, a temporal icon of his eternal begetting in the Holy Spirit. Firstly, as the Son is sent forth by the Father into the world by the power of the Holy Spirit, so the Son is eternally begotten of the Father in the Holy Spirit. Secondly, as the son is conceived in the womb of Mary by the power of the Holy Spirit, and so conforms the Son to be Son now as man, so the Holy Spirit conforms the Son to be the eternal Son of the Father within the immanent Trinity.[712]

The Spirit-formed Son

Weinandy's comment regarding the "conforming" action of the Spirit here seems to be vindicated in the mission of Jesus. From the moment of his baptism – where, once again, he is declared to be God's Son (eg. Matt 3:17) – the Spirit descends on Jesus from the Father and immediately begins directing his words and actions. Henceforth the Spirit that remains on Jesus will be the means by which he is empowered and known (John 1:31-33).

In Luke's account, the effect of this anointing is that Jesus is "filled" and "led" by the Spirit (Luke 4:1). In Mark's telling, the Spirit's first act of conforming is to "drive out" Jesus into the desert – making Jesus the recapitulation of all those who are "driven out" by the Lord.[713] In both

---

For ecumenical affirmations that the mission of Jesus should remain the datum for trinitarian speculations persists see the Klingenthal papers, where the principle is stressed by Bobrinskoy – Vischer, *Spirit of God*, 143; Moltmann – ibid., 165; and in the memorandum itself – ibid., 10.

711 It is instructive to contrast Jesus here with his cousin John – the other great man of the Spirit. Both John and Jesus have the Spirit before their births; yet, while John is described as being "filled with the Spirit" (Luke 1:15) from his mother's womb (thus a difference of extent with respect to other spirit-filled prophets), Jesus is himself *a product* of the Spirit. There is no moment when Jesus receives the Spirit and *becomes* God's man.

712 Weinandy, *Spirit of Sonship*, 42.

713 In the Septuagint the same verb (ἐκβάλλω) is used at key moments such as the exile from Eden (Gen 3:24); Cain's lament over being driven from the ground (Gen 4:14); the expulsion from Egypt (Ex 6:1; 12:33); the exile from the promised land (Dt 29:27-28; Zech 7:14); the jettisoning of Jonah (Jon 1:15 cf. 2:4). Perhaps,

versions, however, it is clear that Jesus' ministry is a spiritual enterprise. The Spirit is upon Jesus to enable him to fulfil the great promises of Scripture (Luke 4:18); to bring help and justice to the oppressed (Matt 12:18); to drive out evil Spirits (Mark 3:22-30); to speak the words of the Spirit (John 6:63; Acts 1:2).

In line with the patriarchal motif identified in all the traditions above, this power and equipping of the Spirit is never presented as an agency that is *coordinate* with or *alternative* to the Father. Thus to say, as Weinandy does, that the Spirit conforms Jesus to his sonship is *also* to say that the Father conforms him through the Spirit. As Peter puts it: "God anointed Jesus of Nazareth with the Holy Spirit and with power; ... he went about doing good and healing all who were oppressed by the devil, for God was with him." (Acts 10:38)

The Holy Spirit, then, is the means by which God is with, and works through, the incarnate Son. And this pattern is filled out in many details. For example, although it is the Spirit who brings about the virgin conception, it is God (presumably the Father) whose paternity is established in the event with the Spirit mediating his power and presence. Although it is the Spirit that fills Jesus for ministry, it is the Father's words that the Spirit enables the Son to speak: "He whom God has sent speaks the words of God, for he gives the Spirit without measure. The Father loves the Son and has placed all things in his hands." (John 3:34-35). Given that Jesus later ascribed this speaking of the Father's words to the Father dwelling in him (14:10); it would seem to be a reasonable suggestion that the Spirit is thus the enabler of the *perichoretic* union of the Father and Son – just as he is the means by which the Father and Son are in *us*:

> "If you love me, you will keep my commandments. And I will ask the Father, and he will give you another Advocate, to be with you forever. ... "I will not leave you orphaned; I am coming to you. In a little while the world will no longer see me, but you will see me; because I live, you also will live. On that day you will know that I am in my Father, and you in me, and I in you. ... "Those who love me will keep my word, and my Father will love them, and we will come to them and make our home with them. (John 14:15-23)

The Mediating Spirit

The suggestion that the Spirit is the means by which Jesus himself comes to us (14:18) is, it must be admitted, not the only possible interpretation of the verse. The coming has been also been interpreted as a reference to the

---

given the testing (Luke 4:4 cf. Deut 8:3) and temptation that ensues, the key contexts here are the expulsion from Eden and the expulsion from Egypt.

The Will of Him Who Sent Me

resurrection appearances and the *parousia*.[714] Yet the general pattern of the Spirit signifying the presence of another person is not so easily avoided, even in the immediate context of this verse. As Godet points out,[715] there is little to be gained in retreating from a Pentecost interpretation of v 18 when v 23 (with its clear parallels to v 15-16) seems to be making the same point with regard to both the Father and the Son.

And the same kind of thing can be elsewhere in the NT:

- In Acts 16:6-7 we find a curious alternation between the "Holy Spirit" and "the Spirit of Jesus".

- In Romans 8 we find the Spirit variously described as "the Spirit of Christ", v 9; the "Spirit of God" (or "the Spirit of him who raised Jesus from the dead"), vv 9, 11, 14; and, most strikingly, as "Christ in you", v. 10.

- In 2Cor 3:17-18 we find the statement that the "the Lord is the Spirit" next to a reference to "the Spirit of the Lord."[716]

The same spiritual mediation can also be found in the body and temple imagery of Paul's epistles. In Eph 2:2 and 1Cor 3:16 the church is respectively the dwelling place where God dwells (ἐν πνεύματι) and "God's temple" where "God's Spirit dwells." In 1Cor 6:19 the expression "temples of the Holy Spirit" reoccurs in the context of the individual Christian – and here the Spirit is *specifically* associated with our union with Christ:

> Do you not know that your bodies are members of Christ? Should I therefore take the members of Christ and make them members of a prostitute? Never! Do you not know that whoever is united to a prostitute becomes one body with her? For it is said, "The two shall be one flesh." But anyone united to the Lord becomes one spirit (ἓν πνεῦμα ἐστιν) with him. (1Cor 6:15-17)

---

714 For a helpful overview see Carson, *John,* 501-502.

715 Godet, *Commentary on the Gospel of St. John with a Critical Introduction,* 145-146. Carson, who resists the spiritual rendering of v 18 becomes slightly unclear when it comes to verse 23 – though he apparently allows that verse at least *includes* a reference to the Spirit; Carson, *John,* 504.

716 Which would seem to make it difficult to interperet "the Lord" as a reference to the third person of the Godhead *in se* – as per the patristic exegesis reflected in the NCC. For this point, and a helpful overview of other issues associated with this controverted text see P. Barnett, *The Second Epistle to the Corinthians. New International Commentary on the New Testament* (Grand Rapids: Eerdmans, 1997), 199-202.

According to Paul's analogy here the Spirit seems to be in some sense equivalent to the physical body such that belonging to Christ represents a similar (but far more profound) bond to that achieved by sexual intercourse.[717] As Thiselton observes,[718] the passage "paves the way" for Paul's more fully developed statement in chapter 12 where the Spirit is also seen as the spiritual bond that holds Christ's body together:

> For just as the body is one and has many members, and all the members of the body, though many, are one body, so it is with Christ. For in the one Spirit we were all baptized into one body... (1Cor 12:12-13)

None of this should be taken to mean that Paul, or any other NT writer has *collapsed* the distinction between Jesus and the Spirit. Some of the passages above might possibly be taken that way – and there are others too: such as 1Cor 15:45 where Christ is described as "life-giving spirit" (πνεῦμα ζωοποιοῦν v. 45); or Eph 4:10 which speaks of him ascending above the heavens to "fill all things." Yet Paul is *also* clear that Jesus is in heaven (cf. eg. Rom 10:6; Eph 1:26); and that he is still embodied (albeit in a "spiritual" body). Neither his contemporary presence by the Spirit, nor the fact of (what would later be called) his mystical corporate body should be taken to mean that he has "turned into" the Spirit.

Yet this close association between the Spirit and Son does fit well with the general mediatory pattern discussed above. The Spirit *still* carries and forms the Word: just as he made him known to the prophets of old through mystery and symbol;[719] just as he brought him into the world; just as he directed and empowered his ministry on earth. Now, with the Son "physically" in heaven, it is the Spirit that makes him present to us;[720] who unites and conforms us to him, making us part of him. It is the Spirit that inscribes him on the face of history, working to complete his greater body (the *totus Christus*) and its

---

717 Here I think Fee and Thiselton are correct to render "Spirit" with a capital – as per verse 19 and 1Cor 12:12-13. See G. D. Fee, *The First Epistle to the Corinthians. New International Commentary on the New Testament* (Grand Rapids: Eerdmans, 1987) 260; Thiselton, *Corinthians,* 458, 469.

718 Ibid. 469.

719 I am thinking here particularly of Peter's reference to the "Spirit of Christ" at work in the "prophets who prophesied of the grace that was to be yours" [1Pet 1:10-12]; and of Paul's insistence that the Israelites were accompanied by the πνευματικῆς ... πέτρας who was Christ (1Cor 10:4). Whatever these difficult passages mean, they would seem to suggest that God's Old Testament work was *already* a work of the Son and Spirit – albeit in a different mode of expression.

720 See comments along these lines in M. Turner, *The Holy Spirit and Spiritual Gifts: in the New Testament Church and Today,* Revised edition (Peabody: Hendrickson, 1998), 81, 85; Grenz, *Theology,* 371-372; D. A. Carson, *The Gagging of God: Christianity Confronts Pluralism* (Grand Rapids: Zondervan, 1996), 265.

sufferings.[721] As Paul puts in Gal 4:19, Christ is *still* being "formed within you".

Yet where does this leave the Son's transition from Spirit-sent to Spirit-sending? My recasting of "Spirit-sent" in the broader category of "Spirit-brought" seems to fit well with the way the Spirit communicates him to us; but can it account for the apparent changes in Christ's own relationship to the Spirit?

Again, and briefly, it is important to note that there is no reason to believe that the Spirit's mediation of the Father-Son relationship has altered with the ascension of the Jesus. The book of Revelation, for example, seems completely unembarrassed to speak of the ascended Christ receiving disclosures from the Father (1:1); or of being wise through the agency of the Spirit (the seven eyes of 5:6). Meanwhile the Spirit that Jesus pours out on all flesh is also depicted as being given by the Father to him (Acts 2:33 cf. v. 17); or sent by the Father: in Jesus' name (John 14:25); or sent at the request of the Son (John 14:26).

Thus the basic intra-trinitarian pattern revealed elsewhere is maintained. The Father is still the source. The Son still receives that which allows him to fulfil his destiny *from* the Father *through* the Spirit such that the Spirit can justly be called both the Spirit of God and the Spirit of Jesus. The Spirit would appear to be remain a *vinculum* and mediator of relationship between the Father and Son – just as he was during Jesus' earthly sojourn.[722]

Spirit-Sent to Spirit-Sending

Nevertheless there *does* seem to be something new in Jesus' sending the Spirit to us. The Spirit-formed and Spirit-sent Son is now also manifest as a kind of *principium* with regard to the Spirit.[723] Does this signify an alteration in trinitarian relations after all? Well, in one sense yes, but the transition does not begin there. Even within his maturation from infant conceived by the Spirit to

---

721 This delineation of the Spirit as the mediator of Christ (again, as per word and breath) avoids the idea that the Christ and the Spirit offer *alternative* mediations (cf. 1Tim 2:5; Rom 8:26) – see Graham Cole's concern along these lines in Cole, *Life,* 113 n. 89. The mediation of Christ on earth *is* through the Spirit. As Calvin insists, the Spirit is the means of union between Christ and his church; *Institutes* 3.1.1-2.

722 Which is to say that Jesus earthly humilition and *kenosis* is not to be associated with the mediating presence of the Spirit – as if his eternal relation with the Father *excluded* the Spirit (and were thus implicitly binitarian).

723 Not, as we have just seen, in such a way that the Father is excluded or displaced as *principium*.

preacher who speaks by the Spirit (Acts 1:2)[724] we already witness changes in his relation to the Spirit. This is due to the fact that his mission is partly the story of his *own* perfecting in his role and humanity. Christ does not arrive from heaven as a grown adult who has already been tested and overcome, or has already gained the scroll of destiny. Rather he must grown into and win this new expression of his sonship.[725] There is a new beginning (his birth of Mary) and a new maturing which gives rise to his being perfected as "son" in a new way (Rom 1:4; Heb 5:5-9).[726]

In this light, salvation history is a kind of model of the "events" of the *opera ad intra*. The movement from caused to cause; from Spirit-breathed to Spirit-sender resonates with the original movement of the first begetting. Just as the Son comes forth from the Father by the Spirit to be another person *like* the Father (without separation); so, in space and time, he comes forth again by that same Spirit and is made to be become like the Father *in relation to us*[727] – which includes his becoming a sender of the Spirit. Or, again, the Spirit that proceeds from the Father to form the Son now perfects him again as the source of that same Spirit in a with regard to us.[728]

---

724 I am grateful to fellow Melbourne Anglican, Megan Curlis-Gibson for pointing this verse out to me.

725 This *process* by which the Son is becomes what he will be by the Spirit corresponds to observations made by Colin Gunton with regard to the Spirit's creative operations through time; C. E. Gunton, *Father, Son and Holy Spirit: Essays Toward a Fully Trinitarian Theology* (London: T&T Clark, 2003), 107-108, 134.

726 So Jean Galot writes, in complementary terms, of the Son *becoming son* in new ways:

> The eternal Sonship is an intra-Trinitarian relationship between the Father and the Son. The Sonship Christ receives by his Resurrection, on the other hand, is explained in terms of a relationship to men. What this new Sonship expresses and defines is the quality of Messiah and hence of Savior of mankind. Even as we point out this difference, we must remember that Christ's new Sonship is essentially an extension of the First. The Son of God now becomes in his human nature what he has been from all eternity. The Incarnation already involved an analogous extension.

J. Galot, *Jesus, our Liberator: A Theology of Redemption*, trans. M. A. Bouchard (Rome: Gregorian University Press, 1982), 395.

727 One modern resonance with what I am arguing for here might be seen in Pannenberg's depiction of the mission of Christ as a contingent expression of the "self-distinction" of the Logos from the Father; Pannenberg, *Systematic Theology*, 2.388-389.

728 A quite legitimate question here must be whether the Son then is also eternally a giver of the Spirit since he is eternally like the Father. This is Augustine's position of course, and may be correct – although I am not sure whether it can be

This last idea, if correct, fits with the objective of salvation history as I have been presenting it in this thesis: that it is a manifestation and installation of the Son as a distinct object of worship alongside the Father. As the Father is praised as creator (despite the Son's involvement creation) so the Son is now honoured as saviour (though the Father remains the source of that too). This new sending of the Spirit is simply the outworking of this development. As the Spirit gives life through the Father's creative lifegiving action, so now, as the Father makes the Son lifegiver (cf. John 5:21-23), the Spirit also goes forth again from *him* – so that all will honour the Son even as they honour the Father who sent him.

The Spirit and the Bride

So once again, as we have already seen in our discussion of the relationship between Christology and anthropology, this pattern also involves us. Another attraction to this scheme is the way it relates the operations of the Spirit to the place of God's people. If, as has just been argued, a function of the Spirit is to mediate the coming forth of the Son, then it should be remembered that the Spirit effects this arrival and τελειότησ by conforming the Son to the patterns he (the Spirit) has already laid down through his previous dealings with the people of God. The Spirit-formed Christ is the true man of God; the true lover of the temple; the true Adam before the tempter; the true penitent at the Jordan; the true recapitulation of the Exodus and the wilderness wanderings; the true Moses, and so on. The Spirit, in other words, does not come fresh from the Father *ex nihilo* to form and conform the Word in his mission, but carries him on wind that bears the scents of history, such that (under God) history and humanity themselves become vehicles of the Christ-forming Spirit. Creatures themselves become caught up in the mediating role played by the Spirit in the *opera trinitatis ad extra*. The Father loves his Son and sets him before us through the Spirit *but also* (shockingly) through us.

The converse is also true, of course. The Son in each successive stage and "state" also responds to the Father by actively conforming himself to the pattern given him by the begetting/sending/resurrecting Father. The Son who is *formed by* the Spirit which comes from the Father, also embraces what the Father is making him and responds to it through that same Spirit. Supremely, this return takes place via the cross, where Jesus "through the eternal Spirit offered himself without blemish to God," (Heb 9:13-14). But the Spiritual response of the Son neither starts nor ends there. As we have seen, the *earthly*

---

established on scriptural grounds. A similar speculation can be found in Donald Bloesch's depiction of the Son giving back the Spirit to the Father; D. G. Bloesch, *God the Almighty: Power, Wisdom, Holiness, Love. Christian Foundations* (Downers Grove: InterVarsity Press, 1995), 202-203 (Thanks to Graham Cole for this reference).

Son is a man wholly directed and driven by the Spirit. And after his ascension (again achieved by the Spirit)[729] the Son continues to respond to the Father by means of his spiritual body. As believers remain in Christ through the Spirit (1Cor 12:12-13), that abiding brings forth fruit which glorifies the Father (John 15:7-8). Thus, the people given to the Son by the Father (John 6:37-40; Eph 1:4-10) through the Spirit (1Cor 2:12-16 cf. 2Cor 4:6) are now returned by means of the same Spirit as Christ assimilates them to himself and his own filial response. The members of the church become fresh instruments by which the Spirit fulfils his subsistent identity as bond, gift and (following Weinandy *et al.*) mediator of filiation *ad extra*. We are the currency by which the Father and Son love each other through the Spirit who is justly called love itself. The 11th century Benedictine, William of St. Thierry comes close to expressing what I am attempting to articulate:

> You love yourself, O most lovable Lord, in yourself, when, from the Father and the Son, the Holy Spirit proceeds – the Holy Spirit who is the love of the Father for the Son and the love of the Son for the Father, such a sublime love that it is the unity of both, such a deep unity that, of the Father and the Son, the substance is one.
>
> And you love yourself in us, when, having sent the Spirit of your Son into our hearts, by the sweetness of the love and the warmth of the good will that you inspire in us, crying 'Abba, Father', you cause us to love you with a great love. You also love yourself in us so much that we, who hope in you and cherish your name of Lord, ... who dare to believe by the grace of your Spirit of adoption that everything that belongs to the Father is also ours and who are your adopted sons, call you by the same name that your only natural son used for you!
>
> In this way, such a firm bond, such a clinging and such a strong taste of your sweetness comes about that our Lord, your Son, called it 'unity', when he said: 'that they may be one in us'. And this unity has such

---

729 Cf. Rom 8:11; 1Pet 3:18. Some modern commentators, such as Cole and Fee, resist seeing any strong connection between the Spirit and the resurrection in these passages. Fee, for example, argues that the Spirit's role in Rom 8:11 is not to resurrect us but to testify to our future resurrection (by the one whose Spirit we have); G. D. Fee, *Paul, the Spirit, and the People of God* (Peabody: Hendrickson Publishers, 1996), 56-58. Cole suggests that the reference should be understood as the Spirit of God *essentialiter* (ie. not the person of the Holy Spirit as such); Cole, *Life,* 167-169. I am not entirely convinced by these arguments, primarily because I am skeptical of the "independent" or "individual" agency of the Spirit they work to deny. I do not think the passage need be taken to mean any more or less than that the Father gives (and will give us) us life through the Holy Spirit which is also (mysteriously) his Spirit. And indeed both Fee and Cole acknowledge that the Spirit – as a person of the Trinity – *must* be involved in the resurrection in some implicit way: ibid., 169. Fee, *Paul,* 57.

dignity and glory that he added: 'As I and you are one'. O joy, O glory, O wealth, O pride-for wisdom also has its pride! ...

We therefore love you, or rather you love yourself in us, we loving with affection, you loving with effectiveness, making us one in you by your own unity, or rather by your own Holy Spirit, whom you have given to us...

Adorable, terrible and blessed one, give him to us! Send your Spirit and everything will be created and you will renew the face of the earth... May the dove bearing the olive branch come! ... Sanctify us with your holiness! Unite us with your unity![730]

The Personhood of the Spirit

At this point we begin to see that a more fully developed Spirit Christology might yield some profound insights into the relationship between history, creation and the Trinity itself. But can it avoid the accusation that plagues almost every pneumatology – especially those in the Augustinian vein – that it pays insufficient regard for the distinct personhood of the Spirit? Well, perhaps not. The scheme that I have been laying it out in this chapter certainly renders the Father and Son with greater definition and clarity. The Spirit here might be described as meta-personal – as the enabler of the other persons in their subsistence and communion.[731]

But whether this is properly to be seen as a weakness is another matter. For if it is a theological deficiency to pay more attention to the Father and Son, then it is surely a deficiency that Scripture itself seems unembarrassed to exemplify:

– While post-Constantinople I Christians find themselves compelled to add "and the Holy Spirit" to every expression of praise and thanksgiving to the Father and Son, the New Testament writers frequently omit him (see, for example, Paul's greetings in Rom 1:7; 1Cor 1:3; 2Cor 1:2; Gal 1:1).

---

730 William of St Thierry, *The Golden Epistle* in Y. Congar, *I Believe in the Holy Spirit,* trans. D. Smith, combined edition (New York: Crossroad Pub. Co, 1997), 86.

731 Thomas Weinandy seeks to reinstate the subjectivity of the Spirit here by describing him as actively "personing" the other *hypostases*:

> The Spirit (of Love) then, who proceeds from the Father as the one in whom the Father begets the Son, both conforms or defines (persons) the Son to be the Son and simultaneously conforms or defines (persons) the Father to be the Father. The Holy Spirit, in proceeding from the Father as the one in whom the Father begets the Son conforms the Father to be the Father for the Son and conforms the Son to be the Son for (of) the Father."

Weinandy, *Spirit of Sonship,* 17

- We search the scriptures in vain for any expression of love toward the Spirit from the Father and Son; or any explicit intent that he should be honoured alongside them. Rather the Spirit is known in his making known the Father and (and the Father *through*) the Son (Jn 15:13-15; 1Cor 2:12-16).

- There is no prayer or praise directed toward the Spirit in either the New or Old Testament.

- When heaven is opened for us in Revelation, the picture is at face value closer to binitarian; God and the Lamb appear on their throne(s) but the Spirit is presented in something like functional or physiological terms – the seven eyes of the Lamb; the seven candlesticks.[732]

All of this is quite disturbing if we think of the Spirit's personhood in the same terms as that of the Father and Son. In that case it is difficult to avoid thinking of him as the poor-relation of the divine family, and that honour given to the Father and Son comes at his (the Spirit's) *expense*. But if his personhood is real but *different* from the first two persons[733] – specifically, if his personhood itself is in some way *mediative* of their personhood and unity[734] – then it might be that honour accorded to the Father and Son in their unity *already is* the appropriate response to the Spirit.[735]

---

732 The point here is not to deny the Spirit's divinity, nor his personal agency, but to reiterate that this agency is transparent and instrumental rather than opaque. In other words, the Spirit *continues* to operate in the same way that both he and the Logos operate before the incarnation.

733 So JürgenMoltmann:

> I have deliberately avoided the terms "hypostasis" and "person" at this point, because I do not wish to blur the differences between the personhood of the Father, and the personhood of the Son, and the personhood of the Spirit, by using a term for person common to them all." The Holy Spirit has a wholly unique personhood, not only in the form in which it is experienced, but also in its relationships to the Father and the Son. Moltmann, *Spirit of Life*, 12.

Karl Rahner also suggests that the term "*hypostasis*" is not to be read univocally in its application to the Father, Son and Spirit – Rahner, *Trinity*, 28-30. Complementary observations are made by Robert Doyle, who observes that the biblical patterns of reference and function as regards the Spirit are quite different from those observed in the case of the Father and Son: "clearly the NT states that the Holy Spirit is God, and Person in God, but that he is God and Person in a different way from Father and Son; Doyle, *Spirit of the Father*, 25-27.

734 Assuming here, of course that the personhood of the Father and Son is inextricably linked to their unity according to their ways of subsisting.

735 Or conversely, rejection of Jesus' works might signify a rejection of the Spirit – cf. Mark 3:29; Luke 12:10.

Precisely how this can be – how a breath, or gift, or bond, or essence can also be an acting subject – is unquestionably mysterious.[736] Yet if it is difficult for us to understand how the Spirit can appear in the modality of discrete agent – *another counsellor* – as well as mediator of other persons then it is worth remembering that orthodox Christology has already prepared us for this kind of tension by presenting us with a person who simultaneously upholds the universe by the word of his power *and* who appears in flesh in space and time; who is both another person like the Father (image, stamp, Son) *and* who proceeds from the Father dynamically like a word or radiance. Although in the case of the Spirit this last balance is reversed – i.e. he is more commonly presented as dynamic unity than distinct agent – the obstacles to understanding are the same: how can we think of the divine persons as one without sacrificing their individuality? How can we think of their individuality without dividing their unity?

Another element to bear in mind in consideration of the Spirit as meta-person is the fact that Western theology's recourse to the divine being as God *simpliciter* already envisages something along the same lines. In fact if, as the likes of Pannenberg and Grenz (and possibly Augustine) would have it, the Spirit *actually is* the personal *essentia* of God, then the *Spirit of sonship* model and western trinitarianism converge remarkably. The western designation of God as triune person is vindicated *without* thereby introducing a fourth *res* onto the stage.

Conclusion

Finally, I would suggest that it is precisely these vindicatory and synthetic qualities that should commend this pneumatology to us for further consideration. If the Spirit and Son are co-processional then the pro-Nicene emphasis on the monarchy of the Father is affirmed *as well as* the Augustininan depiction of the Spirit as bond and the Son as co-determiner of the Spirit. If the Son's eternal relationship to the Father is mediated by the Spirit – as it is on earth; and as is the case in our adoption – then the Irenaean/Christian Neoplatonist tradition is also given new life, for now we see that the story of salvation history does indeed follow the eternal dynamic of the Godhead.

---

736 That he *is* a personal agent in some way is unavoidable in the light of the biblical evidence. The Spirit is a distinct agent who leads (Lk 4:1), drives out (Mk 1:12), teaches (Lk 12:12) and can be blasphemed (Mk 3:29). With regard to us he is another Counsellor (Jn 14:16) who teaches us about Jesus (Jn 14:26); testifies on Jesus behalf (Jn 15:26); speaks what he hears (Jn 16:13). The Spirit can be lied to & tested (Act 5:3,9); bears witness (Acts 5:32); speaks (Acts 8:29; 10:19; 11:12); commands (Acts 13:2; 16:6); has opinions (Acts 15:28); warns (Acts 20:23), intercedes for the saints and is known by God (Rom 8:26-27) etc.

Simultaneously the weakness of the Neoplatonist scheme – its tendency to overlook the Spirit[737] – is now mended.

Also, if, as I have attempted to argue in this chapter, there is a "fit" between the eternal begetting of the Son and the successive forms of Christ, which the Spirit elaborates – as a man; in his ministry; as saviour; as head of the church; as *like the Father* with regard to us in his sending of the Spirit – then the *personalist* strain of Irenaean thought I have defended in this thesis is also strengthened. The divine breathing that forms the first Word now breathes him again into the world. The eternal Son is re-formed as son by the Spirit of Sonship before us, and for us, and through us. By the Spirit, the Father unifies everything in the Son.

---

[737] James Mackey makes the charge that Neoplatonist and Middle-Platonist trinitarianism typically fails to rise higher than binitarianism; J. P. Mackey "Trinity, Doctrine of the" in *A New Dictionary of Christian Theology,* ed. A. Richardson & J. S. Bowden (London: SCM, 1983), 581-589.

Chapter 7

How does RITW Address Contemporary Theological Discussion?

[T]he humanity of Jesus is the product of obedience, the fruit of the loving response of the Son; it is, so to speak, prayer that has taken on concrete form ... the humbling involved in the Cross corresponds on a profound level to the very mystery of the Son. Essentially, the Son is the release and handing back of himself – that is what sonship means.

– Joseph Ratzinger[738]

Introduction

Thus far I have argued at length that Responsive Intra-Trinitarian Willing can be seen as one possible expression of orthodox trinitarianism; that it *has* occurred in a few contexts; and that it can help facilitate a broader systematic framework which might be seen to accord with the patterns of Scripture. Nevertheless, the model here is scarcely the only one offering itself as a potential theological catalyst. In this chapter I will compare the RITW framework with two other important theories currently working their way through modern theology: Hegelianism and Neoplatonism. Indicating points of agreement and contrast between these and RITW, I will suggest that the latter is able to express many of the strengths inherent in these other frameworks, and yet that it is also able to avoid their dangers.

Finally, following another thread in contemporary theology, I will also use the findings of my historical and biblical study as the basis for some comments on the current evangelical debate concerning relational subordination between the Father and Son.

---

738 J. Ratzinger, *The God of Jesus Christ: Meditations on the Triune God* (San Francisco: Ignatius Press, 2008), 67-68.

The Ghost of Hegel and the God who Becomes

As we have already seen in our earlier discussion of Karl Rahner, one of the most important developments in modern trinitarian theology has been the desire to more closely connect the relationship between the Trinity as revealed in salvation history, and that of the immanent Trinity. Arising from diverse concerns,[739] the new stress on the immanent comes in two basic forms; the expressivist kind wherein the Trinity *ad extra* is seen as a *reflection* of the Trinity *ad intra* and – more radically – the determinative (also "narrative" or "relational") variety in which God actually *becomes complete* through the processes of history.

Of these two, it is the latter that first demands our attention, featuring in so much twentieth century trinitarianism.[740] Jürgen Moltmann, in a piece of classic Hegelian dialectic, depicts God as eternally determined by the trans-historical event of the crucifixion.[741] In the moment of abandonment, God the Father is at

---

739 A list of contributing factors might include: the contention that Greek philosophy has displaced biblical and Hebrew ways of thinking about God; an academic predilection for Hegelian models of history (see below); and, and anxieties over God's moral nature in the wake of the sufferings of the twentieth century.

740 Whether Barth himself is implicated here is a complicated question. Certainly it can be argued that he prepares the way for the next generation of Hegelians by beginning his trinitarian discussion from the standpoint of revelation (CD 1/1:296, 339) – raising the question of whether God would have been three if there had been nothing for him to be revealed *to*. Later, in CD 4, he almost reduces the Trinity to the proleptic decision of God to be God for us:

> [I]t is pointless, as it is impermissible, to return to the inner being and essence of God and especially to the second person of the Trinity as such, in such a way that we ascribe to this person another form than that which God Himself has given in willing to reveal Himself and to act outwards. ... According to the free and gracious will of God, the eternal Son of God is Jesus Christ as he lived and died and rose again in time, and none other. He is the decision of God in time ... which was made from all eternity.

CD 4/1:52.

The problem here is that by indicating what he says we cannot know, Barth creates a paradox. Even though elsewhere he *does* talk about the persons of the Godhead apart from creation – see G. Hunsinger, "Election and the Trinity: Twenty-Five Theses on the Theology of Barth", *Modern Theology* 24.2 (2008): 179-198 – it is scarcely surprising that contemporary Barthian studies are riven with disagreement at this very point, with conservative scholars such as Paul Molnar and George Hunsinger holding out against explicitly Hegelian readings of Barth by Eberhard Jüngel and Bruce McCormack (see below).

741 "[T]he form of the crucified Christ is the Trinity;" J. Moltmann, *The Crucified God: The Cross of Christ as the Foundation and Criticism of Christian Theology*,

once dialectically opposed to his Son – and then synthetically reconciled by the Spirit. Wolfhart Pannenberg travels toward a similar goal over different terrain. While retaining the traditional doctrine of generation in regard to the Son and Spirit, Pannenberg also wants to fold into this, the social aspects of the relations *ad extra*: "The Father is the Father only in relation to the Son, in the generation and sending of the Son. The Son is the Son only in obedience to the sending of the Father, which includes recognition of his fatherhood."[742] As Pannenberg sees it, the Father cannot be God while there is resistance to his kingship, thus he is contingent upon the obedience of the Son to be honoured as God, and he also needs the Son to reconcile the world to him. At the same time this honouring of the Son by the Father establishes the Son's deity since his self-distinction as obedient Son means that all the Father's honour is mediated by the Son.[743]

> The lordship of the Son is simply to proclaim the lordship of the Father, to glorify him, to subject all things to him. Hence the kingdom of the Son does not end (Luke 1:33) when he hands back lordship to the Father. His own lordship is consummated when he subjects all things to the lordship of the Father and all creation honours the Father as the one God.[744]

Other schemes that evince the same historic determination of the immanent Trinity by the economic, can be readily found elsewhere. A fuller treatment would include Robert Jenson who seeks to deconstruct the atemporal God of classical theology and replace him with a "reclaimed Hegelian"[745] God who is

---

trans. R. A. Wilson & J. Bowden. *SCM classics* (London: SCM, 2001), 254. Similarly: "He is the Lamb slain, and the Lamb slain from the creation of the world. ... The meaning of the cross of the Son on Golgotha reaches right into the heart of the immanent Trinity;" J. Moltmann & M. Kohl, *The Trinity and the Kingdom of God*, trans. M. Kohl (London: SCM, 1981), 159. "[T]he Son's sacrifice of boundless love on Golgotha is from eternity already included in the exchange of the essential, the consequential love which constitutes the divine life of the Trinity;" (ibid., 167-168).

742 Pannenberg, *Systematic Theology*, 1.428.

743 Precisely by distinguishing himself from the Father, by subjecting himself to his will as his creature, by thus giving place to the Father's claim to deity as he asked others to do in his proclamation of the divine lordship, he showed himself to be the Son of God and one with the Father who sent.

   Ibid., 1.310.

744 Ibid., 1.313.

745 "To reclaim Hegel's truth for the gospel, we need only a small but drastic amendment: Absolute Consciousness finds its own meaning and self in the one historical object, Jesus;" C. E. Braaten & R. W. Jenson (eds), *Christian Dogmatics*, 2 volumes (Philadelphia: Fortress Press, 1984), 2.169.

defined diachronically and eschatologically.[746] Or Catherine Mowry LaCugna, with her insistence that there is strictly *no* knowledge of God (*theologia*) to be discovered beyond that revealed in the incarnate Christ.[747] And it would have to reckon with the controversial readings of Barth by Jüngel and McCormack, that would construe his actualism as a complete identification of the *logos incarnandus* and *asarkos.*[748]

---

746   If instead we follow scripture in understanding eternity as faithfulness to the last future ... the Trinity is simply the Father and the man Jesus and their Spirit as the Spirit of the believing community. This "economic" Trinity is eschatologically God "himself", an "immanent" Trinity.

       Ibid., 1.155

    Elsewhere Jenson still wants to maintain that the Logos would still *be* himself somehow without salvation history, but immediately protests that "what that would have been like, we can know or guess nothing whatever;" cf. R. W. Jenson, *Systematic Theology,* 2 volumes (New York: Oxford University Press, 1997), 1.141.

747   God *is* God by sharing, bestowing, diffusing, expressing Godself. The gift of existence and grace that God imparts to the world is not produced by efficient causality, largely extrinsic to God; the gift is nothing other than God's own self. ... There is no God who might turn out to be different from the God of salvation history, even if God's mystery remains absolute.

       LaCugna, *God for Us,* 210-211.

748   That is to say, that Jesus Christ is not simply all we can *know* about God but is also the means by which God is self-determined. McCormack: "Barth ... wants to insist that when God gives himself over in this way to our contradiction of him ... he is not changed on an ontological level by this experience for the simple reason that his being, from eternity, is determined by this event;" B. McCormack "Grace and Being: The Role of God's Gracious Election in Karl Barth's Theological Ontology" in *The Cambridge Companion to Karl Barth,* ed. J. B. Webster. *Cambridge Companions to Religion* (New York: Cambridge University Press, 2000), 98. This reading has been sharply contested by Paul Molnar: "Barth is clearly stating that God would be the same triune God he was and is with or without deciding to act outside of himself;" P. Molnar, "Can the Electing God be God Without Us? Some Implications of Bruce McCormack's Understanding of Barth's Doctrine of Election for the Doctrine of the Trinity", *Neue Zeitschrift für Systematische Theologie und Religionsphilosophie* 49.2 (2007): 199-222, 203. See additional discussion in E. Jüngel, *God's Being is in Becoming: The Trinitarian Being of God in the Theology of Karl Barth, a Paraphrase,* trans. J. Webster, 2nd English edition (Edinburgh: T&T Clark, 2001) and Molnar, *Freedom,*.

    Most interesting for this present discussion is the recent doctoral work of Shirley H. Martin who argues (against Molnar *and* McCormack) that for Barth, the obedience of the human Christ is an "overflow" of the eternal obedience of the eternal Son; S. H. Martin, "Freedom to Obey: the Obedience of Christ as the Reflection of the Obedience of the Son in Karl Barth's *Church Dogmatics*"

But what can be observed here briefly is that such theories possess a substantial attraction and offer some distinct advantages over classical trinitarian orthodoxy. For example:

- Pannenberg's Father-is-God, Son-is-included scheme does a far better job of approximating Pauline and Johannine monotheism than some other modern trinitarianisms which would personify the essence or simply blur the oneness-threeness question with a vague "*perichoresis*". His depiction of salvation history as the Son securing the Father's kingdom, and through this being lifted up and included in that kingship, corresponds very well to the relational patterns seen in the Fourth Gospel and in other passages such as 1 Cor 15:28.

- Catherine Mowry LaCugna's attempt to break through the *theologia/oikonomia* distinction that would keep us apart from God, expresses a proper desire for real communion. LaCugna's "relational ontology" that refuses a grace that stops at a mere analogical representation,[749] but cries out for a real participation in God's life, resonates with Scripture (cf. Ps 42:1-2; Rev 21:2, 22-23; 22:4) – and surely with our own best aspirations too.

- Bruce McCormack's Barthianism justly reminds us that the first object of God's election is not us, but his Son, whom he has appointed to inherit the world.

- Robert Jenson's Hegelianism points out that, from the perspective of the end and God's providence, the apparent chaos of salvation history is ultimately creative, by which God achieves his assured end, despite (and through) sin, conflict and reconciliation.

Overall these *narrative* or *relational* theologies do better than classical (or "essentialist") theology when it comes to the biblical testimony of Jesus' personhood and achievements. By refusing to speak of "nature" in abstraction from "person" they largely avoid the messy task of dividing the "human bits" of Jesus' life from the bits which really belong to the Logos.[750] They are also

---

(Unpublished Ph.D. dissertation, University of St Andrews, 2008). cf. CD IV/1 209).

749 She quotes Rahner with approval: "What is given in grace 'is not merely a copy or an analogy of the inner Trinity but this Trinity itself, albeit as freely and gratuitously communicated;'" LaCugna, *God for Us,* 235 n. 13.

750 Jesus' human action and presence is without mitigation God's action and presence ... [o]nce it is clear that there truly is only one individual person who is the Christ, who lives as one of the Trinity and one of us, and that he is personal precisely as one of us, then to say that he as creature is our savior ... is simply to say that he plays his role in the triune life and does not need to abstract from his human actuality to do so.

able to take seriously the fact that the person who is Jesus *really* receives and becomes something through his historical work – a very difficult idea for classical theology.

And such accounts as these would, if adopted, be most congenial to a very strong form of RITW. If the connection between the immanent Son and the economic is such that the latter actually creates or defines the former, then the debate over whether Jesus' obedience corresponds to eternal filiality is entirely moot. Although modern authors might strain to offset the filial subordination with theories of the Father *also* depending on the Son,[751] the fact must remain that the obedience of the man Jesus *just is* the relationship of the first two persons of the Trinity.[752]

Jenson, *Systematic Theology*, 1.144-145.

751 Thus, in addition to what we have already witnessed in Pannenberg, Jenson depicts the Spirit (through Jesus) as the means by which "the Father is freed from mere persistence in his pretemporal transcendence;" Braaten & Jenson, *Christian Dogmatics*, 2.156-157.

752 So Moltmann:

[T]he Son's sacrifice of boundless love on Golgotha is from eternity already included in the exchange of the essential, the consequential love which constitutes the divine life of the Trinity. The fact that the Son dies on the cross, delivering himself up to that death, is part of the eternal obedience which he renders to the Father in his whole being through the Spirit, whom he receives from the Father.

Moltmann & Kohl, *Kingdom*, 168.

Jenson:

The "hypostases" are Jesus, and the transcendent will he called Father ... the hypostases' "relations" are Jesus' historical obedience to and dependence on his Father and the coming of the future into the believing community;"

Braaten & Jenson, *Christian Dogmatics*, 1.137.

See Pannenberg as already quoted – Pannenberg, *Systematic Theology*, 1.428.

Catherine Mowry LaCugna is the notable exception to the rule here. Despite conceding that the monarchy of the Father is "defensible ... and perhaps demanded by the standpoint of the economy, and reinforced by the Bible" (LaCugna, *God for Us*, 69), the view she offers of the divine monarchy is baleful and blurry. Monarchy is at once potentially patriarchal and hierarchical, and the *fontalis plenitudo* of mutuality and love: ibid., 398-400. The possibility that both patriarchy *and* mutual love and affirmation might coexist is never considered. As Terence L. Nichols rightly notes: "LaCugna's analysis is hampered because she has no middle term between hierarchy as domination and absolute equality;" T. L. Nichols, *That All May be One: Hierarchy and Participation in the Church* (Collegeville: Liturgical Press, 1997), 278.

But the price of alliance with such theologies is too high. Weak where traditional orthodoxy is strong, they fail to take seriously those scriptural testimonies to the Son's *original* glory; or reduce it into a proleptic expression of that achieved in history (an abstraction just as rarified as anything offered by "Greek" essentialism). In rejecting the language of essence, they surrender the orthodox vocabulary which makes it possible to speak of the *real* sonship of Jesus, and are thus reduced to functionalistic categories.

The ultimate consequence of their elision of immanence and economy is an undermining of the Son's honour and glory. For if he is not *formerly* rich (2Cor 8:9), or in the form of God (Phil 2:6) apart from (and prior to) the incarnation, then the honour that is due to him for his voluntary *kenosis* is lost.[753] If his eternal Sonship is *predicated* on his relationship to humanity then Christ himself is a product of will and history – and thus not just ontologically subordinated to the Father,[754] but *to creation* – deriving his significance from the world of which he is correlate.[755] Perhaps most seriously, if the Trinity itself is a product of decree – even eternal decree – then we are still left with the *logical* implication that behind this decision is the completely unknown God (*deus absconditus*) who makes that primal decision;[756] the status of the persons (or at least the Son and Spirit) in regard to the "prior" unknowable essence becomes deeply problematic.[757]

---

753 The antecedent condition of possibility for such a kenosis is not only God as personal but the trinitarian God, the antecedent relation of Father and Son ... The incarnation is a supreme gift from the Father and a self-gift of the Son in obedience to the Father.

Farrelly, *Trinity,* 133.

754 The same criticism applies to McCormack's scheme. McCormack argues that his Barthianism does not deny the *logos asarkos,* but simply asserts that "there is no 'eternal Son' if that Son is seen in abstraction from the gracious election in which God determined and determines never to be God apart from the human race;" B. McCormack "Grace and Being: The role of God's Gracious Election in Karl Barth's Theological Ontology" in *The Cambridge Companion to Karl Barth,* ed. J. B. Webster. *Cambridge Companions to Religion* (New York: Cambridge University Press, 2000), 100. But here the Word's natural birthright has been turned into an act of contingent grace – an eternal adoptionism.

755 At this point we are right back to Scotus' theory that Christ's significance resides in his being perfect creation; except now it is *far worse* because there is no Logos apart from the Christ at all.

756 " ... when one speaks of God freely determining himself ... one has posited a purely spontaneous force of will logically prior to God's own nature;" Hart, *The Beauty of the Infinite: The Aesthetics of Christian Truth,* 162 n. 8.

757 Robert Lethams's very appropriate concern regarding the relationship between the Palamite doctrine of energies and the persons is relevant here; Letham, *Holy Trinity,* 340-348.

What I have been arguing in the previous chapter, is that we can achieve the same gains promised by narrative/relational theology without abandoning orthodoxy. If we see the events of salvation history as a free initiative by the Father to glorify his true (natural/essential) Son in a fresh context, then everything falls into place:

- Then, with Wolfhart Pannenberg, we contend that the Son and Father reciprocally (re)establish each other's Lordship over the fallen world in line with their characteristic modes of operation but we *deny* that these historical events circumscribe their personal relations.[758]

- With Catherine Mowry LaCugna we affirm that the going forth and return of creation is a real event in the life of God – it artificially creates a new context for that eternal relationship. Yet we deny that Jesus' ascension as functional "son" – revealer, saviour and head – constitutes his *eternal and essential* sonship in relation to the Father.

- With Bruce McCormack we contend that the fundamental object of the Father's election is his Son, who is predestined to inherit the world. But against all radical Barthian existentialism, we deny that this election defines the triune being itself.[759]

- With Jürgen Moltmann we agree that the cross is the *sine qua non* of God's being *for us*. But we deny that God's essence *in se* is thereby established or limited.

- With Robert Jenson we can testify that history *matters* to God and that it is consummated in Christ. Yet we deny that Father, Son or Spirit depend on it (either proleptically or actually) to be themselves.

---

758 That is to reaffirm what Pannenberg identifies as "mythological" and "primitive" and "contradictory" – see, for example, W. Pannenberg, *Jesus - God and Man*, trans. L. L. P. Wilkins, Duane A (London: SCM, 1968), 183, 186 – the idea that the person of the Son was present at the beginning with the Father and *really* (albeit incomprehensibly) came down and took flesh.

759 According to Barth, God's being is most decisively construed by the notion of decision. God is so unmitigatedly personal that his free decision is not limited even by his "divine nature": what he is, he himself chooses ... God *is* the act of his decision.
Jenson, *Systematic Theology*, 1.140.

Neoplatonism Redivivus: A Response to Modern Participationism

Hegelian historicism embodies some interesting points of overlap and disagreement with the RITW framework. But there are different points of connection and disconnection with the second kind of Rahnerianism mentioned above – that is the kind where the economic Trinity is seen to *express* the immanent.

As I have already pointed out in Chapters 2-4, this way of relating the Trinity to salvation history is scarcely an innovation. It finds repeated expression in exemplarist participationism of both East and West. In our own time various forms of Christian Neoplatonism flourish in the writings of diverse figures such as: evangelical Anglican Philip Edgcumbe Hughes (1915-1990);[760] North American Episcopalian Kathryn Tanner;[761] American Orthodox David Bentley Hart;[762] and Joseph Ratzinger (Benedict XVI).[763] Perhaps the most significant contributions come from the Catholic giant Hans Urs von Balthasar (1905-1988)[764] and, in the immediate scene, the leaders of the still burgeoning Radical Orthodox (RO) movement such as John Milbank and Catherine Pickstock.[765]

By now, of course, the themes of Christian exemplarism are familiar enough to us: the Son/Logos is the first and true essential Image of the Father, *after* whom and *through* whom the creation is formed, and *in whom* it is ultimately consummated: the union of Word with humanity in the incarnation being the means by which human nature (especially will) is repaired (and "divinised"). These elements are maintained fairly consistently, and even extended by the (at least non-RO) exemplarists just mentioned, giving rise to modern forms of the doctrine that resonate well with the ideas in this thesis.

---

760 Hughes, *True Image:*.

761 Tanner, *Jesus,*.

762 Hart, *The Beauty of the Infinite: The Aesthetics of Christian Truth,*.

763 For a representative sample see Benedict XVI's address on the centrality of the Word at the opening the 2008 Synod; J. Ratzinger, "God's Word More Stable Than Any Human Reality: Address from the opening day of the Synod, Monday, 6 October [2008], during the Liturgy of the Hours celebration of the Third Hour", *L'Osservatore Romano, Weekly Edition in English* (October 8, 2008): 5.

764 Neoplatonic/exemplarist themes are so deeply embedded and prevalent in Balthasar's massive oeuvre as to make individual references almost arbitrary. For brief introductions see A. Hunt, *What Are They Saying About the Trinity* (New York: Paulist Press, 1998), 49-61. Casarella, *Expression and Form*, 37-65.

765 See, for example, J. Milbank, G. Ward & C. Pickstock, *Radical Orthodoxy: A New Theology* (London: Routledge, 1999); R. Shortt, *God's Advocates: Christian Thinkers in Conversation* (London: Darton, Longman & Todd, 2005), 103-105.

For Kathryn Tanner, stressing the unity of subjectivity in the person who is Logos *and* Christ, the life of Jesus is "the human version of the Son in his relations with the Father".[766] Because humanity is "the Word's proper instrument,"[767] it is possible to see a true *enhypostasia* at work. When Jesus brings his human will into conformity with the Father's, what he achieves is a "conformity that is naturally Jesus' own, in virtue of being the Son of God, the one whose very will is the will of the Father."[768] Although she is very wary of describing the trinitarian conformity as "obedience" – such externality of willing belongs solely to the human[769] – nevertheless she insists that the result is "the triune life in a human form."[770]

An even bolder expression emerges from the theology of Hans Urs von Balthasar. For Balthasar there is a concern to balance the infinite difference between God and finitude with a connection between the Son's humanity and his procession in eternity.[771] As *per* Tanner, Balthasar is impressed with the significance of the fact that Christ and the Logos are one person and, as such, have one relationship with the Father in two modes.[772] For Balthasar this leads

---

766   Tanner, *Jesus,* 20.

767   Ibid., 24.

768   Ibid., 32.

769   Ibid., 52, cf. n. 54. Tanner criticises Barth for presenting "too close" a relationship by characterising the pre-incarnate Son as humble and obedient. We might observe here however that, if McCormack is right about Barth, then for him the Logos *just is* the humble and obedient Christ as set forth in the eternal election of God.

770   Ibid., 50-51.

771   The trinitarian analogy enables the Son ... to do two things: he represents God to the world – but in the mode of the Son who regards the Father as "greater" and to whom he owes all that he is – and he represents the world to God, by being, as man (or rather, as the God-man), "humble, lowly" ... It is on the basis of these two aspects, united in an abiding analogy, that the Son can take up his one unitary mission ... to represent the Father's authority *vis-à-vis* men and to represent mankind's sin in the sight of God, the Judge, achieving its atonement, together with his "brothers", before the Father.

H. U. von Balthasar, *Theo-drama,* trans. G. Harrison, 5 volumes (San Francisco: Ignatius Press, 1988), 3.230 n. 68.

I am indebted to the insights of Nicholas Healy and David L. Schindler here: N. Healy & D. L. Schindler "For the Life of the World: Hans Urs von Balthasar on the Church as Eucharist" in *The Cambridge Companion to Hans Urs von Balthasar,* ed. E. T. Oakes & D. Moss. *Cambridge Companions to Religion* (Cambridge: Cambridge University Press, 2004).

772   On earth "the Son is obedient to the Father in the Spirit ... [as] the intelligible form of his eternal attitude to the Father who begets him, namely, that of primal obedience in willing cooperation and gratitude;" von Balthasar, *Theo-drama,* 5.123.

even to a rejection of the *extra calvinisticum*,[773] and draws him close to Hegelianism at one point, with an insistence that "the incarnation of the second divine person does not leave the inter-relationship of those persons unaffected."[774] More typically however, the obedience of Christ is seen as an analogical manifestation of the trinitarian life;[775] simultaneously a fresh expression of the paternal relationship and (via *analogia entis* perfection of the creaturely response.[776]

The world can be thought of as the gift of the Father (who is both Begetter and Creator) to the Son, since the Father wishes to sum up all things in heaven and earth in the Son, as head (Eph 1:10); thus the Son

---

Balthasar, here, goes further than Tanner in his explicit embrace of the terminology of obedience; Anne Hunt observes that he sees "obedience as constitutive of his identity as Son;" Hunt, *Paschal Mystery - Development*, 65. Nevertheless, there is a careful differentiation: "The obedience with which the Son performs the Father's will is not the obedience of a 'serf' ... it quite evidently comes from God himself;" H. U. von Balthasar, *Prayer*, trans. A. V. Littledale (New York: Sheed & Ward, 1961), 188, cited in Hunt, *Paschal Mystery - Development*, 66.

773 See for example von Balthasar, *Theo-drama*, 3.228.

774 See Edward Oakes' careful treatment of Balthasar's kenoticism here; C. S. Evans, *Exploring Kenotic Christology: The Self-Emptying of God* (New York: Oxford University Press, 2006) E. T. Oakes "'He Descended into Hell': The Depths of God's Self-Emptying Love on Holy Saturday in the Thought of Hans Urs von Balthasar" in *Exploring Kenotic Christology: The Self-Emptying of God*, ed. C. S. Evans (New York: Oxford University Press, 2006).

775 By letting go of the 'form of God' that was his (and so his divine power of self-disposal) he willed to become the One who, in a remarkable and unique manner, is obedient to the Father – in a manner, namely, where his obedience represents the *kenotic translation of the eternal love for the 'ever-greater' Father*.

H. U. von Balthasar, *Mysterium Paschale,* trans. A. Nichols (Edinburgh: T&T Clark, 1990), 90-91, my emphasis.

Balthasar goes somewhat further than I do here, envisaging the cross itself as a drama that is made possible by the kenosis and surrender that occurs in the begetting of the Son; see Hunt, *Paschal Mystery - Development*, 60-64.

776 Thus, quoting the mystic Adrienne von Speyr: "[T]he obedience of Christ is, on the one hand, 'interpretation' (John 1:18) of heaven, of the interior life of the Trinity, and, on the other hand, the 'epitome' (Eph 1:10) of the proper attitude of all creatures before God;" H. U. von Balthasar, *First Glance at Adrienne von Speyr* (San Francisco: Ignatius Press, 1981), 59.

takes this gift – just as he takes the gift of Godhead – as an opportunity to thank and glorify the Father.[777]

Questioning Exemplarism/Participationism

Such Christian Neoplatonism as this, would appear to align very neatly with what I have been arguing for in this thesis – casting filial conformity as the great nexus of God and creation. But there are some dangers here too. If it is the filial *pattern* (participation) that is elevated, then the question arises whether it is the person of the Son, or simply his *filiality itself,* that is primary. In other words: is creation's goal to be for the Logos (filiocentrism) or simply to be *like* him (filiomorphism)? The more it is *solely* the latter, the more participation will simply serve as handmaid to business-as-usual liberalism; Christ becomes the supreme manifestation (or more vaguely, establisher) of a universal *telos*;[778] salvation is conflated with sanctification; and the *eschaton* is remodelled into a general (*apocatastasic*) *methexis*.[779]

---

[777] von Balthasar, *Theo-drama,* 262. See discussion in Healy & Schindler, *Life of the World,* 54-55 also A. Nichols, *The Word Has Been Abroad: A Guide through Balthasar's Aesthetics* (Edinburgh: T&T Clark, 1998), 234-236.

Of course, in pursuing a scheme that considers divine inter-personal relations at both the start and conclusion, Balthasar offers a slightly different Neoplatonism from that of the Western scholastics or Maximus. While the former might look to the Son as archetype and means of the world's perfection, Balthasar makes creation itself serve the aspirations of the divine persons for each other. While the latter would think of the Spirit as gift from God to us, Balthasar (also) depicts creation as gift to the Son (and back to Father).

[778] So, for example, in the work of Teilhard de Chardin, and especially in Lionel Spencer Thornton, for whom the chief significance of the Logos-incarnation connection is a transformation wrought in the imagination, reason and will "towards those otherworldly standards of value which were realized personally by our Lord in his Incarnate life on earth;" L. S. Thornton, *Conduct and the Supernatural: Being the Norrisian Prize Essay for the year 1913* (London: Longmans, Green & Co, 1915), 182. See also J. Macquarrie, *Twentieth-Century Religious Thought: The Frontiers of Philosophy and Theology, 1900-1960* (New York: Harper & Row, 1963), 269-273.

[779] As I mentioned in the previous chapter, the theory that all must ultimately be saved (*apocatastasis*) is a besetting sin of Christian Neoplatonism. For a particularly stark example see Hart, *The Beauty of the Infinite: The Aesthetics of Christian Truth,* 399-402; but even the conservative Balthasar wants to encourage an *active hope* of it; H. U. von Balthasar, *Dare We Hope "That All Men be Saved"?: With a Short Discourse of Hell* (San Francisco: Ignatius Press, 1996). Philip Edgcumbe Hughes meanwhile avoids Origenistic universalism but cannot resist annihilationism; 398-407.

The fact that these temptations are real is readily demonstrated. For example, Kathryn Tanner's explanation of the cross demands a switch of focus from "Jesus' passive sufferings on the cross" to his assumption of "all aspects of human existence":[780]

> Jesus is not punished in our stead ... God saves through unity with the Son in Christ. Jesus' obedience to the Father – a life that reflects the Father's beneficent will for us – is an effect of that unity with the Son, not the very condition of our being saved by Christ.[781]

Here it is very hard to see what the death, or even life, of Jesus achieves at all. Even the active obedience of Christ is in danger of becoming simply exemplary rather than effective. But things could be worse. Tanner's desire to maintain the subjectivity of the Logos contrasts with the still more vague statements of John Milbank, whose recurrent critiques of Balthasar reveal the difference between RO Platonism and its antecedents.[782] Comparing Balthasar to Henri de Lubac, Milbank complains of the former's personalism (as opposed to de Lubac's theism);[783] his tendency to "mythologise" rather than philosophise;[784] his transition from aesthetics to drama; and his belief that "creation can truly give something to God."[785] What Milbank wants here, in preference to Balthasar's messy violent and mythological personalism, is an ontological scheme of essence and self-expression on the side of God and participation on the side of humanity: a "serene" pattern wherein God "brings about a not-God [creation] to

---

780 Tanner, *Jesus*, 75. Once again however, this is a false antithesis; it is the recapitulative/representational unity of Christ with sinful humanity that allows him to die its death. See Cyril of Jerusalem's Catechetical Lecture 13 cited above.

781 Ibid., 87-88.

782 Gerard O'Hanlon notes in his discussion of Balthasar, that there is a difference between the "Stoic cosmic version of the Logos as the idea of the world," and the Christian version which "proposes in this role the eternal Son of God whose eternal freedom as readiness towards the Father is always the same;" G. F. O'Hanlon, *The Immutability of God in the Theology of Hans Urs von Balthasar* (Cambridge: Cambridge University Press, 1990), 58. O'Hanlon rightly makes clear that Balthasar remains on the Christian side of this divide; von Balthasar, *Mysterium*, 31-33. But can the same be said of Milbank? Not easily – even fellow RO theologian Frederick Bauerschmidt seems concerned for Milbank on this score; F. C. Bauerschmidt, "The Word Made Speculative? John Milbank's Christological Poetics", *Modern Theology* 15.4 (1999): 417-432, 420-423.

783 Milbank, *Suspended Middle*, 74.

784 Ibid., 13, 69. Cyril O'Reagan makes a similar critique the basis for his argument that Balthasar is not really a Neoplatonist at all but really a Gnostic; C. O'Reagan, "Balthasar and Gnostic Genealogy", *Modern Theology* 22.4 (2004): 609-650.

785 Milbank, *Suspended Middle*, 77.

share in his nature."[786] Radical Orthodoxy here reveals itself too ready to trade away the particularities of the faith – even Jesus[787] and the Bible[788] – for a mess of generalised Platonist *methexis*. Against such we might invoke the words of the English Puritan John Flavel (1627-1691):

> Christ and his benefits go inseparably and undividedly together ... many would willingly receive his privileges, who will not receive his person; but it cannot be; if we will have one, we must take the other too: Yea, we must accept his person first, and then his benefits: as it is in the marriage covenant, so it is here.[789]

---

786 Ibid., 77, cf. 14.

787 All that survives that is particular in this assumption is the proper name "Jesus". It is certainly the case that by telling stories about a character on earth called "Jesus", and by putting words into his mouth, the gospels minimally indicate reference to a "reality" that is independent of their narration. ... [But] the gospels can be read in another way, which gives to the empty name a logical foundation in their universal proclamation. Along this path, I make my "proper start".

J. Milbank, *The Word Made Strange: Theology, Language, Culture* (Oxford: Blackwell, 1997), 150.

See Frederick Bauerschmidt here; Bauerschmidt, "Speculative". Bauerschmidt notes some qualifications of this radical position, but judges that they are "not really integrated into Milbank's overall theological project;" ibid., 428.

788 Mounting similar attacks on Walter Kasper's personalism and patriarchy, Milbank (Milbank, *Word*, 174ff) concedes that his Western "order of *supposita*" (not transmission of essence) view of the Trinity might be resisted as being against the evidence of the New Testament. But he is unperturbed; the wish "to turn primary discourse and practice into a *foundational* point of reference" is "reverse Platonism" – an unrealistic attempt to go "back to the original data" which fails to understand that it is now "hermeneutically transformed".

789 *The Method of Grace: In The Holy Spirit's Applying to the Souls of Men the Eternal Redemption Contrived by the Father and Accomplished by the Son* in J. Flavel, *The Whole Works of John Flavel: Late Minister of the Gospel at Dartmouth, Devon*, 2 volumes (London: W. Baynes & Son, 1820), 2.17.

Modern heir of Puritanism, J. I. Packer puts the matter still more pithily:

> All constructions in which loving communion with the Father and the Son by the Spirit and unending praise and gratitude for redemption are not central are mere pagan fantasies. So we label them secular and strike them out of our reckoning.

J. I. Packer "Universalism: Will Everyone Ultimately be Saved" in *Hell under Fire: Modern Scholarship Reinvents Eternal Punishment*, ed. C. W. Morgan & R. A. Peterson (Grand Rapids: Zondervan, 2004), 180.

Participation in what? A Question and Proposal

A final question for theology that would deploy participationism is what are we participating *in*.[790] One option, of course is an *analogical* participation in the filiality of the Son such that we relate to the Godhead in a somewhat similar manner to the way the Son relates to the Father.[791] Or the incarnation of the Logos *himself* might be seen as the perfector of that creaturely analogy. Or it might be the divine nature itself that is somehow shared with humans through the *communicatio idiomata*. At the other extreme, its most austere participation might mean that we participate only in the Son's offices and achievements.

I do not wish to dispute any of these possible ways of understanding our participation in the divine or filial life. What I do want to suggest however, is that something can be gained by *also* seeing ourselves as participating in the triune life under the mode of free gift between the persons of the Father and Son. We have now seen how this can work: exemplified in John of the Cross, Jonathan Edwards and (much more briefly) Hans Urs von Balthasar. We have also seen how it might function as a controlling element in a biblical theology.

This kind of participation is both less speculative and yet potentially more radical. Less speculative, because it can be described through normal biblical categories: creation, revelation, calling, regeneration, forgiveness, illumination, sanctification and so on. But it is more radical because, here each of those things *also* has intra-trinitarian dimension, thus making us part of the filial/paternal relationship. For example:

- Our creation, election and calling is also the Father's gift to his Son (John 17:10; Eph 1:3-10; Col 1:15-16);

---

[790] For a helpful survey see Rowan Williams'; R. Williams "Deification" in *The Westminster Dictionary of Theology,* ed. A. Richardson & J. S. Bowden (Philadelphia: Westminster Press, 1983), 106-108. Williams divides classical patristic theories of deification between those that think in terms of the communication of divine attributes, and those that see it in terms of "participating in the intra-divine relationship." The difficulty for this study is that much exemplarist participation gives the appearance of being intra-divine whereas in reality it offers only an analogical participation in divine filiality.

[791] In one sense this analogical approach informs every trinitarianism that sees human love as an expression of the eternal love:

> Love of God and love of neighbour ... both live from the love of God who has loved us first. ... Love is "divine" because it comes from God and unites us to God; through this unifying process it makes us a "we" which transcends our divisions and makes us one, until in the end God is "all in all" (1 Cor 15:28).
>
> Benedict XVI, *Encyclical Letter: Deus Caritas Est,*
> http://www.vatican.va/holy_father/benedict_xvi/encyclicals/documents/hf_b en-xvi_enc_20051225_deus-caritas-est_en.html, (accessed March, 2010).

- Our regeneration, resurrection and vindication[792] come from the Father through the Son, for the Son's honour (John 5:21-25);

- The Son regards his mission amongst us as an opportunity to honour his Father (John 7:18; 17:4) – the cross specifically is the moment wherein both Father and Son are glorified (John 13:31).

- The sanctification of believers by the Son, and his response to their prayers, become a further means by which he glorifies his Father (John 15:8; 14:13).

And so on. The impression begins to form that the real sub-text of human/salvation history is the creation of a new context and currency by which the Father and Son can love each other.[793] By loving us, they love each other. And we, by responding to that love and grace, become conduits for that love.[794] As Reformed theologian Michael Horton rightly observes:

> It is not too extravagant to designate this with the noble title of "divinization." Not only are the adopted heirs the beneficiaries of divine love; their adoption also is itself caught up in the love of the Father and the Spirit for the Son.[795]

---

[792] I am using Reformed terminology for the final judgment of believers here (cf. Rom 5:9).

[793] See again, Williams, *Deflections of Desire*, 119ff.

[794] A particularly intriguing suggestion here is made by Robert Jenson, who draws on Peter Lombard, Martin Luther and Jonathan Edwards to propose that the work of the Spirit *ad extra* in the church is connected to his role as *vinculum caritatis/amoris ad intra*; R. W. Jenson "The Church and the Sacraments" in *The Cambridge Companion to Christian Doctrine,* ed. C. E. Gunton. *Cambridge Companions to Religion* (Cambridge: Cambridge University Press, 1997), 216-217. Although Jenson himself may be guilty of confusing those two *operae* (see comments above), the idea that the church might be a contingent *vinculum* has profound resonance with the perichoretic language associated with the Spirit's coming (John 17:20-23) and would vindicate the traditional association between the church and Spirit. As Tertullian writes: "the very Church itself is, properly and principally, the Spirit Himself, in whom is the Trinity of the One Divinity – Father, Son, and Holy Spirit;" *On Modesty* 21; ANF 4.99 – I am indepted to Anne Hunt for this quote; A. Hunt, "Trinity and Church: Explorations in Ecclesiology from a Trinitarian Perspective", *St Mark's Theological Review* 158.1 (2005): 32-44. 33.

[795] M. S. Horton, *Covenant and Salvation: Union with Christ* (Louisville: Westminster, John Knox, 2007), 295.

Observations Concerning the Current Evangelical Trinitarian Debates

As I stated in my introduction to this thesis, it has not been my intention here to issue a detailed response to the arguments associated with the ongoing intra-evangelical debate over the Trinity and gender relations – there are far more important theological issues to be considered than whether the Son's relationship to the Father is somehow analogous to marriage. Nevertheless, given that it is within evangelicalism that the issues of responsive intra-trinitarian willing are being most vigorously debated at the present time, and given that I am part of this tradition, I will here test the patience of non-evangelical readers by making some brief observations on this current discussion.

Evangelicals and Nicaea

One of the somewhat surprising features of the recent evangelical debates over the filial subordination has been the degree to which it typically occurs outside the bounds of traditional trinitarianism, in that many key theologians on both sides of the divide (egalitarian and complementarian)[796] simply reject the filial bond, as it arises from the begetting of the Son by the Father, and as is spoken of in the NCC as "God from God, Light from Light".[797]

Examples of this approach are readily adduced. On the egalitarian side Millard Erickson consciously sides with Arianism against Nicene patriarchy, concluding that causation or origination necessarily connotes essential

---

[796] I am using "egalitarian" and "complementarian" as broad headings for those evangelicals (though the categories are not necessarily confined to evangelicalism) who, respectively, reject and support the notion that the Pauline teaching on both marriage and ministry (eg. Eph 5 and 1 Tim 2) should still be taken to mean that men and women have different responsibilities in these areas in contemporary life. The terms have not gone without challenge but seem to be generally recognized. For further discussion see P. R. Schemm, "Kevin Giles' The Trinity and Subordinationism: A Review Article", *Journal for Biblical Manhood & Womanhood* 7.2 (2002): 67-78, 70.

[797] This failure is not universal. Welcome exceptions can be found in: J. V. Dahms, "The Subordination of the Son", *JETS* 37.3 (1994): 351-364; Paul A. Rainbow, who highlights this very failure in his response to Gilbert Bilezikian – P. A. Rainbow, *Orthodox Trinitarianism and Evangelical Feminism*, (Council on Biblical Manhood & Womanhood) http://www.cbmw.org/Resources/Articles/Orthodox-Trinitarianism-and-Evangelical-Feminism, (accessed March, 2010) – and, Sydney Diocesan Doctrine Commission, *The Doctrine of the Trinity and its bearing on the Relationship of Men and Women*, http://.www.anglicanmedia.com.au/ old/doc/trinity.html, (accessed January, 2003).

subordination.[798] Gilbert Bilezikian waves away eternal generation as a "creedal construction, subject to aleatory interpretations."[799] Rebecca Merrill Groothuis describes divine fatherhood as a metaphor having nothing to do with "God having reproduced himself."[800] Kevin Giles, demonstrating somewhat greater historical awareness, tries to collapse the monarchy of the Father into a T.F. Torrance-inspired scheme where the divine being itself is the cause of the persons.[801] Meanwhile amongst complementarians there is often a similar misperception that the derivation of the second and third persons from the first is a minor postscript to Nicaea: Bruce Ware relegates it to a footnote, declaring that descriptions of the Son as "only-begotten" or "eternally begotten" are "highly speculative and not grounded in biblical teaching".[802] Others, such as Wayne Grudem, brave an even more daring revisionism, suggesting that the

---

[798] Displaying a frustrating disregard to the painstaking differentiation of begetting and creation clarified by orthodox pro-Nicenes, Erickson asks:

> May the Arians have discovered something in the [the idea that begetting leads to inferiority]. Does the biblical revelation really teach the quasi-subordination or the derivation of one person from the other? [T]o speak of one of the persons as unoriginate and the others as either eternally begotten or proceeding from the father is to introduce an element of causation or origination that must ultimately involve some type of subordination among them.

Erickson, *God in Three Persons*, 229, 309.

[799] G. Bilezikian, "Hermeneutical Bungee-jumping: Subordination in the Godhead", *JETS* 40.1 (1997): 57-68, 62. Bilezikian's somewhat relaxed stance toward creedal orthodoxy is curious given the zeal with which he indicts RITW theology as heterodox.

[800] R. M. Groothuis, *Sexuality, Spirituality and Feminist Religion*, http://www.ivpress.com/groothuis/rebecca/archives/000043.php#more, (accessed February, 2005).

[801] In questioning that the Father alone is to be understood as *monarche* of the being of the Son and the Spirit, I follow no lesser scholar than T F Torrance ... the divine three in unity are the *monarche* of the being of the three persons, the Son is the *monarche* of divine revelation and the Spirit is the *monarche* of empowerment and sanctification for the believer. I think this gives a far better picture/model of the creedal 'co-equal' Trinity than the *monarche* model.

K. Giles, *A Reply to Andrew Moody's 'Review' of Jesus and the Father*, (April 2007) http://www.matthiasmedia.com.au/briefing/webextras/a_reply_to_andrew_moodys_review_of_jesus_and_the_father.php, (accessed April, 2007).

[802] Ware, *Father, Son, and Holy Spirit*, 162 n. 3.

causal language of orthodoxy *really means* social hierarchy.[803] Even the usually careful Gerald Bray stumbles here, implying that the Cappadocians invented the method of distinguishing the persons according to their mode of origin,[804] and reducing Calvin's theology of trinitarian relations to functional order.[805]

In light of the centrality of the causal model in trinitarian tradition, as we have seen it above, it might be argued that evangelicals need to at least gain a greater familiarity with Christian heritage of both the East and pre-Reformation West. Whatever their attitude to the metaphysical mysteries implied by divine begetting, this is the historical and *orthodox* position of both East and West. Moreover, as I discussed above, the pro-Nicene scheme aligns with the Bible's consistent depiction of the derivative and familial language concerning the person who is the Son, Word, Image, Radiance, Stamp of the Father.

A Lack of Clarity in Regard to Intra-Trinitarian Willing

This lack of appreciation of the causal priority of the Father can make it harder for Evangelicals to defend relational order without drifting toward genuine Arianism or, conversely, to oppose it without verging on Modalism. If it is not made clear that the divine will first bespeaks a *nature* that is eternally and wholly transmitted to the Son in his begetting, then it will look like the Son begins with an alien nature that must be directed to conform to the Father's.[806] Yet, at the same time, if it is not also seen that this commonality *results from* transmission/birth then the temptation will be to ward off volitional division by reasserting an essential "Willer" that is prior to the persons – in other words Western unipersonalism finally purged of its pro-Nicene heritage.

Appropriately concerned to avoid these conclusions, both complementarians and egalitarians attempt to compensate, but often without making things clearer. For example, those defending RITW might counterbalance their insistence on the Son's obedience to the will of the Father with a strong assertion that this only pertains to "role" and not to essence.[807] Yet this

---

[803] Grudem thus says that such terms "do not mean *anything more* than 'relating as a Father,' and 'relating as a Son'"; W. A. Grudem, *Systematic Theology: An Introduction to Biblical Doctrine* (Leicester: IVP, 1994), 254 n. 38; my emphasis.

[804] Or at least "retained" it: "It is difficult to see what 'cause' can mean when speaking of an eternal person, and all too easy to reflect that the word represents a lingering trace of pre-Nicene subordinationism;" Bray, *God,* 159.

[805] Ibid., 204. The mistake here is that Calvin does retain a notion of causality, but only in regard to the Son's subsistence, not his divine nature; cf. *Institutes* 1.8.19.

[806] This of course is the complaint issued by Kevin Giles against his complementarian opponents; see for example Giles, *Jesus,* 186-187, 310.

[807] So, for example Thomas Schreiner:

overlooks the fact that will has universally been seen by historical theology *as natural*. To insist that the Son is subordinate to the Father's will (without distinguishing between will and *decision*) and then to assert their oneness as to essence is, in historical terms, a contradiction. How can the Son have the essence of God and need to be told anything?

But a similar lack of clarity can readily be found on the other side too. Kevin Giles, for example, correctly demands that his opponents recognise the absolute singularity of the divine will, yet goes on to present the persons as having voluntary interactions.[808] More generally, egalitarians attempt to solve the oneness/threeness problem by invoking the concept of perichoretic interdependence or interpenetration.[809] This works well if it is deployed along Damascene lines ("*perichoresis*" here simply fleshing out what it means for the Son to share the Father's essence),[810] but what is generally meant here is more

---

> [RITW] would only be a heresy if one asserted that there was an ontological difference (a difference in nature or being) between Father and Son. The point is not that the Son is essentially inferior to the Father. Rather, the Son willingly submits himself to the Father's authority. The difference between the members of the Trinity is a functional one, not an essential one.
>
> T. R. Schreiner "Head Coverings, Prophecies and the Trinity" in *Recovering Biblical Manhood and Womanhood: A Response to Evangelical Feminism*, ed. J. Piper & W. A. Grudem (Wheaton: Crossway, 1991), 120.

See also Ware, *Father, Son, and Holy Spirit*, 21.

808 Giles, *Jesus*, 186-187, cf. 110-111; Giles, "Reply". See my online interaction with Giles on this point; A. Moody, *Relational Subordination in the Trinity: A continuation of the discussion emerging from Kevin Giles' books "The Trinity and Subordinationism" and "Jesus and the Father."*, http://ajmd.com.au/trinity/jatf.htm#L2, (accessed March, 2010).

Millard Erickson objects to Giles' linkage of will to nature at this point – see Erickson, *Tampering*, 215-218 – apparently unaware of the historical issues associated with this.

809 Karen Kilby puts it acutely, observing that for many modern social trinitarians the term "*perichoresis*" is deployed with a vagueness that serves whatever social agenda the exponent desires:

> First, a concept, *perichoresis*, is used to name what is not understood, to name whatever it is that makes the three Persons one. Secondly, the concept is filled out rather suggestively with notions borrowed from our own experience of relationships and relatedness. And then, finally, it is presented as an exciting resource Christian theology has to offer the wider world in its reflections upon relationships and relatedness.;"

Kilby, "Perichoresis and Projection", 442. I am indebted to Anne Hunt for pointing out this article in a personal correspondance.

810 See, for example R. del Colle "The Triune God" in *The Cambridge Companion to Christian Doctrine*, ed. C. E. Gunton. *Cambridge Companions to Religion*

akin to Jürgen Moltmann's idea that somehow the persons *mutually* and symmetrically depend on one another.[811] Thus Paul Fiddes:

> This vision of God lays stress upon the equality, mutuality and reciprocity of the three persons ... [quoting Boff] "each person receives everything from the others and at the same time gives everything to the others."[812]

Unfortunately this helps us very little. By refusing to concede logical priority to any of the persons (or even the essence itself), egalitarian *perichoresis* makes it *harder* to answer fundamental questions like: "Whose power created the world?" "Whence the decision to redeem humanity"? When the perichoretic solution is applied to the RITW question, as it is by Millard Erickson – "there are three wills, but the three, in the pattern known as *perichoresis*, always agree"[813] – the problem reoccurs. *How* is it that the persons agree? Is it because *perichoresis* really just means they have a *common* mind (back to unipersonalism) or are we supposed to see any act of will as something that never begins with *anyone* but is simply juggled between them in infinite regression?[814] As soon as it is applied to any actual problem this "Western"

(Cambridge: Cambridge University Press, 1997), 129-132. Of course such a patriarchal contruction would not sit particularly well with the egalitarian agenda. Paul S. Fiddes thus complains against the causality in the "Eastern" version of *perichoresis* suggesting that "this perception might consequently have an effect downwards into the world, sanctioning ... hierarchies of power;" P. S. Fiddes, *Participating in God: A Pastoral Doctrine of the Trinity* (London: Darton, Longman & Todd, 2000), 76.

811 See Moltmann & Kohl, *Kingdom,* 174-176; J. Moltmann "God in the World - The World in God: Perichoresis in Trinity and Eschatology" in *The Gospel of John and Christian Theology,* ed. R. Bauckham & C. Mosser (Grand Rapids: Eerdmans, 2008), 372-374.

812 Fiddes, *Participating,* 77-78. See similar comments in Bilezikian, "Bungie", 62, 66.

813 Erickson, *Tampering,* 254.

814 The problem here is that we are never offered a *sufficient* cause – the system requires us to accept that an endless series of proximate causes can add up to aseity. Matthew Levering makes some helpful observations along these lines in a critique of both Miroslav Volf (who uses the modern perichoretic model) and John Zizioulas (who creates a similar problem by defining the persons *as* pure relationships): "for Volf, the question remains as to how this 'equiprimacy' can be maintained without a stronger account of 'Person' ... if *no person* possesses anything of its own ... then they can hardly be distinguished from one another and from the divine substance"; M. Levering, *Christ and the Catholic Priesthood: Ecclesial Hierarchy and the Pattern of the Trinity* (Chicago: HillenbrandBooks, 2010), 27.

version of the *perichoresis* (as Fiddes mistakenly calls it)[815] dissolves into incoherence.[816]

Once again, evangelicals on both sides of the line seem to be having trouble expressing a coherent trinitarian theology of willing – in large measure because of a lack of regard for traditional categories, and because of a lack of clarity in the distinction between natural will and contingent willing. Perhaps, on this last point, they can scarcely be blamed – the issue has never been definitively clarified. But the modern willingness to tolerate loose taxonomies and second-hand revisions of trinitarian doctrine is not helping.

The (Ir)revelance of Intra-trinitarian Relations for Human Interaction

One gambit played by some egalitarians in this debate is to depict the RITW debate as an aberration thrown up within evangelicalism purely for the sake of justifying the complementarian "equal-but-different" doctrine on gender relations.[817] Unhappily there is arguably some basis for this: both sides show

---

[815] Fiddes' attempts to pass-off the *filioque* as a justification for this characterisation; Fiddes, *Participating*, 76-78. But the *filioque* was never intended to detract from the principium of the Father. As the Latin party declares at the Council of Florence (1439):

> We Latins ... do not [assert the filioque] with the intention of excluding the Father from being the source and principle of all deity, that is of the Son and of the Holy Spirit, nor to imply that the Son does not receive from the Father ... [but that] since the Father gave to his only-begotten Son in begetting him everything the Father has, except to be the Father, so the Son has eternally from the Father, by whom he was eternally begotten, this also, namely that the Holy Spirit proceeds from the Son.

> Translation from J. Gill, *The Council of Florence* (Cambridge: Cambridge University Press, 1959), 247.

See Pannenberg's observations here too; Pannenberg, *Systematic Theology*, 1.334.

[816] Randall Otto rightly asks what (modern forms of) *perichoresis* can mean if they are severed from its essentialist basis; R. E. Otto, "The Use and Abuse of Perichoresis in Recent Theology", *Scottish Journal of Theology* 54.3 (2001): 366-384, 366-377. Indeed. Furthermore we should add that it is *the Father's* essence that is shared by all three and that actually *gives shape* to the perichoretic union (see Chapter 1).

[817] This argument is made repeatedly by Kevin Giles – most recently in his response to Michael Bird and Robert Shillaker: "I have read every book available to me in English on the Trinity and I have not found one outside of the evangelical circle I mention who endorses the eternal subordination of the Son in function and authority;" K. Giles, "Michael Bird and Robert Shillaker: The Son is Not Eternally Subordinated in Authority to the Father", *Trinity Journal* 30.2 (2009): 257-268, 238 n. 7. The charge can also be found in Bilezikian, "Bungie" and Cary, "The New Evangelical Subordinationism: Reading Inequality into the Trinity", 42.

signs that their real interest is elsewhere.[818] And it is also true that the issue has been more fiercely contested amongst evangelicals than amongst any other branch of the church.

But it is not true that gender relations are the only issue that have been associated with RITW question, nor is it true that evangelicals are alone in worrying about it. A trickle of literature and marginal comments, shows that Catholics, Orthodox, liberals and even Neo-orthodox theologians also express interest in the sociological implications of gender relations; indeed in some cases we can find exactly the same arguments concerning gender, equality and trinitarian order as found amongst complementarian evangelicals. Thus (despite some strenuous arguments to the contrary)[819] Karl Barth applies his own form of the *equal but different* analogy to marriage using the Godhead as template:

> Does subordination in God necessarily involve an inferiority, and therefore a deprivation, a lack? Why not rather a particular being in the glory of the one equal Godhead, in whose inner order there is also, in fact, this dimension, the direction downwards, which has its own dignity? Why should not our way of finding a lesser dignity and significance in what takes the second and subordinate place (the wife to her husband) need to be corrected in the light of the *homoousia* of the modes of divine being?[820]

Similarly Thomas Hopko, Dean Emeritus of Saint Vladimir's Orthodox Theological Seminary, uses a thoroughly patriarchal vision of the Trinity (which he asserts is Orthodox and Nicene) to counter the egalitarian trinitarianism of Paul Jewett.[821] Within the same volume, Bishop Kallistos of

---

818 It is unfortunate, for example, that the first and major evangelical appearances on the topic in the modern time tend to have been published *within* the context of the gender debate; for example P. K. Jewett, *Man as Male and Female: A Study in Sexual Relationships from a Theological Point of View* (Grand Rapids: Eerdmans, 1975), 133; G. W. Knight, *The New Testament Teaching on the Role Relationship of Men and Women* (Grand Rapids: Baker Book House, 1977), 21; J. Piper & W. A. Grudem (eds), *Recovering Biblical Manhood and Womanhood: A Response to Evangelical Feminism (*Wheaton: Crossway, 1991) etc. Ironically, Kevin Giles himself exemplifies the same pattern when, in his 2002 book – Giles, *Subordinationism*, he breaks off half-way through to switch focus to sociological issues (gender relations and slavery).

819 Giles, *Jesus,* 275-305

820 CD 4/1.59.202 (see an even stronger statement in Geoffrey Bromiley's discussion of "ordered equality"; G. W. Bromiley, *God and Marriage* (Edinburgh: T&T Clark, 1981), 71-73).

821 T. Hopko "Women and the Priesthood: Reflections on the Debate - 1983" in *Women and the Priesthood,* ed. T. Hopko (Crestwood: St. Vladimir's Seminary Press, 1999), 237ff.

Diokleia advances an argument that looks entirely familiar to complementatians:

> When it is said that the "head of Christ is God [the Father]": this does not imply any Arianizing subordination of the Son to the Father. Within the Trinity there is indeed an "order" (taxis) or "hierarchy", in the sense that the Father is the first person ... the source, cause and fountainhead. ... If, then, the "headship" of the man within marriage is in some way parallel to the relationship of the Father to the Son within the Godhead, this does not necessarily imply any intrinsic inferiority on the part of the woman.[822]

Another prominent Russian Orthodox priest, Alexander Schmemann argues similarly:

> The principle of hierarchy implies the idea of obedience but not that of subordination, for obedience is based on personal relationship whereas subordination is, in its very essence, an impersonal one. The Son is fully obedient to the Father, but he is not subordinated to him. ... To ordain someone to a hierarchical function does not mean his elevation "above" the others, his opposition to them as "power" and "submission."[823]

Most frequently however, theologians outside evangelicalism apply trinitarian order to the church. To Joseph Ratzinger, trinitarian relations are the key to understanding both church itself – which is a participation in the Son's assent to the Father[824] – and the primacy of the Pope, who is given particular responsibility to testify to the Father by testifying to Christ (himself the Father's self-testimony).[825] Similar arguments are made by other Catholic authorities,[826] and even by the liberal-catholicism of Anglican Bishop Peter Carnley.[827]

---

822 Ibid. Kallistos of Diokleia "Man, Woman and the Priesthood of Christ" in *Women and the Priesthood,* ed. T. Hopko (Crestwood: St. Vladimir's Seminary Press, 1999), 36.

823 A. Schmemann, *Church, World, Mission: Reflections on Orthodoxy in the West* (Crestwood: St. Vladimir's Seminary Press, 1979), 166.

824 Essentially, the Son is the release and handing back of himself – that is what sonship means. When the Son is translated into the creation it means "obedience unto death, even death on a cross" (Phil 2:8). ... We become God by sharing in the gesture of the Son. We become God by becoming "child", "son"; we become God when we enter into the words that Jesus addresses to the Father ... "A body have you prepared for me ... "

Ratzinger, *God of Jesus,* 67-68. See also J. Ratzinger, *Christian Brotherhood* (London: Burns & Oates, 2006), 65.

825 See J. Ratzinger, *Church, Ecumenism and Politics: New Essays in Ecclesiology* (New York: Crossroad, 1988), 39-42.

826 See A. Dulles "The Trinity and Christian Unity" in *God the Holy Trinity: Reflections on Christian Faith and Practice,* ed. T. George (Grand Rapids: Baker Academic, 2006), 77-78, or, for an even more robust treatment, see Terence L. Nichols' response to the egalitarian trinitarianism of LaCugna and Moltmann. Highlighting the inconsistency of LaCugna's attempt to elevate the economic Trinity apart from its obvious subordinationism he writes that if:

> ... the economic Trinity was subordinationist, then it follows the immanent Trinity is subordinationist also, at least in some respect. But just as there can be a hierarchy of relations between two persons who nevertheless are equal in respect to their nature, essence, and substance, so also there can be hierarchical relations within the Trinity while there is commonality of substance and being among the persons. ... Within the Trinity there is total communion and participation of the persons in each other, yet there remains a hierarchy of *relationships*: the Father is greater than the Son, and presumably the Spirit also, since the Father is the source and cause of the Spirit as of the Son. This is a model for the Church as hierarchical communion.

Nichols, *One*, 279-280.

John Zizioulas makes similar (though explicitly differentiated) analogies from the Orthodox perspective; Zizioulas, *Communion and Otherness*, 145-149.

827 The priority of the Father as the eternal "source" and "origin" of the other two persons of equal dignity and status, surely finds its closest ecclesiological expression in the principle of *primus inter pares,* or "first among equals." This principle in turn allows us to articulate an understanding of the role of the Bishop in the Church and of the Primate ... The concept of "monarchy" is appropriately applied to the unique ministry of the Bishop because, as teacher, the Bishop is the one who must on occasion *rule* with respect to what is right and what is wrong in matters of both belief and Christian praxis.

P. Carnley, "In Praise of Hierarchy - A Response to Jürgen Moltmann", *Common Theology* 1 (2002): 9-15, 12-13.

It is interesting to observe Carnley's imputing of Arianism against the Sydney Diocese in the light of this; P. Carnley, *Reflections in Glass: Trends and Tensions in the Contemporary Anglican Church.* vol. 2004 (Sydney: Harper Collins), 232-241. Labouring to differentiate his own Episcopal analogy from that of Sydney's own (gender) analogy, Carnley simultaneously chastises the Diocese for being insufficiently voluntarist in their understanding of Christ's virtue (pp. 233-234), and breaking the unity and equality of divine will (pp. 234-235). In this last argument at least Carnley has a point. But he does not show how it is possible to have it both ways – that is, how to reconcile the volitional separation implied by "equal" with the unipersonal or quasi-physiological implied by the unity of will. And this is still more opaque if there is no ontological basis for the Son's "goodness" – whence *then* the link between the Father and Son which allows us to speak of one will?

Nevertheless how legitimate is this analogising of Trinity with human relations?[828] As Anne Hunt wryly observes, the attempt to use trinitarian taxonomy to derive church structure, generally seems to end up justifying the prior ecclesiology of the theologian despite the "common basis in trinitarian theology."[829] No doubt the same is true of the evangelicals.

But the Bible never depicts the second person of the Trinity as the Father's "wife", nor does it make any such connection between bishops and the first person of the Trinity.[830] Of course there is a profound, and apparently hierarchical analogy between marriage and the Christ/church relationship (Eph 5:22-33) but this, as Gregory Nazianzen suggests,[831] involves a different way of being *homoousios*.[832] Whereas in marriage the wife is seen to be a reunion of that which was taken out of the man *leading* to his completeness, in the filial relation the father is reiterated by the offspring who thus participates in him.[833]

Nor can we overlook the disconnection between these human relations and the perfect union of perfect nature that inheres in the Godhead. Bishops and men are not (in case we had not noticed!) perfect, nor are those they lead ever perfectly in tune with them. Thus all human authority in a fallen world *must* be heteronomous in a way that falls infinitely short of the Trinity's unity of natural will and (responsive) contingent willing. Evangelical complementarians and their traditionalist counterparts who want to create *new* analogies between human relations and divine, are in danger of pursuing a natural theology that is already out of date by the end of Genesis 3, and of finding themselves in the

---

828 See the concurring observations of Bird & Shillaker – M. F. Bird & R. Shillaker, "Subordination in the Trinity and Gender Roles: A Response to Recent Discussion", *Trinity Journal* 29.2 (2008): 267-283 – 280-282. Giles – Giles, "Response to Bird & Shillaker", 237-238.

829 Hunt, "Trinity and Church", 40-41. She might be understating the differences between the trinitarian theologies she discusses here. Though, of course that raises the still more disturbing prospect that theology might be being influenced by social agendas.

830 Indeed Richard Bauckham puts it rather starkly in his critique of Moltmann, observing that the idea that we should see "the Trinity as an external model that human relationships should reflect ... has no biblical basis ... the New Testament does not use the idea of the image of God in this way;" R. Bauckham "Jürgen Moltmann's *The Trinity and the Kingdom of God* and the Question of Pluralism" in *The Trinity in a Pluralistic Age: Theological Essays on Culture and Religion,* ed. K. J. Vanhoozer (Grand Rapids: Eerdmans, 1996), 160.

831 *Or.* 30.20; cf. discussion in Chapter 1.

832 *Or.* 31.11.

833 We might ask whether the current fashion in stressing the Father's dependence on the Son actually tends to convert filiality into conjugality.

same camp as other image makers, such as those who would presume to fashion icons to express God.[834]

But this criticism cuts both ways too. If there are problems with the complementarian co-opting of trinitarian hierarchy, the contrary egalitarian impulse to eschew all paternal priority is equally wrongheaded. The Father may not be head of his Son *in the same sense* that "the head of the woman is the man" (cf. 1Cor 11:3, ASV),[835] yet the idea that he is head – as source and *principium* in regard to the other two persons – is the clear testimony of both Scripture and tradition. Without going over old ground again, the egalitarian rejection of the logic of subsistent equality commits a fundamental category mistake of confusing essence with mode of subsistence – leading to the conclusion that the only permissible distinction between Father, Son and Spirit is one of bare haecceity.[836]

If there is a connection between divine filiality and human gender/church structures it is not to be found in analogy but in the (much broader) categories

---

834 For the negative case, see my comments concerning Rowan Williams' poetic/artistic theories of icon theology; A. Moody "The Hidden Center: Trinity and Incarnation in the Negative (and Positive) Theology of Rowan Williams" in *On Rowan Williams: Critical Essays,* ed. M. Russell (Oregon: Wipf & Stock, 2009), 46, cf. n. 110. Meanwhile Trevor Hart puts the case for a licensed *analogia* beautifully. Drawing on Barth he writes:

> At the end of the day, we can trust that there is an appropriate analogy between our language and God himself at these points, because the basic metaphors are of his making and choosing rather than ours. We can trust, too, that as we deploy them to speak of him, he will be faithful and will speak of himself in and through our speaking, thereby opening out their ultimate reference and meaning for us so that we "know," through something resembling intuition, how these words refer.

> T. Hart "How Do We Define the Nature of God's Love?" in *Nothing Greater, Nothing Better: Theological Essays on the Love of God,* ed. K. J. Vanhoozer (Grand Rapids: William B. Eerdmans, 2001), 112-113.

835 There is little point here in arguments over whether κεφαλή (1Cor 11:3) is to be understood "source" or "authority over". As should be clear by now, my claim is that any "authority" possessed by the Father in regard to the Son is simply the outworking of his monarchy; that is, the Father's monarchy finds its correlate in the Son's natural and responsive filiality.

836 Thus Kevin Giles protests against arguments concerning the necessity of the monarchy:

> To reply that unless the Son is eternally relationally subordinated to the Father differentiated [sic] cannot be upheld is mind numbing. Two human beings can be clearly differentiated and yet be equals in the broad sense of this term; why not two divine persons?

> Giles, "Reply".

of authority and submission themselves. Wherever authority arises amongst humans, and whatever its basis, it finds itself judged and shamed by the Father who delights to share his authority with his Son in every way possible: a Father who, without abdicating his monarchy, uses the initiative it entails to set a course that will glorify, adorn, and manifest his Son.[837] This is the proper and ultimate use of authority – the ultimate rejection of the zero-sum game that is implicit in the will to power.

Conversely the authority and character of this utterly sovereign Father makes submission to proximate authority possible. The Son who "entrusted himself to the one who judges justly" and was vindicated in his deference to human authority, enables us to go on submitting, knowing that the Father's will is finally for our good in Christ. None of this is to argue for, or against, male headship or episcopal authority, merely to observe how the Father's authority for his Son transforms our attitude to "the authority of every human institution" (1Pet 2:13). Even *structurally* inequitable authority such as slavery is potentially transformed for the Christian slave who bears-up after the pattern of Christ (1Pet 2.19-22).[838] Under the Father's authority *everything* – even injustice – can be ultimately for the glory of Christ and for the good of those "in him", who are called according to his purpose.

---

[837] If what I have argued in the previous chapter is correct – that salvation history is geared for the achievement of a *distinct* glory for the Son who dies alone – then in one sense there is a kind of overlap between the kenotic authority of the Father (as per Balthasar) and the self-abnegation of the husband who lays down his life for his wife.

[838] This is from the perspective of the slave. Again, it is not to say that slavery itself is objectively equitable.

Conclusion

I have laboured in this thesis to outline a theory of trinitarian relations that makes sense of the creation, humanity, incarnation and salvation. I have sought to demonstrate that it is both orthodox – in harmony with the heritage and emphasis of Nicaea – and consistent with the themes, typology and plain reading of Scripture.

I have sought specifically to avoid the major pitfalls associated with responsive intra-trinitarian willing and social trinitarianism: division of the nature and will; heteronomy and ontological subordination. I have proposed that the order of subsistence observed by all ancient Christian traditions might allow a model of divine decision-making wherein the Father chooses from within the options afforded by his nature, and the Son – who also shares that same nature – willingly assents. This scheme guards the equality of the Son and Spirit but also makes sense of the biblical testimony that it is the Father who plans for the world to be recapitulated and inherited by his Son. And I have indicated some ancient and modern examples of just such a scheme from Catholic and Reformed sources.

I have also sought to demonstrate that there are some profound *positives* associated with this framework and the ordered trinitarianism it develops. To draw them together:

(1) RITW theory vindicates the biblical claim that God is love; and furthermore, declares that it is this same love that is the reason why there is a world, history, incarnation and redemption. All created reality issues from the desire of the Father for the Son, and is consummated by the return of that love in the active response of the Son.

(2) RITW theory maintains that history is proceeding according to God's plans despite (and even through) the wreckage of human rebellion and evil. The mystery of God was always to have his Son enter creation and save it and thereby become its redeemer, head and perfector.

(3) RITW theory elucidates a Filio-Christocentric anthropology. Humanity is at once:

- a type and anticipation of the Son in his final glory as ruler of creation;
- that which the Father gives the Son to save, wed and possess;
- restored and completed through union with Christ;

Conclusion

      – a contingent object and means of the eternal exchange of love – directed by the Father to honour the Son, and by the Son back to the Father.

(4) RITW theory thus clarifies a form of participation (even divinisation) which works from biblical patterns rather than ontological speculation. The events of salvation history themselves, and our inclusion in it, are our being part of God's life and love.

(5) Finally, in underlining the relational taxis of the Father and Son, RITW theory demonstrates how the persons work together such that their work is "one". Crypto-modalism is avoided (the works of God are one because God is *really* one person); as is the opposite thought that any of the persons might have come to save us *but only one did*. The works of the persons follow the *propria* of their subsistence – thus our worship is neither confused nor divided. Through the Spirit we praise both the Father, from whom issue all things, and the Son, in whom all things come together; first the creator then redeemer.

> To the one seated on the throne
> and to the Lamb
> be blessing and honour
> and glory and might
> forever and ever!

Bibliography

Patristic & Medieval Primary Sources

Ambrose

De Fide ad Gratianum

De Spiritu Sanctu

Anselm

Cur Deus Hom

Monologium

Proslogium

Athanasius

Ad Afros Epistola Synodica

Contra Arianos

Contra Gentes

De Decretis

De Incarnatione

De Synodis

Augustine

Contra Maximinum

De Doctrina Christiana

De Diversis Quaestionibus Octoginta Tribus

De Fide et Symbolo

De Trinitate

In Ioannis Evangelium (Tractates in Ioannem)

Literal Meaning of Genesis

On Genesis

Unfinished Literal Commentary on Genesis

Basil of Caesarea

De Spiritu Sancto

Epistolae

Boethius

Contra Eutychen et Nestorium

Bonaventure

Collationes in Hexaemeron

Commentaria in Quatuor Libros Sententiarum

De Reductione Artium ad Theologiam

Duns Scotus

De Praedestione Christi

Quaestiones Quodlibetales

Reportata Parisiensia

Epiphanius

Panarion

Gregory Nazianzen

Orationes

Gregory of Nyssa

Contra Eunomium

Hilary of Poitiers

De Synodis

De Trinitate

Hugh of St Victor

De Quatuor Voluntatibus in Christo

John of Damascus

De Fide Orthodoxa

John of the Cross

Romance sobre el Evangelio "In principio erat Verbum" acerca de la Santísima Trinidad

Maximus the Confessor

Disputation with Pyrrhus

On Love

Opusculae

Theologia et Polemica

Peter Lombard

Sententiarum Quatuor Libri

Richard of St Victor

De Trinitate

Socrates of Constantinople

Historia Ecclesiastica

Thedoret of Cyrrus

Historia Ecclesiastica

Thomas Aquinas

Contra Errores Graecorum

De Unione Verbi

De Veritate

Scriptum Super Sententiis

Summa Contra Gentiles

Summa Theologiae

Super Ioannem

Bibliography

Miscellaneous Works

Alberigo, G., J. A. Dossetti & P. P. Joannou *Conciliorum Oecumenicorum Decreta,* Bologna: Istituto per le Scienza Religiose, 1973, http://ldysinger.stjohnsem.edu/@magist/1215_Lateran4_ec12/02_lat4_c01-22.htm, (accessed August, 2009).

Anatolios, K. *Athanasius: The Coherence of his Thought.* Routledge Early Church Monographs. London: Routledge, 1998.

– – – "The Influence of Irenaeus on Athanasius" in *Studia Patristica Vol. XXXVI - Critica et Philologica, Nachleben, First Two Centuries, Tertulian to Arnobius, Egypt before Nicaea, Athanasius and his Opponents (Paperback),* ed. E. A. Livingstone. Leuven: Peeters, 2000.

Anon. ("A Benedictine of Stanbrook Abbey") *Mediaeval Mystical Tradition and Saint John of the Cross.* London: Burns & Oates, 1954.

Anselm, *Medieval Sourcebook: Anselm (1033-1109): Monologium,* http://www.fordham.edu/halsall/basis/anselm-monologium.html, (accessed 2009, August).

– – – *Proslogium; Monologium: An Appendix In Behalf Of The Fool By Gaunilo; And Cur Deus Homo,* trans. S. N. Deane. Chicago: The Open Court Publishing Company, 1903, reprinted 1926.

Arndt, W., F. W. Gingrich & W. Bauer *A Greek-English Lexicon of the New Testament and other Early Christian Literature.* Chicago: Cambridge University Press, 1957.

Athanasius, *Urkunden zur Geschichte des Arianischen Streites, 318-328,* ed. H. G. Opitz. vol. 3. Athanasius Werke. Berlin: Berlin Academy, 1934.

– – – *Athanasius: Werke,* ed. H.-G. Opitz & M. Tetz. de Gruyter, 2001.

– – – *Athanasius Werke: Band III/Teil 1: Urkunden zur Geschichte des Arianischen Streites 318-328: Lieferung 3: Bis zur Ekthesis Makrostichos*

(Lieferung), ed. H. C. Brennecke, U. Heil, A. Von Stockhausen & A. Wintjes. Berlin: Walter de Gruyter, 2007.

Augustine, *De Doctrina Christiana,* ed. R. P. H. Green. Oxford Early Christian texts. Oxford: Clarendon Press, 1995.

--- *On Genesis,* trans. E. Hill, ed. J. E. Rotelle. The Works of Saint Augustine. NY: New City Press, 2002.

--- *Responses to Miscellaneous Questions: Miscellany of Eighty-Three Questions; Miscellany of Questions in Response to Simplician; and, Eight Questions of Dulcitius,* trans. R. Boniface, ed. R. F. Canning. The Works of Saint Augustine, Part 1. New York: New City Press, 2008.

--- *Arianism and other Heresies: Heresies, Memorandum to Augustine, To Orosius in Refutation of the Priscillianists and Origenists Arian Sermon, Answer to an Arian Sermon, Debate with Maximinus, Answer to Maximinus, Answer to an Enemy of the Law and the Prophets,* trans. J. E. R. R. J. Teske. New York: New City Press, 1995.

Awad, N. G. "Between Subordination and Koinonia: Toward a New Reading of the Cappadocian Theology", *Modern Theology* 23.2 (April 2007): 181-204.

Ayres, L. "The Fundamental Grammar of Augustine's Trinitarian Theology" in *Augustine and his Critics: Essays in Honour of Gerald Bonner,* ed. R. Dodaro & G. Lawless. London: Routledge, 2000.

--- *Nicaea and its Legacy: An Approach to Fourth-Century Trinitarian Theology.* Oxford: Oxford University Press, 2004.

Baddeley, M. "The Trinity and Subordinationism: A Response to Kevin Giles", *Reformed Theological Review* 63 (2004): 29-42.

--- *Complementarianism and Egalitarianism (part 3): The Coming Divide (iii),* The Sola Panel, http://solapanel.org/article/complementarianism_and_ egalitarianism_part_31/#5772, (accessed November, 2011).

Bailey, K. E. *Poet & Peasant; and, Through Peasant Eyes: A Literary-Cultural Approach to the Parables in Luke,* Combined edition. Grand Rapids: Eerdmans, 1983.

Bibliography

Baillie, D. M. *God was in Christ: An Essay on Incarnation and Atonement.* Faber paper covered editions. London: Faber and Faber, 1961.

Barnes, M. R., review of *The Fatherhood of God from Origen to Athanasius* by P. Widdicombe, *Theological Studies* 56.3, (1995): 574

– – – "Augustine in Contemporary Trinitarian Theology", *Theological Studies* 56.2 (1995): 237-250.

– – – "The Fourth Century as Trinitarian Canon" in *Christian Origins: Theology, Rhetoric and Community,* ed. L. Ayres & G. Jones. London: Routledge, 1998.

– – – *The Power of God: Dunamis in Gregory of Nyssa's Trinitarian Theology.* Washington: Catholic University of America Press, 2001.

– – – "Divine Unity and the Divided Self: Gregory of Nyssa's Trinitarian Theology in its Psychological Context", *Modern Theology* 18.4 (2004): 475-496.

Barrett, C. K. *The Gospel According to St. John: An Introduction With Commentary and Notes on the Greek Text.* Louisville: Westminster John Knox Press, 1978.

Barth, K. *Church Dogmatics,* trans. G. W. Bromiley, ed. G. W. Bromiley & T. F. Torrance, 4 volumes. Edinburgh: T&T Clark, 1956-1969.

Bathrellos, D. *The Byzantine Christ: Person, Nature, and Will in the Christology of St. Maximus the Confessor.* New York: Oxford University Press, 2005.

Bauckham, R. "Jürgen Moltmann's *The Trinity and the Kingdom of God* and the Question of Pluralism" in *The Trinity in a Pluralistic Age: Theological Essays on Culture and Religion,* ed. K. J. Vanhoozer. Grand Rapids: Eerdmans, 1996.

– – – *God Crucified: Monotheism and Christology in the New Testament.* Grand Rapids: Eerdmans, 1999.

Bauerschmidt, F. C. "The Word Made Speculative? John Milbank's Christological Poetics", *Modern Theology* 15.4 (1999): 417-432.

Beach, J. M. "The Doctrine of the *Pactum Salutis* in the Covenant Theology of Herman Witsius", *Mid-America Journal of Theology* 13 (2002): 101-142.

Beckwith, C. *Hilary of Poitiers on the Trinity: From De Fide to De Trinitate.* Oxford Early Christian Studies. Oxford University Press, USA, 2009.

Beeley, C. "Divine Causality and the Monarchy of the Father in Gregory of Nazianzus", *Harvard Theological Review* 100.2 (2007): 199-214.

Behr, J. *The Trinitarian Theology of St. Basil of Caesarea,* 1999, http://www.allsaints-stl.org/Trinitarian%20Theology%20of%20St.%20Basil%20of%20Caesarea%20-%20Web%20Version%202008.pdf, (accessed November, 2008).

– – – *The Nicene Faith.* vol. 2. Formation of Christian theology. Crestwood: St. Vladimir's Seminary Press, 2004.

– – – "Response to Ayres: The Legacies of Nicaea, East and West", *Harvard Theological Review* 100.2 (2007): 145-152.

– – – "Augustine and the Legacy of Nicaea" in *Orthodox Readings of Augustine,* ed. G. E. Demacopoulos & A. Papanikolaou. Crestwood: St. Vladimirs Seminary Press, 2008.

Benedict XVI *Encyclical Letter: Deus Caritas Est,* http://www.vatican.va/holy_father/benedict_xvi/encyclicals/documents/hf_ben-xvi_enc_20051225_deus-caritas-est_en.html, (accessed March, 2010).

Berkhof, L. *Systematic Theology.* Edinburgh: Banner of Truth, 1959.

Berkouwer, G. C. *Divine Election.* Historical Studies in Dogmatics. Grand Rapids: Eerdmans, 1960.

Berthold, G. C. *Maximus Confessor: Selected Writings.* Classics of Western Spirituality. New York: Paulist Press, 1985.

Bibliography

Bezzant, R. "Trinitarian Strategy", *(draft research paper sent to me, April 2008)*

Bibliotheca Augustiana, Augsburg: Ulrich Harsch, http://www.hs-augsburg.de/~harsch/Chronologia/Lspost12/PetrusLombardus/pet_s000.html, (accessed September, 2009).

Bilezikian, G. "Hermeneutical Bungee-jumping: Subordination in the Godhead", *JETS* 40.1 (1997): 57-68.

Bird, M. F. & R. Shillaker "Subordination in the Trinity and Gender Roles: A Response to Recent Discussion", *Trinity Journal* 29.2 (2008): 267-283.

Bloesch, D. G. *God the Almighty: Power, Wisdom, Holiness, Love.* Christian Foundations. Downers Grove: InterVarsity Press, 1995.

Blowers, P. M. & R. L. Wilken *On the Cosmic Mystery of Jesus Christ: Selected Writings from St. Maximus the Confessor: Popular Patristics Series.* Crestwood: St. Vladimir's Seminary Press, 2004.

Boff, L. & P. Burns *Trinity and Society.* Theology and Liberation Series. Maryknoll: Orbis Books, 1988.

Bonaventure, *S. Bonaventurae Opera Omnia,* ed. A. C. Peltier. Paris: Ludovicus Vivès, 1864.

– – – *Opera Omnia S. Bonaventuræ.* Quarrachi: Collegio San Bonaventurae, 1882-1902.

– – – *De Reductione Artium ad Theologiam: A Commentary with an Introduction and Translation,* trans. E. T. Healy, 2d ed edition. New York: The Franciscan Institute, Saint Bonaventure University, 1955.

Bougerol, J. G. "Bonaventure" in *Encyclopedia of Christian Theology,* ed. J. Y. Lacoste. London: Routledge, 2005.

Braaten, C. E. & R. W. Jenson (eds), *Christian Dogmatics,* 2 volumes. Philadelphia: Fortress Press, 1984.

Bray, G. L. *The Doctrine of God.* vol. 1. Contours of Christian theology. Leicester: IVP, 1993.

Brenan, G. *St John of the Cross: His Life and Poetry,* trans. L. Nicholson. Cambridge: Cambridge University Press, 1975.

Bromiley, G. W. *God and Marriage.* Edinburgh: T&T Clark, 1981.

Brown, A. "On the Criticism of Being as Communion in Anglophone Orthodox Theology" in *The Theology of John Zizioulas: Personhood and the Church,* ed. D. H. Knight. Aldershot: Ashgate, 2007.

Brown, D. *The Divine Trinity.* London: Duckworth, 1985.

Brown, R. E. *The Gospel According to John,* 2 volumes. Garden City: Doubleday, 1966.

Bruce, F. F. *The Gospel of John,* 1st paperpack edition. Grand Rapid: Eerdmans, 1994.

Bugnolo, A., E. D. Buckner & J. C. Klok *The Commentary Project,* Boston: The Franciscan Archive, http://www.franciscan-archive.org/bonaventura/I-Sent.html, (accessed November, 2009).

Bulgakov, S. N. *The Comforter,* trans. B. Jakim. Grand Rapids: Eerdmans, 2004.

Bychkov, O. "What Does Beauty Have to Do with the Trinity", *Franciscan Studies* 66 (2008): 197-212.

Calvin, J. *The Eighth Sermon on the First Chapter of Ephesians,* http://www.the-highway.com/Calvin_Eph8.html, (accessed March, 2010).

– – – *The Sermons upon the Epistle of S. Paule to the Ephesians,* trans. A. Golding. London: Lucas Harison & George Byshop, 1577.

– – – *Commentaries on the Epistle of Paul the Apostle to the Hebrews,* trans. J. Owen, ed. J. Owen. Edinburgh: Calvin Translation Society, 1853.

– – – *Commentary on the Gospel According to John,* trans. J. Pringle, 2 volumes, reprint edition. Grand Rapids: Eerdmans, 1956.

Bibliography

– – – & A. Tholuck *Ioannis Calvini Institutio Christianae Religionis.* Berolini: G. Eichler, 1834.

– – – *Institutes of the Christian Religion,* trans. F. L. Battles, ed. J. T. McNeill, 2 volumes. Philadelphia: Westminster Press, 1960.

Carnley, P. *Reflections in Glass: Trends and Tensions in the Contemporary Anglican Church.* vol. 2004. Sydney: Harper Collins,

– – – "In Praise of Hierarchy - A Response to Jürgen Moltmann", *Common Theology* 1 (2002): 9-15.

Carson, D. A. *The Gospel According to John: An Introduction and Commentary.* Pillar New Testament Commentary. Grand Rapids: Eerdmans, 1991.

Cary, P. "The New Evangelical Subordinationism: Reading Inequality into the Trinity", *Priscilla Papers* 20.4 (2006): 42-45.

Casarella, P. J. "The Expression and Form of the Word: Trinitarian Hermeneutics and the Sacramentality of Language in Hans Urs von Balthasar's Theology" in *Glory, Grace, and Culture: The Work of Hans Urs von Balthasar,* ed. E. Block. Mahwah: Paulist Press, 2005.

Chapman, J. *Catholic Encyclopaedia; St Maximus of Constantinople,* New York: New Advent, 1911, http://www.newadvent.org/cathen/10078b.htm, (accessed March, 2007).

Christou, P. *Maximus Confessor on the Infinity of Man,* "Maximus Confessor; Acts du Symposium sur Maxime le Confessor, Fribourg, 2-5 September 1980" Fribourg, Suisse: Éditions Universitaires, 1982, http://www.verujem.org/maksim_ispovednik/panayiotis_christou.htm, (accessed June, 2007).

Clark, M. T. *Augustine.* Outstanding Christian Thinkers. London: Continuum, 2000.

Clark, R. S. *A Brief History of Covenant Theology,* 2001, http://www.spindleworks.com/libraryCR/clark.htm, (accessed November, 2007).

Clines, D. J. A. *On the Way to the Postmodern: Old Testament Essays, 1968-1998*. Journal for the Study of the Old Testament - Supplement Series. Sheffield: Sheffield Academic, 1998.

Coakley, S. *Powers and Submissions: Spirituality, Philosophy and Gender.* Challenges in Contemporary Theology. Oxford: Blackwell, 2002.

Cole, G. A. *He Who Gives Life: The Doctrine of the Holy Spirit.* Illinois: Crossway, 2007.

Collins, P. M. *Trinitarian Theology, West and East: Karl Barth, the Cappadocian Fathers and John Zizioulas.* Oxford: Oxford University Press, 2001.

Cooper, A. G. *The Body in St Maximus: Holy Flesh, Wholly Deified.* Oxford: Oxford University Press, 2005.

Coppedge, A. *The God Who Is Triune: Revisioning the Christian Doctrine of God.* Downers Grove: IVP Academic, 2007.

Corpus Thomisticum, Navarre: Fundación Tomás de Aquino Universitatis Studiorum Navarrensis, 2006, http://www.corpusthomisticum.org, (accessed September, 2009).

Craig, W. L. "John Duns Scotus on God's Foreknowledge and Future Contingents", *Franciscan Studies* 46 (1987): 98-122.

Crisp, O. *Jonathan Edwards and the Metaphysics of Sin.* Aldershot: Ashgate, 2005.

Cross, R. *Duns Scotus.* Great Medieval Thinkers. Oxford: Oxford University Press, 1999.

――― *The Metaphysics of the Incarnation: Thomas Aquinas to Duns Scotus.* Oxford: Oxford University Press, 2002.

――― *Duns Scotus on God.* Ashgate Studies in the History of Philosophical Theology. Aldershot: Ashgate, 2005.

Bibliography

— — — "Divine Monarchy in Gregory of Nazianzus", *Journal of Early Christian Studies* 14.1 (2006): 105-116.

Cullen, C. M. *Bonaventure*. Great Medieval Thinkers. New York: Oxford University Press, 2006.

Cullmann, O. *The Christology of the New Testament,* revised edition. Philadelphia: Westminster Press, 1953.

Cunningham, D. S. *These Three are One: The Practice of Trinitarian theology.* Challenges in Contemporary Theology. Oxford: Blackwell Publishers, 1998.

Dahms, J. V. "Johannine Use of Monogenés Reconsidered", *New Testament Studies* 29 (1983): 222-232.

Danaher, W. J. *The Trinitarian Ethics of Jonathan Edwards.* Columbia Series in Reformed theology, 1st edition. Louisville: Westminster John Knox Press, 2004.

Dante Alighieri, *The Paradiso,* trans. J. Ciardi. Signet Classics Series. New York: Signet Classics, 2001.

de Armellada, B. G. *Cristo Crucifado, Dios-Hombre en San Buenaventura,* http://franciscanos.net/teolespir/bernardi4.htm, (accessed September, 2009).

del Colle, R. "The Triune God" in *The Cambridge Companion to Christian Doctrine,* ed. C. E. Gunton. Cambridge Companions to Religion. Cambridge: Cambridge University Press, 1997.

Delio, I. *Simply Bonaventure: An Introduction to His Life, Thought and Writings.* New York: New City Press, 2001.

— — — "Revisiting the Franciscan doctrine of Christ", *Theological Studies* 64.11 (March 1, 2003): 3-23.

Deme, D. *The Christology of Anselm of Canterbury.* Aldershot: Ashgate, 2003.

Dodd, C. H. *The Interpretation of the Fourth Gospel.* Cambridge: Cambridge University Press, 1953.

— — — *More New Testament Studies.* Manchester: Manchester U.P, 1968.

Doyle, R. "The One True Worshiper", *The Briefing* 236 (1999): 6-9.

– – –. *The Spirit of the Father and the Spirit of the Son,* ed. B. G. Webb. vol. Spirit of the Living God, Part 2. Explorations.

Dulles, A. "The Trinity and Christian Unity" in *God the Holy Trinity: Reflections on Christian Faith and Practice,* ed. T. George. Grand Rapids: Baker Academic, 2006.

Dunham, S. A. *The Trinity and Creation in Augustine.* New York: State University of New York Press, 2009.

Dunn, J. D. G. *Christology in the Making: A New Testament Inquiry into the Origins of the Doctrine of the Incarnation,* 2nd edition. London: SCM Press, 1989.

– – – *The Theology of Paul the Apostle.* Grand Rapids: Eerdmans, 2003.

Duns Scotus et al. *R.P.F. Ioannis Duns Scoti, Doctoris Subtilis, Ordinis Minorum, Opera omnia, quæ hucusque reperiri potuerunt.* Lugduni: Sumptibus Laurentii Durand, 1639.

Duns Scotus, J. *Ioannis Duns Scoti Opera Omnia Ordinis Minorum,* ed. J. B. a Campanea, L. Durand & L. Wadding. Paris: Vivès, 1891-1895.

Dwight, S. E. *The Life of President Edwards.* New York: G&C&H Carvill, 1830.

Edmondson, S. *Calvin's Christology.* Cambridge: Cambridge University Press, 2004.

Edwards, J. *An Unpublished Essay on the Trinity,* http://www.ccel.org/ccel/edwards/trinity/files/trinity.html, (accessed March, 2008).

– – – *Treatise on Grace,* http://www.ccel.org/ccel/edwards/grace/files/grace.html, (accessed March, 2008).

Bibliography

– – – *The Works of President Edwards in Four Volumes. A Reprint of the Worcester Edition.,* 4 volumes, 9th edition. New York: Leavitt & Allen, 1856.

– – – *Observations Concerning the Scripture Oeconomy of the Trinity and Covenant of Redemption,* ed. E. C. Smyth. New York: C. Scribner's Sons, 1880.

– – – *The Miscellanies: a - 500,* ed. T. A. Schafer. vol. 13. The Works of Jonathan Edwards Series ed. P. Miller. New Haven: Yale University Press, 1994.

Egan, J. P. "Primal Cause and Trinitarian Perichoresis in Gregory Nazianzen's Oration 31.14" in *Studia Patristica, vol. XXVII, Papers Presented at the Eleventh International Conference on Patristic Studies held in Oxford 1991,* ed. E. A. Livingstone. Louvain: Peeters, 1993.

– – – "αἴτιος/'Author', αἰτία/'Cause' and ἀρχή/'Origin': Synonymns in Selected Texts of Gregory Nazianzen" in *Studia Patristica, vol. XXXII, Papers Presented at the Twelfth International Conference on Patristic Studies held in Oxford 1995,* ed. E. A. Livingstone. Louvain: Peeters, 1997.

Ellingworth, P. *The Epistle to the Hebrews: A Commentary on the Greek Text.* NIGTC. Grand Rapids: Eerdmans, 1993.

Elowsky, J. C. *John 1-10.* vol. 4. Ancient Christian Commentary on Scripture ed. Thomas C. Oden. Downers Grove: IVP, 2006.

Elsee, C. *Neoplatonism in Relation to Christianity; An Essay.* Cambridge: Cambridge University Press, 1908.

Emery, G. *La Trinité Créatrice: Trinité et Création dans les Commentaires aux Sentences de Thomas d'Aquin et de Ses Précurseurs Albert le Grand et Bonaventure.* Bibliothèque Thomiste. Paris: J. Vrin, 1995.

– – – "Essentialism or Personalism in the Treatise on God in Saint Thomas Aquinas", *Thomist* 64 (2000): 521-563.

– – – "Biblical Exegesis and the Speculative of the Doctrine of the Trinity in St. Thomas Aquinas's *Commentary on St. John*" in *Reading John with St. Thomas Aquinas: Theological Exegesis & Speculative Theology,* ed. M.

Dauphinais & M. Levering. Washington: Catholic University of America Press, 2005.

--- *The Trinitarian Theology of Saint Thomas Aquinas,* trans. F. Murphy. Oxford: Oxford University Press, 2007.

Epiphanius *The Panarion of Epiphanius of Salamis,* trans. F. Williams. vol. 35-36. Nag Hammadi studies Nag Hammadi and Manichaean studies ed. J. R. Robinson & H. J. Klimkeit. Leiden: E.J. Brill, 1987.

Erickson, M. J. *God in Three Persons: A Contemporary Interpretation of the Trinity.* Grand Rapids: Baker Academic, 2003.

--- *Who's Tampering with the Trinity?: An Assessment of the Subordination Debate.* Grand Rapids: Kregel, 2009.

Eunomius *Eunomius: The Extant Works,* ed. R. P. Vaggione. Oxford Early Christian Texts ed. H. Chadwick. New York: Clarendon Press, 1987.

Evans, C. S. *Exploring Kenotic Christology: The Self-Emptying of God.* New York: Oxford University Press, 2006.

Evdokimov, P. *Woman and the Salvation of the World: A Christian Anthropology on the Charisms of Women.* Crestwood: St. Vladimir's Seminary Press, 1994.

Farrell, J. P. *Free Choice in Saint Maximus the Confessor.* South Canaan: Saint Tikhon's Seminary Press, 1989.

Farrelly, J. *The Trinity: Rediscovering the Central Christian Mystery.* Oxford: Rowman & Littlefield, 2005.

Fennema, D. A. "John 1.18: 'God the Only Son'", *New Testament Studies* 31 (1985): 124-135.

Fiddes, P. S. *Participating in God: A Pastoral Doctrine of the Trinity.* London: Darton, Longman & Todd, 2000.

Field, R. *Of the Church, Five Bookes. Vol. 5.* Eccles. hist. soc. Cambridge: J.H. Parker, 1850.

Bibliography

Finlan, S. *Problems with Atonement: The Origins of, and Controversy about, the Atonement Doctrine.* Collegeville: Liturgical Press, 2005.

Flavel, J. *The Whole Works of John Flavel: Late Minister of the Gospel at Dartmouth, Devon,* 2 volumes. London: W. Baynes & Son, 1820.

Florovsky, G. *Cur Deus Homo? The Motive of the Incarnation,* http://jbburnett.com/resources/florovsky/3/florovsky_3-6a-curdeushomo.pdf, (accessed November, 2009).

Frost, B. *Saint John of the Cross, 1542-1591, Doctor of Divine Love: An Introduction to his Philosophy, Theology and Spirituality.* London: Hodder & Stoughton, 1937.

Gatiss, L. "The Inexhaustible Fountain of All Good Things: Union with Christ in Calvin on Ephesians", *Themelios* 34.2 (2009): 194-206.

Geanakoplos, D. J. "Some Aspects of the Influence of the Byzantine Maximos the Confessor on the Theology of East and West", *Church History* 38.2 (1969): 150-163.

Gibson, M. "The Beauty of the Redemption of the World: The Theological Aesthetics of Maximus the Confessor and Jonathan Edwards", *Harvard Theological Review* 101.1 (January 2008): 45-76.

Giles, K. *The Trinity & Subordinationism: The Doctrine of God and the Contemporary Gender Debate.* InterVarsity Press, 2002-09.

--- *Jesus and the Father: Modern Evangelicals Reinvent the Doctrine of the Trinity.* Grand Rapids: Zondervan, 2006.

--- "Michael Bird and Robert Shillaker: The Son is Not Eternally Subordinated in Authority to the Father", *Trinity Journal* 30.2 (2009): 257-268.

--- *A Reply to Andrew Moody's 'Review' of Jesus and the Father,* April 2007, http://www.matthiasmedia.com.au/briefing/webextras/a_reply_to_andrew_moodys_review_of_jesus_and_the_father.php, (accessed April, 2007).

Gill, J. *The Council of Florence.* Cambridge: Cambridge University Press, 1959.

Godet, F. L. *Commentary on the Gospel of St. John with a Critical Introduction,* trans. M. D. Cusin & S. Taylor. Clark's Foreign Theological Library, 3rd edition. Edinburgh: T&T Clark, 1889.

Godfrey, A. W. *Medieval Mosaic: A Book of Medieval Latin Readings,* ed. L. H. Keenan. Wauconda: Bolchazy-Carducci Publishers, 2003.

Goodwin, T. *The Works of Thomas Goodwin, D.D., Sometime President of Magdalene College Oxford,* 8 volumes. Edinburgh: James Nichol, 1861.

Gregory of Nyssa & J. Daniélou *From Glory to Glory: Texts from Gregory of Nyssa's Mystical Writings,* trans. H. Musurillo. Crestwood: St. Vladimir's Seminary Press, 1979.

Grenz, S. J. *The Social God and the Relational Self: A Trinitarian Theology of the Imago Dei.* Louisville: Westminster John Knox Press, 2001.

Grillmeier, A. *Christ in Christian Tradition: From the Apostolic Age to Chalcedon (451),* trans. J. S. Bowden. vol. 1. Christ in Christian Tradition, 2nd edition. London: Mowbray, 1975.

Groothuis, R. M. *Sexuality, Spirituality and Feminist Religion,* http://www.ivpress.com/groothuis/rebecca/archives/000043.php#more, (accessed February, 2005).

Grudem, W. A. *Systematic Theology: An Introduction to Biblical Doctrine.* Leicester: IVP, 1994.

Gruenler, R. G. *The Trinity in the Gospel of John: A Thematic Commentary on the Fourth Gospel.* Eugene: Wipf & Stock, 1986.

Gunton, C. E. "The Doctrine of Creation" in *The Cambridge Companion to Christian Doctrine,* ed. C. E. Gunton. Cambridge Companions to Religion. Cambridge: Cambridge University Press, 1997.

– – – *Father, Son and Holy Spirit: Essays Toward a Fully Trinitarian Theology.* London: T&T Clark, 2003.

Bibliography

--- *The Promise of Trinitarian theology,* 2nd edition. Edinburgh: T&T Clark, 2003.

Gwatkin, H. M. *The Arian Controversy,* 2nd edition. Charleston: BiblioBazaar, 2008.

Gwynn, D. M. *The Eusebians: The Polemic of Athanasius of Alexandria and the Construction of the Arian Controversy.* Oxford: Oxford University Press, 2007.

Haines, V. Y. "Felix Culpa" in *A Dictionary of Biblical Tradition in English Literature,* ed. D. L. Jeffrey. Grand Rapids: Eerdmans, 1992.

Hampton, S. W. P. *Anti-Arminians: The Anglican Reformed Tradition from Charles II to George I.* Oxford Theological Monographs. Oxford: Oxford University Press, 2008.

Hankey, W. J. *Re-Christianizing Augustine Postmodern Style: Readings by Jacques Derrida, Robert Dodaro, Jean-Luc Marion, Rowan Williams, Lewis Ayres and John Milbank,* http://www.mun.ca/animus/1997vol2/hankey1.htm#N_81_, (accessed February, 2010).

--- "Dionysius Becomes an Augustinian: Bonaventure's Itinerarium VI" in *Studia Patristica, vol. XXIX, Papers Presented at the Twelfth International Conference on Patristic Studies held in Oxford 1995,* ed. E. A. Livingstone. Louvain: Peeters, 1997.

Hanson, R. P. C. "Biblical Exegesis in the Early Church" in *The Cambridge History of the Bible,* ed. P. R. Ackroyd, C. F. Evans, G. W. H. Lampe & S. L. Greenslade, 1st paperback edition. New York: Cambridge University Press, 1963.

--- *The Search for the Christian Doctrine of God: The Arian Controversy 318-381.* Edinburgh: T&T Clark, 1988.

Hart, D. B. "The Mirror of the Infinite: Gregory of Nyssa on the Vestigia Trinitatis" in *Rethinking Gregory of Nyssa,* ed. S. Coakley. Oxford: Blackwell, 2003.

‎— — — *The Beauty of the Infinite: The Aesthetics of Christian Truth.* Grand Rapids: Eerdmans, 2003.

Hart, T. "How Do We Define the Nature of God's Love?" in *Nothing Greater, Nothing Better: Theological Essays on the Love of God,* ed. K. J. Vanhoozer. Grand Rapids: William B. Eerdmans, 2001.

Harvey, A. E. "Christ as Agent" in *The Glory of Christ in the New Testament: Studies in Christology in Memory of George Bradford Caird,* ed. L. D. Hurst, N. T. Wright & G. B. Caird. New York: Oxford University Press, 1987.

Hauser, A. J. & D. F. Watson (eds), *A History of Biblical Interpretation: The Ancient Period,* vol. 1. Grand Rapids: Eerdmans, 2003.

Hayes, Z. "The Meaning of *Convenientia* in the Metaphysics of St. Bonaventure", *Franciscan Studies* 34 (1974): 74-100.

— — — *The Gift of Being: A Theology of Creation.* New theology Studies. Collegeville: Liturgical Press, 2001.

Healy, N. & D. L. Schindler "For the Life of the World: Hans Urs von Balthasar on the Church as Eucharist" in *The Cambridge Companion to Hans Urs von Balthasar,* ed. E. T. Oakes & D. Moss. Cambridge Companions to Religion. Cambridge: Cambridge University Press, 2004.

Hellmann, J. A. W. & J. M. Hammond *Divine and Created Order in Bonaventure's Theology.* New York: Franciscan Institute, 2001.

Helm, P. *John Calvin's Ideas.* Oxford: Oxford University Press, 2004.

Hengstenberg, E. W. *Commentary on the Gospel of St John.* vol. 5, 7. Clark's Foreign Theological Library ser. 4. Edinburgh: T&T Clark, 1865.

Hennesey, K. "An Answer to de Regnon's Accusers: Why we should not speak of "his" paradigm", *Harvard Theological Review* 100.2 (2007): 179-197.

Hodgson, L. *The Doctrine of the Trinity.* The Croall Lectures 1942-1943. London: Nisbet, 1944.

Bibliography

Holmes, S. R. *God of Grace and God of Glory: An Account of the Theology of Jonathan Edwards.* Edinburgh: T&T Clark, 2000.

--- "Reformed Varieties of the Communication Idiomatum" in *The Person of Christ,* ed. M. Rae & S. R. Holmes. New York: T&T Clark, 2005.

Hopko, T. "Women and the Priesthood: Reflections on the Debate - 1983" in *Women and the Priesthood,* ed. T. Hopko. Crestwood: St. Vladimir's Seminary Press, 1999.

Horton, M. S. *Lord and Servant: A Covenant Christology.* Louisville: Westminster John Knox Press, 2005.

--- *Covenant and Salvation: Union with Christ.* Louisville: Westminster, John Knox, 2007.

Hughes, P. E. *The True Image: The Origin and Destiny of Man in Christ.* Grand Rapids: Eerdmans, 1989.

Hunt, A. *The Trinity and the Paschal Mystery: A Development in Recent Catholic Theology.* New Theology Studies. Collegeville: Liturgical Press, 1997.

--- *What Are They Saying About the Trinity.* New York: Paulist Press, 1998.

--- "Trinity and Paschal Mystery: Divine Communion and Human Conversation" in *Theology and Conversation: Towards a Relational Theology,* ed. J. Haers & P. d. Mey. Bibliotheca Ephemeridum Theologicarum Lovaniensium. Leuven: Leuven University Press, 2003.

--- "Trinity and Church: Explorations in Ecclesiology from a Trinitarian Perspective", *St Mark's Theological Review* 158.1 (2005): 32-44.

--- *Trinity: Nexus of the Mysteries of Christian Faith.* Maryknoll: Orbis Books, 2005.

--- *The Trinity: Insights from the Mystics.* Collegeville: Liturgical Press, 2010.

Hurtado, L. W. *One God, One Lord: Early Christian Devotion and Ancient Jewish Monotheism.* Philadelphia: Fortress Press, 1988.

– – – *At the Origins of Christian Worship: The Context and Character of Earliest Christian Devotion.* Grand Rapids: Eerdmans, 2000.

– – – *How on Earth did Jesus Become a God?: Historical Questions about Earliest Devotion to Jesus.* Grand Rapids: Eerdmans, 2005.

Jenson, R. W. *Systematic Theology,* 2 volumes. New York: Oxford University Press, 1997.

– – – "The Church and the Sacraments" in *The Cambridge Companion to Christian Doctrine,* ed. C. E. Gunton. Cambridge Companions to Religion. Cambridge: Cambridge University Press, 1997.

– – – "God's Time, Our Time: An Interview with Robert W. Jenson", *The Christian Century* 123.9 (2007): 31-35.

Jewett, P. K. *Man as Male and Female: A Study in Sexual Relationships from a Theological Point of View.* Grand Rapids: Eerdmans, 1975.

John Duns Scotus, *God and Creatures; the Quodlibetal Questions,* trans. F. Alluntis and A. B. Wolter. Princeton: Princeton University Press, 1975.

John of the Cross, *The Collected Works of John of the Cross: Romances,* ICS Publications, http://www.carmelite.com/saints/john/works/p_10.htm, (accessed November, 2007).

– – – *The Poems of Saint John of the Cross,* trans. W. Barnstone. New York: New Directions, 1972.

Johnson, E. A. *She Who Is: The Mystery of God in Feminist Theological Discourse.* New York: Crossroad, 1992.

Jones, D. *Synergy in Christ According to Saint Maximus the Confessor,* 2005, http://energeticprocession.files.wordpress.com/2007/02/synergy-in-christ-according-to-saint-maximus-the-confessor.doc, (accessed March, 2007).

Bibliography

Jones, M. *Why Heaven Kissed Earth: The Christology of the Puritan Reformed Orthodox Theologian, Thomas Goodwin (1600-1680)*. Göttingen: Vandenhoeck & Ruprecht, 2010.

Jowers, D. W. *The Trinitarian Axiom of Karl Rahner: The Economic Trinity is the Immanent Trinity and Vice Versa.* Lewiston: Edwin Mellen Press, 2006.

Jüngel, E. *God's Being is in Becoming: The Trinitarian Being of God in the Theology of Karl Barth, a Paraphrase,* trans. J. Webster, 2nd English edition. Edinburgh: T&T Clark, 2001.

Jungwirth, P. *Maximus Study Guide,* http://9stmaryrd.com/shared/st_maximus_intro.pdf, (accessed April, 2007).

Kallistos of Diokleia "Man, Woman and the Priesthood of Christ" in *Women and the Priesthood,* ed. T. Hopko. Crestwood: St. Vladimir's Seminary Press, 1999.

Kannengiesser, C. "(Ps. -) Athanasius, Ad Afros Examined" in *Logos: Festschrift für Luise Abramowski zum 8. Juli 1993,* ed. L. Abramowski, H. C. Brennecke, E. L. Grasmück & C. Markschies. Beihefte zur Zeitschrift für die neutestamentliche Wissenschaft und die Kunde der älteren Kirche. Berlin: Walter de Gruyter, 1993.

Kelly, J. N. D. *Early Christian Doctrines,* 5th edition. London: Continuum International Publishing Group, 2000.

--- *Early Christian Creeds.* London: Continuum International Publishing Group, 2006.

Kelly, J. N. D. *The Athanasian Creed.* Edinburgh: Adam and Charles Black, 1964.

Kerr, F. *After Aquinas: Versions of Thomism.* Oxford: Blackwell, 2002.

Kilby, K. "Perichoresis and Projection: Problems with Social Doctrines of the Trinity", *New Blackfriars* 81.957 (November 2000): 432-445.

Kinzig, W. *In Search of Asterius: Studies on the Homilies on the Psalms.* vol. 47. Forschungen zur Kirchen- und Dogmengeschichte. Göttingen: Vandenhoeck & Ruprecht, 1990.

Knight, G. W. *The New Testament Teaching on the Role Relationship of Men and Women.* Grand Rapids: Baker Book House, 1977.

Knox, D. B. *The Everlasting God,* reprint edition. Homebush: Lancer Books, 1992.

Kretzmann, N. "A General Problem of Creation: Why Would God Create Anything at All?" in *Being and Goodness: The Concept of the Good in Metaphysics and Philosophical Theology,* ed. S. C. MacDonald. London: Cornell University Press, 1991.

La Due, W. J. *The Trinity Guide to the Trinity.* Harrisburg: Trinity Press International, 2003.

LaCugna, C. M. *God for Us: The Trinity and Christian Life,* 1st edition. San Francisco: Harper, 1991.

Ladd, G. E. *A Commentary on the Revelation of John.* Grand Rapids: Eerdmans, 1972.

Leftow, B. "Anti Social Trinitarianism" in *The Trinity: An Interdisciplinary Symposium on the Trinity,* ed. S. T. Davis, D. Kendall & G. O'Collins. Oxford: Oxford University Press, 1999.

Letham, R. *John Owen's Doctrine of the Trinity in its Catholic Context and its Significance for Today,* http://www.johnowen.org/media/letham_owen.pdf, (accessed January, 2008).

--- *The Holy Trinity: In Scripture, History, Theology, and Worship.* Phillipsburg: P&R, 2004.

Levering, M. *Christ and the Catholic Priesthood: Ecclesial Hierarchy and the Pattern of the Trinity.* Chicago: HillenbrandBooks, 2010.

Lewis, C. S. *God in the Dock: Essays on Theology and Ethics.* Grand Rapids: Eerdmans, 1970.

Bibliography

––– *The Last Battle,* reprint edition. Harmondsworth: Penguin Books, 1971.

––– *The Discarded Image: An Introduction to Medieval and Renaissance Literature.* Cambridge: Cambridge University Press, 1994.

Lightfoot, R. H. *St. John's Gospel: A Commentary,* ed. C. F. Evans, revised edition. Oxford: Clarendon Press, 1956.

Lonergan, B. J. F. & M. G. Shields *The Ontological and Psychological Constitution of Christ.* London: Lonergan Research Institute, University of Toronto Press, 2002.

Lonergan, B. J. F. *The Triune God: Systematics,* trans. M. G. Sheilds, ed. R. M. Doran & D. Monsour. Toronto: Lonergan Research Institute/University of Toronto Press, 2007.

Long, T. G. *Hebrews.* Interpretation Commentary Series. Louisville: John Knox Press, 1997.

Lossky, V. *The Mystical Theology of the Eastern Church.* London: James Clarke & Co, 1957.

Louth, A. *Maximus the Confessor.* Early Church Fathers. NewYork: Routledge, 1996.

–––, review of *Persons in Communion: Trinitarian Description and Human Participation* by A. Torrance, *Heythrop Journal* 42.4, (2001): 529-530

Louth, A. & M. Conti *Genesis 1-11.* vol. 1. Ancient Christian Commentary on Scripture ed. Thomas C. Oden. Downers Grove: IVP, 2001.

Lovejoy, A. O. *The Great Chain of Being: A Study of the History of an Idea.* William James Lectures. Cambridge: Harvard University Press, 1964.

Ludlow, M. *Gregory of Nyssa: Ancient and (Post)modern.* Oxford: Oxford University Press, 2007.

Lukken, G. *Original Sin in the Roman Liturgy. Research into the Theology of Original Sin in the Roman Sacramentaria and the Early Baptismal Liturgy.* Leiden: Brill, 1973.

Macquarrie, J. *Twentieth-Century Religious Thought: The Frontiers of Philosophy and Theology, 1900-1960.* New York: Harper & Row, 1963.

Malina, B. J. *Windows on the World of Jesus: Time Travel to Ancient Judea,* 1st edition. Louisville: Westminster/John Knox Press, 1993.

– – – *The Social World of Jesus and the Gospels.* New York: Routledge, 1996.

Malina, B. J. & J. J. Pilch *Social-science Commentary on the Book of Revelation.* Minneapolis: Fortress Press, 2000.

Marshall, B. "Ex Occidente Lux: Aquinas and Eastern Orthodox Theology" in *Aquinas in Dialogue: Thomas for the Twenty-First Century,* ed. J. Fodor & F. C. Bauerschmidt. Directions in Modern Theology. Oxford: Blackwell, 2004.

Martin, F. & T. C. Oden *Acts.* vol. 5. Ancient Christian Commentary on Scripture ed. Thomas C. Oden. Downers Grove: IVP, 2006.

Martin, S. H., "Freedom to Obey: the Obedience of Christ as the Reflection of the Obedience of the Son in Karl Barth's *Church Dogmatics*". Unpublished Ph.D. dissertation, University of St Andrews, 2008.

Maximus the Confessor *The Disputation with Pyrrhus of Our Father Among the Saints Maximus the Confessor,* trans. J. P. Farrell. South Canaan: Saint Tikhon's Seminary Press, 1992.

McClymond, M. J. "Salvation as Divinization: Jonathan Edwards, Gregory Palamas and the Theological Uses of Neoplatonism" in *Jonathan Edwards: Philosophical Theologian,* ed. P. Helm & O. D. Crisp. Aldershot: Ashgate Publishing Limited, 2003.

McCormack, B. *Reformed Christology and the Westminster HTFC Report,* "*Finitum non Capax Infiniti*" 20 May 2008, http://aboulet.com/2008/05/20/reformed-christology-and-the-westminster-htfc-report/, (accessed February, 2010).

– – – "Grace and Being: The Role of God's Gracious Election in Karl Barth's Theological Ontology" in *The Cambridge Companion to Karl Barth,* ed. J. B. Webster. Cambridge Companions to Religion. New York: Cambridge University Press, 2000.

Bibliography

– – – "Grace and Being: The role of God's Gracious Election in Karl Barth's Theological Ontology" in *The Cambridge Companion to Karl Barth,* ed. J. B. Webster. Cambridge Companions to Religion. New York: Cambridge University Press, 2000.

McCoy, C. S., J. W. Baker & H. Bullinger *Fountainhead of Federalism: Heinrich Bullinger and the Covenantal Tradition,* 1st edition. Louisville: Westminster/John Knox Press, 1991.

McFarland, I. A. "'Naturally and by Grace': Maximus the Confessor on the Operation of the Will", *Scottish Journal of Theology* 58.4 (2005): 410-433.

– – – "'Willing is not Choosing': Some Anthropological Implications of Dyothelite Christology", *IJST* 9.1 (2007): 3-23.

McGuckin, J. A. *St. Gregory of Nazianzus: An Intellectual Biography.* Crestwood: St. Vladimir's Seminary Press, 2001.

– – – *St. Cyril of Alexandria: The Christological Controversy: Its History, Theology, and Texts*. Crestwood: St. Vladimir's Seminary Press, 2004.

Meijering, E. P. *Orthodoxy and Platonism in Athanasius. Synthesis or Antithesis,* corrected reprint edition. Leiden: E. J. Brill, 1974.

– – – "Athanasius on the Father as Origin of the Son" in *God Being History: Studies in Patristic Philosophy,*. New York: American Elsevier Pub. Co, 1975.

– – – "The Doctrine of the Will and of the Trinity in the Orations of Gregory of Nazianzus" in *God Being History: Studies in Patristic Philosophy,*. New York: American Elsevier Pub. Co, 1975.

Meijering, E. P. & J. C. M. van Winden *Hilary of Poitiers on the Trinity: De Trinitate 1, 1-19, 2, 3.* vol. 6. Philosophia Patrum. Leiden: Brill, 1982.

Merrill, E. H. "Image of God" in *Dictionary of the Old Testament: Pentateuch,* ed. T. D. Alexander & D. W. Baker. Downers Grove: IVP, 2003.

Meyendorff, J. *Byzantine Theology: Historical Trends and Doctrinal Themes,* 1st edition. New York: Fordham University Press, 1974.

Meyer, J. R. "God's Trinitarian Substance in Athanasian Theology", *Scottish Journal of Theology* 59.1 (2006): 81-97.

Middleton, J. R. *The Liberating Image: The Imago Dei in Genesis 1.* Grand Rapids: Brazos Press, 2005.

Migne, J. P. *Patrologiae Latina,* 217 volumes. Paris: Migne, 1844-1855.

– – – *Patrologiae Graeca,* 162 volumes. Paris: Migne, 1857-1866.

Milbank, J. *The Word Made Strange: Theology, Language, Culture.* Oxford: Blackwell, 1997.

Milbank, J., G. Ward & C. Pickstock *Radical Orthodoxy: A New Theology.* London: Routledge, 1999.

Milbank, J. *The Suspended Middle: Henri de Lubac and the Debate Concerning the Supernatural.* London: SCM Press, 2005.

Molnar, P. *Divine Freedom and the Doctrine of the Immanent Trinity: In Dialogue with Karl Barth and Contemporary Theology.* Edinburgh: T&T Clark, 2002.

– – – "Can the Electing God be God Without Us? Some Implications of Bruce McCormack's Understanding of Barth's Doctrine of Election for the Doctrine of the Trinity", *Neue Zeitschrift für Systematische Theologie und Religionsphilosophie* 49.2 (2007): 199-222.

Moltmann, J. & M. Kohl *The Trinity and the Kingdom of God,* trans. M. Kohl. London: SCM, 1981.

Moltmann, J. *The Spirit of Life: A Universal Affirmation,* trans. M. Kohl. London: SCM, 1992.

– – – *The Crucified God: The Cross of Christ as the Foundation and Criticism of Christian Theology,* trans. R. A. Wilson & J. Bowden. SCM classics. London: SCM, 2001.

Bibliography

– – – "God in the World - The World in God: Perichoresis in Trinity and Eschatology" in *The Gospel of John and Christian Theology,* ed. R. Bauckham & C. Mosser. Grand Rapids: Eerdmans, 2008.

Moody, A. *Relational Subordination in the Trinity: A continuation of the discussion emerging from Kevin Giles' books "The Trinity and Subordinationism" and "Jesus and the Father.",* http://ajmd.com.au/trinity/jatf.htm#L2, (accessed March, 2010).

– – – "The Hidden Center: Trinity and Incarnation in the Negative (and Positive) Theology of Rowan Williams" in *On Rowan Williams: Critical Essays,* ed. M. Russell. Oregon: Wipf & Stock, 2009.

Moody, D. "God's Only Son: The Translation of John 3:16 in the Revised Standard Version", *JBL* 72 (1953): 213-219.

Moonan, L. *Divine Power: The Medieval Power Distinction up to its Adoption by Albert, Bonaventure, and Aquinas.* Oxford: Clarendon Press, 1994.

Morris, L. *The Biblical Doctrine of Judgment,* 1st edition. London: Tyndale Press, 1960.

– – – *The Gospel According to John.* New International Commentary on the New Testament, revised edition. Grand Rapids: Eerdmans, 1995.

Mounce, R. H. *The Book of Revelation,* revised edition. Grand Rapids: Eerdmans, 1998.

Muller, R. A. *The Rise and Development of Reformed Orthodoxy, ca. 1520 to ca. 1725.* vol. 4. Post-Reformation Reformed Dogmatics, 2nd edition. Grand Rapids: Baker Academics, 2003.

Neri, F. *Cur Verbum Capax Hominis: Le Ragioni dell'incarnazione della Seconda Persona della Trinitá fra Teologia Scolastica e Teologia Contemporanea.* Rome: Editrice Pontificia Università Gregoriana, 1999.

Nichols, A. *The Word Has Been Abroad: A Guide through Balthasar's Aesthetics.* Edinburgh: T&T Clark, 1998.

– – – *Light from the East: Authors and Themes in Orthodox Theology.* London: Sheed & Ward, 1999.

Nichols, T. L. *That All May be One: Hierarchy and Participation in the Church.* Collegeville: Liturgical Press, 1997.

Noble, T. A. "Paradox in Gregory Nazianzen's Doctrine of the Trinity" in *Studia Patristica, vol. XXVII, Papers Presented at the Eleventh International Conference on Patristic Studies held in Oxford 1991,* ed. E. A. Livingstone. Louvain: Peeters, 1993.

O'Collins, G. "The Holy Trinity: The State of the Questions" in *The Trinity: An Interdisciplinary Symposium on the Trinity,* ed. S. T. Davis, D. Kendall & G. O'Collins. Oxford: Oxford University Press, 1999.

O'Hanlon, G. F. *The Immutability of God in the Theology of Hans Urs von Balthasar.* Cambridge: Cambridge University Press, 1990.

O'Reagan, C. "Balthasar and Gnostic Genealogy", *Modern Theology* 22.4 (2004): 609-650.

Oakes, E. T. "'He Descended into Hell': The Depths of God's Self-Emptying Love on Holy Saturday in the Thought of Hans Urs von Balthasar" in *Exploring Kenotic Christology: The Self-Emptying of God,* ed. C. S. Evans. New York: Oxford University Press, 2006.

Oberman, H. A. *The Dawn of the Reformation: Essays in Late Medieval and Early Reformation Thought.* Grand Rapids: Eerdmans, 1992.

Olson, R. E. *The Story of Christian Theology: Twenty Centuries of Tradition & Reform.* Downers Grove: IVP, 1999.

Olson, R. E. & C. A. Hall *The Trinity.* Guides to Theology. Grand Rapids: Eerdmans, 2002.

Osborne, C. "Literal or Metaphorical? Some Issues of Language in the Arian Controversy" in *Christian faith and Greek philosophy in Late Antiquity: Essays in Tribute to George Christopher Stead. In Celebration of his Eightieth Birthday, 9th April 1993,* ed. L. R. H. Wickham, C. P. Bammel, E. C. D. Hunter & C. Stead. Supplements to Vigiliae Christianae. Leiden: Brill, 1993.

Bibliography

– – – *Eros Unveiled: Plato and the God of Love.* Oxford: Clarendon Press, 1994.

Osborne, K. B. *A Theology of the Church for the Third Millennium: A Franciscan Approach.* Boston: Brill, 2009.

Otto, R. E. "The Use and Abuse of Perichoresis in Recent Theology", *Scottish Journal of Theology* 54.3 (2001): 366-384.

Owen, J. *Exposition of the Epistle to the Hebrews with the Preliminary Exercitations.* vol. 1, 4 volumes. Boston: Samuel T. Armstrong, 1811.

Owen, J. & W. Orme *The Works of John Owen,* ed. T. Russell, 21 volumes. London: Richard Baynes, 1826.

Packer, J. I. *Introduction: On Covenant Theology,* http://www.gospelpedlar.com/articles/Bible/cov_theo.html, (accessed May, 2008).

– – – "Universalism: Will Everyone Ultimately be Saved" in *Hell under Fire: Modern Scholarship Reinvents Eternal Punishment,* ed. C. W. Morgan & R. A. Peterson. Grand Rapids: Zondervan, 2004.

Pannenberg, W. *Jesus - God and Man,* trans. L. L. P. Wilkins, Duane A. London: SCM, 1968.

– – – *Systematic Theology,* trans. G. W. Bromiley, 3 volumes. Grand Rapids: Eerdmans, 1988.

Parvis, S. *Marcellus of Ancyra and the Lost Years of the Arian Controversy 325-345.* Oxford Early Christian Studies. New York: Oxford University Press, 2006.

Pauw, A. P. "'One Alone Cannot be Excellent': Edwards on Divine Simplicity" in *Jonathan Edwards: Philosophical Theologian,* ed. P. Helm & O. D. Crisp. Aldershot: Ashgate,

– – – *The Supreme Harmony of All: The Trinitarian Theology of Jonathan Edwards.* Grand Rapids: Eerdmans, 2002.

Payne, S. *John of the Cross and the Cognitive Value of Mysticism: An Analysis of the Sanjuanist Teaching and its Philosophical Implications for Contemporary Discussions of Mystical Experience.* Dordrecht: Kluwer, 1990.

Pelikan, J. *A History of the Development of Doctrine.* vol. 5. The Christian Tradition, 5 volumes, paperback edition. Chicago: University of Chicago Press, 1971.

– – – *The Spirit of Eastern Christendom (600-1700).* vol. 2. The Christian Tradition: A History of the Development of Doctrine, 5 volumes. Chicago: University of Chicago Press, 1971.

– – – *The Growth of Medieval Theology (600-1300).* vol. 3. The Christian Tradition: A History of the Development of Doctrine, 5 volumes. Chicago: University of Chicago Press, 1971.

Pelland, G. "La "Subjectio" du Christ Chez Saint Hilaire", *Gregorianum Roma* 64.3 (1983): 423-452.

Peters, T. *God as Trinity: Relationality and Temporality in Divine Life,* 1st edition. Louisville: Westminster, 1993.

Phillips, W. G. "An Apologetic Study of John 10:34-36", *Bibliotheca Sacra* 146 (1989): 405-419.

Piper, J. & W. A. Grudem (eds), *Recovering Biblical Manhood and Womanhood: A Response to Evangelical Feminism.* Wheaton: Crossway, 1991.

Pitstick, A. L. *Light in Darkness: Hans Urs von Balthasar and the Catholic Doctrine of Christ's Descent into Hell.* Grand Rapids: Eerdmans, 2007.

Plantinga, C. "Social Trinity and Tritheism" in *Trinity, Incarnation and Atonement: Philosophical and Theological Essays,* ed. R. J. Feenstra & C. Plantinga. Notre Dame: University of Notre Dame Press, 1989.

Prestige, G. L. *God in Patristic Thought.* vol. 7. SPCK large paperbacks. London: SPCK, 1977.

Puosi, E. *I Am Love.* Longwood: Xulon Press, 2007.

Bibliography

Rahner, K. *Theological Investigations,* trans. C. Ernst. vol. 1, 23 volumes. London: Longman & Todd, 1961.

--- *The Trinity,* trans. J. Donceel. London: William Clowes & Son, 1970.

--- *Foundations of Christian Faith: An Introduction to the Idea of Christianity,* trans. W. V. Dych. London: Darton Longman & Todd Ltd, 1978.

Ramsey, B. *Ambrose.* Early Church Fathers. London: Routledge, 1997.

Ratzinger, J. *Church, Ecumenism and Politics: New Essays in Ecclesiology.* New York: Crossroad, 1988.

--- *Christian Brotherhood.* London: Burns & Oates, 2006.

--- *The God of Jesus Christ: Meditations on the Triune God.* San Francisco: Ignatius Press, 2008.

--- "God's Word More Stable Than Any Human Reality: Address from the opening day of the Synod, Monday, 6 October [2008], during the Liturgy of the Hours celebration of the Third Hour", *L'Osservatore Romano, Weekly Edition in English* (October 8, 2008): 5.

Ratzinger, J. C. *Behold the Pierced One,* trans. G. H. Ignatius. San Francisco: Ignatius Press, 1986.

Rhee, J. S. *A History of the Doctrine of Eternal Generation of the Son and its Significance in Trinitarianism,* http://www.jsrhee.com/QA/thesis1.htm, (accessed January, 2010).

Richard of St Victor *Richard of St Victor: The Twelve Patriarchs; The Mystical Ark; Book Three of The Trinity,* trans. G. Zinn. Classics of Western Spirituality, paperback edition. New York: Paulist Press, 1979.

Rikhof, H. "Aquinas' Authority in the Contemporary Theology of the Trinity" in *Aquinas as Authority: A Collection of Studies Presented at the Second Conference of the Thomas Instituut te Utrecht, December 14-16, 2000,* ed. P. v. Geest, H. J. M. J. Goris & C. Leget. Publications of the Thomas Instituut te Utrecht. Leuven: Peeters, 2002.

Roberts, A., J. Donaldson & A. C. Coxe *The Ante-Nicene Fathers: Translations of the Writings of the Fathers Down to A.D. 325* ed. Schaff, Philip. Grand Rapids: Eerdmans, 1989.

Roeber, A. G. "Western, Eastern, or Global Orthodoxy? Some Reflections on St. Augustine of Hippo in Recent Literature", *Pro Ecclesia* 16 (2008): 210-223.

Rombs, K. "Gregory Nyssa's Doctrine of Epektasis: Some Logical Implications" in *Papers Presented at the Thirteenth International Conference on Patristic Studies Held in Oxford, 1999,* ed. W. F. Wiles, E. Yarnold & P. M. Parvis. Leuven: Peeters, 2001.

Rosemann, P. W. *Peter Lombard.* Great Medieval Thinkers. Oxford: Oxford University Press, 2004.

Rowe, W. L. *Can God be Free?.* Oxford: Clarendon Press, 2004.

Sanders, F. *The Image of the Immanent Trinity: Rahner's Rule and the Theological interpretation of Scripture.* vol. 12. Issues in Systematic Theology. New York: Peter Lang, 2005.

– – – *The Deep Things of God: How the Trinity Changes Everything.* Illinois: Crossway, 2010.

– – – , "The State of the Doctrine of the Trinity in Evangelical Theology", (Paper presented at the 2004 Annual Meeting of the Evangelical Theological Society, Nov. 18, 2004)

Sauvage, G. "Appropriations" in *The Catholic Encyclopedia,.* New York: Robert Appleton Company, 1907.

Schaff, P. *The Evangelical Protestant Creeds, with Translations.* vol. 3. The Creeds of Christendom with a History and Critical Notes, 3 volumes, 6th edition. New York: Harper & Brothers, 1877.

Schaff, P. (ed), *A Select Library of the Nicene and Post-Nicene Fathers of the Christian Church.* two series, 28 volumes. Edinburgh: T&T Clark, 1895.

Schemm, P. R. "Kevin Giles' The Trinity and Subordinationism: A Review Article", *Journal for Biblical Manhood & Womanhood* 7.2 (2002): 67-78.

Bibliography

Schmemann, A. *Church, World, Mission: Reflections on Orthodoxy in the West.* Crestwood: St. Vladimir's Seminary Press, 1979.

Schreiner, T. R. "Head Coverings, Prophecies and the Trinity" in *Recovering Biblical Manhood and Womanhood: A Response to Evangelical Feminism,* ed. J. Piper & W. A. Grudem. Wheaton: Crossway, 1991.

Scott Clark, R. *A Friendly Response to Bruce McCormack,* "Heidelblog" May 23, 2008, http://heidelblog.wordpress.com/2008/05/23/a-friendly-response-to-bruce-mccormack/, (accessed February, 2010).

Sheppard, J. *Christendom at the Crossroads: The Medieval Era.* Louisville: Westminster John Knox Press, 2005.

Shortt, R. *God's Advocates: Christian Thinkers in Conversation.* London: Darton, Longman & Todd, 2005.

Sibbes, R. *The Complete Works of Richard Sibbes, D.D,* ed. A. B. Grosart. Nichol's Series of Standard Divines. Puritan Period. Edinburgh: J. Nichol, 1863.

Simonetti, M. *La Crisi Ariana Nel IV Secolo.* vol. 11. Studia Ephemeridis Augustinianum. Rome: Institutum Patristicum Augustinianum, 1975.

Smail, T. A. "In the Image of the Triune God", *IJST* 5.1 (2003): 22-32.

--- "The Holy Spirit in the Trinity" in *Nicene Christianity: The Future for a New Ecumenism,* ed. C. R. Seitz. Grand Rapids: Brazos Press, 2001.

--- *Like Father, Like Son: The Trinity Imaged in Our Humanity.* Grand Rapids: Eerdmans, 2006.

Smith, R. A. *The Eternal Covenant: How the Trinity Reshapes Covenant Theology.* Moscow: Canon Press, 2003.

Smith, T. L. *Thomas Aquinas' Trinitarian Theology: A Study in Theological Method.* Washington: Catholic University of America Press, 2003.

Spence, A. "Christ's Humanity and Ours: John Owen" in *Persons, Divine and Human: King's College Essays in Theological Anthropology,* ed. C. E. Gunton & C. Schwöbel. Edinburgh: T&T Clark, 1999.

– – – *Incarnation and Inspiration: John Owen and the Coherence of Christology.* T&T Clark Theology. London: T&T Clark, 2007.

Spijker, W. v. t. *The Ecclesiastical Offices in the Thought of Martin Bucer,* trans. J. Vriend. vol. v. 57. Studies in Medieval and Reformation Thought. Leiden: Brill, 1996.

Stead, C. *Divine Substance.* Oxford: Clarendon Press, 1977.

– – – "The Freedom of the Will and the Arian Controversy" in *Substance and illusion in the Christian Fathers,* ed. C. Stead. Collected studies. London: Variorum Reprints, 1985.

– – – "Why Not Three Gods? The Logic of Gregory of Nyssa's Trinitarian Doctrine" in *Studien zu Gregor von Nyssa und Der Christlichen Spätantike,* ed. H. R. Drobner & C. Klock. Supplements to Vigiliae Christianae. Leiden: Brill, 1990.

Steinmetz, D. C. *Calvin in Context.* New York: Oxford University Press, 1995.

Stewart, A. "Heinrich Bullinger, The First Covenant Theologian", *British Reformed Journal* 39 (2001): 18-26.

Strachan, R. H. *The Fourth Gospel: Its Significance and Environment,* 3rd & revised edition. London: SCM, 1941.

Studebaker, S. M., review of *The Supreme Harmony of All: The Trinitarian Theology of Jonathan Edwards* by A. Plantinga Pauw, *Fides et Historia.* Terre Haute 36.1, (2004): 156

Sullivan, J. E. *The Image of God. The Doctrine of St. Augustine and its Influence.* Dubuque: The Priory Press, 1963.

Swinburne, R. "Could There Be More Than One God?", *Faith and Philosophy* 5.3 (1988): 225-241.

Bibliography

Tanner, K. *Jesus, Humanity and the Trinity: A Brief Systematic Theology.* Scottish Journal of Theology, Current Issues in Theology. Edinburgh: T&T Clark, 2001.

Temple, W. *Christus Veritas: An Essay.* London: Macmillan, 1925.

Tertullian *Qu. Sept. Flor. Tertulliani Opera ad Optimorum Librorum Fidem Expressa, Pars IV,* ed. E. F. Leopold. vol. 4. Bibliotheca Patrum Ecclesiasticorum Latinorum Selecta: Ad Optimorum Liborum Fidem, 7 volumes ed. Gersdorf, E. G. Lipsiae: Tauchnitz, 1841.

Thiselton, A. C. *The First Epistle to the Corinthians: A Commentary on the Greek Text.* NIGTC. Grand Rapids: Eerdmans, 2000.

--- *The Hermeneutics of Doctrine.* Grand Rapids: Eerdmans, 2007.

Thomas Aquinas, *On the Truth of the Catholic Faith: Summa Contra Gentiles,* trans. C. O'Neil, ed. J. Kenny. New York: Hanover House, 1955.

--- *Commentary on the Gospel of St. John,* trans. J. A. L. Weisheipl, Fabian R. vol. 4. Aquinas Scripture Series. Albany: Magi Books, 1980.

--- *The Incarnate Word (3a. 1-6),* trans. R. J. Hennessey. vol. 48. Summa Theologiae, 61 volumes, paperback edition. Cambridge: Cambridge University Press, 2006.

--- *Father, Son and Holy Ghost (Ia. 33-43),* trans. T. C. O'Brien. vol. 7. Summa Theologiae, 61 volumes, paperback edition. Cambridge: Cambridge University Press, 2006.

--- *Creation, Variety, and Evil (1a.44-49),* trans. T. Gilby. vol. 8. Summa Theologiae, 61 volumes, paperback edition. Cambridge: Cambridge University Press, 2006.

Thompson, J. *Modern Trinitarian Perspectives.* New York: Oxford University Press, 1994.

Thompson, M. M. *The God of the Gospel of John.* Grand Rapids: Eerdmans, 2001.

Thornton, L. S. *Conduct and the Supernatural: Being the Norrisian Prize Essay for the year 1913*. London: Longmans, Green & Co, 1915.

Thunberg, L. & A. M. Allchin *Microcosm and Mediator: The Theological Anthropology of Maximus the Confessor,* 2nd edition. Chicago: Open Court, 1995.

Tollefsen, T. *The Christocentric Cosmology of St Maximus the Confessor.* Oxford Early Christian Studies. Oxford: Oxford University Press, 2008.

Törönen, M. *Union and Distinction in the Thought of St. Maximus the Confessor.* Oxford Early Christian Studies. Oxford: Oxford University Press, 2007.

Torrance, T. F. *Theology in Reconciliation: Essays Towards Evangelical and Catholic Unity in East and West,* American edition. Grand Rapids: Eerdmans, 1976.

– – – *The Trinitarian Faith: The Evangelical Theology of the Ancient Catholic Church.* Edinburgh: T&T Clark, 1988.

– – – *Trinitarian Perspectives: Toward Doctrinal Agreement.* Edinburgh: T&T Clark, 1994.

Torrance, T. F. *The Christian Doctrine of God, One Being Three Persons.* Edinburgh: T&T Clark, 1996.

Tozer, A. W. *The Knowledge of the Holy,* reprint (original 1961) edition. Carlisle: Authentic, 2008.

Trueman, C. R. *John Owen: Reformed Catholic, Renaissance Man.* Great Theologians Series. Aldershot: Ashgate, 2007.

Turcescu, L. "'Personal' versus 'Individual', and Other Misreadings of Gregory of Nyssa", *Modern Theology* 18 (2002): 527-539.

van Asselt, W. J. *The Federal Theology of Johannes Cocceius (1603-1669),* trans. R. A. Blacketer. Studies in the History of Christian Thought. Leiden: Brill, 2001.

Bibliography

van den Brink, G. *Almighty God: A Study of the Doctrine of Divine Omnipotence.* vol. 7. Studies in Philosophical Theology. Kampen: Kok Pharos, 1993.

van Rossum, J. "The Logoi of Creation and the Divine 'Energies' in Maximus the Confessor and Gregory Palamas" in *Papers Presented at the Eleventh International Conference on Patristic Studies, 1991,* ed. E. A. Livingstone. Leuven: Peeters, 1993.

Volf, M. *After Our Likeness: The Church as the Image of the Trinity.* Sacra Doctrina. Grand Rapids: Eerdmans, 1998.

von Balthasar, H. U. *Prayer,* trans. A. V. Littledale. New York: Sheed & Ward, 1961.

– – – *First Glance at Adrienne von Speyr.* San Francisco: Ignatius Press, 1981.

– – – *Theo-drama,* trans. G. Harrison, 5 volumes. San Francisco: Ignatius Press, 1988.

– – – *Explorations in Theology,* trans. A. V. Littledale, A. Dru & B. McNeil, 4 volumes. San Francisco: Ignatius Press, 1989.

– – – *Mysterium Paschale,* trans. A. Nichols. Edinburgh: T&T Clark, 1990.

– – – *Dare We Hope "That All Men be Saved"?: With a Short Discourse of Hell.* San Francisco: Ignatius Press, 1996.

– – – *Cosmic Liturgy: The Universe According to Maximus the Confessor,* trans. B. E. Daley. San Francisco: Ignatius Press, 2003.

– – – *Theo-logic: The Spirit of Truth.* vol. 3. San Francisco: Ignatius Press, 2005.

von Harnack, A. History of Dogma, trans. N. Buchanan, 7 volumes. London: Williams & Norgate, 1905.

von Schönborn, C. *God's Human Face: the Christ-Icon.* San Francisco: Ignatius Press, 1994.

Vos, G. *The Doctrine of the Covenant in Reformed Theology,* www.biblicaltheology.org/dcrt.pdf, (accessed October 2010).

– – – *Redemptive History and Biblical Interpretation: The Shorter Writings of Geerhardus Vos,* ed. R. B. Gaffin. Phillipsburg: Presbyterian and Reformed Pub. Co, 1980.

Wainwright, A. W. *The Trinity in the New Testament,* 2nd, corrected edition. London: SPCK, 1962.

Waldstein, M. "The Analogy of Mission and Obedience: A Central Point in the Relation between *Theologia* and *Oikonomia* in St Thomas Aquinas's Commentary on John" in *Reading John with St. Thomas Aquinas: Theological Exegesis and Speculative Theology,* ed. M. Dauphinais & M. Levering. Washington: Catholic University of America Press, 2005.

Walker, N. *Sovereignty in Transition: Essays in European Law*. Portland: Hart Publishing, 2006.

Ware, B. A. *Father, Son and Holy Spirit: Relationships, Roles, and Relevance.* Wheaton: Crossway, 2005.

Warfield, B. B. *The Biblical Doctrine of the Trinity,* http://www.apuritansmind.com/ChristianWalk/WarfieldBBTrinity.htm, (accessed May, 2008).

Waterland, D. *The Works of the Rev. Daniel Waterland: Now First Collected and Arranged,* ed. W. Van Mildert. Oxford: Clarendon Press, 1823.

Weinandy, T. G. *In the Likeness of Sinful Flesh: An Essay on the Humanity of Christ.* Edinburgh: T&T Clark, 1993.

– – – *The Father's Spirit of Sonship: Reconceiving the Trinity.* Edinburgh: T&T Clark, 1995.

– – – *Athanasius: A Theological Introduction.* Great Theologians Series. Aldershot: Ashgate, 2007.

Bibliography

West, A. *Documents of the Early Arian Controversy (Fourth Century Christianity)*, http://www.fourthcentury.com/index.php/urkunde-chart-opitz, (accessed Oct, 2008).

Widdicombe, P. *The Fatherhood of God from Origen to Athanasius.* Oxford Theological Monographs, revised edition. Oxford: Clarendon Press, 2000.

Williams, D. H. "Another Exception to Later Fourth-Century 'Arian' Typologies: The Case of Germinius of Sirmium", *Journal of Early Christian Studies* 4.3 335-357.

——— *Ambrose of Milan and the End of the Nicene-Arian Conflicts.* Oxford Early Christian Studies. Oxford: Clarendon Press, 1995.

Williams, R. "Deification" in *The Westminster Dictionary of Theology,* ed. A. Richardson & J. S. Bowden. Philadelphia: Westminster Press, 1983.

——— "The Deflections of Desire: Negative Theology in Trinitarian Disclosure" in *Silence and the Word: Negative Theology and Incarnation,* ed. O. Davies & D. Turner. Cambridge: Cambridge University Press, 2002.

——— *Arius: Heresy and Tradition,* 2nd edition. Grand Rapids: Eerdmans, 2002.

Wippel, J. F. *Metaphysical Themes in Thomas Aquinas II.* Studies in Philosophy and the History of Philosophy, revised edition. Washington: Catholic University of America Press, 2007.

Witherington, B. *John's Wisdom: A Commentary on the Fourth Gospel,* 1st edition. Louisville: Westminster John Knox Press, 1995.

Witsius, H. *The Economy of the Covenants Between God and Man: Comprehending a Complete Body of Divinity.* Phillipsburg: P&R Publishing, 1990.

Works of Jonathan Edwards Online, Jonathan Edwards Center at Yale University, http://edwards.yale.edu/archive/, (accessed from February, 2008).

Zizioulas, J. *Being as Communion: Studies in Personhood and The Church.* Crestwood: St. Vladimir's Seminary Press, 1985.

Zizioulas, J. D. *Communion and Otherness: Further Studies in Personhood and the Church,* ed. P. McPartlan. London: T&T Clark, 2006.

www.ingramcontent.com/pod-product-compliance
Lightning Source LLC
Chambersburg PA
CBHW061433300426
44114CB00014B/1658